NATHANIEL HAWTHORNE
IN THE COLLEGE CLASSROOM

NATHANIEL HAWTHORNE
IN THE COLLEGE CLASSROOM

Contexts, Materials, and Approaches

Second revised edition

Editors

CHRISTOPHER DILLER

and

SAMUEL COALE

EER
Edward Everett Root Publishers, Brighton, 2018.

EER
Edward Everett Root, Publishers, Co. Ltd.,
30 New Road, Brighton, Sussex, BN1 1BN, England.
www.eerpublishing.com

edwardeverettroot@yahoo.co.uk

Nathaniel Hawthorne in the College Classroom.
Contexts, Materials, and Approaches

First published in Great Britain in 2018.
© Christopher Diller and Samuel Coale 2018.

This edition © Edward Everett Root Publishers Co. Ltd. 2018

ISBN: 978-1-912224-19-7 Paperback
ISBN: 978-1-912224-20-3 Hardback
ISBN: 978-1-912224-21-0 eBook

Christopher Diller and Samuel Coale have asserted their right to be identified as the editors of this Work in accordance with the Copyright, Designs and Patents Act 1988 as the owner of this Work.

All rights reserved. No part of this publication may be reproduced, stored in a retrieval system or transmitted in any form or by any means, electronic, mechanical, photocopying, recording or otherwise, without the prior permission of the copyright owner.

Cover designed by Pageset Limited, High Wycombe, Buckinghamshire
Printed in Great Britain by Lightning Source UK, Milton Keynes.

Contents

Preface
Larry J. Reynolds ix
Acknowledgements xii
Inroduction
Sam Coale and Christopher Diller xiii

Part 1: The Romances

Sophia and Nathaniel Hawthorne: Personal Performance and Cultural Construction of Gender in *The Scarlet Letter*
Patricia D. Valenti 3

The Missing Man of *The Scarlet Letter*
Richard Kopley 13

Giving Shape to Gloom; or, Keeping it Real in *The House of the Seven Gables*
Robert T. Tally, Jr 25

Approaching *The Blithedale Romance* through the History of the Book
Sarah Wadsworth 37

Teaching Hawthorne's Romances and/in the History of American Sexuality
Zachary Lamm 51

Hawthorne's Reconceptualization of the European Gothic Tradition
Monika Elbert 63

Part 2: The Short Stories

The "Minister's Black Veil" and Islam in the Core Curriculum
Rosemary Mims Fisk 77

Teaching "The Minister's Black Veil" and "Rappaccini's Daughter" as Frame Stories
Gabriela Serrano 87

Sympathies of the Heart in Nathaniel Hawthorne's "Young Goodman Brown"
Jonathan Murphy 95

The Eco-Gothic in the Short Fiction of Nathaniel Hawthorne
Jennifer Schell 107

Hawthorne, Kant, and Buber in an Interdisciplinary Humanities Classroom
Nancy Bunge 121

Science and Technology in Hawthorne's Short Fiction
Scott Ellis 131

Cautionary Hawthorne: Science, Ethics, and God in the Teaching of "The Birth-Mark" and "Rappaccini's Daughter"
Aaron Cobb and Eric Sterling... 145

Part 3: Institutional and International Contexts

High School–College Partnerships and the Teaching of Hawthorne
Jason Courtmanche.. 161

The Scarlet Letter in a Community College Composition Course
Chikako D. Kumamoto... 173

Hawthorne's Demanding Skepticism
T. Gregory Garvey 185

A Post-Nationalist Approach to Teaching Hawthorne
Ivonne M. Garcia 197

Hawthorne and the Brontës: A Transatlantic Senior Capstone Course
Donald Ross 211

Studying Hawthorne Abroad: The Italian Writings and Their Contexts
Sandra Hughes 221

Part 4: Performative and Visual Contexts

Reading Disability in Hawthorne: Enabling Student Analyses of *The Scarlet Letter*
Sari Altschuler... 235

Puppets, Automata, and Machinery: Counter-Currents of Transnational Romanticism in Hawthorne's Short Fiction
Michael Demson.. 247

Pre-cinematic Visual Spectacles in *The House of the Seven Gables*
Alberto Gabriele 259

Being Viewed and Viewing Oneself: Gendered Discourse in Two Contemporary Hawthorne Adaptations
Nassim Balestrini... 279

Hawthorne, Scientific Anxiety, and American Mad Scientist Films
Walter Squire.. 291

Teaching Gender Dynamics in *The Scarlet Letter* through Film Adaptations
Elisabeth Herion Sarafidis and Danuta Fjellestad....................... 305

Preface

LARRY J. REYNOLDS

Although the American literature canon has undergone considerable change over the past twenty years, with a number of authors and works making their way into and out of anthologies and syllabi, Nathaniel Hawthorne's writings, and perhaps especially *The Scarlet Letter*, have remained a constant presence. Scholars and teachers have continued to value Hawthorne as an innovator of psychological realism, an incisive moral historian, and one of America's finest prose stylists. Countless classroom discussions and student papers have focused on the plots, settings, characters, imagery, symbols, and themes of his short stories and romances. Today, the challenge of teaching Hawthorne in the college classroom is to go beyond traditional and formalist approaches to his works. The essays in this volume, *Nathaniel Hawthorne in the College Classroom*, comprise a welcome aid to those of us seeking innovative ways to engage, instruct, and inspire students.

In my particular classrooms, at a large state university, students often find Hawthorne a difficult read at first, mainly because of his unfamiliar language, his use of historical materials, and his slow-paced descriptive prose. Even the emphasis on sin and guilt, which lies at the heart of so many of his works, can seem irrelevant to today's students. Nevertheless, Hawthorne purveys a set of values and beliefs of immense value and relevance to those students and teachers willing to engage with them. The obstacles a teacher faces facilitating this engagement go beyond the difficulty of Hawthorne's prose. There are also the assumptions that Hawthorne's religious views are Puritanical and his politics retrograde. Neither assumption is sound, as recent scholarship has shown.

What is true is that Hawthorne was a thoughtful pacifist out of step with his turbulent times, and that a number of his works struggle to solve the plight of the individual who feels estranged from his or her community.

One of the lasting beneficial effects of his works is the questions they raise about the behavior of political and religious authorities—especially the ways these authorities use closed systems of thought to control others, often with harmful effects. The witchcraft hysteria of 1692 provided Hawthorne an unforgettable example. Throughout his career, Hawthorne remained skeptical of "isms," including Puritanism, nationalism, abolitionism, and patriotism, for he believed they could lead to unintended hurtful consequences. He opposed the use of violence and insisted that vengeance and beneficence were matters best handled by God, and that those who presumed to know God's will were deluded. His friend, Ralph Waldo Emerson, on the other hand, took an opposing stand, agreeing with the radical abolitionist John Brown that it was "better that a whole generation of men, women and children should pass away by a violent death than that one word of either [the Golden Rule or the Declaration of Independence] should be violated in this country." Such absolutist thinking Hawthorne found appalling.

In his prefaces and letters to friends, Hawthorne often represented himself as a detached observer of the people and events around him, including the Civil War; however, intellectually and emotionally, he struggled to confront the problems of his age, even in his works set in the historical past. These problems included slavery, imperialism, tyranny, terrorism, revolution, mob violence, and war—all of which form the ominous background of Hawthorne's elegant stories and romances. In the foreground are the psychosocial effects of these political and social ills, including shame, dread, alienation, anger, hypocrisy, revenge, despair, and death. When emphasized, these contexts and their cause-effect relationships can show students links between Hawthorne's world and our own.

More important than this historicist task, however, is to illuminate Hawthorne's own set of values and beliefs that he advances as solutions to the struggles of his characters. As Hawthorne's daughter Rose explained after her father's death, "He wrote with temperateness and in pitying love of human nature, in the instinctive hope of helping it to know and redeem itself." In almost all of his works, redemption lies in acts of sympathy, compassion, and self-sacrifice. Moreover, this conduct, he shows, should extend not merely to members of one's own family, or sect, or nation, or army, but to all humankind, including the lowly, the outcast, and the enemy. As his friend Herman Melville astutely observed, Hawthorne's works contain a "democratic spirit of Christianity in all things." One can see this spirit clearly in Hawthorne's "The Gentle Boy," where the Puritans Tobias and

Dorothy Pearson take in the hated Quaker child with the Muslim name, who has been cast out to die. It also permeates *The Scarlet Letter*, especially when Hester becomes a sister of mercy to the very people who punished and shunned her. Even Chillingworth, before he dies, leaves his property to Arthur's child. For Hawthorne, the key to what he called "holy sympathy" lay not in dogma or doctrine, but deep in the human heart, which was one of his richest symbols. Although the news we encounter every day tells us how much hate and violence there exists in the world, Hawthorne's works, in the college classroom, can suggest a moving and impacting alternative.

Texas A&M University

ACKNOWLEDGEMENTS

The editors sincerely thank especially Albert Rolls for his consummate editing and professionalism, and we wish to acknowledge Berry English major Olivia Murphy who proofread the manuscript and helped to create its index. And finally, we owe a special debt of thanks to Larry J. Reynolds who graciously agreed to write a preface for this volume. His eloquent words about the continuing relevance—nay, indispensability—of casting a Hawthornian eye on this complex and troubled world of ours should inspire readers to revisit Hawthorne and his writing time and again.

Introduction

SAM COALE AND CHRISTOPHER DILLER

In a June 16th, 2007 editorial in *The New York Times* called "The Scarlet Letter," Senator Lindsey Graham was castigated for having been so "burned by the uproar of the hard right" over the issue of immigration that he "feels the need to act tough, lest he be saddled . . . with the scarlet letter A, for amnesty." More recently, some political pundits argued against 2012 presidential candidate Mitt Romney's selection of Representative Paul Ryan as a running mate, cautioning that choosing Ryan would "hand President Barack Obama's campaign a twin-edged blade, letting the incumbent slash Romney on the Wisconsin congressman's Medicare proposal and carve in the challenger a scarlet "C" for the unpopular Congress." Clearly, Nathaniel Hawthorne's *The Scarlet Letter* is still as potent a trope of transgression, shame, and discipline as when it was first published (and almost immediately canonized) in 1850. Moreover, both *The Scarlet Letter* and Hawthorne's frequently anthologized stories, such as "The May-Pole of Merry Mount," "Young Goodman Brown," "The Minister's Black Veil," and "My Kinsmen Major Molineaux," populate high school, undergraduate, and graduate courses in American literature, American studies, women's studies, and religious studies. Additionally, *The Scarlet Letter* regularly reappears in the form of plays and films, and it has recently been republished in Polish, Korean, Chinese, Japanese, Persian, and Turkish, among other languages.

The cultural and pedagogical centrality of Hawthorne's writing creates both opportunities and challenges for classroom teachers that this anthology addresses. For many millennial and newer generations of students, the challenge of understanding the historical contexts and literary stakes of Hawthorne's texts is equaled only, perhaps, by the difficulty of reading his highly descriptive and sometimes dense prose in the first place. In the classroom contexts noted above, Hawthorne is still called upon to teach the virtues of close reading and the complexities of point of view, character, irony, paradox, and ambiguity, even if students all too often learn to *dislike* him because teachers tend to approach *The Scarlet Letter* (and other texts) in terms of thematic "course units" (like the outcast) that end up extracting social allegories like so many teeth. What gets lost in this process is not only the slippery nature of Hawthorne's allegories—which are more than likely "anti-allegories" destabilizing or even contravening their initial premises—but also the opportunity to help students see past the placid surface of his prose and to teach how he uses ambiguity and various forms of irony to critique moral, historical, and political platitudes, whether of the left or the right and whether of his day or our own. As Gordon Hutner notes, "One great service that contemporary criticism has performed is to bring a new, more subtle interest to Hawthorne's social writings: criticism of *The House of the Seven Gables*, *The Blithedale Romance*, and *The Marble Faun* has flourished, no longer dominated, as it once was, by nice determinations of crucial formal issues. Instead, their richness as deliberations over the public sphere is only now being appreciated."[1]

If professional criticism of Hawthorne has existed almost since he began writing earnestly in the 1830s (although his first serious critic was Melville), what may be so unusual about Hawthorne's life (1804-1864) was its conventionality, its lack of drama, its Victorian dullness and sense of duty. His was a largely domestic life, although he took several political appointments to support himself and his family—the Boston Custom House, the Salem Custom House, the consulship in Liverpool—since writing was not going to provide any kind of real financial security. Critics have therefore always speculated about or tried to plumb his psychological depths, because the social surface of his life seems so ordinary. Most writers seek habitual solitude to work, but critics have sought to emphasize this trait in Hawthorne as if it were some kind of mental disorder, and thus the focus on the loss of his father at age four, his habitual shyness, and the darkness at

---

[1] Gordon Hutner, "Whose Hawthorne," in *The Cambridge Companion to Nathaniel Hawthorne*, ed. Richard H. Millington (Cambridge: Cambridge University Press, 2004), 253.

the heart of his fiction. Perhaps he recognized this tendency in himself and chose to illuminate and align himself with his Calvinist, witch-hanging ancestors as opposed to the sea captains and farmers who came after them and from whom he was also descended. The shy, retiring, haunted public image may have been partly one more self-created character to distinguish his fiction in an era when gothic tales and novels—the more sensationalist, the better—provided much of the public's reading material. His notion of the American romance, that is to say, a "neutral territory" between the actual and imaginary realms but informed by both, may have been his way of rising to the latter from the former in order to carve out a shadowy past, house, community, or city that he could call his own.

Biographies and critical studies of Hawthorne from the nineteenth to the twenty-first centuries have wrestled with these two seemingly contradictory images of the man and writer: the Romantic *isolato* as morbid genius and elegant stylist, and the practical family man engaged in social observation and savvy political appointments. In 1853, for instance, George William Curtis created the image of the gloomy "absolute recluse" of the ghostly writer holed up in the Old Manse in Concord, aloof, hermetic, and mysterious, a kind of timid Byron and Romantic icon. This image for good or ill stuck in the public mind and has never been entirely eradicated. So influential was it that Hawthorne's children struck back in an effort to present him as a more conventional husband and father in Julian Hawthorne's two-volume *Nathaniel Hawthorne and His Wife* (1884, a typical Victorian title, alas) and Rose Hawthorne Lathrop's *Memories of Hawthorne* (1897). Thus the fault and battle lines were drawn before the end of the nineteenth-century.

In the twentieth-century, Hawthorne biographers continued to oscillate between "dark" Hawthornes, enriched by psychological studies, and "lighter" Hawthornes, which emphasize his conventional lifestyle and roles as husband, father, and job-seeker. From Newton Arvin's *Hawthorne* (1929) to Edwin Haviland Miller's *Salem is My Dwelling Place: A Life of Nathaniel Hawthorne* (1991) and Walter T. Herbert's *Dearest Beloved: The Hawthornes and the Making of the Middle-Class Family* (1993), this first group of biographers focused on the Freudian-scarred, embattled and repressed victim of grim Calvinist traditions, his psychological triggers—fatherless at four, raised by women, a recluse for twelve years after graduating from Bowdoin College, etc.—driving his wife into an inferior position in his marriage and prodded by unconscious Oedipal struggles with their shadowy tendrils of incest, anxiety, and self-doubt. In reaction to this wounded phantom, other biographers, especially of the 1940s and 1980s, went out of their way to portray Hawthorne in a more socially grounded and detailed manner. These biographies include Randall Stewart's *Nathaniel Hawthorne* (1948), Mark Van Doren's *Nathaniel Hawthorne* (1949), Arlin Turner's *Nathaniel Hawthorne: A Biography* (1980), and James R. Mellow's *Nathaniel Hawthorne in His Times* (1980). Here we discover in depth Hawthorne's political connections, his finances, his family relationships, and his writing of the successful campaign biography for his college friend, President Franklin Pierce, which won Hawthorne the lucrative consulship in Liverpool from 1853–1857.

Perhaps the most balanced biographies we have today, though, are Brenda Wineapple's *Hawthorne: A Life* (2003) and Robert Milder's *Hawthorne's Habitations: A Literary Life* (2013). Wineapple depicts the various facets of the man not as at war with one another but as parts of a living, complex, and indeed sometimes contradictory individual (who isn't?), unable to provide for his family as a writer and yet determined to find ways to add to his limited financial success from his fiction. She also discusses the weight of the past on the man and his fiction but refuses to leave us with either the Romantic phantom or the man so conventional that he couldn't have possibly written the dark fiction that he did. In a more persistently literary vein, Milder pursues Hawthorne's constant battle between literary realism or naturalism, which Milder finds in the *Notebooks* and which suggests no moral cosmic framework for life (or for annihilation after it), and literary romanticism, which he locates in the novels and short stories and sees as created to cast a moral eye on human lives in terms of sin, good, and evil.

Critical studies over the past 75 years or so initially followed the bipolar pattern of the biographies rather than their more recent exceptions. Wading through the long, impressionistic, and sometimes convoluted critical pieces of the nineteenth century, we discover the same ambivalence: the morbid scrutiny of Hawthorne's fiction versus the decorousness of his elegant style. How could he possibly create and engage both? When psychology emerged as the latest and most popular paradigm for American society in the twentieth century— "repression" became the key buzz word of the 1920s—and the New Critics subsequently buttressed and expanded its effects as related to myth and religion, viewing each text as a unified fiction built upon elegant ironies and structural as well as thematic ambiguities, Hawthornian criticism shifted, as we can see in the titles of such publications as Richard Harter Fogle's *Hawthorne's Fiction: The Light & The Dark* (1952), Hyatt H. Waggoner's *Hawthorne: A Critical Study* (1953),

Roy R. Male's *Hawthorne's Tragic Vision* (1957), Harry Levin's *The Power of Blackness: Hawthorne, Poe, Melville* (1958), and culminating in Frederick Crews' full-blown psychological study, *The Sins of the Fathers: Hawthorne's Psychological Themes* (1966). The latter underwrote Hawthorne criticism for years.

Beginning in the 1970s, however, the critical landscape changed radically once again: new approaches to Hawthorne emanating from scholarship in feminism, race, gender, sexuality, linguistics, and deconstruction shattered the New Critical notion of a unified text. Selected titles register the proliferation of vantage points and a new sense of critical urgency: Kenneth Dauber's *Rediscovering Hawthorne* (1977), Richard Brodhead's *The School of Hawthorne* (1986), Richard H. Millington's *Practicing Romance: Narrative Form and Cultural Engagement* (1992), and John Dolis' *The Style of Hawthorne's Gaze: Regarding Subjectivity* (1993). Feminist angles of approach to Hawthorne were especially productive and sparked path-finding scholarship in the form of Nina Baym's *The Shape of Hawthorne's Career* (1976), Monika M. Elbert's *Encoding the Letter "A": Gender and Authority in Hawthorne's Early Fiction* (1990), Emily Miller Budick's *Engendering Romance: Women Writers and the Hawthorne Tradition* (1994), and Jamie Barlowe's *The Scarlet Mob of Scribblers: Rereading Hester Prynne* (2000). Critics working within and from gender and gay studies built upon this feminist legacy and explored how Hawthorne's articulation of emergent middle class subjectivities involved changing views of privacy, masculinity, and homoeroticism; studies in this vein included David Leverenz's *Manhood and the American Renaissance* (1989), Leland S. Person's *Aesthetic Headaches: Women and a Masculine Poetics in Poe, Melville, and Hawthorne* (1988), and David Greven's *Men Beyond Desire: Manhood, Sex, and Violation in American Literature* (2005).

In light of this rich critical tradition and ongoing scholarship, what has been surprisingly neglected over the years is how and why we teach Hawthorne at all. Although one can find a few recent articles that engage the issue of teaching Hawthorne, no book length study exists, which is strange given how regularly Hawthorne's texts appear in secondary, post-secondary, and graduate curricula. *The Scarlet Letter*, as well as Hawthorne's other romances and many short stories, remain at the heart of what Susan Gallagher, following John Guillory, calls our "pedagogical canon"—that is, the required texts that instructors list on syllabi, teach, and ask students to value.[2] In fact, *The Scarlet Letter* remains a top ten book on high school reading lists and receives substantial attention in preparation and presentation materials for high school instructors (in which Hawthorne usually appears as a latter day Puritan haunted writer). The experiences with Hawthorne that high school students bring with them to college further underscore the need for this book, as it is one thing for scholars to grapple with Hawthorne's carefully reconstructed historical and religious contexts, layered ironies, or seeming indirection, for example, but another thing to provoke undergraduates to see how Hawthorne's ambiguous moral moments were deliberate and generative artistic choices. Moreover, undergraduate study of Hawthorne now includes a wide bandwidth of both his well-known and lesser known works, including all his published romances, many tales, and even his sketches, writings for children, and political essays. Heeding Thorstein Veblen's pragmatic dictum "Whatever is, is wrong," then, this book strives to correct a pedagogical lag in regard to Hawthorne in the twenty-first-century college classroom.

~ ~ ~

The essays in *Nathaniel Hawthorne in the College Classroom* are organized into four parts, and we have entitled Part 1 "The Romances" to indicate how Hawthorne's first and most famous novel is now perhaps best considered and studied in the context of his other three completed ones. (Hawthorne's novels are also engaged, albeit less directly, in essays located elsewhere in the book.) No anthology devoted to teaching Hawthorne would be complete without attention to *The Scarlet Letter*, and so we begin with three essays that focus specifically on that text and offer fresh perspectives. In "Sophia and Nathaniel Hawthorne: Personal Performance and Cultural Construction of Gender in *The Scarlet Letter*," Patricia D. Valenti addresses head-on students' frequent tendency to read *The Scarlet Letter* as an allegory of Hawthorne's own life and relationships. Because students of literature are perennially fascinated by the links between an author's life

---

2   Susan Gallagher, "Contingencies and Intersections: The Formation of Pedagogical Canons," *Pedagogy* 1, no. 1 (2001): 54.

and writing, teachers can both acknowledge and deepen this interest by moving from biographical to historical perspectives and back again. For example, Valenti examines how the performance of gender roles by Sophia Peabody Hawthorne and Nathaniel Hawthorne simultaneously derived and deviated from nineteenth-century gender conventions. The tensions thus en/gendered in the Hawthornes' relationship resurface in depictions of Hester Prynne and Roger Chillingworth/Arthur Dimmesdale as refractions of failed or anxious masculinity as Hawthorne himself experienced it. This essay therefore offers a doubly historicized perspective derived from students' tendency to personalize Hawthorne.

Richard Kopley, in his essay, offers a fascinating and detailed account of how he leads his students step by step on a literary detective hunt to find a camouflaged but pivotal historical figure in *The Scarlet Letter*: Anne Hutchinson's ally in the Antinomian Controversy, John Wheelwright, who is never mentioned in the romance but is brilliantly implied. Kopley recounts how he begins this quest with selections from John Winthrop's journal (to recover the theological conflicts and resulting politics of the Antinomian debate), and engages his students in the attempt to establish the authorial identity of a book Hawthorne received in 1842 called *The Salem Belle* (written by Ebenezer Wheelwright, Jr., and also invoked in the novel). Finally, Kopley and his students return to *The Scarlet Letter* itself and consider how the novel's primary characters complexly allegorize the historical challenge made by Hutchinson and Wheelwright (whose disobedience of patriarchal authority and subsequent expulsion alludes to Adam and Eve). Through this inductive mode, students better recognize that Hawthorne's great novel is a meditation on guilt, but now that mediation can be recognized in all its complexity and sad beauty.

Two other Hawthornian romances, *The House of the Seven Gables* and *The Blithedale Romance*, are the focus of the next two essays by scholars Robert T. Tally, Jr., and Sarah Wadsworth. In "Giving Shape to Gloom; or, Keeping it Real in *The House of the Seven Gables*," Tally engages one of the primary difficulties—even frustrations—that students have with Hawthorne's work: the persistent ambiguity with respect to what is "real." (Is Young Goodman Brown's vision "really" just a dream? What "really" is revealed on Arthur Dimmesdale's chest? And so on.) In *The House of The Seven Gables*, Tally argues, Hawthorne exploits this ambiguity, indulging in fantasy while insisting on a kind of realism to the point that he seems to want to have it both ways: a more intense realism made possible by allowing his narrative to partake of the unreal. In the classroom, this can cause consternation, both with respect to the work itself (for example, in regard to Phoebe's gift of making things look real, rather than fantastic, within her sphere), but Tally shows how ambiguity implies questions about the generic place of this text in American literature and literary value more generally: what is the value of this densely symbolic narrative work in relation to more dramatic and explicit texts such as Douglass's *Narrative* or Stowe's *Uncle Tom's Cabin*?

Tally's essay introduces and complements Sarah Wadsworth's essay "Approaching *The Blithedale Romance* through the History of the Book," as she shows how Hawthorne's third novel directly engages questions of authorship, publishing, gender, and power. Describing a "History of the Book" approach that immerses her students in antebellum material culture and publishing practices, Wadsworth uses the vibrant, rapidly expanding, and highly contested arena of the antebellum literary marketplace to equip students to explore the text's dubious supernaturalism as a complex and highly gendered trope hinging on narrative manipulation and power—a valuable framework for reconsidering Zenobia's relation to her docile sister and rival, Priscilla. Resituated in the context of the 1850s boom in women's fiction and the burgeoning debate over women's "true" nature, this essay asks students to consider how Hawthorne both uses and questions the cultural categories of the "strong" and "weak" woman.

If Wadsworth seeks to ground Hawthorne's text in the material culture of the book in the 1850's, Zachary Lamm's contribution provides a broader perspective both on Hawthorne's romances and on questions of gender and sexual normality in the nineteenth century. In "Teaching Hawthorne's Romances and/in the History of American Sexuality," Lamm describes a course, "Gender and Sexuality in Nineteenth Century America," which deploy a selection of theoretical and literary texts, with Hawthorne at the center, that trace the development of sexual normativity across the nineteenth century. Hawthorne's recognition of the romance's visionary work against normativity may have ultimately proven unsuccessful, Lamm argues, but his theory of the romance represents a resistance to and rejection of this normative movement, offering fantasies of alternative intimacies as a revitalized vision of sociality.

Finally, Monika Elbert's "Hawthorne's Reconceptualization of the European Gothic Tradition" explores changing conceptions of the gothic in *The Scarlet Letter* and in *The Marble Faun*. Because students are usually uninformed about the English (and German) origins of the gothic, Elbert first establishes how Hawthorne borrows Gothic trappings from Horace

Walpole's Italian-based *The Castle of Otranto* (especially its preface) and recycles them in *The Scarlet Letter*. In the comparative context created by juxtaposing Hawthorne's first and last novels, Elbert argues that Miriam's story is paradoxically much more American than Hester's, precisely because her origins are so uncertain: given the darkness of both her skin and origins, Miriam becomes both the wandering Jew figure of the traditional Gothic and the quintessential American Gothic figure for Hawthorne (much in the vein of his own "Ethan Brand" or Charles Brockden Brown's Carwin, lurking in the back hills of Pennsylvania). In other words, when Hawthorne gets to his last completed novel, Hawthorne's Gothic becomes less Gothic, in the traditional European sense, than it was in *The Scarlet Letter*.

~ ~ ~

Part 2 of *Nathaniel Hawthorne in the College Classroom* engages Hawthorne's short fiction—both well-known and lesser-known stories. This section opens dramatically with Rosemary Fisk's essay "The 'Minister's Black Veil' and Islam in the Core Curriculum," which offers a provocative recovery of the mesmeric power of the veil in the form of the iconic veils—whether a simple hijab or a veil that is part of a niqab or full burqa—that Muslim women often wear. In the context of the recent burqa ban in France among other precedents, the essay explores both the symbolic power of Father Hooper's black veil and how the Islamic veil creates a multiplicity of responses even as it reifies the wearer's Muslim theology at a glance. In the classroom, Fiske projects a picture of a veiled woman to gaze and to be gazed upon so that students feel the enveloping mystery of the symbol and want to say something in response, however clumsy or contradictory. But at a level beyond language, she suggests, students begin to recognize that the appropriate response to the unknown is not fear, or avoidance, or even feminist rescue but engagement and open dialogue with otherness.

Gabriela Serrano also returns to "The Minister's Black Veil" and to "Rappaccini's Daughter" but in a more traditional way: in "Teaching 'The Minister's Black Veil' and 'Rappaccini's Daughter' as Frame Stories," Serrano draws attention to how paratextual frames—Hawthorne as Aubepine, the *Veil* as a parable with a reference to Joseph Moody's experience—call for an active student reader. While not officially frame stories in their narrative structure, these two tales and the process Serrano outlines nevertheless alert students to how they are being rhetorically positioned and asked to assume an identity and to read a tale before it has actually begun. Similarly, two other essays in Part 2 return to a different chestnut of Hawthorne's short fiction: "Young Goodman Brown." Jonathan Murphy's "Sympathies of the Heart in Nathaniel Hawthorne's "Young Goodman Brown" offers a close reading of Hawthorne's famous short story, buttressed by historical evidence such as the role of Hawthorne's ancestors in the Salem witch trials, the complex use of spectral evidence, and the on-going pursuit of the Puritans in trying to distinguish between natural and supernatural occurrences, between mental disorders and demonic possession. For her part, Jennifer Schell returns "Young Goodman Brown" with an eye to how it and Hawthorne's most powerful Gothic tales—including "Ethan Brand," "Roger Malvin's Burial," and "The Maypole of Merry Mount"—pivot upon wilderness settings. Like Monica Elbert in Part 1, Schell describes how she first creates a comparative context for Gothic literature using excerpts from European works such as Goethe's *Faust*, Coleridge's "Christabel," and Radcliffe's *The Mysteries of Udolpho*. By importing an eco-critical perspective informed by Roderick Nash's *Wilderness and the American Mind* and Greg Garrard's *Ecocriticism*, Schell argues that teachers and students can interrogate the distinctly Puritanical origins of the eco-Gothic and explore how these sensibilities place Hawthorne in dialogue with other American writers, including Charles Brockden Brown, Poe, Melville, and Thoreau.

Offering an interdisciplinary humanities context, Nancy Bunge describes a "Literature and Philosophy" class in which students read philosophical texts and a selection of Hawthorne's short stories with the same theme—as many students do in freshmen seminars—so that they can understand how the sheer presentation and dramatization of an idea matters. Specifically, pairing Hawthorne with Immanuel Kant's *Groundwork for a Metaphysics of Morals* and Martin Buber's *I and Thou* showcases Hawthorne as both an subtle and engaging thinker and writer. Both Buber and Kant emphasize the importance of treating people as ends in and of themselves, obviously an important theme in Hawthorne tales such as "The Birthmark" and "Rappaccini's Daughter," but other tales such as "Young Goodman Brown" and "My Kinsman, Major Molineux" also complicate this theme. After students have waded through Kant's turgid prose and Buber's sometimes vague declarations, they find Hawthorne's short stories vivid and engrossing: they not only see how Hawthorne's stories are more vividly written, but they also see that Hawthorne's tales arguably engage, with greater subtlety, the central issues that Kant and Buber address. The pedagogical endgame of such interdisciplinary pairings is that students can both enjoy literature and see how it tends to present ideas with the complexity of formal philosophical statements.

The remaining two essays in Part 2 also take a philosophical tack toward Hawthorne's short fiction and examine issues of science, religion, and ethics—issues of substantial importance not only to Hawthorne but also to college students today, who are living in a technologically suffused and rapidly changing global environment. As Scott Ellis documents, Hawthorne was fascinated by developments in science and technology, from chemical experiments and automation to radical changes in communication and transportation, and yet he worried about scientific "progress" and "the science of calculation"—a term coined by Charles Babbage and republished by Hawthorne in an excerpt in *The American Magazine of Useful and Entertaining Knowledge* (1836)—for the developing human dominion over the natural world. Ellis places Hawthorne's worries and writing in dialogue with other American and European thinkers—Thomas Carlyle, Robert Owen, Samuel Tyler, and Edward Hitchcock—and such fellow writers as Herman Melville, Edgar Allan Poe, Fitz-James O'Brien, and Rebecca Harding Davis. With these historical and literary perspectives in hand, he suggests, students can be asked to engage directly, through assignments or discussions, with developments in technology and communication of the 21st century—blogs, wiki sites, digital editions, and scholarly web sites that naturally provoke further questions about the artist/scientist relationship that Hawthorne explores in his short fiction.

If Ellis focuses on discourses of science and progress, in "Cautionary Hawthorne: Science, Ethics, and God in the Teaching of 'The Birth-Mark' and 'Rappaccini's Daughter,'" Aaron Cobb and Eric Sterling discuss these two stories in the context of an American literature survey course and how the stories can be used to encourage critical reflection about the ethical intersection of science and religion. "The Birth-Mark," for instance, meditates upon the dangers of scientific experimentation, the dynamics of control and domination in domestic relationships, and the quest for perfection. Yet Hawthorne also addresses these issues, Cobb and Sterling argue, within the context of a spiritual understanding of human life. (God seems to have made his mark on Georgiana, both literally and figuratively, and to have warned Aylmer through his troubling and prophetic dream, the meaning of which the scientist chooses to ignore.) There are similar themes in the well-known "Rappaccini's Daughter," but perhaps most interestingly the authors connect these stories and issues to an intriguing variety of media contexts, including debate at the 2002 Presidential Council on Bioethics (which began with a discussion of "The Birth-Mark"), interviews by NBC's Dr. Nancy Snyderman on the *TODAY* show, and clips from *The Twilight Zone* and the Holocaust movie, *Europa Europa* (1990). In doing so, they illustrate how Hawthorne's meditations on the ethics of science and technology are timeless precisely because they remain topical.

~ ~ ~

Sections 3 and 4 of *Nathaniel Hawthorne in the College Classroom* are titled "Institutional and International Contexts" and "Performative and Visual Contexts," respectively, and they expand discussions of teaching Hawthorne by bringing diverse institutional, international, and visual contexts into play. The first essay of Section 3, Jason Courtmanche's "High School-College Partnerships and the Teaching of Hawthorne," describes a reciprocal partnership between a high school teacher of English Language Arts and Courtmanche's college students in teacher education. Courtmanche rightly points out that whereas college professors are specialists of literary authors and periods and are expected to conduct research in their area of specialization, high school English and Language Arts teachers are generalists who must cover entire national literatures and historical periods for a student body that often surpasses 100 students each term. A high school English teacher, for example, may have read *The Scarlet Letter* in high school or in an undergraduate American Literature survey course, but they may also never have encountered it at all. To turn these discrepancies into opportunities, the two partners meet prior to the academic year to discuss readings and assignments, norm goals and expectations, and to develop ideas for student collaboration. During the term, their respective students read several common texts and then communicate by email and in a shared virtual space such as a wiki. In these ways, college undergraduates help the high school students to read and respond, to develop ideas for their papers, and then provide feedback and response to those papers throughout the drafting process, furthering their own training as prospective high school teachers. The two instructors also trade guest appearances in each other's classes so that the high school teacher provides insight for the education majors into high school students and culture and the university professor provides guest lectures on historical context, literary movements, and literary devices and analysis. This essay thereby approaches the teaching of the literary "canon" as a shared responsibility between and among teachers and students.

As Courtmanche's essay shows, college instructors often must grapple with assumptions about reading literature and Hawthorne from students' high school experiences, but the title and substance of Chikako D. Kumamoto's essay "Teaching *The Scarlet Letter* in a Community College Composition Course" underscores how Hawthorne is also taught in another rapidly expanding educational niche. At a community college, Kumamoto points out, students are often invested in "two cultures" (to adopt C. P. Snow's concept): some are geared toward traditional liberal arts/transfer interests and yet many are there to obtain practical workforce training. Mining this two-fold mentality, Kumamoto describes a composition course that creates a contact zone created by pairing Hawthorne's *The Scarlet Letter* and Max Weber's *The Protestant Ethic and the Spirit of Capitalism*. What links Hawthorne to Weber are affiliations of the Calvinist calling, Puritan work ethic, capitalism, and a germinal discourse on America's national origins. After establishing these affiliations, the essay describes how students are guided step by step through the research and inquiry process—creating their own interpretive context, working from topic to issue or inquiry question, forging a hypothesis—before getting down to drafting, while all the time reading and rereading Hawthorne's novel and testing their evolving views against textual evidence and inference. As Courtmanche and Kumamoto illustrate, the use of Hawthorne's texts to cultivate critical habits of mind and hand is broadly shared.

The remaining essays in Section 3 return to the college classroom but consider the teaching of Hawthorne in a diverse range of instructional settings, including literary survey and upper division literature seminars, an interdisciplinary humanities course, and a senior capstone and study abroad course. T. Gregory Garvey's expansive essay, "Hawthorne's Demanding Skepticism," explores Hawthorne's writing in three different settings: 1) general education introductions to literature or American literature, 2) courses on the basics of literary analysis for English majors, and 3) advanced undergraduate or graduate courses with a generic emphasis such as the novel, or a topical interest such as gender. Whereas Hawthorne's historical sensibility helps to structure the broad scope of survey courses, Garvey suggests, his craftsmanship makes his texts ideal for teaching the basics of close reading and structural analysis. Capitalizing on the stylistic density of *The Scarlet Letter*, his essay describes a sequence of exercises for introductory English majors, including an initial "inside/outside" close reading practice in which students analyze a short passage ("inside") and then bring that reading to bear on a subsequent passage in the same text ("outside"), before moving onto broader structural analyses of the text. The essay concludes by pressing and illustrating the pedagogical value of Hawthorne for advanced students in research-oriented courses. Ivonne M. Garcia offers a case in point for Garvey's concluding point about Hawthorne for advanced students in her essay "A Post-Nationalist Approach to Teaching Hawthorne" in which she describes a literature seminar that juxtaposes (trans)national issues with Hawthorne's many familial relocations and travels. By always locating the author within his political and cultural moment, Garcia illustrates, advanced students can examine how Hawthorne assigns signification to different political categories of representation, such as race, gender, socio-economic class, and sexuality, and how his works often both invoke and challenge specific nationalist ideologies such as Manifest Destiny.

Radiating from Garcia's transnational approach, the next two essays in Section 3 take up intriguing opportunities to study and to teach Hawthorne in international literary and cultural contexts. In his essay "Hawthorne and the Brontës: A Transatlantic Senior Capstone Course," Donald Ross describes a senior capstone course in which students read multiple novels by Hawthorne and the Brontë sisters; however, for the sake of highlighting transatlantic affiliations, Ross focuses upon the final novels of Charlotte Brontë and Hawthorne which were set on the European continent (*Villette* in Belgium and *Marble Faun* in Italy). Noting how this broader setting and "foreign" characters resonate with Hawthorne's frequently articulated frustration with the lack of historical materials imposed on the American novelist, Ross shows how both novels are differently invested in continental art and aesthetics: Hawthorne's novel has many scenes where the characters view and comment on works of Italian art, and *Villette* has an interesting scene where Lucy Snow and her eventual boyfriend are in a gallery. In all cases, the nationality and national prejudices of the characters are part of their reactions to art, so students are able to consider the novel's presentation and discussion of art in its visual context (for example, by projecting a photograph of Hawthorne's Faun of Praxiteles in the classroom) and to consider how these two texts specify how American and British aesthetic assumptions and cultural institutions differ (even though they share some influences and themes).

Sandra Hughes' essay "Studying Hawthorne Abroad: the Italian Contexts and Writings" echoes Ross' focus on *The Marble Faun* and quite literally asks students to follow in that novel and Hawthorne's footsteps in Italy. In the preface to *The Marble Faun*, Hawthorne famously complains about an essential problem faced by American authors, saying: "No author, without a trial, can conceive of the difficulty of writing a Romance about a country where there is no shadow, no antiquity, no mystery, no picturesque and gloomy wrong [...] Romance and poetry [...] need Ruin to make them grow" (*Centenary Hawthorne* 4: 3). Italy, in other words, offered just what Hawthorne needed to revive his career as a novelist after a silence of many years. The art, history, culture, and landscape of Italy appear, in one form or another, on every page of *The Marble Faun*. Indeed, Hawthorne's fidelity to the actual was so great that 19th-century tourists routinely used *The Marble Faun* itself as a guidebook. Hughes explains how to do the same with Hawthorne's novel in the classroom—including "Rappaccini's Daughter"—and the Italian writings of Henry James (including *Roderick Hudson, Daisy Miller, The Aspern Papers,* and *Italian Hours*. She then describes a course that includes traditional classwork but that is crucially supplemented by real or virtual excursions to relevant museums and historical sites in order to help students develop a specific appreciation for the significant thematic and aesthetic role that Italian monuments and works of art play in the texts studied.

~ ~ ~

Hughes' essay serves as an appropriate bridge to the final section of *Nathaniel Hawthorne in the College Classroom*: "Performative and Visual Contexts." Perhaps most provocatively in this section, Sari Altschuler asks us to reconsider *The Scarlet Letter* in light of scholarship emanating from the burgeoning field of disability studies. As she points out, perhaps the most pronounced feature of Nathaniel Hawthorne's modes of characterization is physical variety: from Georgiana's birthmark and Rappaccini's daughter's deadly touch to Clifford's infirmity and Hepzibah's nearsighted scowl, Hawthorne's texts teem with extraordinary and extraordinarily marked bodies. In regard to *The Scarlet Letter*, nearly every major character—

Dimmesdale, Chillingworth, the customhouse officer, and arguably Hester and even the narrator—is, in some manner, disabled, and teachers often frame the corporeal diversity of Hawthorne's characters as pure metaphor. Altschuler offers three possibilities for opening up student readings of disability in Hawthorne. First, she describes how the novel offers teachers and students a discussion of the sheer physical variety of mid-nineteenth century daily life before institutionalization, technological innovation, and modern medical advances. Second, the essay introduces David Mitchell and Sharon Snyder's notion of "narrative prosthesis"—literature's narrative dependence on disability—and shows how this concept can help students to reconceptualize Hawthorne's disabled figures and critique disability's central narrative functions in the novel. And finally, the essay proposes that providing a vocabulary and context for disability in Hawthorne makes *The Scarlet Letter* more broadly useful for less traditional classroom contexts—for example, those of the Medical Humanities and Narrative Medicine. In whatever classroom context, however, bringing disability's marked and unmarked complexity into view enables new and dynamic readings of Hawthorne.

In his essay "Puppets, Automata, and Machinery: Counter-Currents of Transnational Romanticism in Hawthorne's Short Fiction," Michael Demson considers how Hawthorne's short fiction frequently plumbs a disquieting fear of puppets, automata, and machinery; like many texts in British, European, and Russian Romanticism, his stories are filled with figures of artificial life, of simulated inspiration, and of theatrical animations. He describes teaching several of Hawthorne's short stories which instance anxieties and parodies—even mockeries—of automata in the context of a sophomore/junior level course that compares Romantic fiction from a variety of national traditions. To identify foundational themes (including recurrent figures of speech and philosophical questions), Demson's students begin with a close study of several ancient and classical texts, including the creation story from "Genesis," Plato's description of poetic inspiration in *Ion*, Herodotus' discussion of Egyptian puppets, and Ovid's version of "Pygmalion." The course juxtaposes Hawthorne's "Feathertop" with Mary Shelley's second "Preface" to *Frankenstein*, "Rappaccini's Daughter" with E. T. A. Hoffmann's "The Sandman" and "Automata," and "The Artist of the Beautiful" with Nikolai Gogol's "The Nose." What emerges from this series of intertexts is the perennial conflation of the creation of life with the creation of an inspired work of art.

Like Demson, Alberto Gabriele asks us to reconsider how a focus on visual technology sheds new light on a Hawthorne novel in his essay "Pre-cinematic Visual Spectacles in *The House of the Seven Gables*." Gabriele's central claim is that Hawthorne's recurrent gesture toward escape from the minute details of reality is paradoxically carried out with an insistence on visual phenomena and contemporary popular culture to make his romance a realistic rendition of the new spectacles of urban modernity. Several new forms of portraiture and visual culture, besides the traditional painted image, for example, punctuate *The House of the Seven Gables*: daguerreotypes, phantasmagorias, dioramas, kaleidoscopes, proto-cinematographic modalities of vision, print culture, and mesmeric apparitions, all challenge the centrality that the painted portrait had in nineteenth century fiction. The upshot is that teaching the book in parallel with a study of pre-cinematographic forms of popular entertainment helps students to understand challenges to traditional representation and narrative structure posed by industrial modernity. The genre of the portrait, in particular, allows students to focus on the differently gendered formats of artistic representation—large painting, miniature, sketching—and the daguerreotype offered a new and proto-modernist form of portraiture, which Hawthorne finally privileges.

If both Demson and Gabriele suggest how Hawthorne's prose is a kind of *Ut Pictura Poesis*—a "speaking picture," as Simonides of Keos is reported by Plutarch to have said of poetry—the next two essays in Section 4 examine the actual performative and visual voicing of Hawthorne texts on stage and in film. In his essay "Being Viewed and Viewing Oneself: Gendered Discourse in Two Contemporary Hawthorne Adaptations," Nassim Balestrini reports how her students are usually astonished when they learn that adaptations of Hawthorne's work date to the nineteenth century and can be found in numerous artistic genres and media. Balestrini uses two recent appropriations of Hawthorne's *The Scarlet Letter* and "The Birthmark" as cases in point—both of which are set in contemporary high schools. The first, the 2010 California high school film, *Easy A*, shows how elements of Hawthorne's romance—and especially its sexual politics—still resonate in the twenty-first century world of young adulthood, a world in which rumor, backbiting, and scaremongering serve as tools for enhancing or ruining a person's reputation. The second, Hawthorne's tale "The Birthmark" as revisioned in the 2003 short story "Birthmark" (revised, 2007) by the West Coast writer and multimedia artist, Miranda July (b. 1974), again intersects with the real world interests of high school readers and young women, especially as it examines how ideologies of scientific and medical authority invoke gender assumptions and aesthetic norms during a period when adolescents are still forming their own personal and social identities. Walter Squire describes how several of Hawthorne's short stories intersect with famous "mad scientist" films in his essay "Hawthorne, Scientific Anxiety, and American Mad Scientist Films." Like Aaron Cobb and Eric Sterling in Section 2, Squire suggests that since Hawthorne's "mad" scientist stories focus upon human loss, they may encourage students to consider contemporary medical and scientific ethics in terms of effects upon people instead of within abstract notions of morality. The anxieties forwarded by these films range from the disruption/replacement of human conception via birth in the lab to nuclear holocaust, and Squire explains how Hawthorne's skepticism about scientific inquiry often intersects in these films with issues of sexuality, gestation, reproduction and, in particular, to the hotly debated topics of cloning, genetic engineering, and stem cell research. Squire concludes with a rich (and annotated) film bibliography.

The final essay in *Nathaniel Hawthorne in the College Classroom* continues to explore how film adaptations—in this case, of *The Scarlet Letter*—can offer teachers of Hawthorne an illuminating contrastive rhetorical context. Although Elisabeth Herion Sarafidis and Danuta Fjellestad teach American literature in a unique cultural and institutional context (in Sweden), they describe facing pedagogical challenges similar to their American colleagues"—primarily, that their students have scant knowledge of the sociocultural and historical contexts against which the story of Hester Prynne plays out. Their students also have considerable difficulties with the narrative point of view, and they find it a challenge to understand the seriousness of the sexual mores and gender dynamics so central to the story. Nonplussed, students often resort to the clandestine practice of "getting" the basics of the story by reading plot summaries on various Internet sites or watching a movie. Rather than resisting these tendencies to circumvent Hawthorne's novel, however, the essayists describe ways to make use of these practices by teaching *The Scarlet Letter* in dialogue with two dramatically different Hollywood film adaptations: Robert Vignola's 1934 version and Roland Joffé's somewhat infamous 1995 adaptation (with Demi Moore). A set of activities, such as response-papers, small-group discussions followed by minutes, class-discussions, ten-minute lectures, etc., help students return to the novel in order to answer questions about what, actually, happened to the verbal text when it was remediated into the hybrid medium of film. This exercise underscores the importance of historicizing concepts such as adultery and sin; moreover, it raises students' attention of representation of gender dynamics as culturally dependent. Perhaps somewhat paradoxically, the two essayists conclude, it is the scenes added in the film scripts—scenes for which there are no equivalents in the novel—that are especially effective in this regard.

~ ~ ~

Given these engaging essays, we believe that *Nathaniel Hawthorne in the College Classroom* does indeed update Hawthorne for the twenty-first-century classroom by juxtaposing a broad range of texts and contexts that balance traditional and new ways of approaching Hawthorne's literary legacy. Shuttling between Puritan and antebellum and contemporary contexts, moving back and forth between literary and interdisciplinary readings of his texts, and integrating classroom teacher/student interaction with wikis, blogs, and other digital teaching platforms, this anthology confirms the continuing popularity of Hawthorne even as it also documents how today's "Hawthorne" is more of a diverse amalgam than ever before. Amidst this almost dizzying array of texts, intertexts, contexts, theoretical approaches, genres, and media, Hawthorne's singular artistic choices and accomplishments are not lost but rather given a greater depth and resonance. We therefore hope that this collection offers teachers practical resources to design teaching strategies and learning environments to meet their students at points of real need and interest while it also stimulates new conversations about how and why Nathaniel Hawthorne continues to plunge readers into realms that both delight and terrify.

PART 1
THE ROMANCES

Sophia and Nathaniel Hawthorne: Personal Performance and Cultural Construction of Gender in *The Scarlet Letter*

Patricia D. Valenti

> Dearest, I know how sensitive is thy nature—how easily thy heart might be broken—how soon thou wouldst vanish away from the earth, were thy soul to be wronged or violated in any manner.... But thou wilt be happy—we will both be happy.... God hath married us; but to our perfect peace and fulness of security on earth, it is necessary that man should marry us too. It will be an *external pledge* of one eternal and infinite union.[1]

Students of literature are perennially interested in an author's life. Teachers of literature, just as consistently, wonder how to use that interest as an effective classroom strategy. Too often, biographical assignments are little more than scavenger hunts yielding facts, which are then linked in dubious fashion to a text. The astute teacher, however, will use the author's life as the springboard to understanding how literature is

---

1 This quotation, surviving only in Sophia's hand, demonstrates her occasional practice of using commonplace books over decades to copy or draft letters. Though dated April 28, 1840, the quotation is found in *Commonplace Book*, volume 3, 1862–69, MS, the Henry W. and Albert A. Berg Collection of the New York Public Library, Astor, Lenox, and Tilden Foundations.

produced in the complex nexus of an individual's life and the superstructure of cultural forms. Gender, for example, is not experienced as theory; rather, it is mediated through specific individuals. Such was the case for Sophia Peabody Hawthorne and Nathaniel Hawthorne, whose performance of gender roles simultaneously derived and deviated from nineteenth-century expectations. Sophia demonstrated behavior typically relegated to men: sexual assertiveness, success as a wage earner, and activity in the public sphere. Nathaniel's perceived deficiencies in these areas produced his anxieties as lover and husband. The tensions en/gendered in the Hawthornes' courtship and marital relationship inform the rhetoric of *The Scarlet Letter* and the depictions of Hester Prynne, Roger Chillingworth, and Arthur Dimmesdale.

Before Sophia met Nathaniel, she had pursued a career in the visual arts. She had exhibited some of her original oil canvasses, garnering success in the marketplace as well as encouragement from New England's leading artists. Nathaniel's pursuit of a literary career had taken the path of anonymously published short stories. His travel had been relatively circumscribed, no farther than Niagara Falls, while Sophia had spent eighteen months in Cuba, that trip documented in three volumes totaling more than eight hundred pages. Nathaniel first encountered Sophia, as did many others in Salem, through her *Cuba Journal*. With its "great many little bursts & enthusiasms & opinions & notions," Sophia complained somewhat disingenuously that its circulation made her feel as if she had been "stuck up bodily upon a pole & carried about the streets[.] I could not feel more *exposed*," she wrote her mother. In admiration for the *Cuba Journal*'s author, Nathaniel dubbed Sophia the "Queen of Journalizers."[2]

Their ensuing courtship was conducted largely through correspondence. Although Nathaniel's letters to Sophia survive, he burned most of hers, but their content may be surmised by a remnant, dated April 28, 1840, and quoted above. His resistance to an "external pledge" had prolonged their engagement. A letter from Nathaniel, written a full nine months before this just cited, had addressed the same issue but from the opposite perspective: "We *are* married!" Then again: "Yes—we are married; and as God Himself has joined us, we may trust never to be separated, neither in Heaven nor on

---

2 Sophia Peabody to Mrs. Peabody, *Cuba Journal*, December 8, 1834, 3:90, MS Berg. For information about those who read the *Cuba Journal* in Salem, see Claire M. Badarraco's "The Night-Blooming Cereus: A Letter from the *Cuba Journal* of Sophia Peabody with a Check List of her Autograph Materials in American Institutions," *Bulletin of Research in the Humanities* 81 (1978): 56–78.

Earth. . . ." But Nathaniel demurred with regard to some public declaration of their love: "The world might, as yet, misjudge us; and therefore we will not speak to the world." What exactly the "world" might "*mis*judge" is not clear, for surely two fully adult heterosexuals (she was almost thirty, he had just turned thirty-five) would have created no scandal by publicly solemnizing their love in marriage. As one year of courtship rolled into the next, Nathaniel maintained, "I have an inexpressible and unconquerable reluctance to speak of thee to almost anybody. It seems a sin."[3]

Although Sophia's need for public confirmation was inimical to Nathaniel's need for secrecy, she conspired with him in their use of rhetorical strategies that separated their discourse from the commonplaces of everyday speech and hence separated them from the world. Their use of archaic forms for verbs, second-person pronouns (*thee* and *thou* and *thy*), and adjectives fostered a dialect of intimacy, a common phenomenon in nineteenth-century courtship correspondence, as Karen Lystra has pointed out. Nathaniel subverts these conventions, however, with his frequent use of the third person to refer to himself—as, for example, when he writes, "thy husband's soul yearns to embrace thee! Thou art *his* hope—*his* joy . . . ." The third person creates distance rather than intimacy, separating the writer from the intensity of his emotion and obscuring his identity. Designating himself as Sophia's husband more than two years before their wedding conflates sequential stages of their relationship. Becoming simultaneously her lover and husband, he dispensed with a need for an "external pledge."[4]

The peculiar linguistic features of Nathaniel's courtship correspondence surface in *The Scarlet Letter*. Archaic language appropriately establishes the setting of colonial New England while it echoes the Hawthornes'

---

3   Nathaniel Hawthorne to Sophia Peabody July 24, 1839, August 16, 1841, and the August 28, 1840 remnant published as his letter in The Letters 1813–1843, ed. Thomas Woodson, et al. 23 vols., *The Centenary Edition of the Works of Nathaniel Hawthorne* (Columbus: Ohio State University Press, 1984), 15: 329, 560, 452. Citations from *The Scarlet Letter* are taken from vol. 1 of *The Centenary Edition*.

4   Karen Lystra, *Searching the Heart: Women, Men, and Romantic Love in Nineteenth-Century America* (London: Oxford, University Press, 1989). See Patricia D. Valenti, *Sophia Peabody Hawthorne, A Life, Volume I*, (Columbus: The University of Missouri Press, 2004) ch. 15, "Sophie, Naughty Sophie, Dove" for a full analysis of Nathaniel's courtship correspondence. Nathaniel Hawthorne to Sophia Peabody, March 15, 1840, *The Letters 1813–1843*, 15:420, emphasis added.

interpersonal tensions. Dimmesdale repeatedly refers to himself in the third person to distance himself from Hester. He asserts, for example, that "the sinful mother [is] happier than the sinful father" (115), a true statement that cloaks falsehood in the third person. Even at the end of the novel, his Election Sermon obscures truth while he pretends to disclose his sin, his crime, his daughter, his beloved. "*He* hid it cunningly from men,"' Dimmesdale proclaims still hiding himself behind the third person. As Michael Ragussis observes, the minister's "utterances are part of a system of counterspeech where even the truth becomes a hiding place, a deception" (115, 255, emphasis added).

For both the writer of courtship correspondence and his fictional character, third person utterances spring from the same well and serve the same purposes, concealment and obfuscation, and the author's silence about a love that "*seems* a sin" finds its narrative rationale in *The Scarlet Letter* where the minister's love *is* a sin. But what sin, exactly? Dimmesdale knows that he transgressed both the civil and religious laws against fornication, an act he commits when he and Hester are ignorant that her husband still lives. She is a married woman, however, which she realizes during the first scaffold scene when she looks into the crowd and sees her husband, who compels her silence. Thus she knows that she has broken the law against adultery. Just as she conspires with Dimmesdale to keep their transgressive love a secret, so too she conspires with Chillingworth to keep their marriage a secret. Lover and husband are thus conflated into a single character type, that of a man unable or unwilling to proclaim the true nature of his relation to a woman.

Nathaniel validated his peculiar demands for secrecy during courtship by claiming his love was too exalted to be expressed to others, that language was too weak a vessel to convey the magnitude of his emotions. He and Sophia *should* not speak of their love because they *could* not speak of it: "I never use words, either with tongue or pen, when I can possibly express myself in any other way," he informed her; "how much, dearest, may be expressed without utterance of a word! Is there not a volume [excision] in our many glances? . . .;—our minds will enter into each other, and silently possess themselves. . . ." Thoughts and glances also become a means for Dimmesdale's private communication with Hester during the first scaffold scene. With his "deep and troubled eyes," he induces her to remain silent about his paternity. Then at Governor Bellingham's mansion, she issues a silent threat to him when she fights with Boston's leaders over custody of her child. Hester "seemed hardly so much as once to direct her eyes" at Dimmesdale for him to realize that his exposure would result from refusal to defend her. "'Speak thou for me!'" she commands, and he does (68, 113).[5] Hester exerts tremendous power through her silence, though in her art she subversively announces her passion, as did Sophia's.

"Endymion," Sophia's last oil canvas, was painted while her marriage was still in its honeymoon phase. Based upon the mythical figure represented in poems by both John Keats and Henry Wadsworth Longfellow, her painting reprised the theme of the title character's sexual initiation by a woman. "She woke Endymion with a kiss,/ When, sleeping in a grove,/ He dreamed not of her love" are words from Longfellow's poem which would have been known to the Hawthornes' contemporaries. Sophia claimed her painting was the "record . . . of my happy, hopeful days! The divine dream shining in Endymion's face, is it not my dream & my reality too? His body entranced in sleep, his soul bathed in light—every curve flowing in consummate beauty—in some way, it is my life." Sophia's painting thus encoded her relationship with Nathaniel after marriage just as two earlier paintings had represented the couple while they were engaged. Her "Isola" and "Menaggio" depicted a man and woman on a bridge, a fitting location for a betrothed couple. Nathaniel immediately interpreted these figures to represent himself as "the very noble cavalier with whom Sophie is standing." He had "actually trembled" upon receipt of these pictures and sequestered them from all eyes but his own.[6] Executed in the fine materials of oil and canvas, "Isola," and "Menaggio" as well as "Endymion" are aesthetically pleasing, symbolic works that require interpretation by the cognoscenti. These paintings thus meet the criteria of high art, and Nathaniel was their privileged interpreter, thereby confirming his intimacy with a woman whose artistic production yields its meaning to a restricted audience, himself, an audience of one.

---

5   Nathaniel Hawthorne to Sophia Peabody, January 13, 1841, April 15, 1840, *The Letters 1813–1843*, 15: 511–12, 440. In "Hester's Revenge: The Power of Silence in *The Scarlet Letter*," *Nineteenth-Century Literature* 43, no. 4 (1989): 470–71, 466, Leland Person has also observed that Hester's "vengeful" silence has the "effect of action" and the "exercise of power."

6   "Endymion," in *The Complete Poetical Works of Henry Wadsworth Longfellow*, ed. Horace Scudder (Boston: Houghton Mifflin, 1922), 15. Sophia Peabody Hawthorne to Mrs. Peabody, February 6, 1844, MS Berg; Nathaniel Hawthorne to Sophia Peabody, *The Letters 1813–1843*, 15:401–402. The "Isola" and "Menaggio" are now housed at the Peabody Essex Museum in Salem, Massachusetts.

Rose Hawthorne Lathrop would later describe "Endymion" as "a picture in pale brown monochromes, of the most remarkable perfection of finish and beauty of draughtsmanship." Whatever its aesthetic value, its worth was to have been calculated in the marketplace. "Endymion" had been painted in order to produce income for the financially strapped newly-weds, and John Louis O'Sullivan, Nathaniel's editor at the *Democratic Review*, claimed he could fetch as much as one hundred dollars for the painting in a New York gallery. The Hawthornes would never know if O'Sullivan, notoriously derelict in paying Nathaniel for his stories, could have succeeded in obtaining so great a sum because Nathaniel forbade its sale and even prevented its display. He recoiled, as Sophia wrote her mother, at the thought of having "a woman come out of the shade, far less his wife." Sophia attempted to neutralize the demeaning portent of her husband's words by adding that his wishes were "a matter of sentiment, not contempt of *handiwork*." Her choice of word is telling for it suggests not high art, such as "Endymion," but low art, those decorative functional pieces that are accessible and satisfying to the mass market of consumers. This was, in fact, the very type of art Sophia was producing when, after Nathaniel had lost his position at the Custom House, he was writing *The Scarlet Letter* "vehemently morning & afternoon." For a brief moment, her painted lampshades, inlaid handscreens, and illustrations were the vogue among Salem's wealthiest citizens. She struggled to meet the demands for her products, knowing that she provided her family's "bread & butter & rent."[7]

Sophia "possessed an art that sufficed . . . to supply food," the words Nathaniel used in *The Scarlet Letter* to describe how a mother, Hester, turns her talents into wages that pay for household expenses, something that the father, whether in real-life or fiction, did not. Hester generates income by converting a conventionally feminine domestic task, sewing, into highly desirable products for public consumption. With her production of embroidered gloves, ruffs, baby linens, and other apparel, she "had ready and fairly requited employment for as many hours as she saw fit to occupy" (82–83). Her "labor," as Hannah Arendt uses the word to denote what takes

---

[7] For information on the source of Sophia's inspiration for "Endymion," see Nathaniel Hawthorne, *The Letters 1843–1853*, 16:14, fn 1; Rose Hawthorne Lathrop, *Memories of Hawthorne* (Boston: Houghton, Mifflin, 1897), 72. Sophia Hawthorne to Mrs. Peabody, January 21, 1844, February 6, 1844 and September 2, 1849, MSS Berg, my emphasis; Sophia Hawthorne to Mary Mann, September 12 and November 4, 1849, MSS Berg.

place in the private sphere, is thus transformed into *praxis* in the *polis,* thereby and in yet another arena challenged Dimmesdale's (in)capacity as a man. Despite or perhaps because of Hester's indisputable successes, the narrator grudgingly acknowledges the popularity of her "handiwork" (that word again!). With some condescension and absent any praise for its value, the narrator remarks that Hester's "*handiwork* became what would now be termed the fashion," speculating that its popularity derives from "the morbid curiosity that gives a fictitious value even to common or *worthless things* . . . or because Hester really filled a gap which must otherwise have remained vacant" (82, 182, emphases added).

One cannot avoid associating the narrator's denigration of Hester's art with the author's private resentments of his wife's and other women's talents and successes. While Sophia's work had found appreciative audiences with open purses, Nathaniel's career had been foundering. He had been poorly remunerated and ignored by a public that preferred those "common or worthless things" produced by the financially successful "d-----d mob of scribbling women," as he would later (in)famously write his publisher. His envy was palpable, as he continued with his invective: "I should have no chance of success while the public taste is occupied with their trash." In *The Scarlet Letter*, he had already addressed the vagaries of a marketplace which rewarded a kind of genius, both artistic and entrepreneurial, that functioned beyond conventional parameters of genre or gender.[8]

Hester, however, like Sophia, exhibits a range of talent. In addition to decorative adornments for the wealthy, she has transformed her badge of ignominy into a multivalent object of high art, lavishly embroidered "in fine red cloth . . . and fantastic flourishes of gold thread" (53). As Nina Baym has remarked, "by making the letter beautiful, Hester is denying its literal meaning and thereby subverting the intention of the magistrates who condemn her to wear it. Moreover, by applying this art to her own letter, she puts her gift to work in the service of her private thoughts and feelings."[9] Hester's embroidered A—her language, her voice, her proclamation of passion and non-conformity—cleverly encodes Sophia's artistic visual and verbal media, as both painter and "Queen of Journalizers."

---

8 Hannah Arendt, *The Human Condition* (Chicago: University of Chicago Press, 1958), 49, 25, 32. Nathaniel Hawthorne to William Ticknor, January 19, 1855, *The Letters, 1853–1856,* 17:304.

9 Nina Baym, *Readings on The Scarlet Letter*, Literary Companion Series (San Diego: Greenhaven Press, 1998), 93.

Like her who represented heterosexual intimacy in "Endymion," "Isola," or "Mennagio," Hester invests the "A" with sexual signification. No wonder that Dimmesdale, like his creator Nathaniel, is tremulous and convulsive and shudders and shivers at the specter of symbolic revelation of his physical union with Hester. Like his author he is the uniquely privileged interpreter of this representation, for Dimmesdale alone knows that he is the man signified by this "A" for adultery, the crime and sin, and "A" for Arthur. This "scarlet letter" is indeed a *letter*, an item of private correspondence between lovers that invokes Sophia's undoubtedly scarlet letters to Nathaniel during their engagement, letters he assured would remain visible to his eyes alone.

The "A" reproaches Dimmesdale's guilty silence about his love for Hester and its embodiment in Pearl, and that silence has repercussions for mother who must and does assume full economic responsibility for their child, just as she assumes exclusive responsibility for Pearl's nurture and moral development. In these capacities, Hester demonstrates herself to be entirely able, another value signified by the scarlet "A," and represents an extreme type of emerging motherhood. Women had formerly been regarded as passive incubators of their children during pregnancy; after birth, children's discipline and character formation were duties of the father. At the time of *The Scarlet Letter's* composition, however, the departure of fathers from the home to the public sphere coincided with an emerging hereditarian theory that posited far more responsibility for the mother. A child's physical and moral welfare were now believed, by those enlightened by "scientific" theory, to be the result of a dynamic process beginning *in utero* and persisting after birth. Sophia's vigilance about every aspect of her children's lives—the food they ate, the air they breathed, the homeopathic medicine they took to prevent or cure illness—attests to her belief that maternal nurture would triumph over nature. She abhorred the thought of corporal punishment; so exceedingly gentle was her method of discipline that it was invisible to her critics. Such practices inform Hester's attitudes toward Pearl, whose assertion, "'I am my mother's child,'" is a profound affront to patriarchal authority not on theological but on ontological and sociological grounds. Indeed, Hester's independence and her fierce refusal to name the child's father wrests all rights and responsibilities from him, a fearful indictment of manhood.[10]

---

10 Monika Elbert in "Hester's Maternity: Stigma or Weapon," *Emerson Society Quarterly* 36 (1990): 179 examines the consequences of the evolution of separate

A father so constructed is impotent indeed, and "The Custom House" chapter, which introduced *The Scarlet Letter*, allowed Nathaniel to ruminate about his own failures as a provider. He deplored the lassitude of his fellow Custom-House employees who idled their days spinning tales. Even that, however, he was forced to admit, was beyond his power at the time: "My imagination was a tarnished mirror," he admitted, and would-be characters mock him. "'The little power you might once have possessed over the tribe of unrealities is gone! . . . . Go, then, and earn your wages!' In short, the almost torpid creatures of my own fancy twitted me with imbecility, and not without fair occasion" (34, 35). The man whose identity and livelihood should depend upon verbal prowess could not summon words, his impotence as a writer linked to his financial failures. So painful was this admission that it required him to utter it in the third person: "Conscious of his own infirmity,—that his tempered steel and elasticity are lost,—he for ever afterwards looks wistfully about him in quest of support external to himself." This conspicuously phallic metaphor illustrates Charles Rosenberg's observation that, for nineteenth-century American men, "The demand for economic achievement . . . served in synergistic parallel with that for sexual achievement."[11]

Thus the domestic politics of the Hawthorne household, the tensions that arose as a result of Sophia's and Nathaniel's deviations from normative assignments of gendered behavior, informed the composition of *The Scarlet Letter*. Nathaniel Hawthorne depicted the emerging usurpation of male authority as a drama that played out for him at this moment of his perceived failures as provider and wage-earner. Sophia's competences would have

---

spheres during mid-century America and its impact upon "Hester's single motherhood [which] is one of those peculiar feminine mysteries that men have made taboo because it robs them of their power." See Sophia's "Family Journal" portion of *American Note-books* in *Studies in the American Renaissance* (1996): 147–76. My other references here are Nathaniel Hawthorne, *The Scarlet Letter*, 1:110 and Charles Rosenberg, "The Bitter Fruit: Heredity, Disease and Social Thought in Nineteenth-Century America," in *Perspectives in American History* (Cambridge: Cambridge University Press, 1974), 190–94.

11   Charles Rosenberg, "Sexuality, Class, and Race in 19th-Century America," *American Quarterly* 25 (1973): 146. David Leverenz grounds manhood upon the observation that by midcentury, men had begun "to measure their worth primarily through their work." Leverenz, *Manhood in the American Renaissance* (Ithaca: Cornell University Press, 1989), 3.

further eroded his sense of manhood. It was she who had pressed for public acknowledgment, exercised professional talent, earned wages, and assumed responsibility for childrearing, thus wresting from Nathaniel those activities that defined masculinity. Just as depictions of Chillingworth/Dimmesdale encode emasculating biographical circumstances, depictions of Hester represent womanhood as Sophia enacted it.

Nathaniel claimed that *The Scarlet Letter* "broke [Sophia's] heart and sent her to bed with a grievous headache—which I took as a triumphant success!"[12] What broke her heart? What gave her a headache? Did Sophia recognize in Hester her strength, talent, and sexuality? Did she recognize in Dimmesdale/Chillingworth the secrecy of her engagement and the burden of silence placed upon Hester? While biographical evidence answers in the affirmative, the novel itself deconstructs that conclusion, for *The Scarlet Letter* turned the tide in Nathaniel's literary career. By speaking the unspoken, he fashioned from the silencing of female voice and control of female assertiveness an eloquent statement about the power of woman. Exorcizing his fears of inadequacy as a man, husband, and wage earner, he launched his most successful and acclaimed work to that date and began the most prolific period in his life as a writer.[13]

University of North Carolina at Pembroke

---

12 Nathaniel Hawthorne to Bridge, February 4, 1850, *The Letters, 1843–1853*, 16:312.

13 Versions of this article have appeared elsewhere as "'Then, All Was Spoken!' What "The Custom-House" and *The Scarlet Letter* Disclose," in *The Nathaniel Hawthorne Review* 40 (2014): 19–39 and in *Sophia Peabody Hawthorne, a Life*, vol. 2 (University of Missouri Press, 2015): 35–37.

The Missing Man of *The Scarlet Letter*

Richard Kopley

We all like to understand the origins of cultural achievements. We are intrigued to know that Pablo Picasso's 1907 painting, *Les Demoiselles d'Avignon*, was influenced in part by African masks; that Bob Kane's 1939 creation Batman was shaped in part by Zorro; and that the Beatles's 1967 song, *Being for the Benefit of Mr. Kite*, was drawn from a nineteenth-century circus poster.[1] After all, we want to know something about the nature of the imagination. In my one-semester American literature survey at Penn State DuBois, "The Great Traditions in American Literature," I try to appeal to this interest.

It is always satisfying to elicit from students the connection between a great work in the American literary canon and a great work from another literary canon altogether. The Master of Chancery's three denials of Bartleby in Herman Melville's classic 1853 short story are usually recognized by at least one student to be versions of Peter's three denials of

---

1   See Robert Goldwater, "Intellectual Primitivism," *Picasso in Perspective*, ed. Gert Schiff (Englewood Cliffs, NJ: Prentice-Hall, 1976), 35-45; Sarah Boxer, "Bob Kane, 83, the Cartoonist Who Created 'Batman,' Is Dead," *New York Times*, November 7, 1998, http://www.nytimes.com/learning/general/onthisday/bday/1024.html; Steve Turner, *A Hard Day's Write: The Stories behind Every Beatles Song*, 3ʳᵈ ed. (1994; London: Carlton Books, 2005), 127–28.

Jesus in the books of Matthew, Mark, Luke, and John.[2] The elopement of Harney Shepherdson and Sophia Grangerford in Mark Twain's 1884 novel, *The Adventures of Huckleberry Finn*, is typically understood by a few students as an adaptation of the doomed love in William Shakespeare's *Romeo and Juliet*. Sometimes, of course, the students need a little help, so I point out other connections--for instance, Washington Irving's transformation in his 1819 short story, "Rip Van Winkle," of Otmar's "Peter Klaus the Goat-Herd," and Edgar Allan Poe's borrowing of the meter for his 1845 "The Raven" from that of Elizabeth Barrett Browning's "Lady Geraldine's Courtship."[3] There is sometimes a little surprise at the interconnectedness of things. And there is always discussion about the merits of the achievement of the American writer and the virtue of the transformation.

Doubtless, all of us who teach the American literature survey note connections between our canon and other canons. Doubtless, too, all of us observe connections within the American literary canon and try to enable the students to make the connections themselves, when possible. In my experience in the classroom, sometimes students pick out the relationship between Jay Gatsby's schedule of self-improvement and Benjamin Franklin's schedule of self-improvement in the *Autobiography*. When I highlight the early language in "Rip Van Winkle,"—"the blue tints of the upland melt away into the fresh green of the nearer landscape"—it is possible that a

---

2 For my study of the biblical allusions in "Bartleby," see "The Circle and Its Center in 'Bartleby the Scrivener,'" *ATQ* 2, no. 3 (1988): 191–206.

3 For the "Rip Van Winkle" source, see Johann Karl Christoph Nachitigal ["Otmar"], "Peter Klaus the Goatherd," *Great German Short Stories*, ed. Lewis Melville (pseud. for Lewis Saul Benjamin) and Reginald Hargreaves (New York: Boni and Liveright, 1929), 332–35. For Irving's response to those who noticed the source, see his note to "The Historian" in *Bracebridge Hall or The Humorists A Medley by Geoffrey Crayon, Gent.*, (Vol. 9 in *The Complete Works of Washington Irving*), ed. Herbert F. Smith (Boston: Twayne, 1977), 247. For scholarly commentary, see Henry A. Pochmann, "Irving's German Sources in *The Sketch-Book*," *Studies in Philology* 27 (1930): 477–507. T. O. Mabbott discusses Poe's use of Elizabeth Barrett Browning's meter in "Lady Geraldine's Courtship" for "The Raven"—see Edgar Allan Poe, *Collected Works of Edgar Allan Poe*, 3 vols., ed. Thomas Ollive Mabbott (Cambridge, MA: Belknap/Harvard University Press, 1969–78), 1:356–57. I discuss "The Raven" in Richard Kopley and Kevin J. Hayes, "Two Verse Masterworks: 'The Raven' and 'Ulalume,'" *The Cambridge Companion to Edgar Allan Poe*, ed. Kevin J. Hayes (Cambridge, UK: Cambridge University Press, 2002), 191–204.

student, given an appropriate prompt to remember the early tale, will catch the connection when F. Scott Fitzgerald writes in *Gatsby*, "the inessential houses began to melt away until gradually I became aware of the old island here that flowered once for Dutch sailors' eyes—a fresh green breast of the new world."[4] Having studied Edgar Allan Poe's "The Raven," students are likely to recognize echoes in Walt Whitman's "Out of the Cradle Endlessly Rocking" (for example, "Demon or bird!" and "never more shall I cease perpetuating you").[5] What I hope they note, as well--in *Gatsby* again--is that in the scene at the Plaza, the language—"but the silence was unbroken by his 'thank you'"—owes something to "The Raven," too.[6] Having studied Poe's "The Tell-Tale Heart," students will usually recognize in response to a guiding question Hawthorne's transformation of that work in chapter 10 of *The Scarlet Letter* (regarding Roger Chillingworth's approaching the sleeping minister, Arthur Dimmesdale). With a hint or two, they usually also see the link between that Poe tale and Frederick Douglass's *Narrative of the Life of Frederick Douglass,* in which Douglass writes of Hugh Auld, "He raved, and swore," and later states, "I thought I was never better satisfied with my condition than at the very time during which I was planning my escape."[7]

---

4   Washington Irving, "Rip Van Winkle" in *The Sketch Book of Geoffrey Crayon, Gent.* (Volume 8 in *The Complete Works of Washington Irving*), ed. Haskell Springer (Boston: Twayne, 1978), 29; F. Scott Fitzgerald, *The Great Gatsby*, in *Cambridge Edition of the Works of F. Scott Fitzgerald*, ed. by Matthew J. Bruccoli (Cambridge: Cambridge University Press, 1991), 140. I noted this in *The Threads of "The Scarlet Letter"* (Newark: University of Delaware Press, 2003), 112. For the Irving quotation in the survey textbook, see *The Norton Anthology of American Literature*, 7th ed., 2 vols., ed. Nina Baym (New York: W. W. Norton, 2008), 1:456 ("Rip Van Winkle" is 455–66).

5   For the relevant pages of the survey textbook, see *The Norton Anthology of American Literature*, 7th ed., Poe, "The Raven," 1:675–78; Whitman, "Out of the Cradle Endlessly Rocking," 1062–66.

6   Regarding Poe and Whitman, see Joseph M. DeFalco, "Whitman's Changes in 'Out of the Cradle' and Poe's 'Raven,'" *Walt Whitman Review* 16 (1970): 22–27. For an elaboration of the link between "The Raven" and *Gatsby*, see n. 5 in Kent P. Ljungquist's "Fitzgerald's Homage to Poe: Female Characterization in *This Side of Paradise* and *Tender is the Night*," *Poe and Our Times: Influences and Affinities*, ed. Benjamin Franklin Fisher IV (Baltimore: Edgar Allan Poe Society, 1986), 96. The relevant passage in *The Great Gatsby* appears in the 1991 Cambridge, p. 100.

7   For Poe's "The Tell-Tale Heart," see *The Norton Anthology of American Literature*, 1:702–05. For the relevant pages of Douglass's *Narrative* in the Shorter

In all these cases, of course, we explore the interpretive implications of the correspondences noted, from "Bartleby" as a failed Second Coming to Douglass's *Narrative* as a challenge to patriarchy. For many students, our discussions of verbal correspondences constitute their introduction to the power of allusion.

I'd like to discuss how I embed in the American literature survey class a particularly rich set of allusions that I have come upon: Nathaniel Hawthorne's three allusions in his novel, *The Scarlet Letter* (1850), to the novel, *The Salem Belle* (1842). I have discussed the strong relationship between the two novels elsewhere;[8] I will consider here how that relationship may enliven classroom study of Hawthorne's classic. I will proceed chronologically, as I do in the classroom, from the Antinomian Controversy of the 1630s, as recorded by John Winthrop in his journals, to eventually *The Scarlet Letter*, and to that crucial intertext, *The Salem Belle*. This last, obscure volume was published anonymously, but the name of its author is knowable, and that name is no mere bibliographical trifle. Indeed, the name of this novel's author makes possible our understanding the significance of Hawthorne's allusions to it.

After an introductory lecture on the first day of class, I usually proceed on the second day of class with passages from John Winthrop. Although for many of the texts in this course I rely on the shorter (seventh) edition of the *Norton Anthology of American Literature*, for Winthrop I rely on volume 1 of *Winthrop's Journal "History of New England," 1630-1649*.[9] I pass out to the students on the first day, along with the course description and syllabus, six extracts from this volume. The focus in all six is the Antinomian Controversy, the conflict that took place in Boston from 1636 to 1638 between the theocratic government, led by Governor John Winthrop, and a small group of defiant believers, led by Anne Hutchinson and the husband of her sister-in-law, the Reverend John Wheelwright. The issue was the very nature of the divine covenant. Hutchinson and Wheelwright challenged the government, maintaining that it erroneously advanced a covenant of works when it should have propounded the covenant of grace. That is, they

---

Seventh Edition, see 978. I have written of the connection of "The Tell-Tale Heart" to *The Scarlet Letter* in *Threads* 22–35, and of the link between Poe's tale and *Narrative of the Life of Frederick Douglass* in *Threads*, note 31, 130.

    8   Kopley, *Threads*, 64–96.

    9   John Winthrop, *Winthrop's Journal "History of New England," 1630-1649*, 2 vols., ed. James Kendall Hosmer (New York: Scribner's, 1908).

contended that salvation was determined not from without but from within.[10] This early dissent engages students as an instance of principled resistance to authority. I encourage the students as they read to focus on the historical account and to be assured that unfamiliar language and points of doctrine will be clarified in class as we proceed.

The first extract (195-99) introduces Anne Hutchinson, who believes in an inner spirit ("the Holy Ghost"), and the "silenced minister," Mr. Wheelwright, who defends a similar view. The Reverend John Cotton, caught between the theocratic leaders and the two dissenters, tries to resolve matters peacefully. The second extract (210-19) presents Wheelwright at court, attacking the covenant of works; Winthrop discusses other topics, then returns to Wheelwright, who speaks for the covenant of grace. The sentencing of Wheelwright is delayed. The third extract (232–35) offers specific points of belief with which Wheelwright did not agree, and the court ruled that it was "disorderly" for one woman (Hutchinson) to address "sixty or more" "in a prophetical way, by resolving questions of doctrine, and expounding scripture" (234). The fourth extract (239–41) describes the court's eventual decision: since Wheelwright would not recant, nor were his allies able to sway the majority, "he was disenfranchised and banished" (240), given two weeks to leave the colony or be arrested. Hutchinson was also called to the court, for she had attacked ministers "for not preaching a covenant of free grace." She "vented her revelations," and therefore "the court proceeded and banished her" but allowed her to stay in "a private house" since it was winter (240). The fifth extract (259–65) recounts Hutchinson's being given an opportunity to concede her mistakes, which she initially did: "she yielded she had been in error" (261). However, later "she made a retraction of near all, but with such explanations and

---

10 For a helpful presentation of the evidence regarding the Antinomian Controversy, see David D. Hall, ed., *The Antinomian Controversy, 1636–1638 A Documentary History*, 2nd ed. (Durham: Duke University Press, 1990). Relevant supplementary reading includes John Cotton, *The Correspondence of John Cotton*, ed. Sargent Bush, Jr. (Chapel Hill: University of North Carolina Press, 2001); Michael P. Winship, *Making Heretics: Militant Protestantism and Free Grace in Massachusetts, 1636–1641* (Princeton: Princeton University Press, 2002); Francis J. Bremer, *John Winthrop: America's Forgotten Founding Father* (New York: Oxford University Press, 2003); and Eva LaPlante, *American Jezebel: The Uncommon Life of Anne Hutchinson, the Woman Who Defied the Puritans* (New York: HarperSanFrancisco, 2003).

circumstances as gave no satisfaction to the church" and then, according to Winthrop, "she impudently persisted in her affirmation" (that she had not said what she had said). So, "the church, with one consent, cast her out" (264) and she left for Providence Plantation. The sixth and final extract (324–25) reveals that, according to Winthrop, with Hutchinson and Wheelwright gone, "the Lord brought about the hearts of all the people to love and esteem them [Winthrop and Cotton] more than ever before, and all breaches were made up, and the church was saved from ruin beyond all expectation" (324).

This early confrontation with authority in the Massachusetts Bay Colony elicits much interest in the students. Discussion focuses on a variety of matters including the self-serving and self-satisfied view of Winthrop; the courage of Hutchinson and Wheelwright; the irony that the Puritans, persecuted in England, became the persecutors in the colony; the dangers of a theocracy; and the virtues of what we sometimes take for granted in the United States, the separation of church and state. Depending on the students and recent events, we may consider other instances in our history of the arrogance of the enfranchised or the bravery of the disenfranchised. Or we may consider the development of women's public role in society, including its present strengths and limitations. Perhaps we may consider current theocracies and current persecution. Or we might consider the significance of the religious views of our Founding Fathers. The Antinomian Controversy yields much to talk about. At the close, I tell the students that this historical conflict will emerge again, a little past the midway point in the course, when we read Nathaniel Hawthorne's novel, *The Scarlet Letter*. Some students have already read the novel in high school, but I tell them that they will have a new understanding of the work in this course.

For the purposes of this essay, I will skip two months from January to March. We read in that time some of the greats, including Benjamin Franklin, Thomas Jefferson, Washington Irving, Edgar Allan Poe, Ralph Waldo Emerson, Henry David Thoreau, and Margaret Fuller. We have our midterm and then begin with Frederick Douglass. Following spring break, finally, we get to Nathaniel Hawthorne and *The Scarlet Letter*. I allocate four hour-and-fifteen-minute classes to that novel, the first of these to "The Custom-House" and each of the next three classes to eight chapters of the twenty-four chapter work. In the second class of the four, we come upon the reference to "the sainted Anne Hutchinson" in chapter 1, and some student will recall our early reading and consider why she is "sainted."[11] We also come upon the reference to "an Antinomian" in chapter 2 (37). In the third class of the four, we learn in chapter 13 that if Hester Prynne had never born her daughter Pearl, "Then she might have come down to us in history, hand in hand with Anne Hutchinson, as the foundress of a religious sect" (108). So we infer Hester's close association with the female Antinomian leader. But what of the male Antinomian leader?

In the fourth of the four classes on *The Scarlet Letter*, we encounter the three allusions to *The Salem Belle*. In order to enable students to recognize these allusions, I provide them with photocopies of the relevant pages from the 1842 novel. I rely on my own copy, but the novel is available on Google Books. (I have written an introduction to a forthcoming reprint of *The Salem Belle*.) We begin with chapter 17, "The Pastor and His Parishioner."[12] This relates the meeting, in the forest, between the former lovers, Hester Prynne and Arthur Dimmesdale. Hester, who wears the scarlet letter, has been punished, but Dimmesdale, who has hidden his part in the relationship for seven years, has not. We are told that "one solemn old tree groaned dolefully to another, as if telling the sad story of the pair that sat beneath, or constrained to forebode evil to come." The despairing minister asks, "'Must I sink down there, and die at once?'" Hester offers him her strength and encouragement and finally advises, "'Up, and away!'" (126–28). Similarly, chapter 12 of *The Salem Belle* relates the meeting in the forest between brother and sister, James and Mary Lyford. Mary has been accused of witchcraft in Salem, and James provides her with hope and counsel: at first, "'do not sink under this load of sorrow,'" and later "'immediate flight is necessary.'" The author writes, "The wind sighed mournfully along, as if in sympathy with the sadness which had fastened deeply on the minds of brother and sister."[13]

---

11   Nathaniel Hawthorne, *The Scarlet Letter and Other Writings*, ed. Leland S. Person (New York: W. W. Norton, 2005), 37. This is the edition we used in the American literature survey. For the passage in the scholarly edition, see Nathaniel Hawthorne, *Centenary Edition of the Works of Nathaniel Hawthorne*, ed. William Charvat, et al. 23 vols. (Columbus: Ohio State University Press, 1962-97), 1:48. For the sake of accessibility, subsequent references to the novel are from the former edition and are documented parenthetically.

12   The correspondences are more fully treated in Kopley, *Threads*, 84–89.

13   [Ebenezer Wheelwright], *The Salem Belle: A Tale of 1692* (Boston: Tappan and Dennet, 1842): 172–77.

We discuss the parallels, these and others, and agree that they are not conclusive but that they are suggestive. Then we turn to chapters 20 and 21 in *The Scarlet Letter*, "The Minister in a Maze" and "The New England Holiday." We focus on the passages about Boston Harbor. There is a ship, "one of those questionable cruisers, frequent at that day, which, without being absolutely outlaws of the deep, yet roamed over its surface with a remarkable irresponsibility of character." Hester is seeking to book passage to England on board this ship for herself, the minister, and their daughter Pearl. Later, Hawthorne acknowledges, "It remarkably characterized the incomplete morality of the age, rigid as we call it, that a license was allowed the seafaring class, not merely for their freaks on shore, but for far more desperate deeds on their proper element. The sailor of that day would go near to be arraigned as a pirate in our own." He adds, "The Puritan elders, in their black cloaks, starched bands, and steeple-crowned hats, smiled not unbenignantly at the clamor and rude deportment of these jolly seafaring men" (137, 148). Notably, in chapter 15 of *The Salem Belle*, "a little schooner" appears piloted by Captain Ringbolt. The author comments, "How he obtained his merchandise was sometimes a mystery; but the Salem ladies were careful not to inquire too curiously into the matter." The anonymous writer adds, "It was rather wonderful, however, that so much charity was extended towards this gentleman, considering the very strict morals of the Puritans, and the rigid honesty with which they were accustomed to discharge their pecuniary obligations."[14] In both harbor scenes, the Puritans tolerate something akin to piracy. In *The Salem Belle*, a character named Somers again seeks passage on board the uncertain vessel for Mary and James Lyford, as well as her beloved, Strale, and Somers himself and his wife and child.[15]

The class is ready for a third pair of related passages. So we move ahead to "The Revelation of The Scarlet Letter" and "Conclusion." Dimmesdale, having given his Election Sermon, ascends the scaffold and confesses, tearing open his shirt, revealing the scarlet letter on his breast. Hawthorne begins by stating that "all eyes were turned towards the point where the minister was seen to approach among them." The townspeople observe him hold Pearl's hand, rely on Hester's support, then "approach the scaffold, and ascend its steps." He addresses those gathered, "'People of New

---

14   Ibid, 203–04.
15   Ibid., 218.

England! . . . ye, that have loved me—ye, that have deemed me holy!—behold me here the one sinner of the world!'" He declares that his sin was far greater than Hester's, that her scarlet letter "is but the shadow of what he bears on his own breast," and he reveals his own scarlet letter seared into his flesh. As he dies, "the multitude, silent till then, broke out in a strange, deep voice of awe and wonder" (158–63). Yet some denied seeing anything and considered the minister to have been acknowledging only that all men are sinners. I am quiet as we turn to the conclusion of *The Salem Belle*, toward the end of 17, and I wait for the students to recognize the parallels. They do.

The students notice that the vengeful rebuffed suitor, Trellison, the falsely accusing enemy of Mary Lyford, who is unable to live with his guilt, also "mounted the scaffold," and they identify further correspondences. As "[e]very eye in that immense assemblage was fixed upon him," Trellison confessed all. He declared, "'Hear me, magistrates and men, and ye ministers of an insulted God! hear me, old age, middle life and youth! I proclaim in your ears that the maiden who has this day escaped death, was guiltless of the crime for which she was condemned to die!'" He goes on: "'It was this hand that brought down the threatened ruin upon that child of innocence and love.'" After his confession, "he passed through the spell-bound and awe-struck multitude," and when he was gone, "An unbroken silence reigned for a few moments through all that vast assembly, and the first words that were spoken, were an expression of thankfulness that the innocent maiden had escaped." However, some consider the confession untrue, owing to the supposed witchcraft of the escaped Mary Lyford.[16]

The students appreciate the connection and now can consider its significance. Discussion follows regarding why Hawthorne made this series of allusions to *The Salem Belle*. One possibility is that he was linking the Antinomian Controversy with the Salem witchcraft delusion, since both involve the oppression of the innocent by those in power. And, of course, as Hawthorne admits in *The Scarlet Letter*, his own ancestor John Hathorne was one of the persecutors of the so-called "witches" (11–12). I let discussion go on for a few minutes, then bring in a critical new fact: the identity of the author of *The Salem Belle*. A *research path* leading from a copy of the novel at the Lilly Library at Indiana University with the inscription "By Mr.

---

16 Ibid., 228–31. For my earlier presentation of the parallels between *The Scarlet Letter* and *The Salem Belle*, see *Threads*, 84–89. For treatment of my finding the parallels, see my "Adventures with Poe and Hawthorne," *The Edgar Allan Poe Review* 14, no. 1 (2013): 16–35 (see esp. 25–26).

Wheelwright" to the papers of the family of the inscriber, Jane Ann Reed, at the Rare Book and Manuscript Library of Columbia University, including a reference to his address, to Boston directories for 1841 and 1842 reveals the author to be Ebenezer Wheelwright. This is further confirmed by examination of his papers at the New England Historical and Genealogical Society; another copy of *The Salem Belle*, held by the Phillips Library of Salem, Massachusetts, inscribed by "E. Wheelwright"; and another novel with similar theme, plot, and language, *Traditions of Palestine*, whose authorship is acknowledged by Ebenezer Wheelwright in the NEHGS papers to be his.[17] How should we understand the name of the author, I ask my students, in light of his direct descent from John Wheelwright, his great-great-great-great grandfather?

The response may come slowly, but it comes, perhaps with a few hints. Even as we link Hester Prynne with Anne Hutchinson, we may link the minister, Arthur Dimmesdale, with John Wheelwright. Why? Even as Hester and Dimmesdale suffered similarly with public humiliation in *The Scarlet Letter* for what is perceived as a shared crime, adultery, so too did Anne Hutchinson and John Wheelwright suffer similarly with expulsion for a shared crime, the defiance of the theocratic authority. Evidently Hawthorne used the secret authorship of *The Salem Belle*, available to him through his publisher and Ebenezer's, Tappan and Dennet, as well as, perhaps, through his friend, editor James Russell Lowell, and his sister-in-law Elizabeth Peabody, to intimate the Antinomian Controversy. It is John Wheelwright, I would argue, who is the missing man in *The Scarlet Letter*.[18]

At this point we discuss the word "allegory," for *The Scarlet Letter* seems an allegorical representation of the famous conflict from 1636 to 1638. The word is somewhat familiar since we've discussed allegory in Poe's *The Narrative of Arthur Gordon Pym*. I've presented Poe's novel as a double

---

17   Out of deference to time constraints in the classroom, I am brief with the students about the research. For a fuller account, see Kopley, *Threads*, 64–96, 142–53. See also Kopley, "Adventures with Poe and Hawthorne," 23–31. The Lilly Library volume inscription is courtesy Lilly Library, Indiana University, Bloomington, Indiana. The Phillips Library volume inscription is from the C. E. Frazer Clark Collection, Clark ADD 423, Copy 1, Phillips Library, Peabody Essex Museum, Salem, Massachusetts.

18   See also Kopley, *Threads*, 91–94; Kopley, "Adventures with Poe and Hawthorne," 31–32.

allegory, involving both a familial level and a biblical one.[19] Remarkably, I argue, there is a double allegory in *The Scarlet Letter*, too. They look puzzled, and I ask where before they have read a story of a man and woman who disobeyed authority and were expelled. Following a moment or two of quiet, a student will mention Adam and Eve in the Garden of Eden. Thus there is a kind of wonder at the artistry of Nathaniel Hawthorne. He has rendered allegorically in his greatest novel both the Antinomian Controversy and The Fall. He has developed with deftness and intricacy the great theme of his oeuvre, Man's Fall and its consequence. Repeatedly, we discover that the origin of Hawthorne's work involves his concern with Original Sin.

And so the class comes to a close. But there may be one final question: Did Hawthorne really put all that stuff in there? I respond first by asking if it wouldn't be harder to believe that the patterns we've worked out are totally coincidental, and there's usually agreement that it would be. Then I offer an analogy, one I have found that easily engages my students. I ask them to think of their best friend. Consider how he or she seemed on first meeting. Now, consider how he or she seems after you've really gotten to know that person. Is there a difference? (Nods.) What kind of difference? The students may be forthcoming here or not, but even if they would rather not talk about their specific best friend, they're thinking about their answer to the question. A great work of literature, I say, is like a best friend. Over time, after close and perhaps affectionate attention, both may open up and reveal their complexities. Close reading—of a book, of a friend—requires patience and devotion. But the rewards, I say with pleasure, are great.

Penn State University (DuBois)

---

[19] See my introduction to Edgar Allan Poe, *The Narrative of Arthur Gordon Pym of Nantucket* (New York: Penguin, 1999), ix–xxix.

Giving Shape to Gloom; or, Keeping it Real in *The House of the Seven Gables*

Robert T. Tally, Jr.

In what might be considered the climactic moment of Nathaniel Hawthorne's *The House of the Seven Gables*, the mysterious Holgrave proclaims his love for Phoebe and describes the transformative effect she has had upon him. Prior to her arrival, he exclaims, "[t]he world looked so strange, wild, evil, hostile; my past life, so lonesome and dreary; my future, a shapeless gloom, which I must mold into gloomy shapes!"[1] His estimation of Phoebe's power is a more heartfelt version of the narrator's earlier observation regarding "her proper gift of making things look real, rather than fantastic, within her sphere" (297). The scene highlights a theme of the novel as a whole, one announced by Hawthorne himself in the preface, that is, the appropriate relationship between the real and the fantastic. In *The House of the Seven Gables*, the romancer Hawthorne, using a "gift" proper to both Holgrave and Phoebe, shapes the gloom in order to dispel it and

---

1   Nathaniel Hawthorne, *The House of the Seven Gables*, volume 2 of the *Centenary Edition of the Works of Nathaniel Hawthorne*, ed. William Charvat, et al. (Columbus: Ohio State University Press, 1965), 314. References to this edition are hereinafter cited parenthetically in the text.

thereby to transform the material of a romantic, seemingly otherworldly tale into something almost unremarkably mundane.

One of the difficulties students sometimes have with this book and with much of Hawthorne's work is this persistent ambiguity with respect to what is or is not "real." Is Young Goodman Brown's vision "really" just a dream? What "really" is revealed on Arthur Dimmesdale's chest in *The Scarlet Letter*'s finale? In *The House of the Seven Gables*, Hawthorne dramatizes this ambiguity, indulging in fantasy while insisting on a kind of "realism," which is a somewhat anachronistic term when used in this context but which does seem to fit the attitude he wishes his readers to adopt in the end. Actually, he wants to have it both ways, a more intense realism made possible by allowing his narrative to partake of the unreal or fantastic. In the classroom, this can cause consternation, both with respect to the work itself—just what's *really* going on here?—and to the place of the novel in American literature more generally, that is, what is the value of this densely symbolic or ironic narrative relative to works with more explicit messages like Frederick Douglass's *Narrative*, Harriet Beecher Stowe's *Uncle Tom's Cabin*, or Henry David Thoreau's *Walden*? The student's understandable desire for a straightforward meaning and a clear message is thwarted by the author's insistence upon irony and ambiguity. Hawthorne challenges his readers, in more ways than one, warning them in the preface that "[w]hen romances do really teach anything, or produce any effective operation, it is usually through a far more subtle process than the ostensible one," and "[a] high truth . . . is never any truer, and seldom any more evident, at the last page than at the first" (2–3). The challenge to the student lies in figuring out how to perceive this truth, which requires the student to ascertain the real substance amidst the shapeless gloom of the narrative.

Hawthorne's ambiguous approach to reality in this romance is tied to his sense that literary works employing ambiguity provide access to a "higher" truth than the author thinks possible in more realistic writings, including nonfiction. In this, he may have shared Herman Melville's distaste for "plodding" narratives of fact. In a letter that accompanied the manuscript for his third book, 1849's *Mardi: and A Voyage Thither*, Melville asked his publisher not to list him on the title page as the author of *Typee* and *Omoo*, for he wished to "separate 'Mardi' as much as possible from those books." He confessed that, while *Mardi* was originally conceived as a continuation of such travelogues, in "proceeding in my narrative of *facts* I began to feel an incurable distaste for the same; & a longing to plume my feathers for a flight, & felt irked, cramped, and fettered by plodding along with dull common places."[2]

This distinction between plodding personal narrative and soaring romance is not merely one between nonfiction and fiction. After all, we know Melville took many liberties with the truth in *Typee* and *Omoo*. Rather, it had more to do with that authorial "latitude" claimed by Hawthorne in the preface to *The House of the Seven Gables*, according to which the writer of a romance may tell the truth even more effectively than the writer of nonfiction or of realistic fiction, who is limited by facts. Hawthorne himself might have been distinguishing his own romances from the earlier tales and sketches limited to intensely local experiences or regional characters, such that his literary narratives opened up a greater imaginative space for a writer's exploratory adventure than could be possible in the local or personal narrative forms, as these terms are used in Jonathan Arac's T*he Emergence of American Literary Narrative, 1820–1860*.[3]

Melville had not yet met Hawthorne in 1849, but his encounter with Hawthorne the following year, in which *The Scarlet Letter* was also published, famously influenced his much more ambitious project in *Moby-Dick*. *Moby-Dick* is a book only ostensibly based on Melville's personal experiences as a whaleman, but as his narrator breathlessly puts it late in the novel, the narrative really involves nothing less than "the whole circle of the sciences, and all the generations of whales, and men, and mastodons, past, present, and to come, with all the revolving panoramas of empire on earth, and throughout the whole universe, not excluding its suburbs."[4]

In moving from the representational modes of their earlier local and personal narratives, Hawthorne and Melville transformed their literary cartographies partly by reimagining both the spaces to be mapped and the narrative techniques used to map them. This artistic shift required a sort of map-like projection in order to achieve a sense of totality, and the

---

2   Herman Melville, *Correspondence*, ed. Harrison Hayford, Alma A. MacDougall, G. Thomas Tanselle, et al. (Evanston: Northwestern University Press and the Newberry Library, 1987), 114–15.

3   Arac, *The Emergence of Literary Narrative, 1820–1860* (Cambridge: Harvard University Press, 2005).

4   Herman Melville, *Moby-Dick, or, The Whale*, ed. Harrison Hayford, Hershel Parker, and G. Thomas Tanselle (Evanston: Northwestern University Press and the Newberry Library, 1988), 456.

resulting romances expanded the imaginary geography of American literature, moving beyond both place and the individual observer, toward a broader survey of the territory as a whole ... not excluding its suburbs. In Hawthorne's case, in particular, this move was facilitated by an ironic position with respect to realism. The ambiguities of emergent, mid-nineteenth-century literary narrative actually help make sense of the real world, often in hitherto unforeseen ways. The desire for verisimilitude and the pleasure found in flights of fancy are thus not mutually exclusive, even if they are frequently in tension. In examining this tension in a novel like *The House of the Seven Gables*, students can learn to appreciate the aesthetic power both of giving shape to the gloom and of keeping it real in imaginative literature.

Hawthorne famously raises the problem of proportion between reality and fantasy in his preface, where he strikes a distinctively defensive tone in distinguishing the genres of novel and romance, and particularly in drawing attention to the differences in the role and expectations of an author. As Hawthorne explains,

> When a writer calls his work a Romance, it need hardly be observed that he wishes to claim a certain latitude, both as to its fashion and material, which he would not have felt himself entitled to assume, had he professed to be writing a Novel. The latter form of composition is presumed to aim at a very minute fidelity, not merely to the possible, but to the probably and ordinary course of man's experience. The former—while, as a work of art, it must rigidly subject itself to laws, and while it sins unpardonably, so far as it may swerve aside from the truth of the human heart—has fairly a right to present that truth under circumstances, to a great extent, of the writer's own choosing or creation. If he think it fit, also, he may so manage his atmospherical medium as to bring out or mellow the lights and deepen and enrich the shadows of the picture. He will be wise, no doubt, to make a very moderate use of the privileges here stated, and, especially to mingle the Marvellous rather as a slight, delicate, and evanescent flavor, than as any portion of the actual substance of the dish offered to the Public. He can hardly be said, however, to commit a literary crime, even if he disregard this caution. (1)

The paragraph contains a delightful mélange of metaphors, comparing writing to painting or to the culinary arts, but what stands out most vividly is the political or juridical discourse of rights, privileges, and crime. In the opening words of *The House of the Seven Gables*, even before the main story of crime and punishment begins, Hawthorne wishes to absolve himself of even the imputation of a crime himself. Although "as a work of art," the Romance "must rigidly subject itself to laws," the author of a romance, who is free to choose or create both the material of a romance and the way such material is presented, is granted full immunity in advance. The novelist may not have the same freedoms, being confined not only to the possible but also to the probable and ordinary. For Hawthorne, the romancer, operating outside the jurisdiction of the literal-minded or worse, is beyond the reach of the literary constabulary.

Hawthorne, however, does avoid the excesses of fantasy, and one might argue that the entire point of *The House of the Seven Gables* is to indulge briefly in the terrors and delights of the fantastic, before returning to the domestic tranquility of the everyday.[5] In this romance, he supplies several examples of the delicate mingling of "the Marvellous and the Real." The primary method seems to be that he will introduce something that could be interpreted as otherworldly, only to offer a rational, altogether ordinary explanation, one that would utterly dispel the fantastic image and reveal it to be almost uninterestingly mundane.

Take, for example, the story of Maule's well. On the very spot upon which the house of the seven gables stands, there had been a "natural spring of soft and pleasant water—a rare treasure on the sea-girt peninsula" (6). Presumably, this spring is part of what had made the area so attractive to old Colonel Pyncheon, who managed to confiscate the land after Matthew Maule was convicted of witchcraft and executed. The horror of that original sin and of Maule's curse is what gives *The House of the Seven Gables* its ostensibly supernatural effects, but throughout the novel, the fantastic gets mingled with the real. When Colonel Pyncheon builds his house on this ill-gotten acre, the curse first reveals itself in the well: "It was a curious, and, as some people thought, an ominous fact, that, very soon after the workmen began their operations, the spring of water, abovementioned,

---

5   In "Hawthorne and the Real," Millicent Bell, following the lead of Henry James, questions the validity of the romance/novel distinction and argues for Hawthorne as a significant realist (or proto-realist) novelist. See Bell, "Hawthorne and the Real," in *Hawthorne and the Real: Bicentennial Essays*, ed. Millicent Bell (Columbus: Ohio State University Press, 2005), 1–21. Focusing primarily on *The Scarlet Letter*, this entire collection re-examines Hawthorne's purported distance from realism.

entirely lost the deliciousness of its pristine quality. Whether its sources were disturbed by the depth of the new cellar, or whatever subtler cause might lurk at the bottom, it is certain that the water of Maule's Well, as it continued to be called, grew hard and brackish" (10). The "subtler cause" is otherworldly, the curse of a dead warlock, but the everyday explanation of contamination is far more realistic. The authorial narrative voice declines to be authoritative in this matter, preferring to allow both explanations, regardless of likelihood to coexist.

Other examples abound, some involving more supernatural phenomena than others. For instance, we learn that "the world" unfairly and erroneously views Hepzibah Pyncheon as an "ill-tempered old maid," owing to the "scowl" perpetually worn on her face. Hawthorne, however, notes that "this forbidding scowl was the innocent result of near-sightedness" (34). Here, the misperception is not due to any curse but has all too real consequences for Hepzibah. Even in this entirely quotidian detail, a woman's squint mistaken for a scowl, Hawthorne creates an aura of ambiguity and irony typical of his literary narratives.

As Arac has pointed out, literary narrative emerged in the United States around 1850, with such works as Hawthorne's romances and Melville's *Moby-Dick* and *Pierre, or, the Ambiguities*. With the Compromise of 1850, a brief respite from sectarian discord was dearly bought. As Senators Henry Clay and Stephen Douglas had wished, the threat to the Union was averted (or postponed) by this legislation. In the relative calm of the moment of compromise, a small window opened for a new kind of literature, one that would become a highly valued cultural form in the following century. Writers of literary narrative, a form devoted to originality, creativity, and the imagination, in many cases deliberately distanced their work from the concerns of the day and expected such works to be judged according to intrinsically aesthetic standards, rather than being held up to any quotidian reality: "The Compromise of 1850 had displaced politics and opened the possibility for the *literary* narratives of Hawthorne and Melville."[6] At the same time, the outrage occasioned by the compromise poured fuel upon an already fiery commitment to another kind of writing, more directly

---

6   Jonathan Arac, *The Emergence of American Literary Narrative, 1820–1860* (Cambridge: Harvard University Press, 2005), 181. See also Arac, "The Politics of *The Scarlet Letter*," in *Ideology and Classic American Literature*, ed. Sacvan Bercovitch and Myra Jehlen (Cambridge: Cambridge University Press, 1986), 247–66.

political and engaged, which Arac calls *national narrative* that could be typified by the rhetoric of Frederick Douglass and the fiction of Harriet Beecher Stowe. Their writings, along with those contemporaneous works by Hawthorne and Melville, mark an important moment in the history and literature of the United States, a moment when the tensions of aesthetics and politics are made visible in interesting ways.

The politically charged writings of Douglass and Stowe had motivations and functions rather different from the literary fiction of Hawthorne and Melville. In the literary narrative form, the author carved out a space for the imagination and directly set the work apart from the political issues of the day. This is not to say that literary narratives do not also bear on the social and political spheres, but that in their use of irony, allegory, linguistic complexity, and personal interiority or psychological experience, they absent themselves from the most pressing matters of daily social life. For the sensitive reader, these works may edify, but they do not take a firm position. *Moby-Dick* may tell one quite a bit about the nature of work, of human relations, of good and evil, of the darkness in the hearts of men, and of the dignity of human life, plus it teaches us a good deal about whales and whaling, but it will not tell us how to vote in the elections of 1852. The ambiguities and nuances that make for great literature are precisely the things that interfere with an effective political program, where one needs to see clearly what the problem is, what steps may be taken to solve it, and how to organize multitudes to affect the solution.[7]

An animating feature of Hawthorne's romances is that they call into question *agency*, whether conceived as individual or collective action. In challenging the very ability of people to make a real difference, he necessarily removes direct political action from the sphere of literature, contrary to the express aims of such other, more politically active writers as Douglass and Stowe. We can see this in even so outwardly political a writer as Melville. In *Moby-Dick*, for example, a symbolically named fictional intermediary ("Call me Ishmael") is established between the author and the

---

7   For a discussion of the literary historical conflict between literary and national narratives, see my "'Literature Proper': Genre Problems in an Early American Literature Survey," *Teaching American Literature: A Journal of Theory and Practice* 1, no. 2 (Spring 2007): 123–41. See also my foreword to Gerardo del Guercio, *The Fugitive Slave Law in* The Life of Frederick Douglass, an American Slave *and Harriet Beecher Stowe's* Uncle Tom's Cabin: *American Society Transforms Its Culture* (Lewiston, NY: Edwin Mellen, 2013), iii–x.

reader, and this sensitive spectator reports on events and the activities of others without taking much action himself.[8] Indeed, even the great "man of action" himself, Ahab, is cast as a more ambiguous figure, the tragic hero whose will is also subject to fate—"Is Ahab, Ahab? Is it I, God, or who that lifts this arm?"—an actor who is most often *acted upon* by some unseen force. In *The Scarlet Letter*, Hawthorne's narrative style requires the reader to interpret events without directly taking a position. Hawthorne refuses to define his terms but allows multiple meanings to proliferate, most obviously in the ambiguous symbol of the scarlet "A" itself.

As Sacvan Bercovitch has noted, Hawthorne's fiction actually makes ambiguity into a political virtue, as its very uncertainties make possible compromise by establishing that neither party in a given conflict can really know with certainty what is right: "Ambiguity is the absence of conflict.... Process for him is a means of converting the threat of multiplicity (fragmentation, irreconcilability, discontinuity) into the pleasures of multiple choice, where the implied answer, 'all of the above,' guarantees consensus."[9] If "all of the above," however, is the answer, a narrative's very polysemy, its multiplicity of meanings, disengages it from active politics in which choices need to be definitively made for good or ill. Hawthorne establishes an apolitical stance that distances his narrative from the pressing events of the day.

Even more visible is the lack of action in *The House of the Seven Gables*, where the felicitous happy ending is occasioned by mere happenstance, and no action by any character is required to make things right in the end. The putative villain, Judge Pyncheon, dies of seemingly mysterious but wholly natural causes. The fortune that restores our heroes, particularly Hepzibah and Clifford, to wealth and social position falls in their laps by an off-camera stroke of luck, when the rightful heir, Judge Pyncheon's son, who had not been mentioned previously, is revealed to have also died while abroad. Even the radical politics of the enigmatic firebrand character, Holgrave, are literally domesticated by the magic of marriage and home. He who had once raged about the necrocracy of baleful tradition, which weighs like a nightmare on the minds of the living, becomes

---

8   See, e.g., Robert T. Tally, Jr., *Melville, Mapping and Globalization: Literary Cartography in the American Baroque Writer* (New York: Continuum, 2009), especially 50–64.

9   Sacvan Bercovitch, *The Office of The Scarlet Letter* (Baltimore: Johns Hopkins University Press, 1991), 26.

the devotee of "permanence" and an ironically self-acknowledged "conservative" (314–15).

Such turns of events work better in romance than in real life, of course, but it may be that Hawthorne felt that inaction or even the impossibility of action was preferable to the sort of revolutionary activity the younger Holgrave and his Fourierist contemporaries advocated. Elsewhere, in his 1852 campaign biography of his old Bowdoin College classmate, Franklin Pierce, he writes that slavery was "one of those evils which divine Providence does not leave to be remedied by human contrivances, but which, in its own good time, by some means impossible to be anticipated, but of the simplest and easiest operation, when all its uses shall have been fulfilled, it causes to vanish like a dream."[10] Hawthorne defends Pierce's own support of the Compromise of 1850, and the idea that slavery would soon disappear as if by natural processes or according to divine Providence may well have assuaged the guilty consciences of those anti-slavery supporters of the Compromise.

Whether this is wishful thinking, a commitment to romanticism, or a calculated political position, Hawthorne's "fantasy of evanescence" (as Arac calls it)[11] offers cold comfort to those combating the "evil" of slavery and no comfort at all to those in bondage. Douglass, knowing all too well the pertinacity of the slave system, had little patience for the arguments of incrementalists or the wait-and-see crowd of putatively anti-slavery thinkers. In a profoundly artful manner, and yet, without compromising his own political commitments in the least, he combined his own personal experience and eyewitness testimony with a broader abolitionist argument. Although the genre within which he wrote was *personal narrative*, he readily extended his experiences to a national platform that made his arguments more directly graspable as political, not merely personal, action.

Similarly, but operating within the realm of fiction, indeed of sentimental romance, Stowe's *Uncle Tom's Cabin* offered a national narrative with a powerful critique of slavery which all readers could readily discern. Stowe's readers are not encouraged to ponder the complex ambiguities of the plot but actively recruited to adopt a clear ideological position on slavery, the central issue of contemporary national controversy. As a romancer, but

---

10 Nathaniel Hawthorne, *The Life of Franklin Pierce* (1852; New York: MSS Information, 1970), 113.

11 Arac, *The Emergence of American Literary Narrative*, 151.

unlike Hawthorne, Stowe went out of her way to nationalize the narrative, even making the hated villain, Simon Legree, a Northern-born man from New England, as if to emphasize that the sin of slavery is not limited to Southerners or to individual sinners but taints the nation as a whole. With the widespread and largely unprecedented success of this novel, Stowe establishes the political uses of sentimental fiction in the real world. By depicting the horrors of "life among the lowly," *Uncle Tom's Cabin*'s final subtitle, she also describes the dehumanizing condition of a system in which humans are transformed into objects; the subtitle of the original, serialized publication was "The Man Who Was a Thing." Swiftly moving from the discrete experiences of individual characters to the national and even human condition, *Uncle Tom's Cabin*, no less than the writings of Douglass, exhorts its audience to act and to act on behalf of a realizable political and ethical program.

In this sense, *The House of the Seven Gables* has nearly the opposite effect. With its commitment to ambiguity and irony, this romance draws the reader away from any political program that might pit impoverished but high-born ladies, ex-criminals, young radicals, or poor working men (like Uncle Venner) against the grasping, rampant bourgeoisie, although Hawthorne clearly has some fun in introducing the improbability of such a class struggle. With its obliteration of agency, *The House of the Seven Gables* undermines any overtly political reading, since no action is required to render a happy ending, and the only force for good, Phoebe, with "her proper gift of making things look real, rather than fantastic, within her sphere" (297), operates passively by shedding a sort of natural, innate light on the gloominess of others around her. Hawthorne's own "gift" as a writer allows him to present the most fantastic scenes, make them appear altogether real, and in the end cancels out the distinction by bringing the castles in the air back down to earth.

In this project, the author, whether claiming to be a romancer or a novelist, becomes a kind of sorcerer, entrancing the reader by producing visions. As if to underscore this supernatural vocation, Hawthorne includes a chapter in which we learn that the Daguerreotypist Holgrave is also a writer, whose "name has figured . . . on the covers of Graham and Godey" (186). The chapter, "Alice Pyncheon," is really a Holgrave-authored short story, and the plot involves the enchantment of the eponymous Pyncheon by a descendent of Old Matthew Maule and, hence, Holgrave's ancestor. Upon completing the tale, Holgrave discovers that his storytelling has enchanted Phoebe, that she is entirely under his power: "It was evident, that, with but one wave of his hand and a corresponding effort of his will, he could complete his mastery over Phoebe's yet free and virgin spirit" (211–12). The suggestion of sorcery is not to be taken literally, of course, but Hawthorne here implies that there is powerful and dangerous magic in the mere act of telling a story.

The magic of the everyday is part of the ambiguity of Hawthorne's romances and of *The House of the Seven Gables* in particular, but just as Holgrave abjures his power over Phoebe, Hawthorne dispels the otherworldly in favor of the mundane. In one of the most bizarre scenes in the novel, one that really seems out of place, the unnamed narrator directly addresses the corpse of Jaffrey Pyncheon, openly berating him while "indulging our fancy in a freak" (280), a phantasy involving a procession of Pyncheon ghosts. As if repenting this authorial decision, Hawthorne returns to the language of the preface and cautions the reader that "[t]he fantastic scene, just hinted at, must by no means be considered as forming an actual portion of our story. We were betrayed into this brief extravagance by the quiver of the moonbeams; they dance hand-in-hand with shadows, and are reflected in the looking-glass, which, you are aware, is always a kind of window or door-way into the spirit world" (281). Thus, like Holgrave during the same fateful night, Hawthorne himself seems to have been forced to mould a shapeless gloom into gloomy shapes (306). During all of this, Clifford and Hepzibah experience their own wild train-ride, in which the most modern and ordinary conveyance seems almost a magic carpet ride to a bewildering new world, and yet when they step off the train, "[t]he world fled away from these two wanderers" (266).

The dreariness and gloom afflicting these "two owls" are also dispelled by the light of Phoebe, once they return to the house of the seven gables. Thus, the several chapters comprising the death of Jaffrey Pyncheon, which also detail events taking place while Phoebe has been away, find their clarifying and realistic resolution in the mere presence of the girl: "But the house was not altogether so dreary as Clifford imagined it . . . when Phoebe ran to meet them" (308). Phoebe, with her "proper gift of making things look real, rather than fantastic," casts her light upon the scene and allows the "real" to triumph.

In the world without Phoebe, a world of romantic fantasy rather than novelistic realism, the figurative geography and its requisite points of reference are "most fantastically awry." This phrase comes from an early scene in *The House of the Seven Gables*. Hanging in the study of the Pyncheon manse, opposite the portrait of the stern Colonel Pyncheon, is a map of a territory to the east, which is "grotesquely illuminated with pictures of Indians and wild beasts, among which was seen a lion; the natural history of the region being as little known as its geography, which was put down most fantastically awry" (33). As readers know, this "little known" region to the east provides the motive force for much of the plot, and even though it never appears in any substantive way within the text, this place exerts a spiritual power over the fates of the Pyncheon and Maule families for generations. One might say that the resolution of the novel requires the imaginary geography of the place to be "put down aright," as Hawthorne's narrative first invokes, then undermines the shapeless gloom and gloomy shapes of a Gothic or romantic landscape by establishing a clear, orderly, and perhaps a bit too conveniently neat ending in which everything is illuminated, not grotesquely but realistically, in the light of Phoebe. In the end, the haunted house of the seven gables, like the "little known" territory to the east, becomes of place of passing fancy, a hollow old building evacuated of its dense historical content. In Hawthorne's romances, the gloom is dispelled by those who are able to face the truth. "Be true!" is the motto of *The Scarlet Letter*, after all. The mist-enveloped domain of fantasy can be cleared up in the light of a real world sensibility, and Phoebe is the avatar of this concept; the very word *Phoebe*, in fact, refers to a shining light. For all of Hawthorne's delving into the spirits of particular places in New England, the ultimate aim is to set down the geography "aright," making way for the prosaic reality of everyday life.

Texas State University

Approaching *The Blithedale Romance* through the History of the Book

Sarah Wadsworth

Following quickly on the heels of two full-length romances, a children's book, and a collection of tales and swiftly succeeded by a campaign biography, *The Blithedale Romance* (1852) represents the culmination of the most successful, prolific, and varied phase of Hawthorne's career. The third of four romances completed, *Blithedale* departs from his other book-length fictions in several respects. It's the only romance to be set entirely within Hawthorne's own milieu, it's the only romance to feature writers as principal characters, and it's the only one to employ a first-person narrator. Owing in part to its contemporary setting, authors as protagonists, and biographical undertones, *Blithedale* lends itself especially well to pedagogical approaches that attend to nineteenth-century print culture. Inherently interdisciplinary and "hands-on," a "History of the Book" approach offers students new ways to access and understand literary history in general and *The Blithedale Romance* in particular.

Situated at the intersection of three core disciplines—bibliography, history, and literary studies—the History of the Book requires an awareness of printed materials as physical objects as well as "cultural transactions" and forms of artistic expression.¹ Beginning with the artifact itself, book history simultaneously calls on practitioners to examine minute details of the physical text—the closest of close readings—and to open out to investigate the material conditions of authorship, reading, and publishing. As Leslie Howsam explains, book history considers the book as a process, something that *happens*, and "ask[s] questions about relationships" between readers and writers, authors and editors, publishers and markets, and, indeed, among all the parties involved in what Thomas R. Adams and Nicolas Barker refer to as "the whole socio-economic conjuncture" within which books operate.² With the digitization of an endless archive of artifacts, book history is no longer the exclusive province of professional scholars with access to unique objects in special collections. Furnished with a handful of documents easily obtainable on the internet or in scholarly editions, students of *Blithedale* can benefit from a rigorous nuts-and-bolts approach that asks them to attend to the significance of details and nuances within the physical book while exploring connections between the literary text and the historical world outside the text.

I typically spend two to three weeks on *Blithedale*, dividing the text into six sections and building into the schedule a set of exercises focused on specific print artifacts. My first experience teaching *Blithedale* was in an advanced undergraduate course called "Writing in the 1850s," which I adapted from Donald Ross's graduate seminar at the University of Minnesota and transplanted to a small liberal arts college. Since the entire course was grounded in the History of the Book, I wanted the students to explore the archive looking for items that would help situate the assigned readings within the context of 1850s print culture. A largely unsifted collection of books bequeathed to the college and including an unexpectedly marvelous array of mid-nineteenth-century materials proved to be a bonanza. Favored with a library that welcomed guest-curators, I arranged for the class to develop an exhibit of 1850s books. After browsing through a cartload of materials culled from the stacks, students picked items to research

---

1   Leslie Howsam, *Old Books and New Histories: An Orientation to Studies in Book and Print Culture* (Toronto: University of Toronto Press, 2006).
2   Howsam, *Old Books and New Histories*, 4. See Thomas R. Adams and Nicolas Barker, "A New Model for the Study of the Book," *A Potencie of Life: Books in Society: The Clark Lectures, 1986-1987*, ed. Nicolas Barker (London: British Library, 1993), 5–44. Adams's and Barker's conceptual map appears in Howsam, *Old Books and New Histories*, 36.

and write up for a special display. Showcasing the kinds of popular productions David S. Reynolds discusses in *Beneath the American Renaissance* (1989; 2011), the exhibit included the two-volume first edition of *Uncle Tom's Cabin*, a copy of Fanny Fern's bestselling *Ruth Hall*, a book of parlor games, and a popular songbook, all accompanied by placards containing bibliographical details and notes prepared by the students and professionally produced by library staff.[3]

Although this particular exhibit framed an entire course, lasted for several weeks, and was open to the whole campus community, the activity can be downsized easily to concentrate on a cluster of satellite texts centered around *The Blithedale Romance*. In an essay on book history in the American literature classroom, Jean Lee Cole explains a set of assignments she calls "Time Capsules," in which students examine, describe, analyze, and report on artifacts of nineteenth-century print culture.[4] Tailored to *The Blithedale Romance*, such an exercise can mobilize students individually or in small groups to browse through digital archives such as GoogleBooks, Internet Archive, and Making of America to locate and then report on materials that illuminate aspects of the cultural history informing Hawthorne's work: for example, women's history, reform movements, spiritualism, and Transcendentalism.[5]

While these activities serve as a kind of wide-angle lens affording a broad view of contemporaneous print culture, other artifacts can function like a magnifying glass, enabling students to enlarge upon specific moments or problems in the text that reward detailed analysis. The front matter is an excellent place to begin. Since readers often skip front matter altogether, it's worth spending a little time discussing its various functions with the class. In a "smart classroom" clicking through the first edition's opening pages allows students to compare their own paperback copies with the original and observe how components of the physical book, including typography,

---

3   Thanks to Kristi Wermager and the staff of Gould Library at Carleton College for hosting the "Writing in the 1850s" exhibit.

4   Jean Lee Cole, "Book History in the American Literature Classroom: On the Fly and On the Cheap," *Teaching Bibliography, Textual Criticism, and Book History*, ed. Ann R. Hawkins (London, Pickering and Chatto, 2006), 59–61.

5   *The Blithedale Romance: A Bedford Cultural Edition*, ed. William E. Cain (Boston: Bedford/St. Martin's, 1996) and *The Blithedale Romance: A Norton Critical Edition*, ed. Richard H. Millington (New York: W. W. Norton, 2011) provide a useful foundation for exploring these and other contexts.

cover design, and marketing pieces, frame the text. Viewing the lengthy advertisement from *Blithedale*'s publisher, Ticknor, Reed, and Fields, at the beginning of some copies of the first edition, including ones available through Internet Archive and the Hathi Trust, for example, provides a glimpse into the literary marketplace in which Hawthorne participated.[6] The prevalence of genteel poets—Longfellow, Whittier, Holmes, and Lowell—draws attention to Hawthorne's use of a fictional poet as narrator, while the dominance of American authors reflects the distinct brand of literary nationalism promoted by editor James T. Fields.[7] In addition, the appearance of Grace Greenwood (Sara Jane Lippincott) in a list that is almost exclusively male highlights both long-standing gender inequities and the inroads women writers were making in the nineteenth-century literary marketplace.

Other components of the front matter help establish a sense of Hawthorne's personal history, audience, and preferred genre. Paratexts such as prefaces, forewords, and introductions create their own generic expectations, and it's useful to canvass students on their own reading practices. Do they read, skip, or skim them? Why, or why not? After these ice-breakers, the class is poised to evaluate Hawthorne's rhetorical aims in *Blithedale*'s preface. Parsing this document as a set of instructions in which the author positions his text and guides readers in how to read and how not to read can help ensure that students approach the romance itself with some understanding of the Brook Farm experiment, its relation to Hawthorne's life and fiction, and a working definition of "romance" as Hawthorne conceived it.

A convenient bridge from front matter to fiction occurs in the preface's third paragraph, where Hawthorne identifies the four principal characters:

---

[6] The Online Books Page maintains a list of digitized editions of Hawthorne's works. See The Online Books Page: Online Books by Nathaniel Hawthorne, accessed March 3, 2014, http://onlinebooks.library.upenn.edu/webbin/book/search?author=Nathaniel+Hawthorne&amode=words.

[7] On literary nationalism, see Susan S. Williams, "Publishing an Emergent 'American' Literature," *Perspectives on American Book History: Artifacts and Commentary*, ed. Scott E. Casper, Joanne D. Chaison, and Jeffrey D. Groves (Amherst: University of Massachusetts Press, 2002), 165–76. Several early reviewers couched their praise in the discourse of literary nationalism as well. See J. Donald Crowley, ed., *Hawthorne: The Critical Heritage* (New York: Barnes and Noble, 1970), 243, 245; *The Blithedale Romance: A Norton Critical Edition*, 259.

"the self-centered Philanthropist," "the high-spirited Woman," "the weakly Maiden," and "the Minor Poet." It's also worth noting that Hawthorne considered several alternative titles for this novel, including "Hollingsworth," "Zenobia," "Priscilla," and "Miles Coverdale's Three Friends," in addition to "The Veiled Lady," "The Arcadian Summer," and, simply, "Blithedale."[8] Asking students what meaning they attach to these capitalized labels can open up a discussion of Hawthorne's use of character types and initiate a conversation on the four main players. As a professional poet, Coverdale is neither a starving artist shivering in a garret nor a Whitmanesque Bohemian sounding his "barbaric yawp"; he is respectable, bourgeois, and conventional, much like the poets advertised by Ticknor, Reed, and Fields. Making this connection helps students understand the vastly different role of poetry in the nineteenth century, with poets like Longfellow and Tennyson selling in large popular editions to mainstream readers. At the same time, the pairing of the gentleman-poet Coverdale and the lady-magazinist Zenobia highlights tensions between the traditional publishing patriarchy and a new generation of popular, prolific, and often "strong-minded" women writers, such as Fanny Fern and Grace Greenwood, both of whom Hawthorne admired.[9] With some insight into the unprecedented success of such mid-century novelists as Harriet Beecher Stowe, Maria Cummins, and Susan Warner, students can better understand the commercial pressures Hawthorne faced, epitomized by his slur against "a d---d mob of scribbling women" in a letter to publisher William D. Ticknor, as well as the harsh criticisms Coverdale levels at Zenobia, both as a writer and as a woman.[10]

---

8   Fredson Bowers, "Textual Introduction," in *The Centenary Edition of the Works of Nathaniel Hawthorne*, Vol. 3: *The Blithedale Romance* and *Fanshawe*, ed. William Charvat et al. (Columbus: Ohio State University Press, 1964), xix. Subsequent citations from *The Blithedale Romance* are from this edition and are parenthetically documented.

9   For a useful discussion of women writers and "gentleman publishers," see Susan Coultrap-McQuin, *Doing Literary Business: American Women Writers in the Nineteenth Century* (Chapel Hill: University of North Carolina Press, 1990), chs. 1–2.

10   Nathaniel Hawthorne to William D. Ticknor, January 19, 1855, in Nathaniel Hawthorne, *The Letters, 1853–1856*, ed. Thomas Woodson, et al., *The Centenary Edition of the Works of Nathaniel Hawthorne*, (Columbus: Ohio State University Press, 1987), 16:304.

As Scott Casper observes in his chapter on antebellum reading in *Perspectives on American Book History: Artifacts and Commentary,* many nineteenth-century novels included scenes of reading. In these vignettes, books-within-books constitute embedded artifacts that illuminate the literary culture within the text.[11] The excerpts in this invaluable sourcebook provide useful reference points for considering how the convalescent Coverdale immerses himself in the reading matter at hand. The texts he enumerates, including volumes of Emerson, Carlyle, and the *Dial,* form the foundation of an ideal education in Transcendentalist thought. At the same time, the reference to the *Dial,* preceded by a prophetic allusion to Margaret Fuller, points to the most important woman writer associated with New England Transcendentalism while adumbrating the interconnected roles of writers, female characters, and "prophet" figures within Hawthorne's romance. By extrapolation, the example of Emerson's Poet contrasts in varying ways with Hawthorne's failed "Minor Poet," false prophets like Hollingsworth and Westervelt, and the feeble yet "Sybilline" Priscilla.[12] Coverdale also reads popular "romances" by women writers with proto-feminist themes, as indicated by Zenobia's sharing of novels by George Sand. Like the allusion to Fuller, this reference foregrounds the role of the woman writer and lends irony to the fate Hawthorne assigns Zenobia.

Praised by both Henry James and William Dean Howells as the greatest of Hawthorne's heroines, Zenobia embodies the plight of the female intellectual at a time when the Cult of True Womanhood defined women strictly in terms of domesticity.[13] An effective artifact for acquainting students with Victorian gender ideology is the article, "Literary Women" (1864). In this essay, the author argues that successful women writers "[undergo] a defeminizing process" in which they "sacrifice [their] innocence." Identifying George Sand as a cautionary "beacon that points out the rocks and shoals which literary women seldom reach, but in the direction of which most of them are sailing," this critic warns that for a woman "knowledge of life" is "the fruit from off a deadly tree, the taste of which

---

11 Scott Casper, "Antebellum Reading Described and Prescribed," in *Perspectives on American Book History: Artifacts and Commentary,* 160–61.
12 On literary nationalism, writing as prophecy, and women writers, see Williams, "Publishing an Emergent 'American' Literature," 184–92.
13 Henry James, *Hawthorne* (London, 1879), 106-07; William Dean Howells, *Heroines of Fiction* (New York: Harper and Bros., 1901), 175–78.

opens to her the wide world, but closes to her the gates of the enchanted gardens of paradise." Moreover, because women "almost always" lack the "severe discipline" required for a "literary education," their uncontrolled "passion itself becomes weak or luxuriant; and sympathy degenerates into weakness." In conjunction with contemporaneous writing reflecting more positive attitudes toward women writers (*Perspectives on American Book History* and the *Bedford Cultural Edition* provide samples), this artifact succinctly contextualizes one of *Blithedale*'s central conflicts in language that echoes Coverdale's.[14]

Hawthorne's characterization of Zenobia is richly allusive, yet for most students this will be opaque without some shared reference points. Compiling some nineteenth-century visual images into a sequence of slides can demystify Hawthorne's veil of allusions. To begin, a portrait of Margaret Fuller will remind students of the reference to her in chapter 7 as well as Hawthorne's ambivalence towards her, immortalized in his journal.[15] Fuller, whose life was interpreted as a "representative fiction of the time,"[16] became known to contemporaries as "the New England Corinne." A slight digression on Madame Germaine de Staël's germinal novel *Corinne, or Italy* (1807) locates *The Blithedale Romance* as a text that appropriates and revises this immensely popular figure of the tragic female intellectual. Alerting students to Coverdale's role in this act of revision prepares them to interrogate how Zenobia and Coverdale separately deploy historical and mythological allusions to affirm and challenge the nature and extent of women's power.

For nineteenth-century readers, the historical Zenobia (d. 274) carried significant weight as a symbol of female power and ambition. Following the death of her husband, with whom she had reigned jointly, she ruled Palmyra, dispatching her armies across the Near and Middle East in an

---

14   "Literary Women," *Littell's Living Age* 25 (1864): 609–10. Available in its entirety in ProQuest's *American Periodicals*, this article is excerpted in Williams, "Publishing an Emergent 'American' Literature," 181–82, but the excerpt omits the allusions to George Sand, forbidden fruit, and "luxuriant" passion.

15   Nathaniel Hawthorne, Vol. 14: *The French and Italian Notebooks*, ed. Thomas Woodson in *The Centenary Edition of the Works of Nathaniel Hawthorne* (Columbus: Ohio State University Press, 1980), 155–57. The relevant passage is reprinted in *The Bedford Cultural Edition* of *The Blithedale Romance*, 490–92.

16   John Paul Eakin, *The New England Girl: Cultural Ideals in Hawthorne, Stowe, Howells, and James* (Athens: University of Georgia Press, 1976), 51.

attempt to conquer the Eastern Empire. With the defeat of her armies, she was taken captive and exiled in Italy. Numerous artists have depicted Zenobia in painting and sculpture, and slides displaying their work can recreate the associations that would have been familiar to readers who encountered her in popular periodicals of Hawthorne's day.[17]

Students will then have little trouble discussing ways in which Zenobia's self-naming is apt, although they will probably need guidance to see how Coverdale repeatedly recasts her identity, substituting the historic image of tragic warrior queen with mythic images of female sexuality and transgression. His imagining of her in "Eve's earliest garment" is only the first such instance (17). (It's worth pointing out that this passage appears in the manuscript but not in the first edition, although it was restored to the Centenary Edition and subsequent editions based on it.)[18] Coverdale's first impression of Zenobia, in which he insistently directs readers' attention to her voluptuous body and away from her famously sharp mind, can alert students to the way this persistent sexualizing is tinged with suggestions of impropriety, perhaps most memorably in the speculation that "Zenobia has lived, and loved! There is no folded petal, no latent dew-drop, in this perfectly developed rose!" (47). Coverdale also likens Zenobia to Pandora, ostensibly on account of the glow in her cheek (24). (Students may be interested to know that in *A Wonder-Book for Girls and Boys* [published in 1852, like *The Blithedale Romance*], Hawthorne retooled the myth of Pandora's box in the story "The Paradise of Children.")[19] Much later, in the final encounter between Zenobia and Coverdale, she wields a related image, comparing

---

17   These might include the sculpture *Zenobia, Queen of Palmyra* (1857) by Harriet Hosmer, Giovanni Battista Tiepolo's *Queen Zenobia Addressing Her Soldiers* (1752), and Warwick Goble's *Zenobia, Queen of Palmyra* (1880), as well as Herbert Schmalz's *Queen Zenobia's Last Look upon Palmyra* (1888), Sir Edward Poynter's *Zenobia, Captive* (1878), Hosmer's *Zenobia in Chains* (1859), Guy Head's *Zenobia, Queen of Palmyra in Chains* (c. 1780), and William Bouguereau's *Zenobia Found by Shepherd on the Banks of the Araxes* (1850), which depicts the drowned Zenobia recovered from the river.

18   See Bowers, "Textual Introduction," l-liii for a discussion of this and two other deletions, including the lengthy anti-temperance digression in praise of "tippling" in Chapter 21. As Bowers notes, the expurgation may have been suggested by Hawthorne's wife, Sophia.

19   Walter Crane's illustration "Pandora Opens the Box" for *A Wonder-Book* (Boston: Riverside Press, 1892) provides a handy visual to accompany the Pandora reference.

Priscilla to Bluebeard's wife. Like the allusions to Eve and Pandora, this trope evokes female curiosity, sexuality, forbidden knowledge, transgression, and evil, but, in contrast, Bluebeard's wife confronts evil, exposes it, defeats it, and escapes victorious. Although Zenobia's bitter irony makes it clear that the comparison is a despairing mockery of Priscilla's docility and timidity, the ambiguity of her distraught remark that Priscilla "will make as soft and gentle a wife as the veriest Bluebeard could desire" complicates the conventional definitions of "strong" and "weak" women and mirrors the cultural ambivalence surrounding women's increasing power (226).

Given Coverdale's strategic misogynistic repositioning, it's easy to lose sight of Zenobia's status as a popular magazine contributor. "Zenobia's Legend," or "The Silvery Veil," offers a pertinent opportunity to explore the significance of her role as a writer. In this story-within-a-story (like "Fauntleroy" in form), Zenobia gives a dramatic oral performance that heightens the fantasy or "romance" quality that the preface touts while further distancing her rhetorically from the role of professional writer. At the same time, her dramatic storytelling echoes the kind of fairy-tale performance Hawthorne delivered through the narrator of *A Wonder-Book* and its sequel, *Tanglewood Tales* (1853). Coverdale, who absorbs the tale into his own narrative, characterizes Zenobia as more suited to the vocation of stage actress than writer despite her fame, which surpasses his own as a "Minor Poet." Coverdale also makes several pointed criticisms of her writing. A discussion of the ways in which the controversy over women's role politicized women's writing prepares the way for the pivotal debate that unfolds at Eliot's Pulpit.[20]

With the move from country to city in chapter 15, the time is ripe to shift attention to Coverdale and his role in the developing plot, a line of inquiry that leads into questions of authority (who gets to speak and why?), agency (who has the power to act?), and authorship (how do authors shape their material? how do they exert control?). Harkening back to chapter 11, the class can productively reassess Coverdale's claim that his "own part . . . resembled that of the Chorus in a classic play, which

---

20 An impromptu "readers' theater" of the scene at Eliot's Pulpit, conducted in multiple groups of four, can increase students' investment in *Blithedale*'s gender politics. At the conclusion of the novel, a survey of selected reviews reinforces the polarized views the character of Zenobia generated, both within the text and among antebellum readers. See, for example, Crowley, *Hawthorne: The Critical Heritage*, 258, 262, and 266.

seems to be set aloof from the possibility of personal concernment" (97). Here and elsewhere Coverdale imagines himself on the outside looking in, but how involved is he really? Turning to the tropes of masks and veils, as well as the imagery of performance and stagecraft, students might be prepared to consider his claim with skepticism and question the degree to which he's involved in shaping the plot, both as a participant in the "drama" and as its "author." These matters become especially complicated and crucial in the Hotel–Boarding House–Drawing Room sequence, in which stand-offishness gives way to voyeurism, and voyeurism slips into intrusiveness and meddling.[21]

Although few editions of *Blithedale* contain embellishments, a pair of illustrations from the late nineteenth century may prompt further discussion of Coverdale's voyeurism and the ironic link Hawthorne forges among various types of "seers"— observer, voyeur, visionary, prophet, false prophet, charlatan. In the P. Fenelon Collier edition (1900), an illustration depicts Zenobia, looking pensive and vulnerable, as a scowling Hollingsworth towers behind her in an aggressive and menacing posture. Meanwhile, in the background Priscilla and Coverdale look on surreptitiously, the latter nearly concealed by the cover of trees (fig. 1). Similarly, in the Service and Paton edition (1899), Coverdale peeps at the Masqueraders from behind a tree, spying on their revelry from afar (fig. 2). Examining these illustrations may encourage students to think critically about the relationship between image and text and consider how these graphic representations interpret and arguably alter the characters and scenes they portray.[22]

---

21 An entertaining entrée into these chapters is to show the opening scene from Alfred Hitchcock's *Rear Window*, in which a convalescent photojournalist idly trains his eye, and then his telephoto lens, on the apartment facing his flat. Asking students to think about the way the events in the apartments are filtered and mediated through various "lenses" can alert them to the problem of perspective in *Blithedale*.

22 Nathaniel Hawthorne, *The Works of Nathaniel Hawthorne*, ed. Julian Hawthorne, vol. 3, *Twice-Told Tales* and *The Blithedale Romance* (New York: P. Fenelon Collier, 1900). The illustration falls between pp. 234 and 235. Nathaniel Hawthorne, *The Blithedale Romance* (London: Service and Paton, 1899). The illustration, which appears between pp. 250 and 251, is reproduced in Michael Borgstrom, "Hating Miles Coverdale," *ESQ: A Journal of the American Renaissance* 56 (2011): 364.

Like Hawthorne's use of voyeurism, mesmerism as a textual motif raises questions about agency, passivity, manipulation, and power within a gendered, sexualized context. An effective way to explore how mesmerism functions thematically is to have students read the letter Hawthorne wrote to Sophia in anticipation of her attendance at a séance.[23] Working in small groups, students can tease out his objections to mesmerism, as articulated in both the text and the subtext of his response to Sophia. Ask them to "read between the lines" and substantiate their readings with reference to word choice and tone. Class discussion can then readily pursue the larger issues intimated by the letter. Hawthorne's concerns about relinquishing one's free will and exposing one's innermost self (or the innermost self of one's loved one, the "holy of holies," to "intrusion" and violation resonate with Coverdale's unintended eavesdropping on Hollingsworth as he prays, his complaints that he's not free, Priscilla's lack of agency—she is "only a leaf" carried along by the current—and Zenobia's sinister relationship with Westervelt, while raising additional questions about the text's implicit framing of romantic love as a form of spiritual "possession" or thralldom. Finally, mesmerism, both in the letter and in the romance, has an analog in Hawthorne's depiction of Hollingsworth as a charismatic leader who attempts to control his followers, body and soul, with its suggestions of misplaced belief, hypocrisy, and dubious spirituality. Considered from a book history perspective, mesmerism thus emerges as a complex and highly gendered trope hinging on verbal manipulation and narrative power and challenging the literary nationalists' conception of the writer as visionary, cultural prophet, and "representative man."

In composing *The Blithedale Romance,* not only did Hawthorne draw on forty pages of journal-writing devoted to his life at Brook Farm, but he also reworked other journal entries to flesh out details of *Blithedale*'s fictional world.[24] A useful exercise that allows students to practice fine-grained critical reading, while peering into Hawthorne's writing process, involves collating sections of the journal against the text of *Blithedale.* A

---

23 This letter can be found in *The Blithedale Romance: Bedford Cultural Edition,* 423–25 and *The Blithedale Romance: A Norton Critical Edition,* 237–39.

24 The Brook Farm entries (Sept. 26, 1841 to Oct. 27, 1841) appear in *The American Notebooks,* ed. Claude M. Simpson, *The Centenary Edition of the Works of Nathaniel Hawthorne,* vol. 8 (Columbus: Ohio State University Press, 1972), 196–222. The *Bedford Cultural Edition* of *The Blithedale Romance* includes excerpts.

quick introduction to this activity is to model a group collation by reading aloud the "picnic party" journal passage upon which Hawthorne based his description of Blithedale's Masqueraders, a passage that concludes with the entrance of Emerson and Fuller, sparking "much talk,"[25] while students peruse the fictionalized scene. After examining the ways he revised this journal entry, students will be prepared to analyze the entry in which Hawthorne recounts the recovery of Martha Hunt's body alongside the corresponding passage of fiction in which Coverdale describes Zenobia's corpse.[26] Working in pairs, students conduct a word-for-word comparison, with one student reading aloud from the journal while the other marks significant differences in the text of *Blithedale*. By carefully documenting which details Hawthorne retains, which ones he omits, and which new elements he introduces, students gain insight into his composition process and literary technique, especially his use of symbolism. This side-by-side comparison reveals, for example, that he invented details about the posture of Zenobia's corpse that simultaneously suggest prayer and combat. Students will readily grasp that this small revision has a powerful impact as it creates a graphic, highly symbolic image of the drowning woman's physical, spiritual, and emotional struggles. while prompting Coverdale's ensuing reflections on mercy and redemption, which run counter to the grim remarks on "inflexible judgment" Hawthorne inscribed in his diary.[27]

The textual history of *Blithedale*'s ending further illuminates Hawthorne's composition process, as well as the technical dimension of the text's journey from manuscript to bound book. In a notebook entry he recorded: "Wrote the last page (199th manuscript) of the Blithedale Romance, April 30th. 1852. Wrote Preface, May 1st. Afterwards modified the conclusion, and lengthened to 201 pages. First proof-sheet, May 14th."[28] In his introduction to The Centenary Edition of *The Blithedale Romance*, Fredson Bowers explains that "the fact that the first two details have dates and the third none may suggest that the conclusion was not appended before the

---

25 See Hawthorne, *The American Notebooks*, 201–02.
26 Hawthorne, *The American Notebooks*, 261–65. The relevant kernel of this entry is excerpted in the *Bedford Cultural Edition*, 496–96. On Hawthorne's "'method' as a writer of fiction" see Roy Harvey Pearce. "Introduction to *The Blithedale Romance*," *The Blithedale Romance* and *Fanshawe*, *The Centenary Edition of the Works of Nathaniel Hawthorne*, vol. 3 (Columbus: Ohio State UP, 1964): xxiii–xxv.
27 Hawthorne, *The American Notebooks*, 264.
28 Ibid., 314.

manuscript was sent to [E. P.] Whipple on May 2, the day after completion of the Preface." Although, as Bowers notes, "the case is indemonstrable," this scenario raises the possibility that Hawthorne's friend Whipple, to whom he sent the manuscript for critique, "could have suggested the need for a different ending from Coverdale's reflections at Zenobia's graveside."[29] Regardless of the lapse of time between Hawthorne's original completion of the romance and his penning a new conclusion, this late revision encourages students to contemplate the impact of the two endings on the romance as a whole and, in particular, the contrast between "the moral which presents itself to [Coverdale's] reflections" in Blithedale-Pasture and the moral that readers might infer from the belated revelations conveyed in "Miles Coverdale's Confession." The moral Coverdale "draw[s] from Hollingsworth's character and errors" in the Blithedale pasture can also be compared with the impassioned morals Coverdale extracts from Zenobia in their last exchange and his subsequent "softening" of Zenobia's caustic conclusions (224, 241, 243). Finally, readers should consider how Coverdale's renunciation of poetry as a vocation, as disclosed in the new ending, relates to the motif of failed prophecies, doomed prophets, and the inefficacy of the literary artist to effect change.

By the time the class finishes *The Blithedale Romance*, students have gained not only exposure to the History of the Book, but hands-on practice reading and interpreting the kinds of artifacts that book historians seek out and marshal as evidence. By leveraging these artifacts both to broaden the historical and cultural context of Hawthorne's world and to narrow it in order to analyze specific aspects of the literary text, a book history approach gives students insight into Hawthorne's creative process as well as his imaginative response to the gender dynamics and genre expectations of the nineteenth-century literary marketplace.[30]

Marquette University

---

29 Bowers, "Textual Introduction," lii. Hawthorne's letter to Whipple appears in *The Blithedale Romance: A Norton Critical Edition*, 253–54.

30 I would like to thank Donald Ross and Emily B. Todd for their thoughtful criticism of earlier versions of this essay.

Teaching Hawthorne's Romances and/in the History of American Sexuality

ZACHARY LAMM

There is no denying that the politics of sexuality in every sense of the word are central to *The Scarlet Letter*. Any substantial inquiry into that romance will require consideration of both biosocial sexual identity and practices of physical intimacy, as both play vital roles in the narrative trajectory and the moral universe of the text. In the context of feminist discussions of politics and sexuality, Lisa Duggan and Nan D. Hunter emphasize "questions of power, passion, violence, representation, consent, agency, diversity, and autonomy associated with sex" as key to understanding the nature of sexual politics;[1] in the context of *The Scarlet Letter*, these concerns take the form of questions of the nature of adultery and fidelity, same-gender and cross-gender identification and attraction, property rights (including the question of persons as property), the sexual division of labor, the gendered nature of power and authority, the violence that might be done to women and other minorities, the role of sex in forming both individual and communal identities, and the relation of sex as a component of private life to the law.

---

1 Lisa Duggan and Nan D. Hunter, *Sex Wars: Sexual Dissent and Political Culture* (New York: Routledge, 1995), 16.

Discussing *The Blithedale Romance*, another of Hawthorne's provocative romances, Michael Colacurcio has argued that we must understand Hawthorne's "urgent subtext" as "unblushingly sexual," and I believe this perspective is applicable broadly within the oeuvre of Hawthorne's romances, as he tries again and again with somewhat varied results to envision a sexual politics both inside and outside the mores of his contemporary society, which were positioned at an odd crossroads of enlightenment and fanaticism, empiricism and superstition, permissiveness and prohibition.[2] In making this claim, I will focus on *The Scarlet Letter* as an exemplar of the seriousness with which questions of the politics of sexuality must be analyzed and discussed as part of our pedagogical practices when teaching Hawthorne's romances and of the representative function of Hawthorne's romances within a transitional moment for American sexual history.

In this essay, I'm going to describe a course I'll call "Gender and Sexuality in Antebellum America," which I've taught several times in a number of ways for a variety of student audiences, ranging from introductory literature surveys to advanced seminars in Gender and Women's Studies. While the selection of texts and work required has varied greatly, the thesis of the course remains the same: in the decades between the American Revolution and the Civil War, the U.S. underwent massive shifts in terms of sexual politics that trouble the narrative of progress we have come to accept as a truism in the early twenty-first century. At the center of this course (and usually in fact at mid-semester) is Hawthorne, whose romances, I argue, are the documents most conscious and critical of the cognitive dissonance that plagued antebellum American culture on the subject of sex on the one hand—a religiously-driven reform movement that chastised the unvirtuous and the intemperate and on the other—the recognition of sex as a means of pleasure (and that pleasure as a kind of need) for both men *and* women. The notion of companionate marriage as opposed to merely proprietary marriage made sex and sexual desire appealing and, in a growing number of instances, acceptable in ways it had not been previously.[3]

---

2   Michael J. Colacurcio, "Nobody's Protest Novel: Art and Politics in *The Blithedale Romance*," *Nathaniel Hawthorne Review* 34, nos. 1–2 (2008): 25. Colacurcio describes the romance as ultimately chastising the sexual utopianism he claims we must recognize as its ineluctable if sometimes obscured theme, a position from which I depart in no uncertain terms.

3   The most concise and effective description of these historical shifts in sexual beliefs and practices within the nineteenth century comes from John D'Emilio and

More effectively than any of his peers, Hawthorne observed, recorded, and analyzed these tandem movements in attitudes toward sex, and reading his romances as the centerpiece of a rigidly divided and divisive transformation in attitudes toward sex alters both our attitudes toward antebellum understandings of the politics of sexuality and of the romances themselves, which students have often read—and have been taught to read—in a very conservative fashion.[4]

Sexual Positioning

The 1850s represent an unprecedentedly strange (or we might say *queer*) moment in the history of American sexual politics. As the Age of Enlightenment gave way to the Great Awakening, and the social value placed upon reason and empiricism succumbed to the unchallenging appeal of sentimentalism and reform, the relative sexual permissiveness of the mid-nineteenth century often gets swept under the rug of a popular historical narrative that sees pre-twentieth-century sexual culture in the United States as an untroubled migration from prudish Puritanism to squeamish Victorianism. The mistake is, however, easy to understand and often repeated (ask students early on in a course what they think American sexual culture was like in the 1850s, and you will probably get some version of this), but I have found that when provoked by discussions of the ever-growing field of the history of sexuality, students are happy to explore new horizons of the sexual past, especially since they imagine themselves

---

Estelle B. Freedman's *Intimate Matter: A History of Sexuality in America*, 3rd ed. (Chicago: Univ. of Chicago Press, 2012), esp. 109–67.

4   I follow here Peter Coviello, who concurs with Colacurcio's emphasis on reading sex as a major theme of Hawthorne's romances, but warns against too-conservative readings (including Colacurcio's), asking that we instead take seriously *Blithedale*'s introduction, in which Hawthorne warns us against understanding the book as "putting forward the slightest pretensions to illustrate a theory, or elicit a conclusion, favorable or otherwise, in respect to Socialism," which is the subject of *Blithedale*'s explicit political content. See Coviello, *Tomorrow's Parties: Sex and the Untimely in Nineteenth-Century America* [New York: New York University Press, 2013], 147).

to be living on the precipice (and perhaps now even over it) of a new era of sexuality.

Michel Foucault, writing from a Euro-centric perspective that does not cathect American Puritanism as a locus of cultural origin the way our students frequently do, often makes sweeping analytical gestures that juxtapose an idealized, liberal version of the seventeenth and eighteenth centuries, synonymous for him with the Enlightenment, with a morally conservative, though nevertheless guiltily perverse, version of the nineteenth century, which gives a somewhat inaccurate impression of both. Foucault describes the early seventeenth century (in Europe, of course) as "a time of direct gestures, shameless discourse, and open transgressions, when anatomies were shown and intermingled at will, and knowing children hung about amid the laughter of adults; it was a period when bodies 'made a display of themselves.'" To his mind, this era of relative libertinism is countered by a vision of the nineteenth century in which "sex seems to have been incorporated into two very distinct orders of knowledge: a biology of reproduction, which developed continuously according to a general scientific normativity, and a medicine of sex conforming to quite different rules of formation," which led to an era in which sex was publicly debased and disavowed but in which it was nevertheless the subject of extensive discourse. [5]

While understandings of human biology continued along the normal path of developments and discovery without being subjected to social censure, the scientific understanding of sexuality developed in decidedly prejudicial ways that we would now describe as "homophobic" and that were "not based on a fundamental relation to truth."[6] This troublesome sexology

---

5   Michel Foucault, *The History of Sexuality, Vol. I: An Introduction* (New York, Vintage, 1990), 3 and 54.

6   Ibid., 55. An important development for the development of sexual conservatism Foucault describes was, of course, the entry of the term "homosexual" into both scientific nomenclature and popular discourse. This made it possible to conceive of "the homosexual" as a type of person, as a state of being, as opposed to a mere description of types of behavior. The idea of the homosexual made "homophobia" possible, as the censuring of behaviors morphed into the hatred of persons along with the development of the modern rhetoric of "homosexuality." See here, especially Foucault, *The History of Sexuality*, 100-102. On the way this absence of rhetoric on homosexuality might affect our reading of Hawthorne; see Jordan Alexander Stein, "*The Blithedale Romance*'s Queer Style," *ESQ* 55, nos. 3–4 (2009): 211–36.

does not come about until the end of the century—indeed, most of the literature is published in the 1890s—and Foucault's narrative overlooks the diversity and dissent that was happening in sexual cultures both on the Continent and in the New World during the nineteenth century, instead painting a broad picture of a long "Victorian" era in which sexual interest became ineluctably partnered with sexual shame. If anything, Hawthorne proves himself in his romances to be almost proto-Foucauldian in his critique of conservative sexual culture. He is suspicious of a sexually oppressive and reformist society that fails to acknowledge that, all around, one can find examples both private and public of deviance, non-conformity, "queerness," or what you will, and that the perceived need to represent a reform movement at all is indicative of the presence of a counter-discourse that embraces pleasure, desire, and the individual sexual will, embodied both by the bold individualist and the spaces she creates for free self-expression, such as Hester's cottage or Blithedale itself.

The problem with telling the sexual history of the mid-nineteenth century is the awkward bookending of the period by post-Enlightenment religiosity and homophobic sexual pseudo-science. When we speak of the sexual culture of the nineteenth century, we have a tendency to take a totalizing view, to understand it as one thing, which it most certainly was not.7 Students are always fascinated and enthusiastically responsive to Foucault's ideas (which I have advanced students read—they enjoy it even if they don't immediately understand it—and which I explain through short excerpts to students in introductory courses), and we spend much of the semester grappling with how his history works—and falls short—within an American context. Foucauldian-leaning, though much more empirically-oriented, John D'Emilio and Estelle B. Freedman's widely-read *Intimate Matters* provides a grounding for much of Foucault's poststructuralist historiography in their vast archive of American sexual culture, though it also wields a variety of evidence of a world of sexual exploration that was certainly not hidden from public view. Documenting in particular transformations in the ontological understanding of sex in the United States, D'Emilio and Freedman show how "opportunities for sexual expression gradually expanded" during the nineteenth century, noting how

---

7   In my experience, students conceive of the twentieth century and our current era as having distinct eras, often delimited by decade, but other than an overly-simplified sense of ante- and post-bellum periods, the nineteenth century and before seem to have been rendered monolithic in their conception.

utopianism, "free love," same-sex intimacy, and the growth of sexuality within the realm of commerce "offered alternatives to monogamous sexual relations" that had been largely unthinkable and certainly unspeakable just a few generations prior.8 This struggle to understand how to think and how to speak about deviant desires, non-normative sexualities, and the undesirability of the elimination either is central to understanding the place of the Hawthornian romance within the history of sexuality in the nineteenth-century United States.

My "Gender and Sexuality in Antebellum America" course usually progresses from the simultaneously proselytizing and pornographic seduction novels of the late eighteenth and early nineteenth century to the sexually dissident literature of the 1860s, such as Harriet Jacobs's *Incidents in the Life of a Slave Girl* or Elizabeth Stoddard's *The Morgesons*.9 Written across the span of less than a century, the heroines of these fictions represent a transformation of the female subject of American literature from desirous vic-

---

8   D'Emilio and Freedman, *Intimate Matters: A History of Sexuality in America*, 3rd ed. (University of Chicago Press, 2011). "Free love" is the belief that love, not marriage, is the moral prerequisite for engaging in sexual practices, and it was held by a surprisingly large number of individuals in the nineteenth century. Free lovers critiqued marriage as a dehumanizing institution, and they linked it morally to the practice of slavery; not surprisingly, many free lovers were also abolitionists. There was a strong tie between free love and utopian socialist movements in the U.S., and many of free love's advocates—such as John Humphrey Noyes, who founded the community at Oneida, NY in 1848—founded or participated in socialist projects themselves.

9   Representative texts of the seduction novel genre—the earliest popular genre of American fiction—include Susanna Rowson's *Charlotte Temple* (Boston: Bedford, 2011), William Hill Brown's *The Power of Sympathy*, and Hannah Webster Foster's *The Coquette* (New York: Penguin, 1996 [published together in a single volume]). On the publication, popularity, and politics of the genre, see Elizabeth Barnes, *States of Sympathy: Seduction and Democracy in the American Novel* (New York: Columbia University Press, 1997); Christopher Castiglia, *Interior States: Institutional Consciousness and the Inner Life of Democracy in the Antebellum United States* (Durham: Duke University Press, 2008), esp. 17–59; Cathy N. Davidson, *Revolution and the Word: The Rise of the Novel in America*, Rev. ed. (New York and Oxford: Oxford University Press, 2004), esp. 110–150; Marion Rust, *Prodigal Daughters: Susanna Rowson's Early American Women* (Chapel Hill: University of North Carolina Press, 2008); and Julia A. Stern, *The Plight of Feeling: Sympathy and Dissent in the American Novel* (Chicago: University of Chicago Press, 1997).

tim, more or less unable to control the circumstances of her amorous life, trying to protect herself from physical violence and substance abuse, into a kind of oddly self-assured sexual outsider who nevertheless figures within the logic of the literature as representative. Though readers are unlikely to identify biographically with Linda Brent or morally with Cassandra Morgeson, they might nevertheless recognize the representation of female desire in Civil War-era texts as simultaneously validating, abjected, and reflective of a complex psychological reality. With Hawthorne as the bridge between these two points, the nineteenth century proves a fertile ground for exploring what it means to be a sexual subject and how that subject might enter the world of human culture.

The Scarlet Letter: Beyond Sexual Shame

Shame like sexuality is central to *The Scarlet Letter*. Indeed, shame and sexuality are so intertwined throughout the text that it becomes difficult to think of one without the other. Hester Prynne is punished for a sex crime (adultery) and her punishment is public shaming, to be made a spectacle before her community and then to wear for the rest of her life a badge of that shame, the scarlet letter itself, intended to be representative as much of the public act of shaming as the act for which Hester is punished. From the beginning, however, this is problematic. Making her first appearance before the angry public, she is not dull but radiant: "Never before had Hester Prynne appeared more lady-like . . . than as she issued from the prison. Those who had before known her, and had expected to behold her dimmed and obscured by a disastrous cloud, were astonished, even startled, to perceive how her beauty shone out, and made a halo of the misfortune and ignominy in which she was enveloped."[10] In the community's moral logic, the public shame to which Hester is subjected should be more, well, shaming, but she demonstrates herself here to be resilient and self-reliant, even if unconsciously so. In her feminine ethereality, she stands in stark contrast to

---

10   Nathaniel Hawthorne, *The Scarlet Letter* (New York: Penguin, 1986), 50. All subsequent references to the novel are parenthetically noted and taken from this edition.

world-worn neighbors, women whose struggle to survive had made them hearty but hard, women who "stood within less than half a century of the period when the man-like Elizabeth had been the not altogether unsuitable representative of the sex" (48).[11] Hester makes trouble for members of her sex ironically by coming closest to embodying the feminine idea and thereby placing herself outside of the norm. We are, therefore, for the first but certainly not the last time forced to reckon with the complex and, one might even say, inscrutable logic of shame in the romance.

For the last two decades and more, shame has been central to the study of sexuality. Anticipating (and one might argue steering) the driving force of analyses of shame in queer theory, Foucault deconstructed Victorian prudishness to belie its undercurrent of perverse obsession, and the centrality of shame in the critical understanding of sexual subjectivity was assured. Eve Sedgwick famously argues that "the epistemology of the closet has given an overarching consistency to gay culture and identity throughout this century [i.e., the twentieth]," meaning that the feeling of shame that necessitates hiding one's sexual feelings and identity is felt so widely that it is fundamental to the creation of sexual subcultures.[12] Michael Warner pushes this thesis even further, asserting in no uncertain terms, "It might as well be admitted that sex is a disgrace";[13] discussing inquiry into sexual minorities, he declares, "Talk about stigmatized sex is much more than indulgent shamelessness, or lack of respect for privacy. It is a necessary means to identify the political element of shame, to see how disgust and embarrassment are used by some to restrict the sexual autonomy

---

11   This is, of course, a reference to Queen Elizabeth I of England, who was as a familiar a figure to the antebellum audience, thanks to a spate of popular biographies published in the 1840s and 1850s, as she is today, thanks to popular cinematic representations. Elizabeth is an interesting contrast to Hester not simply because of what the narrator understands to be the former's hardness of form compared to the latter's grace but because Elizabeth was widely known as "The Virgin Queen," whereas Hester carries her bastard with her through the town in this first scene.

12   Eve Kosofsky Sedgwick, *Epistemology of the Closet* (Berkeley: University of California Press, 1990), 68. She acknowledges that much of gay activism is based on overcoming the fear that might drive one into the closet, though questions of from whom and why one hides one's sexuality—or does not—have been key to gay culture for the century or so of its being.

13   Michael Warner, *The Trouble with Normal: Sex, Politics, and the Ethics of Queer Life* (Cambridge, MA: Harvard University Press, 2000), 2.

of others" (16). Indeed, the analysis of shame has been a fruitful line of inquiry for many critics and historians of sexuality, but it is perhaps not, many scholars have begun to suggest, the entire story of non-normative or even normative sexual practice.[14]

Shame is key to the story of *The Scarlet Letter*; it is not, however, identical with that story. Indeed, for a protagonist, Hester is a relatively flat character. In her extended reading of the story, Lauren Berlant posits the law as the primary agent of action in the story: "The law makes things possible."[15] Indeed, the central chapter of the story, "Another View of Hester," which is both the major turning point in the narrative and the thirteenth of twenty-four chapters, is not so much about any particular change in Hester that the law or its shaming mechanisms have brought about; instead, it deals with the altered perceptions of the state and its citizens. Her "badge of shame" has become "the softer pillow for the head that needed one," and Hester has herself become "a Sister of Mercy," "self-ordained" because she saw a need. When strangers arrived in town, its residents would ask, "Do you see that woman with the embroidered badge? ... It is our Hester,—the town's own Hester,—who is so kind to the poor, so helpful to the sick, so comfortable to the afflicted!" (142). Instead of being interpolated in Althusser's sense into a state-enabled system of shaming, Hester's "A" has become a source of pride, not so much for her but for the townsfolk, and it is this transformation that keeps her from directly suffering the censure we might presume was intended. Near the chapter's end, the narrator informs us, "The scarlet letter had not done its office," but this is only true from a strictly moralistic and ideological perspective (145).

"Another View" describes numerous potential meanings for the "A," all unintended by those who pronounced Hester's sentence, and in a more denotative way than any other antebellum example, *The Scarlet Letter* embodies the kinds of slippages in meaning poststructuralist theory asserts as inevitable. The letter may not have done its intended office, but its authors cannot control what it comes to mean in the world. When we are told in the final chapter that the letter "now . . . has done its office," it is not because

---

14 This is perhaps most forcefully asserted in two special issues of two journals: "What's Queer About Queer Studies Now?" *Social Text* 23, nos. 3–4 (2005) and "After Sex? On Writing Since Queer Theory," *South Atlantic Quarterly* 106, no. 3 (2007).

15 Lauren Berlant, *The Anatomy of National Fantasy: Hawthorne, Utopia, and Everyday Life* (Chicago: University of Chicago Press, 1991), 59.

it has brought shame on Hester or because it has taught the town a lesson about the implacable nature of sin but simply because it has revealed Hester's co-adulterer, the Reverend Arthur Dimmesdale (223). She flees after his death but returns to quietly resume her role as comforter and confidant, and after her death the townspeople, it would seem, bury her above Dimmesdale, not together, because he is not her husband, but close, "as if the dust of the two sleepers had no right to mingle," and yet they still can't resist (228). The final passage is so carefully worded by Hawthorne as to almost allow for a more conservative reading, in which Hester is buried with her cuckolded husband, Roger Chillingworth, but that seems unlikely, as their dust would have every right to mingle; in fact, it's what the law would dictate. It is instead a final act of defiance against conservative moralism consistent with the sexual antinomianism that Hawthorne theorizes here and elsewhere in his romances. In this light, *The Scarlet Letter* cannot but be read as a resistance to the puritanism of reform movements of the antebellum age, a kind of longing on the edge of coming into being.

Conclusion

Writing about *The Blithedale Romance*, D. H. Lawrence portrays the two male protagonists, Coverdale and Hollingsworth, as unambiguously homosexual: "The two men love one another with a love surpassing the love of women."[16] It is easy to see how this kind of reading becomes possible in a text in which the narrator describes how the utopian socialist community in which he is living "seemed to authorize any individual, of either sex, to fall in love with any other, regardless of what would elsewhere be judged suitable and prudent."[17] It reads like a queer manifesto. Though *The Scarlet Letter* is more subtle in its politics of experimentation, it nevertheless advocates for the necessity of the same kind of space of freedom, and

---

16 D. H. Lawrence, *Studies in Classic American Literature* (New York: Penguin, 1977), 114. In my experience, students also almost unfailingly read the romance as a gay love story between Coverdale and Hollingsworth. Jordan Stein also comments on this phenomenon in "Queer Style," 211.

17 Nathaniel Hawthorne, *The Blithedale Romance* (New York: Norton, 2011), 52.

explicitly of sexual freedom, that was becoming endangered at midcentury. Sedgwick's twentieth-century closet is not in place yet, though it is becoming more of an inevitability. Across the course of the semester, students see a kind of historical ebb and flow and a large-scale public resistance to sexual normativity that they only imagine to have been possible since the late twentieth century. No one tried harder than Hawthorne to critique sexual conservatism and its program of shame and to imagine a freer world, which he can almost envision and almost bring into being.

University of Illinois at Chicago

Hawthorne's Reconceptualization of the European Gothic Tradition

Monika Elbert

Hawthorne seems the perfect specter to haunt the Gothic classroom. There are uninvited ghoulish guests or unhappy ghosts in many of his stories and novels, and the mysterious Hawthorne himself would be a natural to appear in one of his Gothic settings or scenarios. My focus here will be on his four romances: *The Scarlet Letter* (1850), *The House of the Seven Gables* (1851), *The Blithedale Romance* (1852), and *The Marble Faun* (1859–60), as they relate to a growing sense of America as a haunted land, one haunted by demons, demonic children and characters, witch trials and the dark uncharted forest. These novels are texts often taught in a themed course on the Gothic, or, if used in a regular class on the American Renaissance, students often engage in lively discussion about the Gothic dimension of Hawthorne's writing in comparison to Poe's and their literary ancestor Charles Brocken Brown. Although some of Hawthorne's short stories fit the conventional Gothic paradigm of the "mad-scientist" narrative akin to Mary Shelley's and Goethe's work (such as "The Birthmark" or "Rappaccini's Daughter"), I am more concerned here with showing how Hawthorne personalizes and Americanizes the Gothic genre over the course of his writing career.

Hawthorne's early tale, "Alice Doane's Appeal" (1835), shows the direction Hawthorne would take with American Gothic. In this tale, the storyteller evokes a stock figure of European Gothic, a wizard, and the Gothic taboo of an incestuous brother/sister, but to truly terrify his narrator's female audience, Hawthorne brings up the history of Gallows Hill to show the real terror of the American experience—the Salem Witch Trials and atrocities.1 Even within the wizard frame story, however, Hawthorne incorporates a Gothic theme that would haunt him throughout his life and fiction: the "sins of the fathers." It would become his quintessential Gothic plot. Out of jealousy for his sister's love, Leonard Doane kills his supposed rival, Walter Brome, who turns out to be Doane's doppelgänger, and in the end, as Leonard Doane beholds the corpse of Brome, Doane sees an amazing likeness to his father. Leonard's guilt is overwhelming, and hence his visit to the wizard, a type of modern psychologist. The narrator of the story, overcome by the horrors of Gallows Hill, then interrupts his own tale to tell the more frightening story of the witch trials. The fear evoked causes the fair ladies in his audience great distress and tears. This story encapsulates the sense of Hawthorne's deepest guilt for his forebear's bloody hands at the Salem Witch Trials but also the more general communal guilt at the trials that seeped into New England and American cultural memory.

The theme of patricide and fratricide, though, is not limited to the American experience for Hawthorne, and the ideas of the "sins of the fathers" can be traced to the Bible and to its Gothic progenitor in England, Horace Walpole. In the British Gothic genre, this theme often relates to social-class rivalries, wrought by a specter of an emerging middle class, but on American shores, and especially in Hawthorne's writings, it relates to the boundless frontier and the theme of possession and dispossession, as ownership for land and power becomes a strong and indeed escapable national motive. In addition to this struggle for power, Hawthorne's Gothic characters are also often imbued with a feeling of self-hatred, as they see their most hideous features mirrored in the shape of a fiendish character that haunts their every move.

Hawthorne's growing interest in an American type of Gothic had its inception in Walpole, whom he avidly read as a young man.2 In my American Gothic class, I therefore always start with Walpole to show his

---

1   See Charles L. Crowe's similar interpretation of the fearful in Hawthorne's "Alice Doane's Appeal" in *American Gothic*, ed. Charles L Crow (Cardiff: University of Wales Press, 2007), 11–15.

2   Certain parts of this essay relating to *The Scarlet Letter* and *The Marble Faun* are taken from my afterword in the special issue on the Gothic of *Nathaniel Hawthorne Review* 38, no. 2 (2012): 168–74.

influence upon early American Gothic writers like Hawthorne and also to give students a basic understanding of Gothic tropes. In an odd, roundabout fashion, Hawthorne appropriates the characteristics of the Gothic novel from Walpole, whose *The Castle of Otranto* (1764), set within a medieval Italian context, influenced his writing of the *The Scarlet Letter*. (Later he would transform the Gothic setting and dilemma of *The Scarlet Letter* and make them ostensibly Italian in *The Marble Faun*, though the dilemma remains Gothically American, as I will explain.) Indeed, there are many striking parallels to be found between these two novels, especially in their prefaces dealing with the theory of "romance." From the manner in which the authors fabricate their stories—how they found the material for their novels (Walpole's "black letter" and Hawthorne's "scarlet letter") to the way in which both quite literally speak about the "sins of the fathers"—their motivations and authorial postures are remarkably similar. Thematically, Walpole's and Hawthorne's Gothic is involved with the catastrophe following an abuse of power since the "sins of the fathers" are always connected to some past indiscretion that robs the individual of his rights and honor.

In addition, Walpole's discussion of blending "the two kinds of romance, the ancient and the modern," sounds very much like Hawthorne's description of the haunted state of mind which leads up to his famous moonlit romance passage in the preface to *The House of the Seven Gables* (1851) where he articulates his ideas about the blending of "the Actual and the Imaginary" in a "neutral territory." For his part, Walpole claims that in the ancient form of romance, "all was imagination and improbability," and that in the modern form, nature "has been copied with success" but that the adherence to the actual has "cramped imagination."[3] Hawthorne clearly accepts the literary-historical components of Walpole's Gothic paradigm and also the magical narrative framework surrounding its creation. However, though he accepts the existence of a supernatural realm through the various interpretations of the extraordinary, he is never quite as smitten with the "miraculous" in the way that Walpole is. The manner in which Hawthorne secularizes the religious, places the characters' actions outside a domestic space (unlike the castle/home or church in Walpole) and into nature (the forest) or into a public space (the marketplace), and thereby rewrites the struggle between the classes, reveals his attempt in *The Scarlet*

---

3   Horace Walpole, *The Castle of Otranto*, ed. W. S. Lewis (New York: Oxford University Press, 1982), 7.

Letter to make the Gothic a more democratic and American genre. He remains fascinated, though, by the abuse of power and its pernicious effects on society, thinking back perhaps to the role of his own forebear, Judge Hathorne, at the Salem Witch Trials.

Hawthorne thus borrows the Gothic trappings from Walpole's Italian-based *The Castle of Otranto* and transplants them to create one of the first American Gothic novels, *The Scarlet Letter*. The sins of the fathers, mysterious and withheld identities, family intrigue (dysfunctional families and dysfunctional sexuality), supernatural signs, the usurpation of power, the corruption of the church, the degradation of females and of servants—all these are found in *The Scarlet Letter*. Walpole's notion of the two kinds of romance, "the ancient and the modern," can be found in Hawthorne's perception of the romance in his conceptualization of the "neutral territory" in "The Custom-House." In fact, even the Gothic heroine Hawthorne creates is much more like Walpole's than, say, Poe's frequent femme fatales. Hester has more agency than the typical Gothic heroine, but she must deal with the upshot of inequality and hypocrisy in the Puritan settlement. Even in Walpole, the Gothic female who thrives is the one who uses her mind and doesn't rely on her aristocratic lineage to secure a rightful place in society: in *The Castle of Otranto*, Matilda, the daughter of a repressive and power-wielding father, Manfred, dies at his hands, as she symbolically bears the punishment for her father's sinful behavior. Her friend, the smarter woman, Isabella, represents a more balanced and progressive world view, and she is the one who "gets the guy" (Theodore) at the end of the narrative.

Hawthorne's Hester, in effect, is the American Gothic heroine who must deal with a repressive past embodied in her quasi-aristocratic origins, as indicated by the deteriorating coat of arms of her father's ancestral home in England, a past which has created her and her American culture. Two of the quintessential motifs of American Gothic permeate this novel: the Puritan inability to escape from the European past, in this case the intolerant ways of England, and the larger nineteenth-century global dilemma of social-class fluctuations. Even within the supposedly utopian Puritan settlement, the "city upon a hill," there are drastic differences in privilege and class. The pariah Hester spends much of her time embroidering lovely lace cuffs, ruffs, and collars for the Puritan magistrates, who are the public face of her denunciation, and the women of the community despise her for her beauty, which sets her off as special and dangerous. Puritan mythology would have seen the danger of Hester's beauty as a diabolical lure to waylay men, and despite her charitable contributions to the Puritan settlement, she, living on the periphery of town at her seaside cottage, is as much of an outcast as Mistress Hibbins, the eccentric widow who purportedly communes with the devil and who eventually dies condemned as a witch.

Envy and jealousy and the ensuing conflict for power, which accounted for much fanaticism and finger-pointing in the Salem Witch Trials, always an underlying theme of American Gothic, also account for the rivalry between Dimmesdale and Chillingworth. If we exclude Hester for a moment, the battle for male empowerment between the Puritan worthy and the mad scientist, between religion and science, is at the center of the novel's exploration of conflict. Chillingworth, with his "hungry dream of knowledge,"[4] turns into a demon in the American wilderness, not because he associates with Native Americans (a fear that occurs in early American Gothic works, such as those of Charles Brockden Brown's) but because he will abuse that power for his own good. Like the misguided Aylmer in Hawthorne's "The Birth-mark," Chillingworth becomes the Faustian striver who will use his power to destroy those he despises or envies. If Dimmesdale is the witch condemned to die in the last scaffold scene, it is because Chillingworth has become his persecutor. Dimmesdale, though, is also guilty by virtue of his own crime of pride, one that his literary Gothic forebear, Young Goodman Brown, experienced and for which he, too, was condemned. Had Dimmesdale headed out West or even gone back to England in a timely fashion, two options Hester has suggested, he would have averted the catastrophe of his final act, the delivery of the Election Sermon, which was to have been the triumph of his professional life.

In the new American landscape with its frontier and dark forests, there are many devils, and the protagonists in this novel are all cast in that role at various moments. Pearl, for example, is seen not as a triumph of the new child in a new land but as weighed down by the past, the "sins of the fathers" and original sin. She herself is viewed as "an imp of evil, emblem and product of sin" (84) and a "demon offspring" (88). Hester is understandably troubled when she feels that "an evil spirit" had "possessed the child" (87, 17); we also hear that "There was witchcraft in little Pearl's eyes" (135). It is no wonder that at the end of the narrative, Pearl discovers that she can find no happiness in the New World of her parents: ironically, she

---

4 Nathaniel Hawthorne, *The Scarlet Letter. Centenary Edition.* Vol. 1. Ed. William Charvat, et al. (Columbus: Ohio State University Press, 1962), p. 99. Further references are to this edition and are parenthetically noted.

goes back to the Old World, where she thrives in terms of her status because of her New World money—Chillingworth's inheritance—and Old World nobility in her marriage to an aristocrat, as her letters to Hester include "armorial seals" (274). Pearl's happily-ever-after story cannot be told, though, as it seems implausible for the Gothic plot. As Walpole and the other progenitors of classic Gothic such as Anne Radcliffe and Monk Lewis knew, the past cannot be exorcised, and Hawthorne understood that fact as well. Pearl's happily-ever-after story is an American fabrication, much like Phoebe Pyncheon's at the end of *The House of the Seven Gables*.

In "The Custom-House" introduction to *The Scarlet Letter*, Hawthorne puts himself in league with devils and witches as he associates writing and artistry with the demonic. Indeed, he wears a badge of diabolical inspiration when he feels compelled to tell Hester's story and unwittingly allies himself with her, and he describes the diabolical feeling of being possessed and burned: "It seemed to me, then, that I experienced a sensation not altogether physical, yet almost so, as of burning heat; and as if the letter were not of red cloth, but red-hot iron" (62). In Hawthorne's next two Gothic narratives taking place on American soil, *The House of the Seven Gables* and *The Blithedale Romance*, not only does he reveal his allegiance to the diabolical powers of creation as an American writer, but he also cannot dissociate himself from the atrocities of the Hathorne history or exorcise the diabolical American past.

In *The House of the Seven Gables*, Hawthorne exposes a Gothic connection between the Pyncheon family and the Maules, as the victim and victimizer become interchangeable. Surely the "original" sin is caused by the Pyncheons, who used their power and social status to usurp the Maule property, but the Maules, who feel forever cursed, then participate in the same diabolical game of power and psychological torture. The Walpole theme of the "sins of the fathers," as it relates to infractions in social class, can easily be traced through the conflict of Hawthorne's second Gothic romance. The wizard, Matthew Maule, whose land the Pyncheons claim as their own, is hanged as a witch to make the Pyncheon theft of his land legal: Maule's curse, from the scaffold, resonates throughout the narrative—"God will give him blood to drink"[5]—and the entire male line of

---

5   Nathaniel Hawthorne, *The House of the Seven Gables. Centenary Edition.* Vol. 2. Ed. William Charvat, et al. (Columbus: Ohio State University Press, 1964), p. 8. Subsequent references to this novel are parenthetically noted.

Pyncheons seems cursed by apoplexy, as in the case of Colonel and Judge Pyncheon, and by intrigues brought on by Pyncheon greed, as in the case of Jaffrey Pyncheon. A similar curse brings down Manfred's castle at the start of Walpole's *The Castle of Otranto,* where the marvelous event of a gigantic and supernatural helmet falls upon Conrad's head, right before his wedding ceremony, thereby crushing the Otranto line. Hawthorne must definitely be thinking of such power dynamics in writing his tale of the Pyncheons and Maules.

Colonel Pyncheon, the progenitor of the clan, is Hawthorne's typical respectable "Puritan soldier and magistrate" (9), whom he admired and despised in his retelling of the Hathorne atrocities in the "Custom-House" introduction. Matthew Maule's son, Thomas Maule, a first-rate architect who draws up the plans for the doomed House, is one of a long line of wizards and scientists in Hawthorne's Gothic canon, with whom he the writer sometimes allies himself and whom the reader loves to admire, despite the diabolical darkness, because of his transgressive powers as a creator rather than as an imitator. In fact, by the end of the novel, we realize that both Maule and Pyncheon are at fault, as the Maules quickly reveal similar qualities of ownership and power when they have the means to do so. Thus, for example, Matthew Maule, the grandson of the original Maule and a gifted carpenter like his father Thomas, takes it upon himself to vindicate the family name by seducing and destroying Alice Pyncheon. The final turn of the screw, though, is when we hear that the original sin of claiming property was actually against Native Americans. In fact, the new Maule wizard, Holgrave, tells the story of the Gothic American transgression: "The son of the executed Matthew Maule, while building this house . . . [hid] away the Indian deed, on which depended the immense land-claim of the Pyncheons. Thus, they bartered their eastern territory for Maule's garden-ground" (316). The true Gothic horror is the illegal seizure of Native American territory.

While not ostensibly a Gothic novel, *The Blithedale Romance* does include some Gothic conventions dealing with the "sins of the fathers" and the illegal seizure of property and of wealth. We hear that Old Moodie loses any rights to his daughters based upon his shoddy treatment of his wife, bad business deals, and a basic lassitude that he shares with Coverdale. The new Gothic magician in this book, the heir to Maule, is not the sorry excuse of an author, Coverdale, but the capitalist creator of magic based on illusion, Westervelt, who represents all that is worst about Western monetary power. Through his diabolical power, he manipulates the ghostlike waif, Priscilla, as the "Veiled Lady" whom he can hypnotize and use to seduce an audience. Coverdale himself sees the entire Gothic plot in terms of the Salem Witch Trials:

> I saw in Hollingsworth all that an artist could desire for the grim portrait of a Puritan magistrate, holding inquest of life and death in a case of witchcraft;—in Zenobia, the sorceress herself, not aged, wrinkled, and decrepit, but fair enough to tempt Satan with a force reciprocal to his own;—and, in Priscilla, the pale victim, whose soul and body had been wasted by her spells.6

In "The Three Together," Hollingsworth is one of the old patriarchal Puritans, whom Hawthorne finds guilty, but his tirade against women at the end of the chapter sends not Priscilla but Zenobia to drown herself. She shares her Gothic sensuality with other dark maidens like Hester and Miriam, but interestingly, Priscilla is first seen as the victim, when it is clear that Zenobia is the ultimate one. In fact, if we take the comparison to the Salem Witch Trials far enough, we see that Priscilla cannot be the victim of any witch; like the adolescent girls of Salem, she would be more the victimizer of innocent women like Zenobia, accusing her of witchcraft.

In teaching Hawthorne's Gothic novels, one is often inclined to look at his Gothic women, and certainly Hester and Miriam, as exotic "others." In fact, Miriam has such a mysterious past that it cannot even be traced, although one can surmise since Hawthorne taunts us with stories about her foreign lineage, whether Jewish, German, African, or English. By the time it is finally revealed that she is Jewish on her father's side and English on her mother's, she has already been rendered mysterious. In a perverse way, however, her story is much more American than Hester's precisely because her origins are so uncertain. If the "sins of the fathers" is a basic ingredient of European Gothic, it is really not Miriam's curse. Her curse is more or less the stuff of American Gothic—not knowing her class, not knowing her original ethnicity or nationality, not knowing her parents or not wanting to know, and refusing to marry the husband who has been chosen for her. Indeed, like Hester, she wants to forge her own identity and get away from

---

6 Nathaniel Hawthorne, *The Blithedale Romance and Fanshaw. Centenary Edition.* Vol. 3. Ed. William Charvat et al. (Columbus: Ohio State University Press, 1964), 214. Further references are to this edition and are documented parenthetically.

fathers, a situation unheard of in Walpole's *Otranto*: "There was something in Miriam's blood, in her mixed race, in her recollections of her mother—some characteristic, finally of her own nature—which had given her freedom of thought, and force of will."7 Here, her history replicates America's as she comes from "mixed" blood. The racial connotations of her situation soon become more clear: the man she is supposed to marry had "traits so evil, so treacherous, so wild, and yet so strangely subtle, as could only be accounted for by the insanity which often develops itself in old, close-kept breeds of men, when long unmixed with newer blood" (430–31). Thus, racial purity (a badge of aristocracy) is deemed much more evil than intermarriage, whether racially or economically construed.

In Hawthorne's last completed romance, *The Marble Faun*, Donatello serves as the kind of innocent Gothic hero, but he also gets involved with the class dynamics of New World Gothic. He is not involved in a clerical power struggle but rather in a class struggle. Rather like Poe's Usher, he is entombed in his ancient run-down villa and isolates himself in his tower. Old Tomaso and Stella, the servants inherited from his father, seem to be his only friends and the only recorders of history for the family, unlike Donatello, who says he knows "little or nothing of history" (217). As the count of Monte Beni, he appears to be the last of his line. Indeed, one might ask where the family has gone wrong or what sort of social comingling brought down the dynasty. Perhaps Donatello's plight exacerbates the instability wrought by the apparent mingling of different classes. After all, the progenitor of the family was "a sylvan creature," "a being not altogether human, yet partaking so largely of the gentlest human qualities, as to be neither awful nor shocking to the imagination" (233). This sylvan creature marries below his station by stooping to the level of a "mortal maiden" and marrying for love. We hear that the progeny of this marriage were a "pleasant and kindly race of men, but capable of savage fierceness and never quite restrainable within the trammels of social law" (233). Thus, Donatello becomes one of a long line of freaks with furry ears and with a simplicity bordering on imbecility. If Pearl should become a Gothic monster who returns to the Old World to wreak havoc on that social system, as she is the emblem of her mother's sin (love based on passion), then Donatello

---

7 Nathaniel Hawthorne, *The Marble Faun. Centenary Edition.* Vol. 4. Ed. Roy Harvey Pearce et al. (Columbus: Ohio State University Press, 1968), 430. Subsequent references to this novel are to this edition and are parenthetically noted.

is similarly the emblem of his forefather's sin (with the same kind of love based on Hester's passion). In some ways, though, the demon-child Pearl dancing in the forest is much more credible as a Gothic character than the effete Donatello who seems a half-wit but certainly not a terrifying monster. He seems more a product of Rappaccini's incestuous creations or a product of incestuous aristocratic cross-breeding than a real man.

In the end, although Hawthorne casts his last completed novel on foreign shores, the plight of Miriam is much more American than Roman in that she remains homeless. Granted, we are kept in the dark about Hester's final travels to Europe (with Pearl), but she does return to America (she has a home), whereas Miriam becomes the wandering Jew figure of the traditional Gothic, and for Hawthorne, the quintessential American Gothic figure. Though he suggests that the moonlight of Salem is different from that of Rome, it is really very similar, as it illuminates the same kind of homesickness or weariness. In fact, the Roman landscape is much more Americanized than Hawthorne admits in his preface. There is a reason why Daisy Miller succumbs to Roman fever, for she is transplanted into an arena that is very different from the American landscape she has known (Schenectady, NY). Henry James's and Edith Wharton's Rome is really much more Italian than Hawthorne's. Miriam, like a tortured soul of Salem, cannot belong and cannot *not* belong. When the narrator asks, "What was Miriam's life to be?" the question resonates with Hawthorne's "I am a citizen of somewhere else" (stated in his preface to *The Scarlet Letter*). That same dilemma of not belonging is his whether in Salem or in Rome, the inability or lack of desire to combine Americanness with otherness. Hester has made peace and found her home; Miriam, at the end of the book, is still "at large," forever being pursued by the goblins of her mind. She is much more like the troubled Hawthorne than Hester ever was.

These perspectives reflect the nightmare drama played out by Miriam and Donatello. He might as well have been one of Young Goodman Brown's Indians behind a tree or the black man in the forest. There is nothing particularly Roman about Donatello nor about Miriam. If the Capuchin monk, who haunts Miriam, seems Old Gothic, he seems strangely out of place, like a fabrication that does not belong and is really much more like Judge Pyncheon or any other stern Puritan magistrate in the Hawthorne canon. Hawthorne's Gothic therefore becomes less Gothic in the traditional European sense than it was in *The Scarlet Letter* to the point that *The Marble Faun* seems to be almost a parody of the Gothic. Whereas Hester sees a real threat posed by whatever it is that lurks in the American forest, the "Black Man in the Forest" or the Indian, for Miriam, Kenyon, and Hilda, the old Italian countryside is benign, and they even laugh about Donatello's furry ears. (True, Miriam's model/monk is far more frightening, but that is because his identity is so mysterious, if one-dimensional.) As one reviewer wrote of Hawthorne after reading *The Marble Faun*, "We trust ere long to meet him again on his own natural soil; real as her mountains, broad-thought as her prairies, fresh as her primeval forests. He is not at home among the hybrid mythologies and the mouldering ruins of the antique world."[8] Although this critic is a bit too effervescent about Hawthorne's pleasant New England landscape, he is right in claiming that New England is his rightful home, and Hawthorne, we now know, has created his own diabolical Gothic mythology in that supposedly pristine landscape.

Montclair State University

---

8   "New Novels," *Literary Gazette: A Journal of Art, Science, and Literature* [England], 10 March 1860, in John L. Idol and Buford Jones, eds. *Nathaniel Hawthorne: The Contemporary Reviews* (New York: Cambridge University Press, 1994), 250.

PART 2
THE SHORT STORIES

"The Minister's Black Veil" and Islam in the Interdisciplinary Core Classroom

ROSEMARY MIMS FISK

Teachers of American literature survey classes know that few selections help students understand the concept of ambiguity better than does Hawthorne's enigmatic tale, "The Minister's Black Veil." As with the ending of *The Scarlet Letter*, no explanation for Father Hooper's motives or actions satisfies, and more than a century and a half later, critical interpretations continue to reflect the subjectivity and context of the individual reviewer. In fact, the layered complexities—the religious, racial, and gendered politics—behind Hawthorne's decision to give us a veiled Puritan parson ironically discourage anyone from assigning this text in a freshman core class where students are likely to dismiss the central symbol as a sight gag in a comedy irrelevant to their lives. Even in my upper-level classes of English majors, the occasional student presentation by a black-veiled speaker fails to capture either the symbolic power of the veil or the villagers' confused response. I wondered instead whether the story might return to a live village and work better in a post 9-11 interdisciplinary core classroom if we assume the central character to be a Muslim woman.

My university's interdisciplinary core curriculum features a sequence titled *Cultural Perspectives*, a history-of-ideas survey that frames the freshman year and ambitiously seeks to lay a liberal arts foundation with emphasis on cultural literacy and critical thinking. We begin with Plato's cave and Sophocles' *Antigone* in order to introduce our students to dialectical reasoning and the productive tension of oppositional ideas within western culture for the first weeks. After the fall of Rome, we include a unit on Islam that provides the basic Islamic cultural literacy recommended by Muslim colleagues: a brief history of the Prophet, the Five Pillars, a close reading of the Imrans surah of the Qur'an, the split after the Prophet's death into Shi'a and Sunni identities among others, and maps of the geographical spread of the faith through the asabiya, the Golden Age of Islam contemporaneous with the European Middle Ages. Our agenda isn't merely tolerance of but a full appreciation for the beauties of Islamic culture and its religious kinship with Judeo-Christianity. In fact, close readers of our European common texts will begin to identify the significance of the veil, both literal and figurative, in those texts as well. The spring semester then concludes with a unit on the Global Village, where faculty select their own nonwestern titles. Most classes include at least one novel by a Muslim author and thereby reinforce Islamic themes encountered in the first semester. My students read novels by the Egyptian, Naguib Mahfouz, and the Afghan-American, Khaled Hosseini, and they discover the seduction of the Arabian oral storytelling tradition and the tensions of modernity within these traditional cultures. Thus, Islam bookends my academic year, but I had neglected to tie the Islamic thread anywhere in the middle of the courses until the post 9-11 backlash hit my home state like a Puritan mob.

In January 2004, as my class was trudging through John Calvin's *Institutes* as part of the unit on the Protestant Reformation, Alabama's Department of Public Safety passed and then quickly rescinded a policy to ban all head coverings in drivers' license photographs. The state's politicians were acting in response to similar bans in other states immediately after 9-11 and possibly also in unconscious solidarity with European leaders who sought to ban headscarves, under the phrasing of "all overt religious symbols," from public schools. Curiously, however, Alabama had so few veiled Muslim women to whom this policy might apply that the politicians failed to make the hysteria outlast the expected legal challenges. Even so, in reacting to a perceived threat to the status quo by any veiled Muslim woman, popular opinionators in Alabama as elsewhere reenacted the scene in the village of Milford when Parson Hooper steps beyond his own door with his face covered by a simple black cloth. "The Minister's Black Veil" thereby found its way into my course.

My students who would have been bored discussing Hooper's veil now wanted to know why the Muslim veil creates such hysteria in some communities, why it goes by so many names, and what it even *means*. Like Parson Hooper's veil, the Islamic veil creates a multiplicity of responses even as it often reifies the wearer's theology or ethnicity at a glance. The veil can be a simple *hijab*, a fashionable head covering, that is equally at home in Arabia or London, much as Calvinism is at home today in the pulpits of mainstream churches in the Reformed tradition. Or the veil can be the black face cover, the *niqab*, added to the *jilbab* (long dress) or full *burqa*. To avoid confusion, most Muslim scholars tend to use the word *hijab* to mean any facial veiling. In the original Arabic, *hijab* refers not to a piece of cloth but to ideas about separation and keeping apart.[1] Thus, it is never simply a piece of cloth.

As class begins, I project various images of the *hijab* from recent news stories and fashion-marketing websites to illustrate the range of color and choice available and to underscore the point that for most Muslims worldwide, the veil is not a big deal unless others make it so. Students seem to agree, and at this point they still may feel superior to the gawking villagers

1   For a representative discussion of the geographic and national complexities of evolving terminology related to the veil, see F. El Guindi. *Veil: Modesty, Privacy and Resistance* (New York: Berg, 1999). Recent media reports on the "burqa ban" in France, which went into effect on 11 April 2011, actually refer to a *niqab* ban, a phrase which lacks the alliterative appeal of the phrase in use.

of Milford. Then, I project a single large image of a woman obscured behind a black veil (an Istock photograph), except for her eyes, in full frontal gaze:

The image always elicits a murmured response and a noticeable change in breathing patterns throughout the classroom. I have often wished to snap a photo of my class at this moment, for the veil of this woman most closely evokes the mystery and fear of Father Hooper's veil with its power to haunt. Our literary character now becomes a Muslim woman *who has willingly donned* the full burqa as a sign of strict adherence to religious tradition. Muslim academic Amina Wadud and others clarify this choice as necessary for Muslim women who follow Qur'anic teachings strictly and meaningfully and who claim the power and agency of *Allah* for themselves. Significantly, Wadud, like Parson Hooper, makes no attempt to appease the patriarchal authority figures in her religion. Rather than use the word "submission," she prefers to use the term *Islam* to mean "engaged surrender" because the latter avoids the connotation of involuntary and coerced duties. "Engaged surrender," the woman's thoughtful choice, emphasizes that she is the agent who has adopted *din*, the Arabic word for a complete way of life and more comprehensive than the English word "religion." [2] Perhaps Hawthorne's parson also sought *din* in a new world that was falling away from its earlier religious vision.

I leave the veiled image above my shoulder to face the students as we turn to the text for a close reading. One by one, the students take turns reading aloud a villager's spoken or unspoken response and then probing it for meaning. I take the first quote so that I can illustrate the difference between textual analysis and simple restatement:

Sexton: "But what has good Parson Hooper got upon his face?" [Villager is startled as the black figure comes into the periphery of his visual field. Simple curiosity, astonishment. Emphasis on *what*, an attempt at identification.]

Goodman Gray: "Are you sure it is our parson?" [Curiosity has now focused on the veil and its wearer. Emphasis on *sure*. A question, uncertainty. Veil obscures identity and disturbs comfortable community of conformity.]

---

2 Amina Wadud. *Inside the Gender Jihad: Women's Reform in Islam* (Oxford: Oneworld Publications, 2006), 23–34.

Authorial narrator: Unnamed parishioners are too "wonderstruck" to return his greeting. [No reciprocity. Communication is interrupted, and their silence predicts his future of isolation.]

Sexton: "I can't really feel as if good Mr. Hooper's face was behind that piece of crape." [More uncertainty. The wearer must not be someone we know; therefore he must be an outsider, an Other.]

Old woman: "I don't like it. He has changed himself into something awful, only by hiding his face." [I believe he's dangerous, although I know my opinion is not rational. I trust my feelings and instincts over reason.]
Goodman Gray: "Our parson has gone mad!" [Sensational judgmentalism. Attempt at some explanation and categorization, however out of proportion to the offense.] [3]

To the visibly Muslim woman in a culture where she is part of a distinct minority, this initial confusion as a result of her mere appearance is an everyday experience. She may intend one meaning only, such as a return to traditional values or adherence to Sharia teachings on modesty, but she loses control over the power of her material symbol. Students might research any recent feminist scholarship for the ironies and contrasts implicit in the decision to veil or not to veil.[4]

We return to the story, as rumors precede Parson Hooper into the meeting house and uncomfortable body language replaces spoken words like the tacit "magic circle" of silence, which invariably surrounds Hester Prynne as she moves about in her community. After the service, the author

---

3   Nathaniel Hawthorne, "The Minister's Black Veil," in *Nathaniel Hawthorne: Selected Tales and Sketches*, ed. and intro. Michael J. Colacurcio (New York: Penguin), 185–186. Further citations from the tale are from this edition and are parenthetically noted.

4   In this order, I recommend for further reading Chandra Mohanty, *Feminism Without Borders: Decolonizing Theory, Practicing Solidarity* (Durham: Duke University Press, 2003); Nimat Hafez Barazangi, *Woman's Identity and the Qur'an: A New Reading* (Gainesville: University of Florida Press, 2004); Marnia Lazreg, *Questioning the Veil: Open Letters to Muslim Women* (Princeton: Princeton University Press, 2009); and Emma Tarlo, *Visibly Muslim: Fashion, Politics, Faith* (New York: Berg, 2010).

reports, "None, as on former occasions, aspired to the honor of walking by their pastor's side" (188). Even Old Squire Saunders neglects the customary dinner invitation, making Hooper's social isolation complete. The villagers' gossip focuses on the veil's effect on *themselves*, culminating in the lady's remark: "I would not be alone with him for the world. I wonder he is not afraid to be alone with himself" (189).

The silliness of the gossiper's remark—"I would not be alone with him for the world" and underscored by the off-handed speculation about his deserved fear of himself—would be at home in any of the mob scenes that pass for debates on western streets or more often on internet blogs. I ask the class to move the action again, this time to a current setting even more comparable to little Milford village, a small-town Alabama courthouse where local citizens stand in line to secure a driver's license. We also assume that this Muslim woman in line at the courthouse has *chosen* to express her religious freedom, however paradoxically, with this often-religiously-mandated symbol in cloth,[5] and that the locals do not have the cultural knowledge to grasp that her choice probably has no connection to neat binary oppositions such as East vs. West, Feminist vs. Islamist, or Oppressed vs. Liberated. Nevertheless, the locals do agree that the veiled figure has unsettled them "only by hiding [her] face." They notice that the veil, like Hooper's, "entirely concealed [her] features, except the mouth and chin, but probably did not intercept [her] sight, further than to give a darkened aspect to all living and inanimate things" (186). To these observers, the wearer's entire identity is reduced, again in Hawthorne's words, to "something singular" (187).

In response to this imagined scene, an Alabama blogger in 2004 posted, "What's the point of taking an identification photo of someone covered from head to toe in a shapeless blue burqa? If she were later asked to present her license as I.D., there would be no telling whether it was really her or Osama bin Laden behind that veil."[6] We might ask: does the modern blogger protest an exception to license standards or the shapelessness of

---

5   Conservative mandates follow Sharia teachings on modesty and the averted gaze based on Surah such as 24:30 and 31 of *The Holy Qur'an* (Pickthall translation). "And tell the believing women to lower their gaze and be modest . . . and to draw veils over their bosoms, and not to reveal their adornment save to their own husbands or fathers . . . ."

6   "Alabama Driver's Photo Rule Changed to Allow Hijab," *Labor Law Talk* (blog), February 21, 2004, accessed May 30, 2008, http://www.laborlawtalk.com.

a garment that prevents him from gazing intrusively on an exotic feminine form? In the blogger's tangled and ungrammatical reasoning, Muslim feminists would note not only remnants of Orientalist aggression towards hostile political leaders such as bin Laden but also racist condescension towards the women supposedly veiled and dominated by these leaders.[7]

Our blogger's unintended conflation of piety with sexuality actually belongs in Milford as well, for the funeral scene more than hints at a past connection between the minister and the dead young woman. Later in the wedding scene, the happiness of the occasion dissolves as the minister's veil attracts sexual gossip to himself when the focus should be on the purity of the veiled bride. British Muslim Humera Khan confesses that to her, the *hijab* protects one's spiritual self and creates a sacred space for sexuality, "an incredibly powerful thing." It creates an important divide between the public and private."[8] Yet to the Alabama blogger and to Father Hooper, this boundary has been transgressed to some extent or at some earlier time so that the veil serves as a reminder either to stay away or to stay within. In class, if time and internet access permit, students might take a few minutes to locate online discussions about *hijabi* fights over traditional dress and to identify statements, pro and con, which likewise entangle piety with sexuality.

In the media frenzy that follows our veiled figure in the story, for mediums of communication in Milford create the news even as they deliver it, we see a society troubled by any presence of diversity or difference. Hawthorne's narrator intervenes to comment sadly, "It was remarkable, that, of all the busy-bodies and impertinent people in the parish, not one ventured to put the plain question of Mr. Hooper, wherefore he did this thing" (191). Amina Wadud agrees: "My dress choice [of the *hijab* and *jilbab*] has radical, self-inscribed meaning—not apparent to an outside observer. . . . It can *only* be heard by the voice of the woman who wears it."[9] Yet the veiled woman facing the class seems to signal that she prefers not

---

7 See "Introduction" in Lamia Ben Youssef Zayzafoon, *The Production of the Muslim Woman: Negotiating Text, History, and Ideology* (New York: Lexington Books, 2005), 2–3.
8 Quoted in Tarlo, *Visibly Muslim*, 40.
9 See Wadud, *Inside the Gender Jihad*, 177. See also the introduction "May Muslim Women Speak for Themselves, Please?" in Gisela Webb, ed., *Windows of Faith: Muslim Women Scholar-Activists in North America* (Syracuse: Syracuse University Press, 2000), i–xiii.

to be approached. Within the sacred space of the veil, only a spouse, close family, or friends may share a bond with the wearer. Father Hooper denies himself even this much sacred space for earthly intimacy when he will not speak his heart even to Elizabeth, his plighted wife. Her womanly intuition knows she must help him quiet the rumors of the menacing, ostracizing mob. She steps forward with the civility expected in a pluralistic society, and, with the indirectness of a southern lady employee of the county courthouse, remarks disarmingly, "'There is nothing terrible in this piece of crape, except that it hides a face which I am always glad to look upon'" (193). This act of religious tolerance and even affection does not work for her, however, so she moves towards religious accommodation: "'Lift the veil but once, and look me in the face,'" said she" (194). And the courthouse employee today might add, "and smile for the camera." "'Never! It cannot be!' replied Mr. Hooper" (194). "'Then farewell! said Elizabeth" (194). No driver's license will be processed today. Neither will the Hoopers ever share the same reality that allows for mutual trust, for their separation is reflected in Elizabeth's need to attempt the stronger legal language of accommodation, its failure now implying that the gulf between them will only produce separation and endless silence.

The theme of isolation now on the table, I turn to traditional Hawthorne scholarship as students often recall other isolated Hawthorne characters. In the early tales, Michael Colacurcio sees Hawthorne leaning towards pragmatism amid the hermeneutics of suspicion that make up the villagers' and our readings of the veil and the tale itself. Colacurcio concludes his moral history of these tales: "No one can show forth his inmost heart. But cannot one show his face? The literal face will be, of course, partially deceptive: a parson will smile and smile and be a sinner still. . . . But the alternative turns out to be worse: the symbolic veil will always be destructive of available community; it will continuously heighten and feature what cannot be overcome. Better not wear it. Better do what one can."[10]

Yet is this decision to veil or not to veil another's to make? The newly pragmatic Alabama Department of Public Safety policy states the need for accommodation of otherness: "the photograph of each applicant must be a 'full face' photo. Although variations in hairstyles and head covering make it difficult to rigorously define the term 'face' in general, the head of the

---

10 Michael Colacurcio, *The Province of Piety: Moral History in Hawthorne's Early Tales* (Cambridge: Harvard University Press, 1984), 385.

applicant shall be shown from the top of the forehead to the bottom of the chin and from hairline side-to-side . . . Head coverings and head gear are *only acceptable due to religious beliefs* or medical conditions [emphasis mine]."[11]

Like Colacurcio, Clark Davis would imagine Hawthorne tentatively applauding this new, relaxed policy. Davis recognizes that the face is itself a mask, a veil for private feelings, but adds, "and yet, the face . . . is the site of public identity, the set of features that determines the public self, the face one shows to the world. . . . The only ethical response is to receive the infinite complexity of otherness for what it is and avoid attempts to reduce or control it."[12] Can we know what the veiled woman in the classroom is thinking? Is she even thinking about us at all? If she removed her veil to reveal her face, would we then know? Can we not accept that she is her own beautiful person apart from us and rightfully entitled to protection of privacy?

The inner life of one who adopts the veil with its muffling of sounds and restrictions on bodily movements, not to mention the darkened world one sees through the cloth, is the subject of other studies and discussions. My students will enter this world with the protagonist Mariam when they read Hosseini's *A Thousand Splendid Suns* near the end of the semester. For now, my approach joins Pakistani-born scholar Riffat Hassan in shifting the attention away from the veiled one and back to the harassers and oglers who make daily life miserable for others. One of the first to call herself an "Islamic feminist," Hassan includes not just abusive men but western feminists in her spotlight when they fixate on the veil to reinforce the colonial stereotype that Muslim women are passive victims in need of rescue. She accuses these feminists of not respecting faith-based women's movements.[13] Do we respect and not just tolerate the religiously conservative choice? Why cannot Muslim women be allowed to reform their religious culture from within, as Father Hooper hopes to do by making parishioners aware of their own sinfulness? Why? Perhaps because the wish to bring back "all the gloom and piety" of an earlier theocracy no longer appeals to most modern citizens, East or West. Both the Puritan "city on a hill" and

11   "Alabama Driver's Photo Rule."
12   Clark Davis, "Facing the Veil: Hawthorne, Hooper, and Ethics," *Arizona Quarterly*, 55, no. 4 (1999): 9.
13   Riffat Hassan, "Challenging the Stereotypes of Fundamentalism: An Islamic Feminist Perspective," *Muslim World*, 91 (Spring 2001): 55–70.

the Muslim *khilafah* (or caliphate) with no separation of church and state remain inspirational as symbols but alarming for persons who do not share their religious vision.

In this one class period devoted to Hawthorne's enigmatic tale, it is possible to identify dialectical tensions between conservatism and modernity, individuality and community, and piety and privacy that even today threaten to pull apart our experiment in democracy. I always leave time for the death scene, for it offers one last hope that Hawthorne will help us out of this tension and mystery. Rev. Mr. Clark rushes to the bedside into the privacy of Hooper's home, bearing our questions, but when his attempted hegemony fails, his language takes on judgmental, racist tones: "'Dark old man! With what horrible crime upon your soul are you now passing to the judgment?'" (199). Hooper's response, for he won't be colonized but will speak for himself, is to imagine himself in a scene like a *hijabi* protest movement, where "on every visage" appears a Black Veil, significantly capitalized in the end as the metaphor outlives the wearer (199).

For the duration of the class period, I have allowed the picture of the veiled woman to gaze at the class. Students now look exhausted. They seem to feel the mystery of the symbol and want to say *something* in response, usually to keep the image literal and within the context of driver's license requirements and public safety, but at a level beyond language they also feel the hypnotic power of the *icon* that critic Samuel Chase Coale recognizes is Hawthorne's real exploration of the mystery of guilt, sin, isolation, and the sacred.[14] The range of response in the classroom can be ambiguous and contradictory—by turns fearful, charitable, or transgressive—and often relies on rumors and speculation rather than on open dialogue with others. Hawthorne had created a little Puritan village that appears homogeneous on the surface but can barely accommodate one citizen's pious isolation and difference. Is a nation made up of these little villages ready for the challenges of a multicultural democracy?

Samford University

---

14 Samuel Chase Coale, "Hawthorne's Black Veil: From Image to Icon," *CEA Critic: An Official Journal of the College English Association*, 55, no. 3 (1993): 79–87.

Teaching "The Minister's Black Veil" and "Rappaccini's Daughter" as Frame Stories

Gabriela Serrano

When teaching Nathaniel Hawthorne's "The Minister's Black Veil" and "Rappaccini's Daughter," I draw the following parallels on the whiteboard before beginning class:

"Rappaccini'sDaughter"	"The Minister's Black Veil"
Beatrice/Giovanni = reader/student	parishioners = reader/student
flower = narrative	veil = narrative
Prof. Rappaccini = Hawthorne/college professor	Rev. Hooper = Hawthorne/college professor

Students are curious as to how they compare to characters within the stories. When we discuss, however, how Professor Rappaccini and Reverend Hooper are arguably egomaniacal, sinful characters (if in different ways and to different degrees), and that these characters compare to their own English professor, then students are truly intrigued. Frame stories make students aware of themselves as a reading audience, empowering them to engage more critically when analyzing Hawthorne's two tales. They often read them from the point of view of a strict morality, but the lessons they learn make them question their own values after considering how the characters within the texts react to moral dilemmas. For Hawthorne overtly implies that his stories teach a moral lesson by labeling "The Minister's Black Veil" "a parable" and pointing to the author's "love of allegory" in "Rappaccini's Daughter."[1] When students consider how framing devices such as these prompt them to analyze from a perspective both within and without a text, they are better equipped to probe Hawthorne's message about his peculiar relationship to his readers (in particular) and the human condition (in general).

A useful starting point for our class discussion on Hawthorne's frame narratives is to consider what the term "frame" means. John Frow argues that a frame is determined "by the covers of a book . . . by the author's name . . . by the dedicatory material."[2] In other words, a frame is comprised of paratextual or metadiscursive materials, and I apply this term even more broadly than Frow, as I consider the book I assign for survey courses, the first volume of *The Norton Anthology of American Literature*, as itself yet another frame for "The Minister's Black Veil" and "Rappaccini's Daughter." This anthology, I would argue, gives students a preconceived notion about this collection of early American literature: before they even open their anthology, the collection creates the impression that these stories must be noteworthy literary contributions to the early American literary canon because they appear in lower and upper-level literature courses. If we think further about the anthology itself, how thick it is, how heavily annotated it is, and definitely how expensive the book is, this already erects a wall between students and the literary works in these anthologies. When combined with Hawthorne's unfamiliar and often opaque literary style, for students this institutional and literary barrier can seem unsurmountable.

To overcome these difficulties and to demystify Hawthorne's narrative style, I tell students that despite the appearance of a veil, the author does want us to get to know him and open up his text to multiple interpretations. He is actually trying to make his text more and not less approachable and even entertaining with narrative teasers in the form of two footnotes. I explain that "The Minister's Black Veil" is simply a story within a story

---

1   Nathaniel Hawthorne, "Rappaccini's Daughter," *Mosses from an Old Manse* in *The Centenary Edition of the Works of Nathaniel Hawthorne*, vol. X, ed. William Charvat, et al. (Columbus: Ohio State University Press, 1974), 91. Subsequent citations from this tale are from this edition and parenthetically documented.
2   John Frow, "The Literary Frame," *Journal of Aesthetic Education* 16, no. 2 (1982): 26.

that begins with a personal narrative where the narrator tells us about himself before he begins his fictional tale. When students question whether "The Minister's Black Veil" is a frame narrative, I point to specific clues that Hawthorne provides at the beginning of the story prompting us to read his twice-told tale as such. First, he immediately includes two footnotes before we even get past the title of his story, which focus our attention on another one of Hawthorne's tales,[3] and the story of another minister who wore a similar veil, and so we need to consider how "The Minister's Black Veil" relates to the narrator in "Sights from a Steeple."[4] Second, it is a twice-told tale in at least two respects because the tale is based on a real story, according to Hawthorne, and it is part of a collection of stories, appropriately titled *Twice-told Tales*. Unlike *The Scarlet Letter* and "Rappaccini's Daughter," which are more traditional frame narratives beginning with a short, personal story about the narrator that relates to the fictional tale, "The Minister's Black Veil" is not a clear-cut frame story. What I do emphasize, however, is that a frame most generally is a rhetorical device the author utilizes to help us get to know him. He wants us to know more about his narrative idiosyncrasies to make himself more personable to his readers. "The Minister's Black Veil," therefore, provides a perfect segue to begin our discussion of frame narratives and how they are indicative of Hawthorne's approach to writing.

Moreover, the veil itself is a good symbol for Hawthorne's writing style, which often frustrates students due to its obscurity, even as "The Minister's Black Veil" actually makes teaching him easier. This symbol tells us that there will not be one clear-cut interpretation of the text, and Hawthorne invites us to come up with various, diverse interpretations of his story, so students are free to approach his text openly. Thomas R. Moore considers how Hawthorne developed his writing style during his years as an undergraduate at Bowdoin as a student of Hugh Blair's *Lectures on Rhetoric and Belles Lettres*.[5] Moore explains that this early text on style urged students to

---

3   Hawthorne first published "The Minister's Black Veil" in 1836 in *The Token* and identified himself as the author of "Sights from a Steeple."

4   Nathaniel Hawthorne, "The Minister's Black Veil," *Twice-told Tales* in *The Centenary Edition of the Works of Nathaniel Hawthorne*, vol. 9, ed. William Charvat, et al. (Columbus: Ohio State University Press, 1974), 37. Subsequent citations to this tale and "Sights from a Steeple" are taken from this edition and documented parenthetically.

5   Thomas R. Moore, "A Thick and Darksome Veil," *Nineteenth-Century Literature* 48. 3 (1993): 310.

develop a clear, concise style and prompted students to strive toward "simplicity" but, Moore argues, Hawthorne's "outward adherence to Blair's rules for 'Structure of Sentences' masks a socially and culturally variant subtext."[6] Moore further analyzes Hawthorne's stylistic approach in other short stories and sketches, including "Sights from a Steeple," and determines that "[t]he sketches frequently begin with cues of uncertainty: modals suggesting doubt, 'if' clauses introducing conditions, 'perhaps' clauses provoking speculation."[7] This writing style forces us to more actively approach and analyze his texts.

If Hawthorne's framing devices and style provoke introspection from the start, the physical placement of his narrators in "Sights from a Steeple" and "The Minister's Black Veil" points out how a writer has complete control over a reader's interpretation of his narrative if we do not work to formulate our own individual interpretation of a text. The setting of "Sights from a Steeple" provides students with a nice visual image for how the narrator situates himself not only a higher physical plane but also an intellectual and spiritual one: "Here I stand, with wearied knees, earth, indeed, at a dizzy depth below, but heaven far, far beyond me still. O that I could soar up into the very zenith, where man never breathed, nor eagle ever flew, and where the ethereal azure melts away from the eye, and appears only a deepened shade of nothingness!" (191). Similarly, Reverend Hooper in "The Minister's Black Veil" places himself physically and, from his perspective, morally, in the pulpit above his congregation. Arguably, Hawthorne signifies here upon his own position in relation to his reader: he is not only warning them of a Transcendentalist writer's tendency to isolate himself from the rest of the world, but he is also reminding himself to reconnect with his reading audience. He acknowledges his tendency to distance himself from his readers, but because we are more aware of ourselves as readers through his use of frame narratives, we understand the importance of making a human connection between author and text. Perhaps the moral lesson we learn after all is that our attempt to see beyond the veil is what ties us to him; attempting to reach another human being beyond place, time, and text is what establishes human connection.

I begin my discussion of Hawthorne's use of frame stories with "The Minister's Black Veil" to introduce what the literary term "frame" can

---

6   Ibid., 311.
7   Ibid.

mean, but I delve further into its uses and possibilities in "Rappaccini's Daughter." "The Minister's Black Veil" ends when Hooper dies isolated, in his old age, his isolation self-inflicted, whereas Beatrice Rappaccini's dies young and a victim of her father's ambition. We can interpret both stories as about individuals of higher intellectual knowledge who lack the moral judgment to understand the consequences of their "experiments," and with the latter tale we come to understand how knowledge may not only poison the mind but the soul as well. Rappaccini is a professor, and he is responsible for the intellectual development of his daughter (and Giovanni to a certain extent). Because of his selfish quest for knowledge, his experiment fails, and Beatrice's death symbolizes the death of his failed investigation and failed contribution to the canon of scientific knowledge.

I therefore ask students how they think Professor Rappaccini compares to their own English professor. They respond by characterizing him as evil, mean, egomaniacal, etc. I remind them that like Rappaccini, I exert a kind of control over their fate when determining final grades for the course. The narrator's "love of allegory" allows us to consider the story in the context of students' own lives: "Rappaccini's Daughter" can be about a young person's relationship with an authority figure—whether with his or her parents or a boss, but for our purpose, we focus on the relationship between the authority figure of the professor and her students. Then, we return to the text. The first crucial clue students might miss is the subtitle of the story "from the writings of Aubepine" (91). Aubepine, a French name that alludes to the Hawthorn[e] shrub, makes us question why Hawthorne would include what seems to be such an insignificant detail as a subheading for his story. Here as elsewhere, according to Michael Dunne, Hawthorne "intensif[ies] [the] self-referentiality" in his frame narratives:[8] Dunne notes how Hawthorne is pointing to himself, so the gaze of the reader will always go back to the author, and this forces us to consider how we must constantly go back to the introduction itself throughout the story. As the Hawthorne plant is a thorny shrub, we must approach his text with caution, or we will be hurt by this unwelcoming plant. The thorny bush, though, also protects the flowers and fruit it bears. Perhaps Hawthorne is protecting his readers from something, from a writer's poisonous tendency to want to control his reading audience's interpretation of the text?

---

8   Michael Dunne, *Hawthorne's Narrative Strategies* (Oxford: University Press of Mississippi, 2007), 72.

We then move to discuss the tale's romantic pair—Beatrice and Giovanni—and we first question whether Hawthorne intentionally underdeveloped Beatrice's character to the point that it is difficult to make a human connection or identify with her because we know so little about her. She has led a very sheltered life, to say the least, and she does not question her father's science. And as we are preconditioned to draw strict lines between victims and villains, we consider whether Beatrice is truly the victim when Giovanni may actually be the tragic hero or vice versa. Although the death of Beatrice is tragic, Bernard McCabe claims that the story instead "is Giovanni's tragedy since he is the only dramatically developed character."[9] McCabe concludes that as we "accept the experience of Giovanni, we come nearer to a satisfactory reading of Hawthorne's tale."[10] Giovanni looks at Beatrice from far away and must remain physically removed from her because she is poisonous, although he finally joins her in the garden, even when he is suspicious of the poisonous flower, which Beatrice refers to as her "sister" (102). If some students do not empathize with her character and plight, Hawthorne nevertheless teaches us here about our tendency to label people as victims or villains and our need to sympathize with them.

The story's setting, Italy in the distant past, offers a final clue as to how we should approach the narrative. McCabe, for example, notes that Rappaccini "is a variant of that personification of Renaissance Humanism, the Roger Bacon, the Paracelsus, the 'Overreacher,' an obsessed, single-minded usurper of the divine."[11] Considering that Rappaccini is a scientist in Italy in the distant past, we can imagine that the story could have taken place during the Italian Renaissance when humanists emphasized the importance of learning how to interpret poetry allegorically to find a moral lesson. Individuals can pick and choose how to apply an allegory for their own purpose, since so much of the tale remains ambiguous and mysterious. Students must therefore create an informed judgment about Hawthorne's narrative just as they must decide how to approach the course itself. They must ask themselves whether they are passive or active in their own quest for knowledge, and the answer to this question depends in part on their interpretation of Beatrice's last act—whether it is one of defiance or surrender or both. If, for instance, students assume she is defiant, then

---

9 Bernard McCabe, "Narrative Technique in 'Rappaccini's Daughter,'" *Modern Language Notes* 74. 3 (1959): 214.
10 Ibid., 217.
11 Ibid., 214.

she actively takes the antidote to escape from her father's control and even Giovanni's taunts and doubts. The frame narratives and pedagogical experiments in "The Minister's Black Veil" and "Rappaccini's Daughter," then, ultimately teach us to be more accountable for our own fates as readers, students, and professors.

Angelo State University

Sympathies of the Heart in Nathaniel Hawthorne's "Young Goodman Brown"

Jonathan Murphy

"Young Goodman Brown" (1835) has long been recognized as one of Hawthorne's earliest masterpieces and most frequently anthologized and taught texts. As a critical commentary upon the historical atrocities committed by the Puritan colonists from religious intolerance and racial warfare to the witchcraft hysteria, it therefore remains an unrivalled text for pedagogical relevance and reappraisal. Whether one reads the tale as a philosophical reappraisal of the Calvinist doctrine of depravity, a psychological examination of the various forms of religious and racial panic that have left such an indelible mark upon the American psyche and which continue to do so—witness the current "War on Terror," for instance—or as a political study of the ever evolving "moral-historical" imbrication of good and evil, it seems impossible to exhaust its significance for the study of American culture. The central problem posed by this tale may be summarized by the following formula: in a world unmoored from moral absolutes, how do we decide the difference between good and evil, and most importantly, how do we avoid repeating the errors of the past?

The basic mistake of the Puritans was not that they succumbed to immoral prejudices but that in their attempt to establish a city on a hill, they committed acts of evil *in the name of* the good. In a related manner,

Hawthorne asks his readers to reflect upon the multifaceted legacy of New England Puritanism, still at the root of the American literary canon as taught to high school and college students, and he does so not to shy away from a critical indictment of its criminal history but also to be wary of wholesale denunciations of the past that turn Salemites into religious fanatics who share little in common with our enlightened present. He asks his readers to turn their critical eye inward at the same time that he redirects them outward to the annals of New England history, and he likewise warns them that hypocrisy, like the devil, can assume many forms—even appear as the likeness of God.

David Levin was the first to point out that Hawthorne understood the importance of what was called "specter evidence" in the witchcraft trials. As he noted, "This was evidence that a specter, or shape, or apparition ... had tormented the witness or had been present at a witches' meeting."[1] After it was decided by Thomas Brattle and the Mathers that spectral evidence was no longer to be admitted as evidence on the grounds that it was or just might be the devil's testimony, the death toll peaked at a total of nineteen unjustly accused men and women.

Michael Colacurcio suggests that spectral evidence in the witchcraft trials was symptomatic of a larger spiritual malaise that afflicted New England Puritanism, namely, the ecclesiastical positivism that characterized its quest to establish a church of visible saints. According to him, "Young Goodman Brown" does not so much dramatize the problem of specter evidence as it "enfigures the ultimate breakdown of the Puritan attempt to define the human form of the Kingdom of God: 'specter evidence' turns out to be only the negative test case of the definitive Puritan problem of 'visible sanctity.'"[2] This is because Puritan orthodoxy depended equally upon the visible identification of saints as it did the spectral condemnation of witches. Hawthorne's tale represents the failure of all empirical evidence of spiritual states of either grace *or* damnation. Colacurcio concludes that Hawthorne's tale "could *only* end in nightmare," for it represents the path "by which the quest for visible sanctity leads unavoidably into the realm of spectral evidence."[3]

---

1   David Levin, "Shadows of Doubt: Specter Evidence in Hawthorne's 'Young Goodman Brown,'" *American Literature* 34, no. 3 (1962): 344–52.
2   Michael Colacurcio, *The Province of Piety: Moral History in Hawthorne's Early Tales* (Cambridge: Harvard University Press, 1984), 286–87.
3   Ibid., 313.

The Salem hysteria was not only an ugly symptom of ecclesiastical positivism, nor was it just a matter of public record. For Hawthorne, of course, the stakes of the debate were very personal indeed, as his great-great grandfather, John Hathorne, was one of the judges who presided in the trials.[4] In fact, the first shape the devil assumes in Hawthorne's fiction is not that of a serpent or horned demon or even a universal inclination of the human species but rather that of old Goodman Brown. Satan appears as the protagonist's father, and he looks a lot like his son but has the "indescribable air of one who knew the world, and who would not have felt abashed at the governor's dinner table."[5] John Hathorne (1641–1717) and his father, William Hathorne (1606-1681), were capital fathers of Salem who occupied prominent positions in the myriad affairs of the town.[6] The devil has them in mind when he informs Goodman Brown, "the select men, of divers towns, make me their chairman; and a majority of the Great and General Court are firm supporters of my interest" (77). He alludes to some of their more lurid exploits when he tells Goodman Brown that he helped his grandfather, "the constable, when he lashed the Quaker woman so smartly through the streets of Salem. And it was I who brought the pitch-pine knot, kindled at my own hearth, to set fire to an Indian village, in King Philip's War" (77).

William and John both played major roles in various conflicts with Native Americans, but it was William who was responsible for the persecution of

---

4   See Charles Upham's *Salem Witchcraft* (1867), which provides lengthy transcripts that document John Hathorne's McCarthy-esque style of interrogation. He operated on the assumption of guilt, posed leading questions, encouraged witnesses to identify their guilty associates, and maliciously interpreted every innocent utterance of the accused.

5   Nathaniel Hawthorne, *Mosses from an Old Manse* in *The Centenary Edition of the Works of Nathaniel Hawthorne*, Volume X, ed. William Charvat et al. (Columbus: Ohio State University Press, 1974), 76. All citations from the story are from this edition and are parenthetically documented.

6   Joseph Felt's *Annals of Salem, from Its First Settlement* (Salem: W. & S. B. Ives, 1827), an objective record of the military, economic, and juridical history of Salem, was one of Hawthorne's primary references in reconstructing his blood relative's role in the unsavory debacle. Hawthorne first borrowed this book from September 21 to October 30, 1833. He borrowed it a second time from December 30, 1834 to January 30, 1835. These withdrawals suggest that Hawthorne composed "Young Goodman Brown" between September 1833 and January 1835. See Marion Kesselring's *Hawthorne's Reading, 1828–1850* (New York: New York Public Library, 1949) for a complete listing.

Quakers. Joseph Felt reports that the eldest Hathorne was Deputy of the General Court when the judgment was passed that Quakers "shall be made bare from the middle upwards, tied to a cart, and whipped through the town towards the boundary of Massachusetts; and, if returning, that they shall be similarly punished, with the addition, that some of them shall be branded with an R on their left shoulder."[7] The "R" stood for "Ranter,"[8] which was a pet epitaph the Puritans had for the voluble religious sect. John was appointed Assistant of the General Court in 1684, and it was not long before he inherited his father's sunny disposition, along with his savvy penchant for imprinting his judicial sentences in alphabetical letters upon the recipients of his perverse sense of justice. In 1694, the unrepentant judge enacted legislation that forced adulterers "[t]o sit an hour in the gallows, with ropes about their necks, be severely whipt not above 40 stripes; and forever after wear a capital A, two inches long, cut out of cloth coloured differently from their clothes, and sewed on their arms, or back parts of their garments."[9] John was a bit softer than his father, electing to have the symbol sewn into the clothing instead of branded upon the skin of his victims, but both forms of punishment characterized the person's sinful soul as a blighted object, thereby rendering the spiritual state of the convicted visible to the physical eye of every beholder and ossifying the immaterial freedom of the will in the process. Sometimes the letter of the law really did kill the spirit after all.

7   Felt, *Annals of Salem*, 210–11.
8   Ibid., 192.
9   Ibid., 317. Herein, of course, resides the historical seed of *The Scarlet Letter* (1850) In "The Custom-House," Hawthorne informs us that William Hathorne, his "grave, bearded, sable-cloaked, and steeple-crowned progenitor,—who came so early, with his Bible and his sword, …. was a soldier, legislator, judge; he was a ruler in the Church; he had all the Puritanic traits, both good and evil. He was likewise a bitter persecutor; as witness the Quakers, who have remembered him in their histories, and relate an incident of his hard severity towards a woman of their sect, which will last longer, it is to be feared, than any record of his better deeds, although these were many. His son, too, inherited the persecuting spirit, and made himself so conspicuous in the martyrdom of witches, that their blood may fairly be said to have left a stain upon him." Hawthorne added the "w" to his name to distance himself from the bloody curse incurred by his ancestors, thereby taking "shame upon myself for their sakes." See *The Scarlet Letter* in *The Centenary Edition of the Collected Works of Nathaniel Hawthorne*, Volume 1, ed. William Charvat et al. (Columbus: Ohio University Press, 1962), 7–9. Hawthorne borrowed Felt's *Annals* a third time from January 2 to March 22, 1849.

The next "Shape of Evil" that Goodman Brown encounters in his midnight ramble is Goody Cloyse (88). He overhears her telling the devil that Goody Cory stole her broom while she "was all anointed with the juice of smallage and cinque-foil and wolf's-bane—" (79). The devil interjects at this point, "Mingled with fine wheat and the fat of a new-born babe (79). Francis Bacon has been identified as the source for Hawthorne's derivation of his recipe for witch ointment[10] from his *Natural History* (1627): "The ointment that witches use, is reported to be made of the fat of children digged out of their graves; of the juices of smallage, wolf-bane, and cinque-foil, mingled with the meal of fine wheat."[11] In a related passage, not previously cited by critics, Bacon discredits the popular superstitions regarding witchcraft by subjecting them to his more enlightened point of view. He cautions his readers:

> It is worthy observing, that ... (in) the meetings of witches that have been recorded by so many late confessions, the great wonders which they tell, of carrying in the air, transforming themselves into other bodies, *etc.* are still reported to be wrought, not by incantations or ceremonies, but by ointments, and anointing themselves all over. This may justly move a man to think, that these fables are the effects of imagination: for it is certain, that ointments do all, if they be laid on anything thick, by stopping of the pores, shutting in the vapours, and sending them to the head extremely. And for the particular ingredients of those magical ointments, it is like they are opiate and soporiferous.[12]

The crux of the debate for Bacon thus pivots on whether the ointment enabled witches to levitate or to transmogrify (or, and this amounts to *almost* the same thing, to spectrally dissociate from their physical bodies), or if it instead acted as a soporific that induced hallucinations of flight.

10   Fannye Cherry, "The Sources of Hawthorne's 'Young Goodman Brown,'" *American Literature* 5, no. 4 (1934): 342–48.
11   *The Works of Francis Bacon*, Volume II (London: H. Bryer, 1803), 69. Hawthorne borrowed the second volume of the 1803 edition of Bacon's *Collected Works*, which contains his *Natural History*, in June 1832. He recited Bacon's recipe in his 1836 article on "Witch Ointment" for the *American Magazine of Useful and Entertaining Knowledge*.
12   Ibid, 45–46.

Hawthorne's narrative application of witch unguent points in yet another direction entirely, which is towards his own homegrown tradition of witchcraft delusion and in particular to Increase Mather's *Essay for the Recording of Illustrious Providences* (1684).[13] Indeed, in many respects, "Young Goodman Brown" may be read as pitting the empirical method advanced by Bacon in his *Natural History* against the supernatural history of New England recounted by Mather in his *Remarkable Providences* as the book's running caption reads. Mather intended his book to be a faithful record of divine intervention in the shape of shipwrecks, floods, thunder storms, earthquakes, apparitions, witchcrafts, possessions, judgments, and deliverances. His *Remarkable Providences* was marshaled as a broadside against the more rationalist tendencies in natural history as well as in the Christian church, which, like Bacon, tended to dismiss ghosts and witches and other evidences of revealed religion as superstitious relics of a primitive past. Increase was, of course, the father of Cotton, and his son's extremist disposition, as evidenced in *The Wonders of the Invisible World* (1693), was clearly imbibed from his father at an early age. In any case, as a piece of ideological propaganda, *Remarkable Providences* in large part set the stage for the witchcraft trials in Salem, which took place a mere eight years after its publication.

Increase Mather's central preoccupation is not so much whether to adopt a natural or a supernatural principle of interpretation regarding historical events as it devolves upon how to tell the difference between honest and deceptive spirits. Remarkable providences, in other words, are the epistemological *donnée* of his book. His historiographical task is to distinguish good manifestations of the supernatural from the bad. He argues, for instance, that Satan can appear in the spectral form of saints and even imitate the likeness of Christ and furthermore, that demons exist and may take possession of souls. His sixth chapter on "Demons and Possessed Persons," is especially relevant to "Young Goodman Brown." Mather cites scripture as his authority on the subject, but he admits, "Sometimes indeed it is hard to discern between natural Diseases and Satanical Possessions; so as that persons really possessed have been thought to be only molested with some natural Disease, without any special finger of the Evil Spirit therein."[14] His

---

13 Hawthorne borrowed Mather's book in March 1834, less than two years after reading Bacon's *Natural History*.

14 Increase Mather, *Remarkable Providences Illustrative of the Earlier Days of American Colonisation*, ed. George Offor (London: John Smith, 1856), 169–70.

equivocal language anticipates Hawthorne's own when Goodman Brown loses his faith and becomes a "demoniac" as a result. Hawthorne observes on this illustrious occasion, "The fiend in his own shape is less hideous, than when he rages in the breast of man" (84), but he calls this supernatural interpretation into doubt when he has the devil inform his congregation that "the deep mystery of sin, the fountain of all wicked arts … supplies more evil impulses—than my power at its utmost!—can make manifest in deeds" (87). The author's wry implication is that the devil does not have a shape of his own, and thus no amount of spectral evidence or manifest deeds can point the finger to the Evil Spirit. Increase Mather adopts a more "natural" approach. He indicates that violent convulsions, secret knowledge, strange tongues, powerful strength, an inflexible body, a distended belly, and the vocal haranguing of neighbors are all physical signs that distinguish demoniacal possession from a merely corporeal ailment or imaginative delusion.

The Puritan divine's uneasy settlement of the porous divide between natural madness and supernatural possession is evidenced by his peculiar definition of *lycanthropia* as a condition, "wherein men *believe* themselves to be wolves. This form of madness is actually demoniac possession, not mental illness."[15] Like Bacon, he maintains that it is "A blind heathenish phansie … that witches can transform themselves or others into another sort of creatures."[16] Although he dismisses such heathenish beliefs, he confesses, "Though I deny not but that the Devil may so impose upon the imagination of Witches as to make them believe that they are transmuted into Beasts."[17] *Lycanthropia* is thus rooted in possession, but it is of a type that the demon makes the person suffer from delusions that he or she has been transformed into a beast. For *Lycanthropia*, like spectral evidences, intersects with the topic of witch ointment as well, as is demonstrated by the curious anecdote that Mather recounts about an Irish witch who insisted that she could transform herself into a wolf. Her local magistrate asked her to prove it: "Accordingly, she anointed her head, neck and armpits; immediately upon which she fell into a most profound sleep, for three hours."[18] When she awoke, she claimed to have killed a cow and a sheep some miles distant. Upon inspection, it was discovered that both animals

---

15 Mather, *Remarkable Providences*, 173.
16 Ibid., 177.
17 Ibid., 177-78.
18 Ibid., 178.

were dead. Mather's providential interpretation of this incident is remarkable, indeed. Instead of suspecting that she spectrally committed this offense while her physical body slept, he concludes that it is evident "the Devil himself did that mischief, and in the mean time the Witches who were cast into so profound a sleep by him, as that they could not by any noises or blows be awakened, had their Phansies imposed upon by Dreams and Delusions according to the pleasure of their Master Satan."[19] While it may be superstitious to believe in *lycanthropia*, it is another matter to believe in the devil's power to delude the senses while physically manipulating the material course of history.

Mather proceeds to link the delusional testimonies extracted from witches to the false confessions exacted by the Catholic Inquisitions: "Sometimes persons have been tried for witchcraft by hot, sometimes by cold water ... sometimes by pricking them, sometimes by sticking awls under their seats, sometimes by their ability, or otherwise, to repeat the Lord's Prayer."[20] Hawthorne was, of course, well aware of the infamous execution of George Burroughs that marked the beginning of the end of the trials in New England. In his *More Wonders of the Invisible World* (1700), a rebuttal of Cotton Mather's earlier legitimation of the trials, Robert Calef provides his own eyewitness account of the event. He reports that Mr. Burroughs "made a Speech for the clearing of his Innocency, with such Solemn and Serious Expressions, as were to the Admiration of all present; his Prayer (which he concluded by repeating the Lord's Prayer), was so well worded, and uttered with such composedness, and such (at least seeming) fervency of Spirit"[21] that many felt that it would result in a stay of his death sentence. Such was not to be the case. Cotton Mather proceeded to denounce Reverend Burroughs in no uncertain terms, admonishing the crowd, "That the Devil has often been transformed into an Angel of Light."[22] He might have been quoting directly from his father's book. In his own *Wonders of the Invisible World*, Cotton prefaces his description of "The Tryal of G. B." with the following words: "Glad should I have been, if I had never known the Name of this man; or never had this occasion to mention so much as

---

19   Ibid., 178–79.
20   Ibid., 178.
21   George Lincoln Burr, *Narratives of the Witchcraft Cases; 1648–1706* (New York: Barnes and Noble, 1959), 360.
22   Ibid., 361.

the first letters of his Name."23 Either Burroughs was Satan speaking in the guise of a man whose body he demoniacally possessed, or he was the devil surfacing in the details of Cotton Mather's ecclesiastical positivism. In either case, he was the glitch in the puritanical system that could no longer be concealed and whose cadaver thus had to be left exposed in the ground, a Polyneices-figure whose rotting corpse incited the popular judgment to rise against the spectral evidences and the dishonorable edicts of the chief justices of the scene.

The final person that Brown encounters in his errand beyond the forested precincts of Salem Village is none other than his wife, Faith. Threatened by the loss of his religion in the allegorical form of a pink ribbon fluttering from the heavens, Brown holds onto it ever tighter, but whatever moral substance it may have signified is crushed in his paranoiac grasp. "Think not to frighten me with your deviltry!" he calls out to the forest of shadows that accosts him. "Come witch, come wizard, come Indian powow, come devil himself! and here comes Goodman Brown. You may as well fear him as he fear you!" (83). Desperate to cling to his wife's skirts, the demoniac "rushes onward, with the instinct that guides mortal man to evil" (83). He arrives on the diabolical scene only to find that Faith is irredeemably caught in the baptismal grip of original sin. The devil proceeds to inform the diverse cast of sinners gathered before him that "Evil is the nature of mankind. Evil must be your only happiness. Welcome, again, my children, to the communion of your race!" As Satan prepares to lay the mark of sin upon them, Brown cries out to his wife, "Faith! Faith! ... Look up to Heaven, and resist the Wicked One!" (88). He does not ascertain if she obeys his command, for at that moment he awakens as if from a dream.

Indeed, the entire episode takes place in the uncertainty of a dreamworld so that the reader is left to wonder with the narrator: "Had Goodman Brown fallen asleep in the forest and only dreamed a wild dream of a witch meeting?" (89). The status of his mystical encounter does not really matter for his dogmatic slumber is never really interrupted. He merely exchanges the somnambulistic faith of his forefathers for its nightmarish inversion. He returns to his village an alienated misanthropist doomed "to behold the whole earth one stain of guilt, one mighty blood-spot, ... more conscious of the secret guilt of others, both in deed and thought, than (he) could now be of (his) own" (87–88). Instead of gaining a vision of evil, Brown is cursed

---

23 Ibid., 215.

with an evil optics. He can now only see evil in others, and he views himself as the only chosen person among the elect. He is the reduction to absurdity of the solipsism that defined the church of visible saints in New England, a people who could not stand the sight of sin in themselves and thus had to project it onto a demonized other, be it Quaker, Native American, witch or adulterer, all the better to exorcize their demons and to cloak their depravity with the spectral phantom of visible sanctity.

The implication of "Young Goodman Brown" in the fold of mythology loosens its proper locality as a tale twice told. This is because the story of good and evil is one that has been told and retold since the dawn of history. Hawthorne's fable perversely renders the Edenic narrative as it does Plato's allegory of the cave. Goodman Brown ventures out on a speculative limb, but the only fruit to reward his labors is his fall from grace. Unlike the Platonic dialectician, Brown is not intent upon reflecting upon the essence of the good. Instead of fixing his attention upon the light of the sun, he advances further into the shadowy recesses of his troglodyte faith. His ultimate vision terminates in a total lack of insight. His blindness is not merely expressive of the constitutional finitude of sight, however, but more properly signifies that the dogmatic lenses he adopted that night precluded his rational encounter with the moral shape of evil. No matter how well-intentioned on his part, his misguided turning away from the devil and his dogmatic turning towards the starry heavens leaves him prone to further delusion and despair. Although he began his metaphysical journey guided by his naïve belief in "Heaven above and Faith below" (82), he loses the simplicity of his faith in the myriad complications that beset him on his path. He finally arrives at the cynical conclusion that "There is no good on earth; and sin is but a name" (83). He wards off the nihilistic implications of such a skeptical worldview by retreating into the fold of his conservative religion, which he attempts to surmount by repudiating, but his simplistic reversal of the Puritan logic of visible sanctity does not remedy its ecclesiastical positivism. Regarding the Puritans as angels *or* demons, instead of as moral-historical beings who sought salvation but fell far short in their pursuit of redemption, misses the point of Hawthorne's tale.

Notwithstanding the vast metaphysical heritage alluded to above, Coleridge's mediation of the respective claims of dogmatism and skepticism in *Aids to Reflection* (1825) clearly helped Hawthorne navigate the contentious topics of witch ointment, spectral evidence, demoniac possession, mystical revelation, and other such instances where spirit and matter collide.[24] Both authors take as their primary object of study the radical evil of the human condition, and both link the mystery of our moral condition to the spectral limitations of our sensible comprehension. Coleridge's stated aim in his book is "to establish a general rule of interpretation and vindication applicable to *all* doctrinal tenets, and especially to the (so called) mysteries of the Christian faith: to provide a *Safety-Lamp* for religious inquirers."[25] The target demographic he sought to reach was the unreflecting Christian who "walks in twilight among snares and pitfalls! He entreats the heavenly Father not to lead him into temptation, and yet places himself on the very edge of it, because he will not kindle the torch which his Father had given into his hands."[26] The torch he mentions in this passage symbolizes the divine light of reason, and it is a luminescent and ambulatory metaphor he employs throughout his text and to which he returns in his closing discussion of mysticism.

Coleridge tells his readers to imagine a pilgrim venturing in the dark with only his flickering lantern to illuminate his way. He has a mystical communion with the divinity, and the "shadows and imperfect beholdings and vivid fragments of things distinctly seen" by his lamplight make "deep, vivid, and faithful impressions" upon the way-wearied man. "Fancy modifies sight," writes Coleridge. "His dreams transfer their forms to real objects; and these lend a substance and an *outness* to his dreams."[27] The mystic thus comes to believe in the sensible reality of his supersensible visions, which are at best only inspired imaginations or hallucinated sensations, the spiritual significance of which he misinterprets in accordance with his dogmatic tradition. The allegory or parable that Coleridge shadows forth at the end of his book is "germane to the subject" of "Young Goodman Brown" for he does not merely retell the mystic's erroneous version of the events but displaces his testimony by subjecting it to another logos or law.[28] In a word, he holds the mystic's *illumined* lantern up to the romantic torchlight of *enlightenment* reason and argues that this latter vessel outshines the paltry glow of the former.

---

24   Hawthorne borrowed the American edition of *Aids to Reflection*, first published in 1829, in July 1833.
25   Samuel Taylor Coleridge, *Aids to Reflection* (New York: Cosimo Classics, 2005), 114.
26   Ibid., 10.
27   Ibid., 263.
28   Ibid., 262.

The conclusion of Hawthorne's story does leave room for doubt that its author may have been more uninspired by his readings in skepticism than bedazzled by the "*Safety-Lamp*" of reflection proffered by Coleridge. Indeed, the most obvious lesson of "Young Goodman Brown" is its critique of dogmatism, but an analysis that stops here fails to uncover the more positive directions embedded in the seemingly pathless thickets of Hawthorne's parable. This moral can only be gleaned by standing before the aporia of good and evil and staring it in the face as it were, thereby enduring the crisis of incomprehension precisely *as* a crisis of faith. Although the theoretical enigma of our moral existence must remain an unsolvable problem for our sensible understanding, the irreducibility of this mystery opens unto the practical autonomy of the will, which must form the basis of every ethical decision and hermeneutical imperative.

Goodman Brown's fatal flaw was not merely that he succumbed to the lure of spectral illusion and was, therefore, not able to bear witness to reason in its highest power of self-affirmation. Rather, whether through indolence or ignorance or sheer indifference on his part, and all three attitudes are culpable of the same offense, Brown allowed his free will to become subjugated by the immoral mandates of his dogmatic religion, which confused the epistemological separation between reason and understanding and blurred the ontological distinction between freedom and nature. He was irresponsible before the call of duty sounded by the voice of conscience, and whether he is to be judged a fool or a knave in this regard, the disastrous consequences of his failure to reflect aright are the same. Although we tend to think of enlightenment as a noun, then, it is first and foremost a verb that is uniquely personal inasmuch as it denotes lifting the fetters of tradition in order to think for oneself. Secondarily, it is a movement of thought that requires constant vigilance in order to avoid falling into the pitfalls of dogmatism and skepticism time and again. Finally, this critical vigilance must be turned inwards in an autoimmune fashion in order to avoid morphing into the infernal agency it was meant to safeguard us from. Only then might we learn that the specters that haunt us, whether witches or Puritans or darker skinned people living abroad, are often the estranged and self-destructive projections of our own calcified and terror-stricken imaginations.

Texas A&M University

The Eco-Gothic in the Short Fiction of Nathaniel Hawthorne

JENNIFER SCHELL

For many students, one of the most striking features of Nathaniel Hawthorne's "Young Goodman Brown" (1835) is its description of the witches' coven, which occurs deep "in the heart of the dark wilderness." The allegorical aspects of the story aside, what especially appeals to readers is the Gothic imagery of the scene, namely "the four blazing pines," "the smoke-wreaths," "the fiend-worshippers," "the hell-kindled torches," and the "unhallowed altar."[1] When I teach "Young Goodman Brown" in both American literature surveys and courses for English majors, I emphasize these characteristics, what I call the story's ecoGothic elements, because they fascinate students, and they speak to a recognizable and important trend in both Hawthorne's short fiction and early American nature writing, namely the tendency to locate the Gothic in the forests of the New World. While some of Hawthorne's Gothic stories take place in New England's bustling towns and villages, many others are set in the wilderness.[2] In

---

1   Nathaniel Hawthorne, "Young Goodman Brown," *Mosses from an Old Manse* in *The Centenary Edition of the Works of Nathaniel Hawthorne*, vol. 10, ed. William Charvat, et al. (Columbus: Ohio State University Press, 1974), 83, 86, 87. Subsequent citations from "Young Goodman Brown" and "Roger Malvin's Burial" are from this edition and are documented parenthetically.
2   Here, I use the term "Gothic story" to refer to pieces which contain Gothic elements as well as those which more strictly follow that generic tradition.

addition to "Young Goodman Brown," the list includes "Roger Malvin's Burial" (1832), "The Ambitious Guest" (1835), and "The Great Carbuncle" (1837). As I point out to my students, for Hawthorne the darkness of the human heart is often revealed when men and women experience nature in its wildest forms.

Teaching students about the ecoGothic aspects of Hawthorne's short fiction has numerous advantages, one of which is that it allows them to make connections between his well known and his more obscure texts. Most often, I pair "Young Goodman Brown" with "Roger Malvin's Burial," two tales which contain ecoGothic elements but which differ with respect to their representations of wilderness. In "Young Goodman Brown," the secrets of the villagers, including the historical crimes of the elders and the inner wickedness of the titular character, only become evident when they enter the dark and mysterious forest outside Salem. Here, wilderness functions as a place where men run riot, where they indulge their malevolent tendencies without inhibition. In "Roger Malvin's Burial," Rueben Bourne's pleasant dream of colonizing the woods of northern New England is shattered when he returns to the scene of his ambiguous actions, mistakes his only son for an animal, and accidentally shoots and kills him. Here, Hawthorne's ambivalent representations of wilderness work to criticize antebellum American frontier fantasies of pioneer life and wilderness settlement.

Not insignificantly, scrutinizing Hawthorne's short fiction according to an ecoGothic approach presents English majors, many of whom have already read "Young Goodman Brown," with a fresh mode of analysis, which draws and builds on their prior knowledge of Hawthorne's writing. Because "Young Goodman Brown" is often taught in secondary schools as a Faustian allegory or as a rite-of-passage tale, students tend to be very familiar with it. When confronted with this story for a second or third time, they often chafe against what they perceive to be its apparent simplicity, heavy-handed symbolism, and well-worn themes. Focusing on the ecoGothic features of the tale helps my students to think about "Young Goodman Brown" in a new way and locate it as part of a different tradition, that segment of early American nature writing which stresses the fearsome, not the wholesome, aspects of the natural world.[3] Ultimately, I have found

---

3   Other examples include: Charles Brockden Brown, *Edgar Huntly; or, Memoirs of a Sleepwalker*, ed. David Steinback (New Haven, CT: College and University

that adopting this approach enables students to arrive at a more complete understanding of the scope of American environmental literature and its range of attitudes toward nature.

II

When I introduce my students to Hawthorne's Gothic writings, I stress both the transnational and ecological aspects of the genre. While I emphasize that locating and defining the characteristics of any genre can be both difficult and problematic, I invite my students to discuss collaboratively some of the key elements of the Gothic: its sensational features, its supernatural elements, its traditional themes, and its typical settings. We consider the genre's obsession with history, paranoia, escapism, and violence. And we attempt to come to some understanding of the Gothic's depictions of gender and sexuality, its representations of superstition and religion, its exploration of the uses and abuses of power, and its treatment of extreme states of mind. As our discussion unfolds, I make sure to contextualize our remarks historically so that students can gain an awareness of the development of the genre over time. Thus, as a class, we develop a working definition of the Gothic, which we augment and alter as needed as our discussions unfold.

Taking a cue from Teresa A. Goddu's seminal study, *Gothic America: Narrative, History, and Nation* (1997), I suggest to my students that "Once imported to America, the gothic's key elements were translated into American terms, and its formulas were also unfixed."[4] To enable us to interrogate this statement and discern what it might mean for our conceptualization of the Gothic, I distribute excerpts from such relevant

---

Press, 1973); Edgar Allan Poe, *The Narrative of Arthur Gordon Pym of Nantucket* (New York: Random House, 2002); Herman Melville, *Moby-Dick* (Evanston, IL: Northwestern University Press, 1988); Henry David Thoreau, *The Maine Woods* in *A Week on the Concord and Merrimack Rivers; Walden; or, Life in the Woods; The Maine Woods; Cape Cod* (New York: Literary Classics of the United States, 1985), 589-845.

4   Teresa A. Goddu, *Gothic America: Narrative, History, and Nation* (New York: Columbia University Press, 1997), 4.

British works as Ann Radcliffe's *The Mysteries of Udolpho* (1794) and Mary Shelley's *Frankenstein* (1818).[5] According to Chris Baldick, the first belongs to a "mainstream group" of Gothic texts, which are characterized by their "uniform costume of lurid effects and trappings," whereas the second belongs to an "unorthodox group," which "carries a much lighter cargo of chains and cowls."[6] In this formulation, *Udolpho* represents a more traditional form of the Gothic, while *Frankenstein* represents a variant on the tradition. Each in its own way is useful for foregrounding discussions of Hawthorne's short fiction and its treatment of New England landscapes.

Although *Udolpho* contains detailed depictions of sublime wilderness environments, many of which have Gothic overtones, these passages tend to be overshadowed by those portions of the novel which describe the horrors hidden in Europe's crumbling castles. With respect to Emily St. Aubert's journey to Udolpho, the narrator explains:

> The immense pine-forests, which, at that period, overhung these mountains, and between which the road wound, excluded all view but of the cliffs aspiring above, except that, now and then, an opening through the dark woods allowed the eye a momentary glimpse of the country below. The gloom of these shades, their solitary silence, except when the breeze swept over their summits, the tremendous precipices of the mountains, that came partially to the eye, each assisted to raise the solemnity of Emily's feelings into awe; she saw only images of gloomy grandeur, or of dreadful sublimity, around her. (224)

As this passage indicates, Emily is awestruck by the mountains and forests she passes through on her fateful journey, and as a result she suffers from an onslaught of fear. Though intense, these emotions pale in comparison to those she experiences while imprisoned at Udolpho. Exploring one of

---

5   Ann Radcliffe, *The Mysteries of Udolpho*, ed. Bonamy Dobrée (Oxford: Oxford University Press, 1970); Mary Shelley, *Frankenstein or The Modern Prometheus*, ed. Maurice Hindle (New York: Penguin Books, 1992). Sometimes, I employ selections from Johann Wolfgang von Goethe, *The Sorrows of Young Werther*, trans. Victor Lange, ed. David E. Wellbery (New York: Suhrkamp Publishers, 1988), 11: 1–87 or Matthew Lewis, *The Monk*, ed. Howard Anderson (Oxford: Oxford University Press, 1985).

6   Christopher Baldick, intro. to *Melmoth the Wanderer* (Oxford: Oxford University Press, 1989), x.

the castle's secret dungeons, she stumbles across a horrific sight: "Beyond, appeared a corpse, stretched on a kind of low couch, which was crimsoned with human blood, as was the floor beneath. The features, deformed by death, were ghastly and horrible, and more than one livid wound appeared in the face."[7] What differentiates the two quotations is that in the latter highly sensational and macabre images heighten the emotional import and create an atmosphere of terror. Taken together, these passages and many, many others like them indicate that, for Radcliffe, horror tends to be concealed in manmade structures, not in the natural world.

While Radcliffe maintains the dichotomy between the artificial and the natural worlds, throughout *Frankenstein*, Mary Shelley constantly juxtaposes descriptions of wilderness and the monster in order to highlight the sublimity of the former and condemn the hideousness of the latter. This contrast is most apparent in the scene, which occurs just before the monster tells his story to his maker. At the beginning of chapter 2, Frankenstein provides a detailed description of his wilderness retreat:

> [T]he icy wall of the glacier overhung me; a few shattered pines were scattered around; and the solemn silence of this glorious presence-chamber of imperial Nature was broken only by the brawling waves or the fall of some vast fragment, the thunder sound of the avalanche or the cracking, reverberated along the mountains, of the accumulated ice, which, through the silent working of immutable laws, was ever and anon rent and torn. (93)

As he immerses himself in this wintry wilderness and contemplates the glacier's grandeur, Frankenstein recognizes the existence of powerful natural forces, what he calls "immutable laws," which are beyond the control of mankind. He takes great comfort in this observation until he notices the presence of his monster: "I perceived, as the shape came nearer (sight tremendous and abhorred!) that it was the wretch whom I had created. . . . He approached; his countenance bespoke bitter anguish, combined with disdain and malignity, while its unearthly ugliness rendered it almost too horrible for human eyes."[8] Tonally speaking, the language Frankenstein uses to describe his creation differs markedly from that which he uses to describe

---

7   Radcliffe, *Udolpho*, 348.
8   Shelley, *Frankenstein*, 93–95.

the glacier. As a representative of man's handiwork, the monster is "unearthly" and "horrible," but as a representative of nature's creative capacities, the river of ice is sublime. By characterizing the manmade as monstrous and lauding the natural as awe-inspiring, Frankenstein reinforces an idea advanced elsewhere in the book: man should not overreach himself in his scientific or spiritual quests for knowledge.

As the above extracts demonstrate, both *Udolpho* and *Frankenstein* contain detailed descriptions of sublime wilderness. Even though they depict some of the more intimidating aspects of these environments, neither one of these novels presents them as malevolent or horrifying. No one is buried by an avalanche or swamped by a tsunami; no one is mauled by a bear or incinerated by a forest fire. In *Udolpho* and *Frankenstein*, the horror is almost always human. Emily's well-being is endangered by the duplicitous machinations of her guardians, who imprison her in a crumbling castle filled with dank dungeons and moldering skeletons. Meanwhile, Frankenstein is tormented by a creature he created because he aspired to possess god-like capacities. In these two texts, sublime nature tends to represent a welcome alternative to the malignity or hubris of humankind.

III

Because it is one of his most famous stories and because its use of eco-Gothic imagery is fairly straightforward, I ask my students to begin their consideration of Hawthorne's writing with "Young Goodman Brown." Then, I have them segue into a more complex and ambivalent piece, such as "Roger Malvin's Burial." Since we return to this subject at the conclusion of our discussion of the short stories, I suggest that, as my students read, they think about how Hawthorne's representations of wilderness contrast with those advanced by the British writers.

In "Young Goodman Brown," the first description of the forest outside Salem appears in the exposition and establishes a foreboding tone which continues throughout the story:

> He [Goodman Brown] had taken a dreary road, darkened by all the gloomiest trees of the forest, which barely stood aside to let the narrow path creep through, and closed immediately behind. It was all as

lonely as could be; and there is this peculiarity in such a solitude, that the traveller knows not who may be concealed by the innumerable trunks and the thick boughs overhead; so that, with lonely footsteps, he may yet be passing through an unseen multitude. (75)

Though "gloomy," "dreary," and "lonely," the forest is a fearsome place primarily because it obscures Goodman Brown's sight, such that he does not know who or what might be lurking in the dense foliage. That the threat is human or a construct of the human imagination is confirmed by his worry that "There may be a devilish Indian behind every tree ...What if the devil himself should be at my very elbow!" (75). When juxtaposed, these quotations indicate that, however overgrown or impenetrable it might be, the forest by itself is not necessarily harmful. The mysterious human and supernatural entities, which the woods might conceal, are another matter entirely.

All Goodman Brown's fears are realized when he happens upon a mysterious man sitting under a tree. Together, the two travelers make their way deeper into the wilderness, and the devilish stranger tells him about the hypocrisy of his pious, Puritan ancestors: "I helped your grandfather, the constable, when he lashed the Quaker woman so smartly through the streets of Salem. And it was I that brought your father a pitch-pine knot, kindled at my own hearth, to set fire to an Indian village, in King Philip's war" (77). This conversation is noteworthy, for it describes the ruthless and violent process by which Salem's early residents colonized the wilderness. Engaging in a systematic course of persecution and extirpation, they attempted to purge their settlement of religious dissenters and indigenous peoples. Thematically speaking, this exchange is significant, for it reveals some of the sins of Salem's fathers—their more serious religious transgressions are revealed at the coven—which will come to haunt Goodman Brown for the rest of his life. As I stress to students, this theme was popular with many British and American authors working in the Gothic tradition, and it was one of Hawthorne's particular preoccupations.

Devastated by this knowledge and torn by indecision, Goodman Brown momentarily reconsiders his errand into the wilderness. After he hears distant voices and decries one of his wife's pink ribbons falling from the sky, he recommits himself to his original purpose. As he travels deeper and deeper into the woods, the Gothic imagery intensifies:

The road grew wilder and drearier, and more faintly traced, and vanished at length, leaving him in the heart of the dark wilderness, still rushing onward, with the instinct that guides mortal man to evil. The whole forest was peopled with frightful sounds; the creaking of the trees, the howling of wild beasts, and the yell of Indians; while, sometimes, the wind tolled like a distant church-bell, and sometimes gave a broad roar around the traveller, as if all Nature were laughing him to scorn. But he was himself the chief horror of the scene, and shrank not from its other horrors. (83)

Despite the fact that this passage describes the woods as resounding with a terrible cacophony of discordant natural sounds, it proclaims Goodman Brown, the human, to be the "chief horror of the scene." Along with the road, all signs of his humanity vanish, and, like a wild animal, he follows his "instinct" into "the heart of the dark wilderness," where he is transformed into a "fiend" and a "demoniac" (84). Much like the representations of the forest, which appear earlier in the story, this one indicates that man is much worse than nature when it comes to embodying malevolence.

Finally arriving at the witches' coven, Goodman Brown finds himself confronted by a terrible scene. As he watches, the members sing:

And, with the final peal of that dreadful anthem, there came a sound, as if the roaring wind, the rushing streams, the howling beasts, and every other voice of the unconverted wilderness were mingling and according with the voice of guilty man, in homage to the prince of all. The four blazing pines threw up a loftier flame, and obscurely discovered shapes and visages of horror on the smoke-wreaths, above the impious assembly. At the same moment, the fire on the rock shot redly forth, and formed a glowing arch above its base, where now appeared a figure. With reverence be it spoken, the figure bore no slight similitude, both in garb and manner, to some grave divine of the New-England churches. (85–86)

The Gothic imagery here is intense, particularly because of its sensory appeal, the bright flames, the acrid smoke, and the uproarious singing. The entrance of the devilish figure, dressed as a Puritan elder, only amplifies the hellish atmosphere of the scene and underscores the religious hypocrisies of the villagers. All of this vivid description perfectly sets up the scene in which Goodman Brown, on the verge of being inducted into the coven, exclaims, "Faith! Faith! . . . Look up to Heaven, and resist the Wicked One!" (88). With this utterance, the villagers and their leader vanish, leaving him alone in the dark, damp forest. Although he returns to Salem the next morning, he is profoundly affected by his adventure in the wilderness. Unable to cope with the hypocrisy of those around him or the darkness of his own heart, he is transformed, completely and permanently, into a "distrustful, if not a desperate man" whose "dying hour was gloom" (89, 90).

Like "Young Goodman Brown," "Roger Malvin's Burial" revolves around the idea that the historical crimes of one generation are visited upon the next. The stories are also similar in that they are both set in the wilderness of the distant historical past.[9] With respect to their representations of New England's dense woods, though, these pieces differ dramatically. In "Roger Malvin's Burial," the forest does not represent a riotous place of refuge for men and women seeking to indulge their devil-worshipping tendencies; rather, it functions as a contact zone, a liminal space where colonists encounter indigenous people, their own frailties, and rugged nature. Thus, the descriptions of the woods in "Roger Malvin's Burial" are multifaceted, diverse, and contradictory. While these various representations of wilderness might appear to be discordant, they are coherent insofar as they all work together to discredit popular nineteenth-century American ideals about the romance of pioneering life and value of rugged individualism.

The first description of wilderness in "Roger Malvin's Burial" appears early in the tale, and, for the most part, it characterizes the forest of northern New England as a rather pleasant natural environment:

> The early sunbeams hovered cheerfully upon the tree-tops, beneath which two weary and wounded men had stretched their limbs the night before. Their bed of withered oak-leaves was strewn upon the small level space, at the foot of a rock, situated near the summit of one of the gentle swells, by which the face of the country is there diversified. The mass of granite, rearing its smooth, flat surface, fifteen or twenty feet above their heads, was not unlike a gigantic grave-stone, upon which the veins seemed to form an inscription in forgotten characters. (338)

---

9   "Roger Malvin's Burial" is set in 1725, shortly after "Lovell's Fight," a conflict between 34 English colonists and an unknown number of Pequawket warriors which occurred near what is now the town of Fryeburg, Maine. Pat Higgins, "Lovewell's Fight," *Maine Stories*, accessed June 28, 2013, http://www.mainestory.info/mainestory/Lovewells_Fight.html.

Even though the large rock resembles a headstone, Roger and Reuben appear to be comfortably ensconced in their leafy bower underneath the protective branches of the oak trees. Significantly, the passage lacks the Gothic imagery that appears throughout "Young Goodman Brown"; the skies are sunny and cheerful, not dark and gloomy, and the terrain is gentle and rolling, not steep and craggy. Here, nature is endowed with human qualities, for it is characterized as a benevolent force, which seems to have a vested interest in preserving Roger and Reuben's well-being.

Subsequent descriptions of the forest differ dramatically from that quoted above, however. After promising to return to the woods to look for Roger and bury his body, Reuben departs on his long trek back to the settlements:

> On the second day, the clouds, gathering densely over the sky, precluded the possibility of regulating his course by the position of the sun; and he knew not but that every effort of his almost exhausted strength, was removing him farther from the home he sought. His scanty sustenance was supplied by the berries, and other spontaneous products of the forest. Herds of deer, it is true, sometimes bounded past him, and partridges frequently whirred up before his footsteps; but his ammunition had been expended in the fight, and he had no means of slaying them. His wounds, irritated by the constant exertion in which lay the only hope of life, wore away his strength, and at intervals confused his reason. (346)

This passage also lacks Gothic imagery; however, it somehow manages to characterize the forest as a dangerous and threatening place. Endowing wilderness with antagonistic and punitive aspects, Hawthorne describes how various natural forces coalesce to derail Reuben from his journey and chastise him for his actions, warring against the Pequawket and leaving his wounded friend to die alone in the woods. The clouds obscure the sun, making it impossible for him to navigate accurately the rough terrain, which eventually begins to aggravate his wounds. The land, with its apparently sparse supply of berries, refuses to provide him more than a "scanty sustenance" (349). The animals, seemingly aware that Reuben has exhausted his ammunition fighting the Pequawket, taunt him with their presence. Solely because of his indefatigable will to live, he propels himself onward until he collapses underneath a tree, where he is discovered by members of a search party, who bring him home to Dorcas, Roger's daughter.

When Dorcas asks about her father's death, Reuben's "moral cowardice" prevents him from telling her the truth, and he leads her to believe that he buried Roger as best he could (351). After a few months, Reuben and Dorcas marry, and he inherits Roger's expansive and productive farm, which he manages to bankrupt because he is so tormented by guilt that he neglects his agrarian duties. Left with one option, Reuben decides to remove his family, including his fifteen-year-old son Cyrus, to the northern frontier "to throw sunlight into some deep recess of the forest, and seek subsistence from the virgin bosom of the wilderness" (352). What is remarkable about this sentence is that, insofar as its descriptions of nature are concerned, it reverses the logic of the preceding passages. Here, the active agents are not benevolent or antagonistic forces of nature but are British North America's pioneers, intrepid and self-reliant individuals capable of imposing their will upon an entirely passive landscape. As the narrator indicates, this idea is an attractive one:

> Oh! who, in the enthusiasm of a day-dream, has not wished that he were a wanderer in a world of summer wilderness, with one fair and gentle being hanging lightly on his arm? In youth, his free and exulting step would know no barrier but the rolling ocean or the snow-topt mountains; calmer manhood would choose a home, where Nature had strewn a double wealth, in the vale of some transparent stream; and when hoary age, after long, long years of that pure life, stole on and found him there, it would find him the father of a race, the patriarch of a people, the founder of a mighty nation yet to be. (346)

Acknowledging the appeal of "day-dream," the narrator proceeds to elaborate upon it, using Biblical terms and nation-building metaphors. Much like Adam and Eve, a young man and woman traverse the "summer wilderness," finally settling in some beautiful locale where they establish a patrimony and grow old together. Figuratively speaking, this passage describes how new nations, a word used here both in the Biblical and modern senses, are created. They are carved out of the wilderness through a process that, though confrontational, appears to be relatively easy.

The next paragraph characterizes the "day-dream" as an idyllic fantasy, quite different from the reality that the Bournes experience in the woods: "The tangled and gloomy forest, through which the personages of my tale were wandering, differed widely from the dreamer's Land of Fantasie; yet there was something in their way of life that Nature asserted as her own;

and the gnawing cares, which went with them from the world, were all that now obstructed their happiness" (352). Employing Gothic images and emphasizing the dark, maze-like aspects of the woods serves to contrast this environment with the "summer wilderness" of the prior passage and reveals some of the inefficacies of the day-dream. At the end, though, this quotation returns to the idea that "Nature" is an active, benevolent force, which cares about the Bournes and their fate. Thus, the only difficulties they experience while traveling through the forest stem from the fact that Reuben is unable to forget his worldly worries, most of which revolve around his guilt about concealing the circumstances surrounding Roger's death.

As the Bournes depart from their intended course and travel deeper into unfamiliar tracts of wilderness, the narrator's portraits of the forest become more complex. While describing one of the Bournes' campsites, he expresses a great deal of ambivalence:

> There is something chilling, and yet heart-warming, in the thought of these three, united by strong bands of love, and insulated from all that breathe beside. The dark and gloomy pines looked down upon them, and, as the wind swept through their tops, a pitying sound was heard in the forest; or did those old trees groan, in fear that men were come to lay the axe to their roots at last? (354)

Speaking generally at first, the narrator characterizes the Bourne family and their solitary frontier adventure in highly contradictory terms. Then, he anthropomorphizes the pine trees by endowing them with conflicting emotions. Because the narrator cannot decide how the trees feel about the Bournes' frontier endeavors, he concludes with a rhetorical question, a strategy which intimates that nature remains ultimately inscrutable.

If the above description of wilderness is both ambiguous and ambivalent, then those that relate to the scene of Roger Malvin's death are somewhat clearer. As he wanders the woods near camp following the "supernatural voice" that he believes is directing his actions (356), Reuben hears a rustle in the bushes and fires his musket at what he thinks is an animal. When he approaches the thicket, he realizes that he is standing before the oak tree, which marks the location of Roger's body. Not insignificantly, he discovers that its appearance has changed: "a blight had apparently stricken the upper part of the oak, and the very topmost bough was withered, sapless, and utterly dead. Reuben remembered how the little banner had fluttered on that topmost bough, when it was green and lovely, eighteen years before" (357). With its Gothic elements of the mysterious voice and the dark imagery, this passage foreshadows the story's tragic ending. What's more, it indicates that sometimes nature can serve as a man's conscience, embodying his emotions and reminding him of his ambiguous actions.

Eventually, the narrator reveals that, when Reuben shot his musket into the bushes, he killed Cyrus, who was also hunting in the area. Thus, the blighted oak tree marks the site of not one but two tragic deaths in the wilderness. Despite the sorrowful events and the Gothic elements, "Roger Malvin's Burial" concludes with an optimistic statement about the redemptive qualities and healing capacities of nature: "At that moment, the withered topmost bough of the oak loosened itself, in the stilly air, and fell in soft, light fragments upon the rock, upon the leaves, upon Reuben, upon his wife and child, and upon Roger Malvin's bones" (360). At this point, Reuben believes that his crimes are expiated, and he prays for the first time in many years.

Taken altogether, the representations of wilderness, which appear in "Roger Malvin's Burial," are varied, and my students are often confused by them. As I suggest, though, they all work to debunk romantic American fantasies about colonizing the wilderness with nature viewed as a passive subject subordinated to the dictates of humankind. Whether it portrays the woods as benevolent or malevolent, agreeable or antagonistic, intelligible or inscrutable, "Roger Malvin's Burial" demonstrates some of the problems involved in trying to build a nation through the colonization of its wilderness environments. By emphasizing Roger and Reuben's involvement in Lovell's Fight, it criticizes the wars waged against North America's indigenous peoples. By describing the way in which Reuben torments himself with guilt, it emphasizes the moral frailties of human beings, and by characterizing nature as an active force, it stresses the ultimate impossibility of subduing it.

Over the course of our discussion of "Young Goodman Brown" and "Roger Malvin's Burial," we mark the way in which Hawthorne deploys ecoGothic imagery in each tale. Once we have come to some understanding of the operations of this imagery, I ask my students to return to the extracts from *Udolpho* and *Frankenstein* and contrast them with Hawthorne's stories. Employing this strategy enables them to recognize some of the significant differences in British and American attitudes toward nature. As they often astutely point out, Radcliffe and Shelley tend to appreciate and admire the sublime qualities of nature far more than Hawthorne does.

Both of the British writers go to great lengths to stress the awe-inspiring aspects of wilderness, and, even though they indicate that nature can be dangerous, they prefer to characterize humans, their desires and their actions, as horrific. In this way, Radcliffe and Shelley make an explicit contrast between man and nature. As my students note, Hawthorne refuses to make such neat distinctions; instead, his stories attempt to articulate the complexities inherent in humanity's relationship to the natural world.

University of Alaska (Fairbanks)

Hawthorne, Kant, and Buber in an Interdisciplinary Humanities Classroom

NANCY BUNGE

When teaching Hawthorne in a literature survey, especially if the course fulfills a general education requirement, one inevitably encounters student complaints about his complexity and old-fashioned language, particularly if his writings come accompanied by other "boring" work that shares similar "problems." I have discovered, however, that when teaching Hawthorne in a sophomore-level general education course, "Philosophy in Literature," where my students read philosophic and literary texts with the same themes, Hawthorne's stories usually go over well. When I dreamt up my version of the course, I saw it as a way to help students understand how much the way they present an idea matters, but over the years we have also learned an unintentional lesson about literature's richness and power.

I divide this course into three units, each focusing on a different concept; Hawthorne's tales appear in a section dealing with morality, along with Immanuel Kant's *Groundwork for a Metaphysics of Morals* and Martin Buber's *I and Thou*. Although these pairings may seem strange, Hawthorne shares with these writers the idea that people need to treat each other as ends rather than means. Indeed, Kant presents an almost compulsively logical argument that concludes by treating others as ends in themselves, which provides the basis for all moral behavior. Some students fall in love with Kant's logical intricacies, but most complain about his wordy, abstract language. And they have a point. Here's a sample of what the students struggle through:

> Among the *rational* or reason-based foundations of morality, the ontological concept of *perfection* is better than the theological concept that derives morality from divine and supremely perfect will. It is of course empty, indefinite, and consequently useless for discovering in the boundless field of possible reality, the greatest sum which is appropriate to us; and, in trying to distinguish specifically between the reality here in question from every other reality, it inevitably tends to move in a circle and cannot avoid tacitly presupposing the morality it is meant   to explain. Still, it is better than the theological concept, which derives morality from an all-perfect divine will, not merely because we cannot directly apprehend God's perfection and can only derive it from our own concepts, among which that of morality is pre-eminent; but because, if we do not do this (and to do it would be to give a grossly circular explanation), the concept of God's will that remains for us is made up of such attributes as lust for glory and dominion, bound up with frightful ideas of power and vengefulness—inevitably the foundation for a moral system that would be directly opposed to morality [Kant's emphases].

Because Kant wants to establish a universal basis for his conclusions, he avoids the empiricism which he believes would contaminate his argument's purity. As he explains, "*Empirical principles* are never fit to serve as a foundation for moral laws. For the universality with which these laws must hold for all rational beings without exception—the unconditioned practical necessity that they thus impose—is lost if their basis is taken from the *particular constitution of human nature* or from the accidental circumstances in which it is placed."[1] He uses here a minimal number of examples for fear of particularizing his arguments. In class discussion, we cling to the few concrete models he offers to clarify his ideas.

---

1   Here and above, see Immanuel Kant, *Groundwork for the Metaphysics of Morals*, trans. Arnulf Zweig, ed. Thomas E. Hill and Arnulf Zweig (Oxford: Oxford University Press, 2002), 242–43.

In contrast, Martin Buber offers a much more intuitive argument; he makes very little effort to offer either rational or empirical evidence. He essentially makes pronouncements and leaves it to the reader to rely on his or her responses to them to determine their truth. He trusts that the reader will feel such an intimate connection with his notions that they will seem irrefutable. One student remarked that even talking about Buber's ideas in class undermined their power for her because it weakened the intense connection she felt with his thought. Since most students require some explanation to comprehend Buber's insights, my understanding of her objection has not in any way eliminated the much needed in-class analysis of Buber's ideas.

For instance, Buber opens *I and Thou* by setting out his central concepts in characteristically enigmatic fashion:

> The world is twofold for man in accordance with his twofold attitude.
> The attitude of man is twofold in accordance with the two basic words he can speak.
> The basic words are not single words but word pairs.
> One basic word is the pair I-You.
> The other basic word is the word pair I-It; but this basic word is not changed when He or She takes the place of It.
> Thus the I of man is also twofold.
> For the I of the basic word I-You is different from that of the basic word I-It.
>
> *
>
> Basic words do not state something that might exist outside them; by being spoken they establish a mode of existence.

Buber suggests here that we relate to the rest of the world as a You or an It, meaning we see it as either something we engage or something we objectify. When Buber writes, "The basic word I-You can only be spoken with one's whole being. / The basic word I-It can never be spoken with one's whole being,"[2] he implicitly argues for treating others as ends in themselves, suggesting that the more our attitude allows us to see the world, not only other people, as a You, the richer our lives become. In other words,

---

2 See Martin Buber, *I and Thou*, trans. and ed. Walter Kaufmann (New York: Scribner's, 1970), 53–54.

Buber believes enormous benefit follows from treating others respectfully, or as he explains, "The actual and fulfilled present—exists only insofar as presentness, encounter, and relation exist. Only as the You becomes present does presence come into being."³

Moreover, the I-You stance is so fundamental, it undergirds our very humanity: "And in all the seriousness of truth, listen: without It a human being cannot live. But whoever lives only with that is not human."⁴ In Buber's system, the person who enters into relation with another enjoys massive rewards. Kant, on the other hand, argues that treating others as ends only has moral worth if one does it solely to fulfill the moral law. If one receives benefits of any kind, including a sense of satisfaction for behaving kindly, in Kant's ethical universe, one's act has no moral value. According to him, to behave morally, one must act entirely out of good will, so while Buber and Kant recommend essentially the same treatment of other people, Kant's ethics require an authoritative determination to behave well that Buber's do not.

Not only does reading Hawthorne give the students more pleasure and freedom than reading Kant and Buber, but they more easily see the connections between the tales we read and Kant's and Buber's theories. That one short-story writer, who produces work rich enough to hold two quite different philosophic systems, deserves the admiration from students and often receives it; this too helps them understand that despite the pleasure of reading literature, it can often offer more complexity and depth than theory. Hawthorne's tales about scientists present clear examples of people using others in "Ethan Brand," "Rappaccini's Daughter," and "The Birth-Mark." Students have no difficulty seeing both Buber's and Kant's warnings against this use in these stories; moreover, having these ideas fleshed out in particular situations clarifies them while complicating them, raising issues not addressed by either Kant or Buber. The title character in "Ethan Brand," for instance, claims to regret using others or putting so much emphasis on his intellect that his heart "had withered—had contracted—had hardened—had perished! It ceased to partake of the universal throb."⁵ Brand

---

3   Ibid. 63.
4   Ibid. 85.
5   Nathaniel Hawthorne, "Ethan Brand," *The Snow-Image* in *The Centenary Edition of the Works of Nathaniel Hawthorne*, vol. 11, ed. William Charvat et al. (Columbus: Ohio State University Press, 1974), 99. Subsequent references to "The Celestial Railroad" and "My Kinsman, Major Molineux" are from this edition and are documented parenthetically.

confesses that while searching for the unpardonable sin, he destroyed at least one person, Esther, the daughter of a man named Humphrey who spends his life looking for her. Still, when he meets townspeople who treat others, including himself, as objects, it "made him doubt—and, strange to say, it was a painful doubt—that he had indeed found the Unpardonable Sin, and found it within himself" (93). He manages to conquer this uncertainty, declaring himself an unpardonable sinner. After announcing, "'My task is done, and well done!'" (99), he incinerates himself, leaving behind his hardened heart. When the operator of the lime kiln where Brand commits suicide appears the next morning, he calculates the market value of Brand's heart, establishing that he has no trouble regarding other people as objects, and that despite Brand's demise, unpardonable sinners still exist. Brand's inability to own defeat makes him good company for Aylmer in "The Birth-Mark" who would prefer killing his wife to admitting imperfection into his life. Dr. Rappaccini also worships his power so unconditionally that his daughter's lack of gratitude for his making her poisonous astonishes him. While Buber and Kant leave the motivation for treating others as objects unidentified, Hawthorne clearly links it to arrogance.

Hawthorne's locating this behavior in scientists also invites the question of whether scientific development and the expansion of its influence in society necessarily brings with it a self-destructive arrogance, a question that could be further explored by requiring students to read Hawthorne's tale, "The Celestial Railroad," where he suggests that not just the inventors but everyone else participating in society shaped by scientific advancement has come to regard themselves as superior to human frailty. Brand's destruction of Esther, Rappaccini's proclamation to his daughter—"Wouldst thou, then, have preferred the condition of a weak woman, exposed to all evil, and capable of none?" (127)—along with Georgiana's urging Aylmer not to let her death interfere with his self-confidence because he "aimed loftily" (55)—connects these issues of power to gender with males firmly in control and women either happily complying like Georgiana, making claims for themselves like Beatrice Rappaccini, or vanishing like Esther.

In a different way, "My Kinsman, Major Molineux" suggests that ideological political commitment also nurtures arrogance. In this tale, young Robin arrives in colonial Boston from the country, hoping his successful kinsman will help him rise in the world, and he instead finds himself cruelly treated by virtually everyone he encounters when he asks where he lives. At the tale's end, he learns why: the townspeople have turned against Major Molineux, the British representative. Hawthorne's narrator questions the legitimacy of their complaints, explaining that "the people looked with most jealous scrutiny to the exercise of power, which did not emanate from themselves, and they usually rewarded the rulers with slender gratitude, for the compliances, by which, in softening their instructions from beyond the sea, they had incurred the reprehension of those who gave them" (208). As the colonists parade Molineux through town, the narrator's description suggests little pride in their revolutionary fervor: "On they went, like fiends that throng in mockery round some dead potentate, mighty no more, but majestic still in his agony. On they went, in counterfeited pomp, in senseless uproar, in frenzied merriment, trampling all on an old man's heart" (230).

If "My Kinsman" pivots upon political pretension and democratic anxieties in the early American republic, "Young Goodman Brown" implies that the titular character's religious society has inculcated in him a self-righteous absolutism. As far as the Puritans are concerned, people are entirely good or evil. When Brown discovers himself rushing towards a witches' Sabbath, he turns away from the corrupt celebration at the last moment, urging his wife Faith to do the same. Then, he projects the sin he has discovered in himself onto others. He spends the rest of the tale despising everyone else for their immorality. Thus, ironically, his conviction of his own purity ruins his life: "A stern, a sad, a darkly meditative, a distrustful, if not a desperate man, did he become, from the night of that fearful dream."[6] Whereas Buber and Kant simply define evil behavior without attempting to identify possible causes of it, Hawthorne therefore suggests a number of sources for this behavior: religion, politics, science, and gender, but he takes the analysis even further. Behind this wide variety of specific causes, he consistently finds arrogance. "Young Goodman Brown" suggests that arrogance often comes from a lack of self-knowledge. While Buber and Kant acknowledge no benefit in failure, "Young Goodman Brown" suggests that by admitting flaws, people connect with each other. The person conducting the service in the woods ironically but somewhat accurately declares that "Evil is the nature of mankind. Evil must be your only happiness. Welcome, again, my children, to the communion of your race!" (88)

In fact, some Hawthorne tales combine both a condemnation of mistreating people with hints of the Buberian rewards for resisting this

---

6   Nathaniel Hawthorne, "Young Goodman Brown," *Mosses from an Old Manse* in *The Centenary Edition*, vol. 10, 89. Subsequent references to this tale and "Egotism: the Bosom Serpent" are to this edition and are parenthetically documented.

behavior. For example, "Egotism: The Bosom Serpent" and "The Maypole of Merry Mount" set out the contrasting rewards for seeing people as objects, regarding them as ends, or between an I-It stance towards the world and an I-You approach to life. Roderick Elliston's bosom serpent, the snake in his chest, draws his attention inward. Like most of Hawthorne's lost characters, narcissism consumes him: he sometimes proudly displays this snake to others and at other times attempts to hide it, but he experiences great misery until his wife Rosina advises him to lose himself "'in the idea of another!'" (283). He turns his attention towards her, and this move saves him: the snake departs. The residents of Merry Mount and the Puritans, too, offer a kind of syncretic view in their opposing ideologies, which lock them both into judgmental and detached views of the world. The Puritans see everyone other than themselves as possessed by the devil and treat them accordingly while the Merry Mounters make the same absolute commitment to life as positive, which leaves them so disconnected from reality that they treat funerals as a joke. Although originally Merry Mounters, when conquered by the Puritans, Edith and Edgar accept this fate because love has introduced them to the reality of sadness: "From the moment that they truly loved, they had subjected themselves to earth's doom of care, and sorrow, and troubled joy, and had no more a home at Merry Mount."[7] They do not, however, abandon the joy they experienced at Merry Mount. They synthesize the truths embraced by the two groups, moving into a truer, more nuanced point of view: "As their flowery garland was wreathed of the brightest roses that had grown there, so, in the tie that united them, were intertwined all the purest and best of their early joys" (67).

After reading Kant and Buber, students have no trouble seeing and appreciating the manifestations of their ideas in Hawthorne's tales, but more importantly, the experience of reading his work and contrasting its construction and impact with that of the books they read by Kant and Buber helps them understand the richness of literature. The course juxtaposes literature and theory in a way that helps students see that although literature has much higher entertainment value than theory and makes more room for its readers to shape its meaning, its specificity and allusiveness also allow it to achieve a greater complexity. Furthermore, Hawthorne places the

---

7   Nathaniel Hawthorne, "The Maypole of Merry Mount," *The Snow-Image* in *The Centenary Edition*, vol. 9, 58. Subsequent references to this tale are parenthetically documented.

ideas of Buber and Kant in real life contexts, inviting students to appraise their validity. He clearly suggests that arrogance invites people to use others and that cultivating humility discourages it, encouraging students to ask themselves if this makes sense. He further links this arrogance to the development of science. This poses another relevant idea for students to consider and discuss. The abusive scientists are men and their victims, women. As a result of reading the stories and thinking through multiple ideas, students develop their own conclusions.

To keep the students reading in the course and to provide me with a sense of what they understand, I give daily reading tests. These also help them see that despite their struggles with particular sentences in Kant or Buber, they do in fact grasp the central concepts in the reading. At the end of every class, I also give them writing exercises, which offer them opportunities to use what we just finished discussing to draw and defend their own conclusions. They come to comprehend not only Kant and Buber, but they also develop answers on their own that define what they think of them—and of Hawthorne. For instance, they might be asked to evaluate Kant's notion that morally good behavior must always be a result of good will, meaning that the actor must do good purely for the sake of obeying moral law. Or they may be asked whose philosophy they consider superior, Kant's or Buber's, and to defend their perspective with at least two examples. I return these with grades and any needed comments at the start of the next class. And to make certain that the students grasp the course materials, there is a short-answer exam at the end of each unit, before they begin the paper for that section of the course. The paper topics require them to compare all three authors and develop their own views. For example, a writing prompt make to the form of the following question: "What would Hawthorne think of X claim/idea in Buber and Kant? Why?" Or, I might ask students to "Do a Buberian analysis of at least two stories and a Kantian analysis of at least two stories and analyze at least a total of five stories. Which analysis do you find the most satisfying? Why?" Or, finally, to bring the issues closer to home, I sometimes pose the following hypothetical rhetorical situation for writing: "You and your significant other are having issues. Whose work would you suggest your partner read, Hawthorne, Buber, or Kant? (You could also write about whose work would give you the clearest insight into your issues.) It would help give your paper focus if you defined the central issue in your relationship that needs addressing."

One of the course's most important functions is to remind the students that other truths exist besides those defined by science and logic. For instance, although Kant's argument that no act that one enjoys has moral worth may make logical sense, it does little to persuade or motivate people to behave well. Although Buber may assert that unless one remains open and responsive to the world, life has little value, one best understands his sense Ernest's celestial conversations with the poet or the pleasant environment the family enjoys in "The Ambitious Guest" before the young man joins them. Moral truths finally rest on and grow from intuitions, and their most powerful rendition takes literary form. As one student pointed out, "While Buber and Kant focus on substantiating theories that exist outside the realm of common experience, Hawthorne appeals to the common man as his works depict the shadows of human existence and the camaraderie made possible by our faults." As other students have noted, however, reading the philosophy also enables them to recognize the relevant themes in the literature, and thus the philosophy and literature used in the course enrich each other.

The improvement in students' language may seem a more unexpected development than their improvement in critical thinking. Those students whose sample papers had a tendency to ramble like Kant, actually turn in much more concise work by the end of the term; similarly, those who traded heavily in abstractions and proclamations like Kant got more specific. I like to believe this outcome results from their experiencing how difficult vague writing makes things for the reader. For example, one student's early diagnostic paper started like this:

> Aiming to define mankind's flawed nature is hardly a reasonable target for a poem, yet "An Essay on Man" by Alexander Pope achieves the feat. The extensive piece can best be described as a study of human nature, and is renowned for its success in doing so. Richard Bevis wrote in a critical overview of the poem that, "[it] remains one of the great statements of the human condition," testifying to its credit (Bevis). In "An Essay on Man," Alexander Pope's efficient and specific word choice embodies the tools of repetition, rhythm, and paradox to convey his meaning. Through diction, Pope describes the conflicting nature of man and the obligation to accept it.

Here's the introduction the same student wrote for the last paper in my course where he used Nietzsche's *Birth of Tragedy* to evaluate "The Birth-Mark:"

Can eyes be art? When staring into the eyes of your significant other, it seems a reasonable question. You look, gaze, dive into the colors that mix and shade and seem to pulse; more dynamic than any painting and more full than any chord. You do not find yourself merely observing or glancing—in fact, you have no self-awareness at all. You, the eyes, and the universe they contain are one. Your partner reciprocates this as though by gravity, not by purpose. Catching a glimpse of a truth within, you both continue to focus as the world around you blurs. Amidst this ecstasy you realize that what you have created together must end. The stormy sea of color will settle and fade; the planets will grind to a halt at the humming's decrescendo; you will have to look away from those eyes. For the first time, you know sorrow and say to yourself, "Certainly this is the 'birth of tragedy.'" Yet you are grateful for the experience and delighted that life contains such an art form as love.

Although some professors would not appreciate such an introduction, in the context of this class it illustrates how many of my students improved both their thinking and writing.

Michigan State University

Science and Technology in Hawthorne's Short Fiction

Scott Ellis

In 1836, the second volume of the *American Magazine of Useful and Entertaining Knowledge* reprinted an excerpt from Charles Babbage's *On the Economy of Machinery and Manufacturers*,[1] in which Babbage methodically examines recent developments in science and technology. Even with the improvements in chemistry, electricity, and other localized sciences, Babbage argues that there is a "higher science," one that is "preparing its fetters for the minutest atoms that nature has created. . . . It is the science of *calculation,*—which becomes continually more necessary at each step of our progress, and which must ultimately govern the whole of the applications of science to the arts of life." In the excerpt, he extols the dominance that humanity is exhibiting over the world—"the dominion of mind over the material world advances with an ever-accelerating force"— and although this dominance is at its earliest stages, it is rapidly advancing as mankind and human reason, the "altar of truth," will soon dispel myth and fraud and lead humanity to far-reaching knowledge and control.[2]

---

[1] Hawthorne checks out Babbage's book from the NY Public Library at least in Jan. 1836. See Marian L. Kesselring, *Hawthorne's Reading 1828–1850: A Transcription and Identification of Titles Recorded in the Charge-Books of the Salem Athenaeum* (New York: New York Public Library, 1949), 37.

[2] *The American Magazine of Useful and Entertaining Knowledge* (1836; Google

Interestingly, this excerpt appears in the March 1836 issue of the *American Magazine*, which was the first issue edited by Nathaniel Hawthorne in his short tenure as editor. Given the volume of newspapers, magazines, and books that he with the help of his sister Elizabeth excerpted to fill the pages of his own magazine, we cannot know how much time he spent with this particular passage. However, I want to suggest that Babbage's "science of calculation" serves as a useful concept to help students understand Hawthorne's engagement with science and technology throughout his career in letters. In this selection, Babbage engages in a different type of prolepsis that Hawthorne brings to his Manse tales and later writings: Babbage tries to predict the benefit of future knowledge, the dominion over nature, whereas Hawthorne engages with such dominion often to reveal its potential dark side.

The categorization and definitions of both "science" and "technology" were in flux during the early nineteenth century, so I stress to students the importance of considering Hawthorne's writings at this crucial historical moment, even as writers and thinkers were still refining their understanding of these terms, concepts, and widespread notions of "progress."[3] In general, Hawthorne engaged with three themes that fall under the umbrella of "science" and "technology," and I have found it helpful to list these themes for my students before we begin. First, he often grappled with the developments of power, such as the growing proliferation of the steam engine and the production of work, often in contrast to artisanal labor. Second, he explored the increasing emphasis on regulating time, whether with a clock or via

---

Books, 2009), 293, https://play.google.com/store/books/details?id=NGrXAAAAMAAJ. Hawthorne's selection omits Babbage's paragraphs about the inevitable decline of non-renewable resources such as coal and his attention to solar and water power and Icelandic hot springs. Such a change—one that structurally alters the antecedent to "these anticipations of the future" in Babbage's original text from non-renewable resources to the advances of the "science of calculation"—might be worth exploring in class.

3   For some courses, I ask students early on to define "science" and/or "technology" according to the authors of some of the essays I mention below before moving on to the definitions from the *Oxford English Dictionary*. For helpful introductions to the science and technology of this period, see George H. Daniels, *American Science in the Age of Jackson* (New York: Columbia University Press, 1968); and John F. Kasson, *Civilizing the Machine: Technology and Republican Values in America, 1776–1900* (New York: Grossman, 1976).

changes in one's life expectancy. Finally, he examined the widespread desire to understand and thereby control the natural world. All three themes touch upon scientific and technological developments either initiated or put into broad use during the first two-thirds of the nineteenth century, and all give Hawthorne fuel for his literary fire.

It would be reductive, however, to consider Hawthorne simply as an outspoken opponent of scientific and technological progress. Indeed, even he reveals admiration for industrial machinery during his 1856 visit to the Mersey Iron Foundry in England, where the machinery delights him, despite his lack of understanding of how it all works, and where the "stalwart workmen . . . seemed to be near kindred to the machines amid which they wrought."[4] Instead, he honed his critique of the moral transformation that such developments produced on the men and women whose lives they touched. At issue, for instance, was not the locomotive but its effect on Clifford's understanding of "home" and the past in *The House of the Seven Gables*. The problem in "The Birth-Mark" is not science per se but on its poisonous moral transformation of Aylmer and his quest for perfection. *Septimius Felton* explores the desire for immortality, but this quest is rendered immoral only by the actions of the title character. In other words, like other conscientious cultural observers, Hawthorne carefully absorbed the developments of his age and constructed story worlds that became his own "what if?" artistic experiments.

Over the years, I have taught Hawthorne's tales and novels to students of all levels from introduction to literature courses for first-year non-English majors to junior-level American Renaissance courses to graduate seminars, and the attention that I give to scientific and technological issues varies according to the course. I usually discuss these themes in relation to other common attributes of his work, such as his attention to history and sin, but I have also taught his work in courses specifically exploring literary responses to scientific and technological developments in the nineteenth century. In other words, the time I give to these issues varies course by course, but I have found that these topics attract students, even reluctant ones, to Hawthorne's work, so I always include some discussion on these topics. In this essay I seek to offer suggestions that any instructor could use to help students engage with his writings that examine scientific and technological issues.

---

4   Hawthorne, *The English Notebooks by Nathaniel Hawthorne* ed. Randall Stewart (New York: Russell & Russell, 1962), 279.

The "Higher Science"

When I speak with my students about the relationship between Hawthorne's fiction and nineteenth-century developments in science and technology, both of which fit under Babbage's general phrase "higher science," my goal is to have students understand how he positioned himself in these broader social discourses. Although he rarely sets out to criticize directly such developments, they instead provide a relevant and understandable context through which he could present themes of morality, cupidity, and justice.[5] To give students a clearer perspective on how these developments would resonate with his readers, I find it fruitful to identify specific writers and texts that either Hawthorne read—and the scholarship of Kesselring, Warren, Turner, Cody, and others is very helpful on this count—or those that address keys issues about these topics that can help situate his fiction alongside general public discourse.[6] Moreover, the proliferation of free, online texts from Google Books and Project Gutenberg to the "Making of America" website offers teachers and students a vast array of texts that were accessible only to diligent researchers less than a decade ago. For undergraduate students, I therefore find it useful to talk about and have students read excerpts of key texts that address these topics.

One of the key debates during the first half of the nineteenth century involved the moral dimensions of scientific and technological developments: do scientists, inventors, and innovators have a moral obligation to the public to ensure that their developments not only *can* work but *should* work? Such debates, still familiar to us today, influenced public discourse during this era. These discussions played out in nearly every facet of print culture as well as local pulpits and Lyceum lectures, and they shaped the way that Hawthorne framed his characters' moral decisions. Before we begin a section on his "scientific" tales—"The Birth-Mark," "Rappaccini's Daughter," "Dr. Heidegger's Experiment," etc.—I therefore direct students to read texts

---

5 For a solid introduction to Hawthorne's representation of technology, see Henry G. Fairbanks, "Hawthorne and the Machine Age," *American Literature* 28 (1956): 155–63.

6 Austin Warren, "Hawthorne's Reading," *New England Quarterly* 8 (Dec. 1935): 480–97; Arlin Turner, *Hawthorne as Editor* (University: Louisiana State University Press, 1941); David Cody, "Hawthorne as Burrower," *Literature in the Early American Republic* 1 (2009): 169–96.

from writers who extol the seemingly limitless benefits of developments in science and technology.

In his *Elements of Technology* (1829), for instance, the American doctor and botanist, Jacob Bigelow, catalogs recent developments in mechanical design from the arts of printing to growing plants to heating one's home. Although his book is largely illustrative of such advancements, literally including many illustrations, he couches these developments in a standard narrative of civilizing progress. In the "Advertisement" and "Introduction," Bigelow argues that "There has probably never been an age in which the practical applications of science have employed so large a portion of the talent and enterprise of the community, as in the present; nor one in which their cultivation has yielded such abundant rewards." To prove this point, he asserts that the combination of the "sciences," defined by their empirical processes, and the "arts," which depend upon ingenuity and the imagination, have led to such inventions as the printing press, the steam engine, and gunpowder. These civilizing productions have "not only affected the physical, but has changed the moral and political condition of society" all for the betterment of humanity.[7]

Bigelow's claim about the "moral" improvement that is caused by technological developments is indicative of the attitude of many similar writers from the United States and Great Britain alike, and it gives students a chance to wrestle with Hawthorne's approach to such a claim. After reading these introductory sections along with a few of the more neutral descriptions of developments, including the section on railroads, I direct students to explore Hawthorne's literary response. For instance, how have the railroads affected the "physical," "political," and "moral" condition of the titular character in his sketch, "The Old Apple-Dealer"? How does Hawthorne's narrator react to the "steam-fiend"? Why does he suggest that the wizened merchant and the railroad are "antipodes"? What perspective does his sketch bring to Bigelow's text? Similarly, when teaching *The House of the Seven Gables*, I ask students to reflect and write about Clifford's likely response to Bigelow's introduction. Would Hawthorne's character likely agree with Bigelow? Might there be differences in their assessments? How does the portrayal of the railroad in *Seven Gables* or more directly in "The Celestial Railroad" engage more broadly with assessments of "moral advancement"?

---

7   Jacob Bigelow, *Elements of Technology* (1831; Google Books, 2006), iv and 4, https://play.google.com/store/books/details?id=ed8JAAAAIAAJ.

One could find similar ideas about the inevitable benefits of "progress" in many additional contemporary writings. Selections from Robert Southey's *Thomas More, Or Colloquies on the Progress and Prospects of Society* (1829), Timothy Walker's "Defense of Mechanical Philosophy" in *North American Review* (1831), Andrew Ure's *The Philosophy of Manufacturers* (1835), and "Physical Science and the Useful Arts in their Relation to Christian Civilization" in *New Englander* (1851), to name just a few, all explore in different ways the social impact of technological and scientific developments and form an interesting starting point for exploring Hawthorne's works. Although I often give students the specific texts to read, I have also directed students to find, read, and summarize texts themselves. Of particular help with this assignment is the "Making of America" website, formed through a collaboration between the University of Michigan and Cornell University, as students have found articles from the journals on this database on nearly every topic that Hawthorne explores from railroads and steam engines to automata and mesmerism.

Hawthorne and His Peers

When I direct students to examine Hawthorne's writings in the context of the broader intellectual discourse about science and technology, I also usually do so by also including other literary writers who were exploring similar ideas: reading selections from books and periodicals alongside the poetry and fiction of Walt Whitman, Rebecca Harding Davis, James Kirk Paulding, or Herman Melville gives students a better understanding of different nineteenth-century perspectives. For my students, one of the most interesting topics during this period was the rise of automation and automata. Developments in energy sources led to machinery that could replicate the work of living laborers, and these inventions often originated in automata designed for entertainment, such as Henri Maillardet's writing automaton and Jacques de Vaucanson's automaton duck, which were widely popular in the eighteenth century. Reflecting on the array of automata that were showcased in public throughout Europe and the United States in the late eighteenth century, David Brewster in his *Letters on Natural Magic*

(1832) to Sir Walter Scott, a book that Hawthorne checked out in 1837,[8] writes about the practical application of such tinkering:

> The same combination of the mechanical powers which made the spider crawl, or which waved the tiny rod of the magician, contributed in future years to purposes of higher import. Those wheels and pinions, which almost eluded our senses by their minuteness, reappeared in the stupendous mechanism of our spinning-machines and our steam- engines. The elements of the tumbling puppet were revived in the chronometer, which now conducts our navy through the ocean; and the shapeless wheel which directed the hand of the drawing automaton has served in the present age to guide the movements of the tambouring engine. Those mechanical wonders which in one century enriched only the conjurer who used them, contributed in another to augment the wealth of the nation; and those automatic toys which once amused the vulgar, are now employed in extending the power and promoting the civilization of our species.[9]

As Brewster notes, automata designed for amusement have led to machinery designed for production, a beneficial transition that is spurring the advancement of civilization.

This shift toward automation, though, led many thinkers and writers to question such rosy pronouncements. For Hawthorne, automata give rise to questions of work, free will, and artistic labor. In his tale, "The Seven Vagabonds," and "The Arched Window" chapter in *The House of the Seven Gables*, for instance, the hand-crank barrel organs allow the figures to "come alive" temporarily before the loss of power brings their movement to a close. By connecting these moments to developments in automation, I ask my students to examine the implications on work, leisure, and free will. What do these figures represent? Are these shows for amusement, or do they reflect a broader reality? What is the relationship between the figures and the man who controls them? Similarly, Owen Warland's automaton butterfly in "The Artist of the Beautiful" reveals the quest for non-utilitarian automation, a contrast to the steam engine that caused Warland

---

8   Kesselring, *Hawthorne's Reading*, 40.
9   David Brewster, *Letters on Natural Magic* (1832; repr., London: Chatto & Windus, Piccadilly, 1883), 336.

to turn "pale" and "sick."[10] What is the "value" of the butterfly to Annie, Robert, and Peter? How is this value different for Owen? What does the butterfly suggest about the expanding utilitarian functions of automata? In exploring automata in Hawthorne's work, one could also examine supernatural figures brought to life, such as those in "Feathertop," "Drowne's Wooden Image," and "Monsieur du Miroir," or mesmerism in *Gables* or *The Blithedale Romance*.[11] In all of these tales, he presents figures/characters that are not quite alive or in control of their movements and thoughts, traits that parallel the effects of automation.

Hawthorne was not the only literary writer attuned to this growing interest, and in classes I have found it helpful to compare and contrast his presentations with those of his peers. Incorporating "pure" automata in their tales, Fitz-James O'Brien and Herman Melville present dystopian and destructive creations that challenge the beneficial pronouncements of automata advocates. In "The Wondersmith"[12] O'Brien portrays Herr Hippe/Duke Balthazar as an immigrant gypsy who owns a curiosity shop complete with a variety of toys and automata. Seeking revenge for the death of his son, he unleashes an army of miniature manikin automata who will, he hopes, "spill blood like Christians." The destructive nature of these figurines, alongside the various other spectra of automata in the tale, from a disembodied eyeball to fairies to a monkey, directs us to ask about the symbolic effect of such creations and creatures.

Equally destructive and much more menacing is Melville's Talus/Haman from "The Bell-Tower." Designed by the mechanician/artist, Bannadonna, a distinction worth pursuing in discussion, to strike a large bell to mark time, the automaton instead kills its creator in a gesture that suggests the revolt of a servant or slave.[13] Students always find both tales interesting and rich, and when combined with Brewster's or similar writers' selections

---

10   Nathaniel Hawthorne, "The Artist of the Beautiful," in *Nathaniel Hawthorne: Tales and Sketches* (NY: Library of America College Editions, 1996), 909.

11   For mesmerism, see Samuel Coale, *Mesmerism and Hawthorne: Mediums of American Romance* (Tuscaloosa: University of Alabama Press, 1998).

12   Fitz James O'Brien, "The Wondersmith," *The Atlantic Monthly* 4 (1859): 463–82.

13   The standard edition of Melville's tales is *The Piazza Tales and Other Prose Pieces, 1839-1860*, vol. 9, *The Writings of Herman Melville*, eds. Harrison Hayford, Hershal Parker, and G. Thomas Tanselle (Evanston and Chicago: Northwestern University Press and Newberry Library, 1987).

and Hawthorne's works, these tales lead to rewarding thoughts and discussion about the potential drawbacks of automata. What is the effect of creating not merely neutral but murderous automata in O'Brien's and Melville's tales? How does this destruction contrast with Owen Warland's butterfly or Drowne's figure? What "work" do these automata perform? How do they function in the different story worlds of each author?

Similarly, Melville and other writers, canonical and lesser-known alike, present a correlation between laborers and automata in ways that blur boundaries between human and machine. If automation was increasingly constructed to replace the drudgery of repetitive labor, then what do we make of these early portrayals that instead reveal how automation reshapes rather than replaces the laborer? James Kirk Paulding's "Man Machine" from *The Merry Tales of the Three Wise Men of Gotham* (1826),[14] for instance, presents the reader with a portrayal of the "New View of Society," a likely satire of Robert Owen's view of socialism, that posits the "perfection" of humanity, especially men and children. As the title suggests, the fine line between humanity and machinery is crossed, but what exactly is the benefit?[15] Is this a better world? I have also found it useful to combine Paulding's text with Edgar Allan Poe's "The Man That Was Used Up," Melville's "The Paradise of Bachelors and the Tartarus of Maids," Rebecca Harding Davis's "Life in the Iron Mills" (*Atlantic Monthly*, 1861), and/or "A Night Under Ground" (*Atlantic Monthly*, 1861). All four texts explore workers' conditions under industrial processes, and the resulting class discussion and projects allow students to compare Hawthorne's "tamer" visions of labor and automation with the satirical vision of Paulding, the bleak machine/maid hybrid of Melville, and the mid-century shift in Davis and "A Night Under Ground."

Innovation and inventions in automation led to a reconceptualization of time itself, and many writers portrayed this transformation in their work. When Owen Warland repairs the town's church clock, for instance, "the merchants gruffly acknowledged his merits on 'Change [commercial exchange]; the nurse whispered his praises as she gave the potion in the sick chamber; the lover blessed him at the hour of appointed interview; and the town in general thanked Owen for the punctuality of dinner time." Similarly,

---

14   *The Merry Tales of the Three Wise Men of Gotham* (New York: Carville, 1826).

15   For a helpful analysis of Paulding's text, see Klaus Benesch, *Romantic Cyborgs: Authorship and Technology in the American Renaissance* (Amherst: University of Massachusetts Press, 2002).

the railroad reconfigured notions of time as well as space, and such representations ("The Celestial Railroad," *The House of the Seven Gables*) offer a glimpse into these changing ideas of time. Such considerations work well when placed in comparison with *The Lowell Offering* and Edgar Allan Poe's "The Devil in the Belfry," both of which reveal the effects of this transformation in management of time.[16] The operatives in *The Lowell Offering*, for instance, embody the strict regulation of time that emerges in a burgeoning industrial setting, while the foreigner in Poe's tale revels in his destruction of the clock-driven order of the idyllic town of Vondervotteimittiss. In both instances, the regulation of time that was becoming increasingly important in industry and travel in the early nineteenth century directly affects and at times controls the characters and citizens, and this developing norm gave these writers an opportunity to portray the results of such regulation.

Of course, such literary connections are not limited to the subject of automata. Students have found equally fascinating the comparison between Hawthorne's scientists/alchemists Rappaccini and Aylmer and O'Brien's Linley from "The Diamond Lens" (1858) and Cipriano in "Seeing the World" (1857).[17] The latter two scientists' obsession with their science and the microscopic world leads them towards their own destruction and raises questions about new forms of scientific knowledge. In his 1830 defense of scientific discoveries, with particular and repeated attention to the practicality of such work, the prominent Yale chemist, Benjamin Silliman, writes, "Knowledge is nothing but the just and the full comprehension of the real nature of things, physical, intellectual, and moral; it is co-extensive with the universe of being; reaching back to the dawn of time, and forward to its consummation" (23). Do Hawthorne's and O'Brien's scientists share Silliman's proclamation about "knowledge"? Do they all gain full comprehension of the "moral" essence of things? What are the drawbacks of these fictional scientists, and why do Hawthorne and O'Brien present them not as pioneers but as destructive forces?[18]

---

16   Benita Eisler, ed., *The Lowell Offering: Writings by New England Mill Women* (New York: Norton & Company, 1997) and Edgar Allan Poe, *Tales and Sketches* in *The Collected Works of Edgar Allan Poe*, vols. II & III, ed. Thomas Ollive Mabbott (Cambridge: Belknap Press of Harvard University Press, 1978).

17   Fitz James O'Brien, "The Diamond Lens," *The Atlantic Monthly* 1 (1858): 354–67; and "Seeing the World," *Harper's New Monthly Magazine* 15 (1857): 542–46.

18   Benjamin Silliman, *Elements of Chemistry in the Order of the Lectures Given in Yale College*, vol. 1 (New Haven, 1830). For general analysis of the scientist as

Current Technologies

As we all know, scientific and technological developments reshaped early-nineteenth-century witnesses' understanding of knowledge, communication, work, time, and space during the burgeoning industrial revolution, and during our course discussions, combined with their experiences in history courses, students grapple with such powerful transformations. Viewed from this historical vantage point, the changes are clearly marked: microscopic and telescopic research revealed worlds previously little known to us; steam power transformed production and transportation capabilities; the railroad altered conceptions of distance and time. What is not always clear to students, though, is how subtle such changes were for most people, who did not suddenly wake up one day and realize that their world had changed. Only with the help of thinkers and cultural observers like Hawthorne can we comprehend the magnitude of these changes.

The "digital revolution" is analogous to its industrial predecessor as computer technologies have reshaped our understanding of knowledge (Google, Wikipedia), communication (email, Skype, blogs), work (teleconferencing, work from home capabilities), and time and space (microsecond stock trading, Facebook and Twitter erasing distance). These transformations have significantly affected the lives of millions of people, but it is not always easy to grasp the significance of these changes when we are living in their midst. To help students understand the experience of living through such transformative times, I therefore incorporate assignments that direct students to use and reflect upon the changes in which they themselves are embroiled today. After they complete each of these assignments, I direct students to reflect upon the effect the technology had on their learning, work, and communication, that is, to become a cultural observer like Hawthorne.

The most basic and readily useable assignment directs students to conduct primary and secondary research on Hawthorne and/or the science and technology he examines. To do so, they will automatically gravitate

literary character, see Glen Scott Allen, *Master Mechanics & Wicked Wizards: Images of the American Scientist as Hero and Villain from Colonial Times to the Present* (Amherst: University of Massachusetts Press, 2009). See also Taylor Stoehr, *Hawthorne's Mad Scientists: Pseudoscience and Social Science in Nineteenth-Century Life and Letters* (Hamden, CT: Archon, 1978).

to their computers and digital devices, but by directing them to complete some of their research in the physical library combing through books, journals, and newspapers, even in microfiche, students get a very clear "before and after" understanding of the impact of the web. Many of us are old enough to remember the need to travel to libraries to view many of the materials we can currently access instantly on our screens, and as our students share a similar experience, they can better reflect on the digital effect on knowledge.

During the semester, I also direct students to respond weekly to questions I pose about our course readings, but to do so, they complete two different assignments. During the first month or so of class, they must respond to one of my questions in a traditional response paper which they type and submit to me in class. After this initial period, though, I alter the assignment and ask students to post their responses to a course blog that I set up using either the course management system our institution provides or a free online blog site such as wordpress.com. In their blog responses, students must now engage with the ideas in at least one previous student post, unless s/he is the first to respond, and explain if they disagree and why or agree and develop the point further. At the end of the semester, I ask students to reflect upon this shift in assignment. How did they approach the task differently when the initial reader is only me to when the entire class could read the response? Did reading others' posts affect their own understanding of the question or literature? What are the benefits and drawbacks of posting their ideas on a blog? In sum, how did the blog as a technological tool affect their writing and thinking?[19]

In a few courses, I go a step further and assign students a final wiki project. As an easy-to-edit website, a wiki gives students a tool for collaboration and communication to an audience beyond the instructor. Using the wiki function in a course management system or free wiki sites, such as wikispaces.com, I direct students to complete group projects that they then showcase to the rest of the class. In one such project, students conducted primary research on the topics I mention in section one above, and they

---

[19] For an account of how I use blogging as a teaching tool, see my "Early American Print Culture in a Digital Age: Pedagogical Possibilities," *Pedagogy: Critical Approaches to Teaching Literature, Language, Composition, and Culture* 3, no. 2 (Spring 2003): 288–92. I also address the impact of anonymous blogging in "Pseudonymous Writing and Improved Course Engagement" (co-authored with A. Fiona Pearson) *Writing and Pedagogy* 5 (forthcoming 2013).

post annotations and analyses to their wiki pages. For instance, one group researched the rise of the railroad in New England and located and summarized primary articles relating to the railroad. On another page, they completed an analysis of Hawthorne's representation of the railroad and what his representation communicated. In a different assignment, students completed "interviews" with various nineteenth-century literary characters. (I have shifted between group and individual interview projects depending on the course objectives and other assignments in the course.) I gave mandatory interview questions: How would your character respond to Emerson's idea of "self reliance"? What would your character say about the difference between artisanal and industrial production?—and students post their interviews to a course wiki site. After the initial drafts are complete, I then direct students to engage with and create hyperlinks between their interview pages and those of their classmates. Why would your chosen character respond differently to Emerson than another character? What does this tell us about both characters?

Much like blogs, wikis direct students to present work for a broad audience and engage with each others' ideas online. The wiki, though, also opens the possibility for collaborative work, which has its obvious benefits and drawbacks. Observing this collaboration reveals interesting work patterns: many students choose to work in the early morning hours from 2:00 a.m. to 4:00 a.m. and others feel compelled to take editorial control over the pages. I design the assignment for students to think deeply and carefully about the topic and literature, but I also ask students to write a reflection on how the wiki shaped their work. How did online collaboration—students can meet exclusively online if they so desire—differ from face-to-face group work? How did instant editing capabilities affect their writing? How did time flexibility of the wiki affect their work? How did the public nature of the wiki shift their understanding of the assignment? Did the collaborative wiki help or hinder their work?

In all of these assignments, students experience first-hand the technological tools that were not available twenty or even ten years ago. Many students are so immersed in the world of Facebook, Google, and texting that they do not comprehend the significant transformation of the "digital revolution." By directing students to use and reflect upon elements of this transformation, though, they get a better understanding of the experiences of Hawthorne and his contemporaries. Scientific and especially technological developments may be only one part of a student's life experiences, but they have the potential to shape the moral, cultural, and political landscape of our time, which is the approach Nathaniel Hawthorne took when he presented such developments in his own work. If Charles Babbage argued that the "science of calculation" would lead to better knowledge about and control of our world, then Hawthorne and his contemporary writers sought to use their own writing as "laboratories" to see how this world would turn out.

Southern Connecticut State University

Cautionary Hawthorne: Science, Ethics, and God in the Teaching of "The Birth-Mark" and "Rappaccini's Daughter"

AARON D. COBB AND ERIC STERLING

INTRODUCTION

Science, technology, ethics, and religion exercise great influence on students entering the college classroom, but few students have had the opportunity to reflect seriously on the nature of these influences and the manner in which they affect their lives. This lack of opportunity is problematic, in part because each discipline offers a vision of how one can and should navigate life. Religious views can provide a narrative for students to frame their own lives and understand the nature and value of human life and action. Unreflective assent to religious dogma, however, can have damaging effects on individuals and society. Science and technology, on the other hand, offer a means to exert control over one's life, to fashion or re-make a life better for oneself and others. Although these capacities are alluring, there is an ambiguity in this promise especially if the use of technology is unaligned with what is considered to be good. There may be a desire to recreate oneself through technological means, but one may destroy something of inherent worth in the process. One of the challenges in teaching today's college students, then, is finding ways to encourage critical reflection about religious conceptions, ethics, and the ambiguities of science and technology.

Literature can facilitate this kind of reflective engagement with religion, ethics, science, and technology. In fact, narratives, such as Nathaniel Hawthorne's "The Birth-Mark" and "Rappaccini's Daughter" directly illustrate some of these dynamics. The historical and literary distance of these texts from the contexts in which students live their lives makes them particularly effective for encouraging deep reflection among students. "The Birth-Mark," for instance, is more than merely a short story about a scientist who removes his wife's birthmark, resulting in her unfortunate and unnecessary death. The story deals with moral issues, the ethics and dangers of scientific experimentation, the dynamics and hubris of control and domination in domestic relationships, the value of human life, and the quest for perfection. Hawthorne also addresses these issues within the context of a spiritual understanding of the characteristic qualities of human life. God seems to have made his mark on Georgiana, both literally and figuratively, and to have warned Aylmer through his troubling and prophetic dream, the meaning of which the scientist chooses to ignore. There are echoes of similar themes in "Rappaccini's Daughter," along with allusions to a new but subverted "Garden of Eden" whose creator, Rappaccini, breathes life into a poisonous creation, a new "Eve" marked for a life cloistered within a protective gate.

In this essay, we discuss our approach to teaching "Rappaccini's Daughter" and "The Birth-Mark" in a sophomore-level Survey of American Literature I class, which covers literature from the Puritans through the Civil War.[1]

---

1   Another possibility involves including "Rappaccini's Daughter" and "The Birth-Mark" in a class on nineteenth-century literature (or scientific literature) or adding them, for a class period, in a survey of English Literature II (from the Romantics to the present). After teaching Mary Shelley's Frankenstein, or the Modern Prometheus and Robert Louis Stevenson's Strange Case of Dr. Jekyll and Mr. Hyde, for example, assign these two short stories to explore transcontinental Romantic relationships between literature and science. How do British writers Shelley and Stevenson portray their scientists in regard to scientific experimentation and medical ethics compared to the American Hawthorne? Ask students if they believe that Hawthorne might have been influenced by Shelley and if Stevenson might have been influenced by Hawthorne. Ask students if Aylmer and Rappaccini are modern Prometheuses like Frankenstein.

Our goals are (i) to engage students in a careful and contextualized reading and analysis of the texts, (ii) to explain major themes and concerns in Hawthorne's writing, and (iii) to connect these themes and issues to the contemporary contexts that might elicit from us similar concerns and criticism. In the next section, we discuss the manner in which we engage students in the reading of these stories. We explain the kinds of questions we use to direct students to the various features of these texts and to help them draw connections between these two stories. As we discuss these texts with them, we and they discern and articulate Hawthorne's themes. In the third section, we discuss the manner in which one can draw parallels to challenges in contemporary society. Drawing on various resources, we show how we engage students in reflection on technology and science, religion, and ethics in our own context. Finally, we conclude with a brief account of what this approach to teaching Hawthorne's stories affords.

Reading the Texts

We start class discussion with Hawthorne's introductory remarks to "Rappaccini's Daughter" in which the narrator claims to introduce a work by Monsieur Aubépine (French for "Hawthorn"), a mediocre writer of "allegory." Although some students have a general idea about allegories, it is helpful to ask them to define the term for the class in order to ensure that everyone understands the concept. After a student defines the literary term, and the class discusses it briefly, it is essential to have students relate the concept of allegory to the two Hawthorne stories. Knowing the abstract meaning of allegory means little unless students can employ their critical thinking skills by applying the concept to actual stories. Likewise, applying a clear understanding of the nature of allegory enables them to understand the themes that pervade Hawthorne's work, such as morality, scientific experimentation, and the danger of hubris and excessive ambition. The fact that Hawthorne clearly identifies himself as an allegorist, whose preoccupation with the trope pervades his fiction, suggests to his readers that he wants his works to be read as allegories and for his readers to correlate the real and the abstract.

When asked about allegory in "Rappaccini's Daughter," students compare and connect both the plot and the setting to that of the Garden of Eden in the Book of Genesis. Students compare Giovanni to Adam, Beatrice to Eve, and Rappaccini's garden to the Garden of Eden; the mysterious purple flower may represent, they say, the Tree of Knowledge in regard to its foreboding power and the knowledge of taboo scientific information that it embodies. Students sometimes add the relationship between Rappaccini in Hawthorne's story and God in the Garden of Eden, but if they omit it, the instructor could elicit or even provide this connection because of its paramount significance. Moreover, instructors may want to caution students that a connection might exist between Rappaccini and God, but a connection does not equate the two. Students can then expand upon this correlation, realizing that in Hawthorne's story, Rappaccini perceives himself as a God figure or perhaps that the scientist believes that his unusual experiment, which brings him knowledge beyond that which human beings should know, renders him like a deity, far above the average scientist such as his rival Baglioni.[2] Rappaccini acts like a God,

> a creator who engineers an experimental world tainted by evil and whose noblest creature, deliberately exposed to the taint, partakes of it. The experiment is conducted at the creature's expense, whose fulfillment is made all but impossible by the poison that has been allowed to flourish. The only available "antidote" . . . is death. [3]

Student discussion sometimes leads to the presumption that scientists who venture beyond socially acceptable experiments consider themselves deities by delving into the exploration of knowledge forbidden by God, just as Adam and Eve or Prometheus do. The experimentation is taboo, unethical, and unnatural not because Baglioni disapproves of it or expresses jealousy but because Rappaccini willingly sacrifices the happiness and welfare of his daughter from birth.

---

2   For additional discussion of the rivalry between Rappaccini and Baglioni, see M. D. Uroff, "The Doctors in 'Rappaccini's Daughter,'" Nineteenth-Century Fiction 27 (1972): 61–70. Also, for discussion of "Rappaccini's Daughter" as an allegory about science itself, see Edward H. Rosenberry, "Hawthorne's Allegory of Science: 'Rappaccini's Daughter,'" American Literature 32 (1960): 39–46.
3   Bill Christophersen, "Agnostic Tensions in Hawthorne's Short Stories," in Critical Insights: Nathaniel Hawthorne, ed. Jack Lynch (Pasadena: Salem, 2010), 295.

Surprisingly perhaps, some students defend Rappaccini, calling him a devoted father who loves his daughter so much that he wants to protect her from dangerous men and the temptations of the world. Not wanting his daughter to be seduced or hurt by a deceptive, seductive man, the scientist insulates her from trouble by creating a poisonous barrier that protects her from men and allows the scientist to view and control her courtship in its entirety because she is confined to the garden.[4] Although we do not concur with this line of argument, it is a plausible line of thinking, and we want to encourage not discourage class participation and student engagement with the texts. Rather than openly disagreeing with them, we have found that it is more productive to respond with questions that encourage them to reconsider their interpretations:

- How can Rappaccini be protecting his daughter when he has rendered her poisonous?
- If he truly cared for Beatrice, wouldn't he have waited until she was old enough to decide her fate for herself?
- How can compelling Beatrice to spend her life in the garden and have virtually no human contact be considered love?

Given these questions we hope students will create more complex views of love, especially the kind of suffocating love that would do violence to a person in order to protect her/him from possible harm.

In order to give students a visual perspective on "Rappaccini's Daughter," we recommend showing a film version, introduced by Henry Fonda,[5] as many students are visual learners and welcome the opportunity to see a production of the story. The video cannot be a precise, objective production, of course, but rather serves as the director's and actors' interpretations of Hawthorne's work. For instance, when students witness in the film the stoic reaction of Rappaccini to his daughter's death, it reinforces their interpretation of the scientist's apathy toward his daughter's health and her life itself. This well-done production adds a dream sequence in which Giovanni dreams briefly of Rappaccini kissing Beatrice on the lips, suggesting the possibility of an incestuous relationship. Students are usually

---

4   M. D. Uroff, "The Doctors," 68 ff., suggests such an interpretation.
5   Rappaccini's Daughter, directed by Dezsö Magyar (Monterey, CA: Monterey Video, 1998), VHS.

startled by this brief moment in the film, yet rather than dismissing it as an overreaching interpretation by the director, some connect the possibility of incest to the fact that through his science Rappaccini has imprisoned his daughter, preventing her from venturing out into the world and meeting men; until the arrival of Giovanni, the father does indeed have his daughter to himself. The film invites the students to think of alternative interpretations and allows them to visualize what they merely read on the page. Watching the video inspires them to rethink the written text of Hawthorne's tale.

Although we do mention the link between the young Italian woman Beatrice and the Beatrice in Dante's *Divine Comedy*, the suggestion of incest leads us to the connection between the heroine in Hawthorne's work and Beatrice Cenci, an Italian incest victim violated by her notorious father. Beatrice Cenci, like Hawthorne's Beatrice, eventually finds a lover and turns against her father. It is well documented that Hawthorne and his wife expressed curiosity concerning the Cenci family.[6] If Rappaccini's relationship with Beatrice is incestuous, the allegory involving poison could actually represent syphilis, a disease that links them together.[7] After the discussion and the film, few students consider Rappaccini a protector, but it is their choice. And even students who still defend Rappaccini should at least consider the possibility that the man is an ambitious and amoral scientist who willingly exploits his daughter to further his career.

This description of Rappaccini is significant because it allows for a transition to Hawthorne's "The Birth-Mark," which could also be taught as an allegory involving an arrogant scientist.[8] To facilitate the transition, it is beneficial to ask students to construct a list of connections between the two

---

6   For an in-depth study of Hawthorne and the Cenci family, see Robert White, "'Rappaccini's Daughter,' The Cenci, and the Cenci Legend," Studi Americani 14 (1968): 63–86.

7   For an intriguing study on "Rappaccini's Daughter" as an allegory of the conflict between Benvenuto Cellini and Doctor Jacopo (Giacomo) Da Carpi in sixteenth-century Italy (represented by the rivalry between Rappaccini and Baglioni) and Beatrice's poisonous affliction being syphilis, see Carol Marie Bensick, La Nouvelle Beatrice: Renaissance and Romance in "Rappaccini's Daughter" (New Brunswick: Rutgers University Press, 1985), 93–112.

8   For more discussion of Hawthorne's depiction of scientists see Taylor Stoehr, Hawthorne's Mad Scientists: Pseudoscience and Social Science in Nineteenth-Century Life and Letters (Hamden: Archon, 1978).

male protagonists and between the two heroines of the stories. Students usually link Rappaccini to Aylmer in regard to their obsession with science and their desire to experiment on women. The latter connection is significant because professors can approach these stories by focusing on gender issues in Hawthorne. Women, some students suggest, serve as guinea pigs to their male scientist father/husband, indicating that Hawthorne implies that some hubristic men considered females as expendable pawns whom the scientists willingly destroy for the sake of knowledge. The decisions about the fate of women in both stories are clearly made by men; even when Georgiana decides to have the birthmark removed, it is because she has been manipulated by her husband, who shudders at the sight of her.

In "The Birth-Mark," the narrator and Aylmer focus extensively upon Georgiana's physical beauty and her birthmark. It is important to ask students why there exists such a preoccupation with her looks. They believe that this obsession with her physical appearance derives from her being courted by Aylmer and other suitors, the jealousy of other women, and the belief that she would be physically perfect except for this one defect. Ask students to locate passages that support their ideas. It is then important to ask them to find textual descriptions of Aylmer's looks. Students then realize a significant point that although the narrator and Aylmer dwell upon Georgiana's looks, no mention is made of the scientist's physical appearance, as if it does not matter. Students believe that a gender double standard exists in the story and that Hawthorne suggests that many men feel that a woman's physical appearance, unlike a man's, correlates with her stature in society. What does this distinction signify about the value of physical beauty and gender issues in Hawthorne's society and the desire to employ science to correct physical imperfections?

Contemporary Connections

Although "The Birth-Mark" should not be interpreted as a criticism of science per se, the story reflects the manner in which human desire and the aspiration for perfection can corrupt its practice. Aylmer's quest to "perfect" his wife by removing her birthmark becomes an obsession, and, in the process, he loses sight of her inherent worth as a human being. She is no longer his beloved; instead, she becomes an object of study and experiment.

Aylmer devotes all his time to the singular task of removing this mark that serves for him as "the symbol of his wife's liability to sin, sorrow, decay, and death."[9] He and Rappaccini, as Jennifer Banach Palladino suggests, "are enraptured by the possibilities of science but often lack moral concern—unselfish concern—regarding its proper and noble application. The characters are, rather, divorced from humanity, caught up in the idea of self and the possibility of attaining perfection."[10]

Our students are disturbed by Aylmer's obsession with Georgiana's birthmark. Why is he so concerned with this superficial blemish? To encourage discussion of this obsession and to draw their attention to some of the deep issues this birthmark might represent, we focus on how Hawthorne describes it. They note that the birthmark, although small, is intimately connected with her heart, the very core of her being. Hawthorne indicates that it is

> the fatal flaw of humanity, which Nature, in one shape or another, stamps ineffaceably on all her productions, either to imply that they are temporary and finite, or that their perfection must be wrought by toil and pain. The Crimson Hand expressed the ineludible gripe, in which mortality clutches the highest and purest of earthly mould, degrading them into kindred with the lowest, and even with the very brutes, like whom their visible frames return to dust (38-39).

The birthmark, then, constitutes a mark of humanity; to be human is to be constrained, mortal, finite and subject to the vicissitudes of life.

We then discuss with our students the idea that Hawthorne links Aylmer's obsession with the mark and its removal to the preoccupations of the great philosophers of the Middle Ages who "stood in advance of their centuries, yet were imbued with some of their credulity, and therefore were believed, and perhaps imagined themselves, to have acquired from the investigation of nature a power above nature, and from physics a sway over the spiritual world" (48). Aylmer himself enjoys a reputation among the intelligentsia

---

9   Nathaniel Hawthorne, "The Birth-Mark," *Mosses from an Old Manse* in *The Centenary Edition of the Works of Nathaniel Hawthorne*, vol. X, eds. William Charvat, Roy Harvey Pearce, and Claude M. Simpson (Columbus: Ohio State University Press, 1974), 39. Subsequent citations to this tale are from this edition and are parenthetically documented.
10 Jennifer Banach Palladino, "Hawthorne and American Romanticism," in *Critical Insights*, 67.

for contributing greatly to the production of scientific knowledge. But as Hawthorne notes, he has quit his study of humankind in the

> recognition of the truth, against which all seekers sooner or later stumble, that our great creative Mother, while she amuses us with apparently working in the broadest sunshine, is yet severely careful to keep her own secrets, and, in spite of her pretended openness, shows us nothing but results. She permits us indeed, to mar, but seldom to mend, and, like a jealous patentee, on no account to make (42).

Taking up this study again, he attempts to discover how to remove his wife's defect, even while knowing that his greatest experimental efforts invariably have been failures. In class, students probably should be asked to explicate the preceding quotations rather than relying upon us to interpret them and to ponder why Aylmer wants to proceed with his experiment on his wife, knowing that all his previous efforts have failed. What does his stubbornness indicate about his character, his feelings for his wife, and his views on science?

Interestingly, Hawthorne's depiction of Aylmer's experimental exploits and marital failure has become the object of study in public discussion of bioethics in the United States. In class we mention the 2002 Presidential Council on Bioethics, which began its work with a discussion of "The Birth-Mark."[11] The context of the discussion involved the pressing ethical concerns of our day occasioned by advances in scientific understanding and the advent of new technology. James Quinn Wilson, Commission member, winner of the Presidential Medal of Freedom, and member of the Human Rights Commission, expressed his concerns:

> Suppose we update Mr. Aylmer and bring him into the 21st Century and he now has a Ph.D. and teaches at a leading university as a scientist and biologist. He is a consultant to a major gene technology

---

11   They took up this discussion in the second session, January 17, 2002. For complete transcript details see "Council discussion of "The Birth-Mark" by Nathaniel Hawthorne," President's Council on Bioethics, last accessed 3/4/2014, http://bioethics.georgetown.edu/pcbe/transcripts/jan02/jansession2intro.html. For critical discussion of the use of Hawthorne's "Birth-Mark" in this context, see William R. Newman, Promethean Ambitions: Alchemy and the Quest to Perfect Nature (Chicago: University of Chicago Press, 2005), 1–10.

company and on the basis of prior animal and some human researches he believes there is a reasonable chance, though no guaranteed certainty, that by in vitro—by intrauterine action or by gene transplants he can done [sic] one of [sic] more of three things. First he can reduce significantly the problem that the child will have a Birth-Mark. Secondly, he can reduce significantly the chance that the child will have one leg shorter than the other. And, thirdly, he can increase the probability that the person can dunk the basketball from outside the free throw line. . . . Do we think that interfering with unborn life to achieve any or all of these objectives is legitimate? . . . If there is a therapy that has presumably little down risk and much up side benefit that will prevent the Birth-Mark from appearing, I think the public desire to do this will be overwhelming. If it has to do with making one leg the same length as the other, I think the public will be remarkably supportive. What happens, however, if what we want to do is not remove defects but enhance abilities by increasing IQ or being able to get them to be the next Michael Jordan, or if you prefer the next Pamela Anderson? That raises a very entirely different sort of question. So when we talk about this as being a story about science, we should update the science but then we should not lose track of the issue of what are people's responsibilities toward life. Is enhancement, the elimination of defects acceptable or not? Is improvement, the increase in ability beyond what you would normally predict acceptable? Because I am convinced that by the end of this century all of these things will be possible.[12]

Contextualized in this way, we note that Aylmer and subsequently Georgiana consider the birthmark a defect that must be removed for them to live a happy and fulfilling life. We direct the conversation to these sorts of questions by focusing on a birthmark of another sort, the marks of disabilities that our latest technologies allow physicians to diagnose *in utero*. With the advent of new pre-natal diagnostic tools, many couples can learn of the genetic fate of their potential children and make decisions concerning their care and existence long before their children are born. In the past,

---

12 "Science and the Pursuit of Perfection," The President's Council on Bioethics, last accessed on 3/4/2014, http://bioethics.georgetown.edu/pcbe/transcripts/jan02/jan17session2.html.

we have shown our students a panel discussion on the *Today* show focused on a new safe and effective blood test for diagnosing *Trisomy 21* (Down Syndrome).[13] In this discussion, Dr. Nancy Snyderman argues that this technology could eliminate diseases and disabilities. She maintains that this technology "gives parents a chance to decide whether they're going to continue that pregnancy or not. This is the science of today," later adding that she is "pro-science, so . . . this is a good way of preventing disease." We then discuss the video with the students, steering clear of political and religious controversies, instead tying the discussion to Hawthorne's story.

We ask students what Snyderman means when she says that she has a "pro-science" position. One student noted that she might be referring to technology that allows physicians to correct or alter inherited conditions *in utero*, thus preventing future diseases or disabilities a child might have to suffer. Although this is certainly possible, we wonder aloud what this technology would mean for individuals with conditions such as *Trisomy 21*. These chromosomal abnormalities cannot be "corrected" or "altered" without bringing about the death of the individual. In this sense, they are analogous to Georgiana's birthmark, the removal of which destroys her life because it is part of who she is. To draw this connection explicitly, we ask our students if Aylmer's experiment on Georgiana is successful. Students initially are nonplussed by the question. Of course it's not! His wife dies from the experiment, so how could it possibly be successful? But we point out that because Aylmer's intent is solely to remove the birthmark, and the blemish is removed, he accomplishes his goal. His wife's demise is merely a side effect—collateral damage—manifesting Aylmer's belief that scientific discovery should transcend human life. Students generally accept that because he achieves his goal and, like Rappaccini, expresses no regret over the death of a loved one, the experiment could be perceived as a success from his perspective.

We raise this point about Aylmer's "success" and Snyderman's "pro-science" belief with the students, asking whether the desire to achieve a more "perfect" child through the use of these technologies resembles Aylmer's quest to achieve a more "perfect" Georgiana. We also discuss whether and to what extent we should have the same kinds of attitudes toward the

---

13 Nancy Snyderman, Today, NBC, June 8, 2012. Television. http://www.all.org/article/index/id/MTA1MzU. Our discussion of these texts coincided with World Down Syndrome Day (March 21).

modern desire to eliminate disabilities and diseases through preventative medicine and the use of technologies that could terminate the lives of individuals diagnosed with these imperfections. This incites a particularly dynamic exchange with the students, who are inclined to be skeptical of the use of the technology in this way.

The discussion results in two important outcomes. First, we can focus more carefully on the subtle role of human desire in both Aylmer's quest and modern forms of preventative medicine. While there may be a noble goal associated with attempting to eliminate disease and disability—these are not as superficial as Georgiana's birthmark—underlying both of these is the desire for a human being unmarked by imperfection. Some imperfections may be superficial and others more serious, but they all indicate the flawed state of the human condition, inviting the question of how to deal with and tend to the defects that may be an essential aspect of human nature. Do we seek to rid ourselves of these defects even if it means the destruction of human nature? Or is the quest to remove these defects itself a hubristic failure to see ourselves as we truly are? Is there something important about our mortality, about our dependence and vulnerability, that we must come to appreciate rather than overcome?

Second, we can isolate and focus our discussion more carefully on the desire for perfection and its effects on our actions. While it may be clear that we aspire to better ourselves and to remake ourselves, a tension exists between this kind of transformation and the kind of appreciation we ought to have for our essential human worth. In one sense, Aylmer's obsession with removing Georgiana's mark signals that he is repulsed by the gift he has been given of her presence in his life. In seeking to remake her, he rejects her and her love. By focusing our attention on the issues in modern biotechnology, we may ask students to think seriously about what it would mean to eliminate children marked or coded for disease and disability. Is this a rejection of the gift of human life? Is this a rejection of ourselves, for we are all marked and coded for death in our own mortality? These kinds of questions effectively engage students in a deep discussion of the ethical issues that seem the object of Hawthorne's concern.

There are additional ways teachers can address ethical issues and science in the context of these stories. They could employ the famous "Eye of the Beholder" episode (1960) of *The Twilight Zone* and a YouTube clip from the Holocaust movie, *Europa Europa* (1990). In the former, students see a woman with a bandaged face waiting eagerly for the outcome of her plastic surgery. She is considered so ugly that she cannot live in society. When the bandages are finally removed, students realize that she is a beautiful woman played by Donna Douglas, Elly May Clampett from *The Beverly Hillbillies*. Students are shocked to see that the doctors, who are also not shown until the end, are ugly and have faces like pigs. From the students' perspective, the woman is beautiful, and the other members of the society are ugly, yet the culture perceives the reverse and thus banishes her. They discuss how physical appearance is subjective and may apply this episode to "The Birth-Mark," in which Georgiana's suitors wish to kiss the birthmark, yet Aylmer kills her to remove it. The obsession with physical appearance in Hawthorne's story is still relevant today, including the creation of *The Plastic Surgery Channel*.

Additionally, one could show a video clip from the movie, *Europa Europa* because the film provides students with another perspective on science, hubris, and the treatment of "inferiors" or "the other" by egocentric people. In the scene from this Holocaust film, which is a true account, a German Jew, Solomon Perel, hiding in plain sight from the Nazis as a member of the Hitler Youth, watches a eugenics teacher explain to the Hitler Youth students how to recognize a Jew based on their supposedly inferior genetic makeup. This discussion relates to the class discussion on Hawthorne because it demonstrates how some people like Aylmer use science in their attempt to create earthly perfection. The eugenics teacher announces proudly that "Science is objective. Science is incorruptible."[14] It is important to remind students that although the Nazis murdered Jews, homosexuals, gypsies, Jehovah's Witnesses, Communists, and others, their first victims were the physically and mentally disabled and that their success in killing these initial targets emboldened them to spread their genocide to other victims whom they considered blemished and physically and genetically inferior. The Nazis began their killing with those they considered to have imperfections and thus were unworthy to be members of the Master Race.

---

14   This moment occurs one hour and six minutes into the film. See Europa, Europa, Director Agnieszka Holland (1990), Film. The clip, entitled "How to Recognize a Jew," is available at https://www.youtube.com/watch?v=drjpLdq9x-s.

Conclusion

In our teaching of "Rappaccini's Daughter" and "The Birth-Mark," we thus stress the connections between the stories, the significance of allegory, and Hawthorne's possible views on scientific experimentation. We focus on distinctions between the application of science for the sake of self-aggrandizement and for the advancement of society and humanity, as well as between the abuse of unethical scientific experimentation and the thirst for knowledge that will help people. The employment of our combined training in literature, the history and philosophy of science, and medical ethics proves beneficial as we lead a provocative, interdisciplinary exploration of Hawthorne's stories. Our use of film and YouTube clips allows students to visualize the arguments and perceive them from other perspectives. Furthermore, we attempt to show our students how Hawthorne's themes transcend time—that the concerns in the stories remain relevant today and perhaps especially to our students. When they realize that these issues affect their lives today, they naturally become more intellectually and emotionally invested as students and citizens in the twenty-first century.

Auburn University at Montgomery

PART 3
INSTITUTIONAL AND INTERNATIONAL CONTEXTS

High School–College Partnerships and the Teaching of Hawthorne

Jason Courtmanche

I was a high school English teacher, and now I teach teachers. Because of this "dual" experience and perception, I recognize that there are significant differences in the training and expectations of high school and college. For instance, as higher education faculty, we are expected to be specialists. Those of us who specialize in Hawthorne have read his letters and notebooks, his children's stories, his nonfiction, his early work, his ghost writing, and his posthumous work. The result is that we possess a detailed knowledge of Hawthorne and his writing. High school English teachers by contrast are expected to be generalists who must cover the entire field in broad ways, and by entire field, I mean not just American but British literature, world literature, genre studies, and often times related fields such as journalism, not to mention skills such as how to read and how to write. This is true even though many high school English teachers around the country do not have undergraduate degrees in their content area. A typical high school English teacher will have read *The Scarlet Letter* in high school and in an undergraduate survey course but then never again.

Taking this into consideration, I would caution us to draw the conclusion that as college professors of English we must disabuse our students of deficiencies caused by their high school English teachers. Instead, I approach the teaching of our students as a shared responsibility, and what I do in my position is develop partnerships between myself and area high school teachers. These partnerships take many different forms and sometimes involve both undergraduate and graduate students as well as the high school teachers and their students. In a typical collaboration, the high school teachers and I will meet to discuss and plan readings and assignments and then develop ideas for visits to each others' classes, guest lectures by me, and, when possible, ways for our students to collaborate. In the most elaborate of these collaborations, high school and college students read several common texts and then communicate electronically. My undergraduates gain practical experience, applying the theories they are studying in my class as they mentor the high school students. I am given the opportunity to keep a finger on the pulse of the high school classroom, and the high school teachers gain the kind of specialized knowledge that university professors possess.

Why Partnerships?

High school-college partnerships are not common. Schools of education engage in them as part of the training of future teachers, but otherwise they are hard to find. But they exist. For example, Richard Kopley, past president of both the Nathaniel Hawthorne Society and the Poe Studies Association and Distinguished Professor of English at Penn State-DuBois, has for thirteen years partnered with his former school, New Rochelle High, to provide guest lectures on American authors that he gives or arranges for others to provide.

Several years ago in Manchester, Connecticut, a high school-college partnership arose from a book challenge. Parents of students at Manchester High School challenged the inclusion of *Adventures of Huckleberry Finn* in the high school English curriculum. Without going into detail about the case, the outcome was that the novel remained on the curriculum but with the provision that teachers had to attend an advanced workshop offered by the Mark Twain House and Museum and co-taught by Education Program Director Craig Hotchkiss, himself a retired teacher, and University of Saint Joseph English Professor Kerry Driscoll, who happens to be a Twain specialist. I have always felt that, although this partnership evolved from a contentious battle, the resolution was positive. For example, Amanda Lister, one of the teachers at the center of the challenge is a former student of mine who is an exceptional teacher. Like Lister, a winner of the Co-Teacher of the Year for her district, other high school teachers lack specialized knowledge of canonical authors such as Hawthorne. Currently, I have five active partnerships at three local high schools, including two at E. O. Smith High School, which is where the University of Connecticut is located, and two at RHAM High School, where I taught for twelve years. I will describe two here, one from each of these schools. At E. O. Smith, I am partnered with my former student, Tiffany Smith, a relatively new teacher who inherited the partnership from Denise Abercrombie, a former Teacher of the Year who was my graduate student. Denise passed this collaboration to Tiffany after Denise became department head. At RHAM High School, I work with Deb Anger, who was my colleague for two years and who now teaches the Advanced Placement American Literature course whose curriculum I wrote.

Email Partnership with E. O. Smith High School

Each spring I teach a class called Advanced Composition for Prospective Teachers, which is a required course for English education students. The students take it during their second semester in the School of Education. At this point in this program, they have only completed one clinical placement in a public school, and this may have been in a lower grade level or outside their content area, so they have had minimal or no contact with students from secondary English classes. The class is capped at nineteen. Approximately fifteen of the students are pursuing dual undergraduate degrees in English and Education, and then I will have four or five additional students, maybe elementary or special education students, pursuing an English degree, or just English majors thinking about going into teaching.

Tiffany and I pair my college juniors with high school sophomores from three sections of academic track American Literature, which means that these students are not likely to attend college, or if they do it will be at a community college. There are two or three high school students assigned to each college student. Early in the semester, Tiffany comes to my class to discuss her students and her course. Likewise, I visit her students and have a similar conversation. Because of scheduling constraints, the students do not meet in person but communicate by email or within a course wiki where they can participate in threaded discussions. We do give the college students an open invitation to contact Tiffany and arrange visits, and when our schedules allow, we make additional visits to each other's classes. The students do meet at the end of the semester.

In preparation, Tiffany and I meet in the fall to discuss books and assignments. Spring semester aligns with her study of Romanticism. She assigns traditional texts such as *The Scarlet Letter,* "Young Goodman Brown," *Walden,* "Resistance to Civil Government," and Emerson's essays such as "The American Scholar." Although in past years the students participating in this partnership have read and discussed *The Scarlet Letter,* in recent years we have focused on the work of Emerson and Thoreau. However, this model of collaboration can be replicated with any author or text—in past years we have read *The Great Gatsby, The Catcher in the Rye,* and *Of Mice and Men*—and so it is worth describing here as a template for a collaborative model. Anyone interested in further research into email partnerships can begin with Carlin Borsheim's "Email Partnerships: Conversations That Changed the Way My Students Read."[1]

Tiffany and I require the college students to serve as reading and writing mentors to the high school students, helping them to think about and discuss the works, to generate ideas for their essays, and then to provide responses to drafts of essays. She generates questions each week that we distribute electronically, and these guide the students' discussions. A similar process takes place with the drafting of essays. Tiffany works with her students to generate topic ideas, which are then shared with my students, and then drafts of essays are exchanged electronically with my students making suggestions for revision. The high school students go to the computer lab once each week to write to their mentors or share drafts of essays, and my students have to respond promptly.

Of course, coordinating such an elaborate collaboration presents challenges. We always wish we could find more opportunities to visit each other's classes and to have the students meet more often. The college students sometimes have to deal with high school students who don't participate effectively, but more often than not, students report that the collaboration is beneficial. The college students comment, "I enjoyed the experience and thought that it really helped to get a concrete grasp on high school students

---

1   Carlin Borsheim, "Email Partnerships: Conversations That Changed the Way My Students Read," *The English Journal* 93, no. 5 (May 2004): 60–65.

and their level of writing," and "I feel like I was actually able to help my students." According to Tiffany, "the email correspondence helps the [high school] students to understand and interpret the readings, and I see a huge improvement in their literary analysis essays from the writing they do earlier in the year." She and I receive mutual benefit from our discussions and also from the third-person point of view we take as we observe our students and their learning processes.

Guest Lecture Partnership with RHAM High School

The partnership I will describe from RHAM High School is different from this partnership at E. O. Smith High School. The main differences are that the high school course is for advanced placement juniors, and the partnership takes place in the fall when I am teaching a survey course in American literature that is not populated by education students but by many students who are not even English majors. As such, this partnership is primarily between me and the high school teacher. Whereas most of my partnerships are with former students, this one is with a former colleague. When I first approached Deb Anger about working together in this capacity, I wanted to find out how she taught Hawthorne's work, and I was also curious about her level of familiarity with Hawthorne's work. I was particularly interested in her attitude and approach toward "The Custom-House," which strikes me as a crucial but neglected text. One of the first things I learned is that, although Deb has been teaching American literature for almost a decade, during that time she has only occasionally required her students to read "The Custom-House" and not at all in recent years. She said that the students found it dense and difficult and felt it was disconnected from the novel. She didn't really disagree with those assessments herself. She generally also required students to read "The Minister's Black Veil" and "Dr. Heidegger's Experiment," which appear in the anthology for the course, but these stories were not tied in any direct way to the study of the novel, other than to point out that they were also written by Hawthorne. Although the curriculum is chronological in design, Deb sometimes teaches *The Crucible* prior to teaching *The Scarlet Letter*. She also teaches a unit on Edgar Allan Poe just prior to the unit on Hawthorne.

A Survey of Teachers

Deb's personal experiences with *The Scarlet Letter* and "The Custom-House" are typical of most high school English teachers. She read the novel in high school and then again as an undergraduate. She could not recall if she had been required to read "The Custom-House." When I surveyed about 200 high school English teachers from across Connecticut, I got similar responses. Of the teachers who replied to my survey, about half had read it both in high school and as an undergraduate, but many had only read it once. Most remarkable of all was that fully a fourth of the respondents had never read the novel until they became teachers and encountered it as a required text in a curriculum. The responses of my undergraduate students were consistent with these replies. Of 19 students, 5 had never been required to read the novel, ten had read it in high school only, and only 4 had read it in both high school and college.

As for "The Custom-House," only a few teachers recall having read it at all. Similarly, only four of my undergraduate students had ever read it. As far as teaching *The Scarlet Letter* and "The Custom-House," only half of the responding teachers said they teach the novel at all, and most of those do not require their students to read "The Custom-House." If they do, typically it is only in advanced classes. As one teacher said, "I did require them to read 'The Custom-House,' but I don't think they got much enjoyment or significance out of it. They seemed bewildered how it connected." Echoing this sentiment, another teacher, recalling her own reading of the novel and "The Custom-House" as an undergraduate said, "I remember not really understanding why 'The Custom-House' was there."

The responses made it clear to me that teachers were caught in a vicious cycle regarding the reading and teaching of *The Scarlet Letter*. Most only read the novel once or twice and often without being required to read "The Custom-House." Then they found themselves with a curriculum that required *The Scarlet Letter*. The best they could do was draw upon their memories from having read the book in high school and perhaps in a college survey course, and because "The Custom-House" wasn't required then, they, too, do not require that it be read. And the cycle repeats itself.

Homework for the Teacher

Deb and I decided to make "The Custom-House" required reading and make a discussion of this work central to the novel as a whole. For her, this meant developing a better understanding of it and its relationship to the novel. The first step was to re-read the whole work. Then we met to talk about it, peer to peer. Our discussion focused on a several things. One was the role of ancestors. Because Hawthorne references his prosecutorial great-great-great and great-great grandfathers,[2] we wanted to emphasize the central role they play. Second, we wanted to capitalize on Hawthorne's early comments about the "autobiographical impulse" (3) that compels him to write this work. Here I felt that requiring students to read Nina Baym's "The Romantic *Malgré Lui*: Hawthorne in 'The Custom-House'"[3] could help them think about ways in which "The Custom-House" and the novel are related. This would also give the students a critical framework for discussing the role of Hawthorne's ancestors, and it would introduce the students to literary criticism, which is often neglected in high school classes, even though the students will typically be required to imitate literary criticism in their essays. Lastly, I suggested revamping the unit's approach to both Hawthorne's short stories and to its relation to the preceding unit on Poe. I suggested we read some different stories from those she had used in the past and to use Poe's "The Fall of the House of Usher"[4] as an explicit complement to the students' reading of "The Custom-House," in order to shed light on the similar ways Hawthorne and Poe use Gothic tropes in their treatment of physical spaces.

Subsequently, I gave Deb several reading assignments. We decided to keep "The Minister's Black Veil," but we tabled "Dr. Heidegger's Experiment" and

---

2 Nathaniel Hawthorne, *The Scarlet Letter* in *The Centenary Edition of the Works of Nathaniel Hawthorne*, vol. I, eds. William Charvat et al. (Columbus: Ohio State University Press, 1974), 9. Subsequent references are to this edition and are parenthetically documented.

3 Nina Baym, "The Romantic *Malgré Lui*: Hawthorne in "The Custom-House," *ESQ: A Journal of the American Renaissance* 19, no. 1 (1973): 14–25. Subsequent references to this essay are parenthetically documented.

4 Edgar Allan Poe, "The Fall of the House of Usher," *The Collected Works of Edgar Allan Poe. Volume II: Tales and Sketches, 1831–1842*, ed. Thomas Mabbott (Cambridge: Harvard University Press, 1979), 392–422.

replaced it with "Young Goodman Brown" and "Rappaccini's Daughter." So those two additions had to be reread. Then Deb read Baym's article as well as Claude Lévi-Strauss's "The Structural Study of Myth,"[5] which I hoped would provide a theoretical framework for the study of patterns between and among the novel, "The Custom-House," Hawthorne's short stories, and Poe's "Usher." These readings became the basis for two lectures I gave her students and ultimately formed the foundation of the class's discussions and the students' final essay.

Guest Lectures

The first lecture, given in September, "The Gothic Tradition in American Literature: Guilt, Ghosts, Haunting, and Proto-Psychology," not only discussed Gothic tropes in the context of Hawthorne and Poe but also situated Hawthorne, in particular, within the trajectory of the Gothic tradition in American literature. This talk focused heavily on "The Custom-House" and on Baym's essay, as well as on "The Fall of the House of Usher." I also made brief mention of the ideas of early psychological theorists like Freud and James and to works by Toni Morrison and William Faulkner, authors the students would be reading later in the year and who clearly fell within the Gothic tradition. The second guest lecture took place in October and was on Structuralism and Hawthorne. In this lecture and following discussion, I focused on the work of Lévi-Strauss, with references to work by Freud[6] and Raymond Williams.[7] These theorists provided me with useful ideas during the writing of my book on Hawthorne,[8] and I wanted to share

---

5   See Claude Lévi-Strauss, "The Structural Study of Myth," *The Critical Tradition: Classic Texts and Contemporary Trends*, ed. David H. Richter (Boston: Bedford/St. Martin's, 1998), 835–44.

6   For specific lecture content, see Sigmund Freud, "The Theme of the Three Caskets," *The Critical Tradition*, 488–94.

7   For my use of Williams, see Raymond Williams, "From *Marxism and Literature*," *The Critical Tradition*, 1153–72.

8   Jason Courtmanche, *How Nathaniel Hawthorne's Narratives Are Shaped By Sin: His Use of Biblical Typology in His Four Major Works* (Lewiston, NY: Mellen, 2008).

this with the students. I walked the students through a banding exercise like that used by Lévi-Strauss in his essay[9] to tease out source myths and narrative patterns within Hawthorne's work. This allowed the students not only to reveal influences and patterns but also to see the transformation of ideas from his early stories such as "Young Goodman Brown" (1835), "The Minister's Black Veil" (1836), and "Rappaccini's Daughter" (1844) as they appear later in *The Scarlet Letter*. For her part, Deb spent about five weeks total on the works of Hawthorne and Poe as part of a larger unit on the Gothic Tradition in American Literature. Her final assignment to her students required them to select and write critical summaries of any three essays from the appendices of the Norton Critical Edition of *The Scarlet Letter*. (This edition, of course, also includes the Baym essay.) Then students were required to use or respond to the critical stance of at least one of those essays in their analysis of the novel. In this way, students learned to apply theory and to imitate literary criticism using actual critical essays as mentor texts.

Benefits to Teachers and Students

Post-collaboration, I interviewed Deb Anger to gauge her assessment of the benefits of our collaboration to her and to her students. She felt that the students benefitted most from three things. First of all, she felt that the structuralist banding exercise offered her students interpretive possibilities that they had not foreseen. Second, she thought that the discussion of Baym's essay alongside a close reading of "The Custom-House" provided insight into the connection between Hawthorne's ancestral biography and the content of *The Scarlet Letter*, as well as insight into his personal and psychological motives for writing the novel. And lastly, she saw benefit in the discussion of the connections between psychology and Gothic tropes, particularly those provided by physical spaces and by ghosts that we looked at in "Usher" and Hawthorne's short stories.

Several students said that the banding exercise helped them see connections between "The Minister's Black Veil" and *The Scarlet Letter* that

---

9 Lévi-Strauss, "The Structural Study of Myth," 840.

they had not considered previously, such as the suggestion that Reverend Hooper and the dead girl may have had an adulterous relationship like that of Dimmesdale and Hester. Deb said, "With 'The Minister's Black Veil,' we had talked about the scandal [prior to your visit], but when you talked about the possibilities of other interpretations of the story, the students were blown away."

In terms of our discussion of "Hawthorne in 'The Custom-House,'" Deb felt that both she and her students developed a better understanding of "The Custom-House" and its relationship to the novel. Several of her students are interested in psychology or are taking AP Psychology, and so Baym's discussion of "psychological autobiography" and "*psychological* imperatives" (14-15), as well as Hawthorne's use of physical spaces such as the attic or the prison to represent phenomena such as repression and guilt, was exciting to the students. She said, "the students loved thinking about the significance of architectural structures as characters and thinking about psychology as something these early authors were kicking around." The reading and discussion of "The Custom-House" also provided a better understanding of how the novel relates to Hawthorne's relationship with his ancestors and how this provided context for the work. According to Deb, the students "liked when you talked about Hawthorne's ancestors. They really came to understand him as a person who was truly trying to reconcile some of the feelings of guilt and trying to reconcile it by channeling it through his writing."

As a teacher, Deb felt that our collaboration helped her develop a new appreciation for "The Custom-House" and its importance to the novel as a whole. She found the attic scenes with the ghost of surveyor Pue to be especially important and plans to continue teaching it from now on. But most importantly, she saw a direct benefit from the collaboration upon the quality of her students' thinking and writing. My lectures and her following discussions helped the students to make better connections among the novel, the stories, "The Custom-House," the work of other authors such as Poe, and the fields of history, biography, and psychology. The inclusion of critical essays was especially helpful. She found that the students had a better understanding of how to take and argue a critical stance as a result of having read and discussed several critical essays: "It was a good experience for them to talk about the stories at such a deep level, and that allowed them to do a really good job with the critical essay."

Conclusions and Recommendations

The testimonials of Tiffany Smith and Deb Anger demonstrate how effective and beneficial high school-college collaboration can be. The high school teachers gain degrees of knowledge that enhance the training they receive in the teaching of literature. The high school students benefit from the expertise of a college professor and, when possible, of undergraduate students who have anywhere from a little to a lot more sophistication in their skills at reading, interpreting, and writing about literature. The college students who participate learn much from mentoring younger students, and this is especially beneficial for those students who are studying to become high school English teachers. The experience helps me to know what incoming high school students are and are not learning about major authors and works of literature, and as such I am better prepared to teach them when they become my students. I also learn about the kinds of advanced training that high school teachers would benefit from, and this helps me to better design the professional development I offer teachers.

There are many ways I would like to improve upon these partnerships. For instance, I would like to do more with the students in my sections of American literature so that my fall semester partnerships could function more like my collaboration with Tiffany Smith's students. To truly apply that model to the sections of American literature, I might need more of my education majors to take the course or perhaps create special sections just for them, but this points to other ideas. My experience with high school-college collaborations suggests that we should be reconsidering the way colleges prepare students to become high school English teachers. Perhaps more courses should be co-listed as English and Education courses, so that pedagogy could be discussed in the context of a literature class. These could even be co-taught by English and Education faculty. To my larger point, more professors should reach out to local high schools. In our case, the University of Connecticut is a public land-grant university and has public outreach within its mission. There is no better way for English professors to reach out to the public than to work with their secondary peers. Rather than blaming the high school teachers when students don't meet our expectations, high school-college partnerships treat the education of our students as a shared mission that benefits everyone involved.

University of Connecticut

The Scarlet Letter in a Community College Composition Course

CHIKAKO D. KUMAMOTO

In his Rede Lecture, "The Two Cultures," delivered at Cambridge University in 1959, C. P. Snow described an unbridgeable cognitive gulf between scientists and nonscientists, resulting in the loss of a common culture in contemporary Western society. For Snow, such gulf and loss were perhaps nowhere seen more clearly than in the discord between scientists and literary intellectuals. Christening this state of affairs "the two cultures," he illustrated his thesis in the following passage:

> A good many times I have been present at gatherings of people who, by the standards of the traditional culture, are thought highly educated and who have with considerable gusto been expressing their incredulity at the illiteracy of scientists. Once or twice I have been provoked and have asked the company how many of them could describe the Second Law of Thermodynamics. The response was cold: it was also negative. Yet I was asking something which is the scientific equivalent of: *Have you read a work of Shakespeare's?*[1]

---

1 Quotations from Snow's lecture are drawn from *The Two Cultures and the Scientific Revolution* (New York: Cambridge University Press, 1961), 15–16.

Setting aside the subsequent controversies his lecture stirred up,[2] Snow here invites a consideration of a unique analytical site wherein college students in the first-year composition course can create a contact zone of a common cognitive culture[3] and compose a new vision of literacy. Especially serendipitous is Snow himself who, both as a man of science and a man of letters, is at home in "the two cultures," while bridging literature represented in Shakespeare and science represented in the Second Law of Thermodynamics. Snow as a model of accord is particularly meaningful for community college students who are invested discretely in traditional liberal arts courses on the one hand and those determined to obtain training for the workforce on the other. Snow can thus encourage these students' two cultures to intersect and cross-fertilize one another.

This premise becomes particularly fruitful in a course dedicated to writing formal, research-based papers in a community college setting. In such a course, students can link their maturing interests in literature to their more utilitarian needs for issue-based projects and critical thinking skills. Deriving from their cultivation of classic literature as a contact zone wherein diverse human lives are critically interpreted on their terms, students can connect literature to their lives in pedagogy and classroom applications. They can foster their good writing with what Ophelia calls Hamlet's "scholar's eye,"[4] i.e., transformative knowledge-making through integrating different texts, information, thinking, and human experiences (abilities equally useful and desirable for both student-humanists and student-careerists in our fast-changing world). In other words, the instructor and students can meet in their mutual endeavor to make sense of literary and nonliterary cultures. This is what the scholar of composition, Cheryl L. Johnson, proposes when she posits that the teacher is actually "the third party," providing "another voice and text to be deciphered" in the dynamics of a contact between the text and its reader.[5] Felicitously revisioning Snow's

---

2   For instance, see F. R. Leavis and Michael Yudkin, *Two Cultures? The Significance of C. P. Snow* (New York: Pantheon, 1963).

3   This concept—a site for complex cultural and cognitive interplay—is adapted from Mary Louise Pratt's essay, "Arts of the Contact Zone," *Profession* 91 (1991): 33–40.

4   William Shakespeare, *Hamlet,* eds. Barbara A. Mowat and Paul Werstine (New York: Washington Square Press, 1992), 133.

5   Cheryl L. Johnson, "Participating Rhetoric and the Teacher as Racial/Gendered Subject," *College English* 56 (1994): 4409.

emphasis on cultural and cognitive continuity in the context of a writing class, Johnson defines the instructor as a cultural agent and as a practicing writer in order to help students negotiate contact zones for their own research-based papers.

Built on this "pedagogy of possibility,"[6] one contact zone I created for students was that of the meeting of Hawthorne's *The Scarlet Letter* and Max Weber's *The Protestant Ethic and the Spirit of Capitalism*. The novel was chosen for various reasons, the first being students' accessibility to Hawthorne's fictional world through their familiarity with the Salem witch trials of 1692. The second was its link to Weber's interpretations of the Calvinist calling, the Protestant work ethic, and capitalism. All of these concepts are worth investigating by students who will soon enter the real world of advanced academic and career pursuits. Last was the discursive attraction of America's mythic origin as Hawthorne re-imagines an early American Puritan society and its sociological phenomena. In it, he offers the prototype of American society that anticipates the functionally inclusive character of several conceptions of individuals and community commented upon by Weber. The novel is a work of fiction about and not a historic document of seventeenth-century New England, but as critics have shown, Hawthorne exhibits his intimate and legitimate knowledge of Puritan history, community dynamics, and religious ethos, while his attitude toward the American Puritans reveals his searching and informed criticism of them.[7] Because of his close family ties to the New England Puritan past, he writes as an insider, a personal status tempered by his sensibility filtered through an artist's ability and freedom. In what Robert Friedrichs calls "the prophetic mode," Hawthorne plays "the sociologist as a critic of society, an engaged, committed scholar who seeks to influence

---

6   The expression is taken from Kay Halesek's *A Pedagogy of Possibility: Bakhtinian Perspectives on Composition Studies* (Carbondale: Southern Illinois University Press, 1999), 115. Hers is a Bakhtin-informed pedagogy with which she reimagines "the writing classroom as a dynamic site of education and intellectual challenge that recognizes both the constraints and possibilities of language in students' struggles to locate themselves in the university . . . and beyond."

7   See Edward Dawson, *Hawthorne's Knowledge and Use of New England History* (Nashville: Joint University Libraries [Vanderbilt University]), 1939; Charles Ryskamp, "The New England Source of *The Scarlet Letter*," *American Literature* 31, no. 3 (November 1959): 257–72.

the future through his analysis of the present."[8] A close reading of the novel's protagonist and related scenes reveals that Hawthorne presages the advent of Weber's "iron cage"[9]—a concept I explain in a moment—and seems to prophesy that the resulting effect of such a society involves the emerging outcasts and outsiders who are paradoxically needed and depended upon for the maintenance of society's integrity and continuance.

No more perfect nexus between Hawthorne's rendering of the Calvinist calling and the ascetic Protestantism defined by Max Weber can be found than in the Hester Prynne who comes to understand herself by reorienting her work ethic in a calling from a strictly religious responsibility to a much more personalized meaningfulness. With this premise, Hawthorne allows Hester to enact Weber's view that "the fulfillment of worldly duties . . . alone is the will of God, and hence every legitimate calling has exactly the same worth in the sight of God" (81). Especially in making her artwork a passport to gain reentry into her community that had rejected her, Hawthorne seems to suggest a way to mitigate the pessimistic future intimated in Weber's "iron cage" metaphor. A brief review of Weber's work can clarify the functional relevancy of the notion of the calling and work ethic for both works.

Throughout his text, Weber argues how the work ethic of Protestant Christianity and the rise of the capitalistic and market economy nurtured each other. In particular, he shows how the Protestant ethos paved the way by encouraging capitalism as a natural expression of it. He goes on to say that modern capitalism required a certain type of personality that matched

---

8   Robert Friedrichs, *A Sociology of Sociology* (New York: Free Press, 1970), 57; *Humanistic Sociology*, ed. John F. Glass and John R. Staude (Pacific Palisade, CA: Goodyear, 1972), xii.

9   Max Weber, *The Protestant Ethic and the Spirit of Capitalism*, trans. Talcott Parsons and introd. Anthony Giddens (New York: Charles Scribner's Sons, 1959), 181. Subsequent citations are to this edition and appear in the text parenthetically. Though I do not foreground this aspect of Weber's sociology here, his brief reflections on the complex interplay between the spheres of art and religion are relevant. See *The Sociology of Religion*, trans. E. Fischoff (Boston: Beacon Press, 1963), 223–24; also, "Religious Rejections of the World and Their Directions" in *Max Weber*, trans. and ed. H. H. Gerth and C. W. Mills (London: Routledge & Kegan Paul, 1948), 323–59. Linking Weber further still to Hawthorne, Hester's art of embroidery, having independent and self-justificatory values, might be viewed as a possible displacement of Puritan religion.

the capitalist enterprise itself—self-discipline, hard work, the careful use of time, the reinvestment of one's gains, personal honesty, creative innovation, and faith in the rewards of a just God, a good exemplar being Benjamin Franklin (48–52).[10] What was also required, though, was a religious ethic that provided for conduct and sanctions for lapses. In Luther's and Calvin's world views, all work from the highest to the lowest was a calling and was sanctified, as opposed to the view that work was punishment for man's sin of disobedience (81–83). The idea of a calling, then, became a moral obligation that projected religious behavior into the workaday world. As Weber suggests, "the valuation of the fulfillment of duty in worldly affairs as the highest form . . . inevitably gave every-day worldly activity a religious significance, and . . . created the conception of a calling" (80). This is the core of Weber's "rational ethics of ascetic Protestantism," and it encourages men to apply themselves rationally to their work. Particularly in terms of Calvinism, "God requires social achievement of the Christian because He wills that social life shall be organized according to His commandments . . . in the interest of the national organization of our social environment" (108, 109).

Toward the end of his book, Weber uses the famous image of the "iron cage," symbolizing a technically ordered, rigid, dehumanized capitalistic society where material wealth will be pursued under institutional constraints. This cage, constructed by human desires themselves but contrary to their original intentions to remodel the world and to work out their Protestant ideals in the world, Weber predicts will trap us within its confines with no exit. The heart of the irony for him is that the "iron cage" results from the rationality-maximized Protestant work ethic gradually losing its original "religious and ethical meaning" and its "spirit of religious asceticism" and the sense of a calling (182). He concludes the book with the following dark prophecy:

> No one knows who will live in this cage in the future, or whether at the end of this tremendous development entirely new prophets will arise, or there will be a great rebirth of old ideas and ide-

---

10 Franklin's more up-to-date model is F. Scott Fitzgerald's Jay Gatsby who emulates Franklin's moral perfection project in Chapter 9 of *The Great Gatsby*. See Floyd C. Watkins, "Fitzgerald's Jay Gatz and Young Benjamin Franklin," in *F. Scott Fitzgerald's The Great Gatsby: A Literary Reference*, ed. Matthew Joseph Bruccoli (New York: Carroll & Graf, 2000), 117–21.

als, or, if neither, mechanized petrification, embellished with a sort of convulsive self-importance. For of the last stage of this cultural development, it might well be truly said: "Specialists without spirit, sensualists without heart; this nullity imagines that it has attained a level of civilization never before achieved." (182)

It was in 1930 that Weber expressed this pessimistic indictment of a capitalistic future dystopia built upon an adulterated practice of the Protestant work ethic and calling. However, more than one hundred years earlier in 1850, Nathaniel Hawthorne had already intuited the inevitable erection of the iron cage on American soil in fictionalizing a community of holy work, John Winthrop's "city on a hill,"[11] supported by Calvinist morality and capitalist ideologies. By anchoring his iron cage in colonial, theocratic Boston, he examines the effects of unchecked male-dominated capitalistic behavior upon the feminine productiveness achieved by the sinner outcast, Hester Prynne. Because she lacks financial support from Chillingworth or Dimmesdale, she must work, relying on her talent in needlework to earn a modest living necessary to support herself and Pearl. Seen within the prism of Hawthorne's particular colonial society, her devotion to needlework can be understood as assigned to a special Calvinist calling translated into a personalized exercise of the Weberian Protestant "spirit of religious asceticism" (181). Her needlework thus renews her calling into a kind of feminized moral capitalism that is necessary for her with economic survival and family's stability.

This shift from the adultery-centered to the sociological construction of Hester complicates her transgression[12] and can be iterated particularly in the chapters "The Governor's Hall," "Hester at Her Needle," and "The Market-Place."[13] Hawthorne's sociological tone is apparent when he suggests Hester's economic liminality by way of physical liminality. "Hester at

11 John Winthrop, "A Model of Christian Charity," in *The Norton Anthology of American Literature*, 3rd ed., ed. Nina Baym, et al. (New York: W.W. Norton, 1983), I, 41.
12 For a similar ideological shift, refer to Myra Jehlen, "The Novel and the Middle Class America," in *Ideology and Classic American Literature*, ed. Sacvan Bercovitch (Cambridge: Cambridge University Press, 1986), 125–44.
13 Nathaniel Hawthorne, *The Scarlet Letter: A Romance*, introd. Nina Baym and notes Thomas E. Connolly (New York: Penguin Books, 1986). Subsequent citations appear in the text parenthetically.

Her Needle" is thus decisive in registering the full range of her marginality with her "small thatched cottage" being located in the border region between city and forest, between the urban and the wild, between haves and have-nots (105–06). As she attempts to become a good mother following her "lapse," however, she is depicted as a self-reliant, self-sufficient earner at the margins of the Puritan iron cage. As a telling signifier of the Calvinist measure of the calling and work ethic, Hawthorne stresses her native traits ("her native energy of character, and rare capacity" [108]), while her needlework makes her self-supporting: "it is certain that she had ready and fairly required employment for as many hours as she saw fit to occupy with her needle" (107). She supplies ceremonial dresses, robes, gloves, bands, and even baby-linen adorned by her embroidery (107).

Just as Weber also discusses the redemptive powers of art over religion, even more important is Hester's artwork that acts as her personal connection between her outcast's state and her reentry into the community, which thrives on its bourgeois values: Hester's "art," and "her delicate and imaginative skill" (106), allow her "to have a part to perform in the world" (108), as she is gradually accepted by the community, and eventually "her handiwork became what would now be termed the fashion" (107). Living on the ethical, social, and economic fringes and plying her calling in needlework, Hester thus "incurred no risk of want. She possessed an art that sufficed, even in a land that afforded comparatively little scope for its exercise, to supply food for her thriving infant and herself" (106). Hawthorne here can be said to portray Hester as one who has made a private covenant of conscience that would highlight the artificiality of her community's economic well-being. Furthermore, Hawthorne juxtaposes Hester's gradual progress in her calling and work ethic with the patriarchal-capitalist economic gains as seen in the sumptuary excess of "The Governor's Mansion." There the duty in one's calling in the holy work for "the New Jerusalem" "prowls about in our lives like the ghost of dead religious beliefs" (240, 182).[14] As if anticipating Weber's dystopia, Hawthorne presents Governor Bellingham as an oligarchical personification of a Puritan success story, while endowing him with many materialist manifestations that Weber attributes to rich capitalists without the true sense of a calling. Indeed, as

---

14 A revisionist view of the mercantile Massachusetts Bay Colony as proving a counterweight to unbridled capitalistic behavior is Stephen Innes's study, *Creating the Commonwealth: The Economic Culture of Puritan New England* (New York: Norton, 1995).

Hester and Pearl walk through his garden to his mansion, he has Hester note Bellingham's failure to reproduce in the hard soil his "native English taste for ornamental gardening" (129); a pumpkin vine "deposited one of its gigantic products directly beneath the hall-windows; as if to warn the Governor that this great lump of vegetable gold was as rich an ornament as New England earth would offer him" (129). Other images of reproductive excess in vegetation suggest unbridled capitalist behavior to denote what Shari Benstock terms "the ability of gold to reproduce itself,"[15] including Bellingham's mansion befitting "Aladdin's palace, rather than the mansion of a grave old Puritan ruler," with its elaborately carved furniture, featuring "wreaths of oaken flowers," in the hallway (126–27).

This seeming incompatibility between Hester's emerging and the community's established notions of a calling and its capitalist applicability, however, deepens as Hawthorne has them interact and converge in ways that make it difficult to discriminate between them. This is because he leaves such notions to work in large part by determining the boundaries of marketability. Folded ambiguously into one another are Hester's private application of a calling and the community's public display of its corruptibility, as seen in the chapter appropriately called "The Market-Place." Hester stands on the punitive marketplace of the scaffold, reduced to a wearer of the letter "A," but Hawthorne has her counter the community's narrow market perspective of the letter with her own new economic epistemology. Embroidering the mark of shame "in fine red cloth, surrounded with an elaborate embroidery and fantastic flourishes of gold thread" (80), she upsets the community's gold standard; the gold thread, more than the letter itself, becomes her means to inscribe and transmit her own assaying of gold to the community.

What the community inflicts on Hester is the hypocrisy and artificiality not only of Puritan morality, however, but also of its economic value system. When she displays the gold-threaded scarlet letter as the very currency of her own worth, she at the same time converts the official valuation of herself into her own sense of person. Fashioning her own figural typology from the community's ready reduction of her to "a [moral] type" (274),

---

15 Shari Benstock, "*The Scarlet Letter* (a)dorée, or the Female Body Embroidered," in *The Scarlet Letter*, ed. Ross C. Murfin (Boston: Bedford Books of St. Martin's Press, 1991), 294. However, I differ from her associative images of excessive reproduction as emblematic of "unrestrained female sexuality."

Hester views the gold-fringed "A" as casting "humanizing doubts"[16] on the economic standard whose unchecked behavior is symbolized by decoration and sumptuary excesses in this community.[17] Her doubts are echoed in the community's valuation also beginning to fluctuate as the female spectators in the crowd begin to doubt the wisdom of her official valuation of her (76 and 78–83). Charles Swann notes that Hester is "more subversive than is usually recognized in that she desires and prophesies a radical subversion of the patriarchal structures of her society."[18]

Weber's "iron cage" concept thus signifies the organizational constraints that would eventually emerge in the capitalist society, killing the spirit of the original Protestant ethic and serving to eviscerate spiritual freedom, selfhood, and creativity. In Hawthorne, the iron cage is the hereditary social conventions and the Puritan values that masquerade as a legitimate system. From the Weberian sociological view, Hester proves that she has illuminated such a system's limitations and unnaturalness while speculating about not only the future human condition but also the economic future:

> though it [her speculation of the patriarchal custom and value system] may keep woman quiet, as it does man, yet makes her sad. She discerns, it may be, such a hopeless task before her. As a first step, the whole system of society is to be torn down, and built up anew. Then, the very nature of the opposite sex, or its long hereditary habit, which has become like nature, is to be essentially modified before a woman can be allowed to assume what seems a fair and suitable position. (184)

Hawthorne seems to prophesy that instead of losing oneself in the iron cage of predestination, one can reinvigorate the Protestant (and Weber's) sense of the calling by forming new social relations on a principle of a different kind of rationality and spirituality developed in homemaking, mothering, concern for others, and the feminine and nurturing aspects of

---

16   Breyten Breytenbach, *End Papers: Essays, Letters, Articles of Faith, Workbook Notes* (New York: Farrar, Straus, & Giroux, 1986), 74.

17   As this section argues, I tend to differ with Nina Baym who regards Hester's turning "the letter into a work of art by gorgeous embroidery" is "fundamentally amoral," in "Passion and Authority in *The Scarlet Letter*," *The New England Quarterly* 43, no. 2 (June 1970): 218.

18   Charles Swann, "Hester and the Second Coming: A Note on the Conclusion of *The Scarlet Letter*," *Journal of American Studies* 21 (1987): 264–68.

human existence. As Hester Prynne is depicted performing such things toward the end of the novel, hers is a social and economic system that allows one person to make an impact on the world:

> Hester comforted and counseled them (people with all their sorrows and), as best she might. She assured them, too, of her firm belief, that, at some brighter period, when the world should have grown ripe for it, in Heaven's own time, a new truth would be revealed, in order to establish the whole relation between men and women on a sure ground of mutual happiness. (275)

As Bakhtin and others have shown,[19] what social outcasts exercise is a perspective from the outside through which they can "see" what the insiders cannot; such is their special epistemology where their minds move transformatively toward epiphanic moments, and whereby civil and religious powers are questioned and even subverted. What Hawthorne seems to suggest is the need for a humanized ethical epistemology beyond the Puritans' rigid capitalistic patriarchal one. Puritans are wrong in reducing individual actions to simplified abstractions or objects, such as "sin" or "adultery" or the rigid duality of good and evil. The act of the heart is infinite, irreducible, complex, and full of possibilities. To exemplify this truth is Hester's role as an outcast, and this is the reason why the community "could not entirely cast her off" (108).

As seen from Weber's point of view, Hawthorne's classical work both presents and prophesies about contemporary American society by hinting that our effort to achieve a well-integrated society could lead to tragedy. The social principles of contemporary American society, like those of the Puritans, are laudable in their mythic idealism but often become in reality an antithesis to the original aspirations. Perhaps a full realization of the potential of human society may be accomplished through Hester's vision of "the whole system of society . . . torn down, and built up anew." For me,

---

19 For discussions on epistemological powers of outcasts or outsiders, refer to Mikhail Bakhtin, "Response to the Question from the *Novy Mir* Editorial Staff," in *Speech Genres and Other Late Essays*, ed. Caryl Emerson and M. Holquist (Austin: University of Texas Press, 1986), 1–7; Michel Foucault, *The Order of Things: An Archaeology of the Human Sciences*, reprint (New York: Vintage, 1994); and Julia Kristeva, *Powers of Horror: An Essay on Abjection*, trans. Leon S. Roudiez (New York: Columbia University Press, 1982).

the Snow-inspired instructional approach to Hawthorne, aided by Weber, could not be more apt than in the heterogeneous, vocationalist-privileging classroom of the community college. I therefore encourage students to expand and enlarge their minds in the context of immediate practical issues, geographical boundaries, and cultural sovereignty.[20]

College of DuPage

---

20 John Henry Newman, *The Idea of a University*, ed. Frank M. Turner (New Haven: Yale University Press, 1996), 99.

Hawthorne's Demanding Skepticism

T. Gregory Garvey

In "Earth's Holocaust," a sketch published by *Graham's Magazine* in the spring of 1844, Hawthorne parodies the reformist spirit that characterized his New England. In this story, reformers create a bonfire onto which people come to throw the "worn-out trumpery" of the world. Every now and then a dissenting voice pipes up to express skepticism, but it is quickly hooted down by the utopian enthusiasts. The reformers begin with politics. They throw all symbols of aristocracy and hereditary rank onto the fire. This affirmation of democracy leads to the immolation of liquor, then of titles to private property, the gallows, guillotines, and weapons of all sorts. Soon, the crowd starts to burn books. Finally, they burn Bibles. Midway through, when a skeptic demurs as the pacifists are throwing armaments onto the fire, the narrator gets so caught up in the fervor that he confronts the onlooker:

"Why, Sir, . . . do you imagine that the human race will ever so far return on the steps of its past madness, as to ever weld another sword, or cast another cannon?"

"There will be no need," observed, with a sneer, one who neither felt benevolence, nor had faith in it. "When Cain wished to slay his brother, he was at no loss for a weapon."[1]

---

1 Nathaniel Hawthorne, "Earth's Holocaust," *Mosses from an Old Manse* in *The Centenary Edition of the Works of Nathaniel Hawthorne*, vol. X, ed. William

At the time Hawthorne published "Earth's Holocaust," utopian pacifism was more than just an idealistic dream. After the Napoleonic Wars ended in 1815, Peace Societies sprang up in both the United States and Britain. They promoted basic human rights, disarmament, international arbitration, and laws curbing the power of monarchs to conscript subjects into dynastic wars.[2] Ralph Waldo Emerson addressed a meeting of the Peace Society in Boston in 1838 and despite his reservations about most reform associations, he heartily endorsed the Peace Movement: "It is not a great matter how long men refuse to believe the advent of peace: war is on its last legs; and the universal peace is as sure as is the prevalence of civilization over barbarism, of Liberal governments over feudal forms. The question for us is only *How soon?*"[3]

Hawthorne was far too skeptical, however, about progress to embrace such an inevitability. His point of view in many respects is more like that of the skeptic in "Earth's Holocaust" than it is that of the narrator who embraces the reforms. He had deep reservations about the reformers' ability to improve long-standing institutions. He suspected both their motives and their actual ability to overcome the power of historical inertia. This skepticism extended to his attitude toward the positive or cognitive faculties of human beings. He questioned people's ability to understand accurately the causes and implications of events in the world. He was also doubtful that new institutions, crafted by human willfulness and embodying the self-satisfied virtue of the reformers, would not also introduce ills that canceled out the gains they intended.

From its origins in ancient Greece, skepticism has provided a kind of rigor to substantive moral questions about good and evil and, more abstractly, to epistemological questions about cognition and perception. To be skeptical of something is not to reject it. Rather, it is to call the

---

Charvat, Roy Harvey Pearce, and Claude M. Simpson (Columbus: Ohio State University Press, 1974), 391. All subsequent citations from Hawthorne texts are taken from this twenty-three volume series and documented by respective volume and page number.

2   David Cortright, *Peace: A History of Movements and Ideas* (New York: Cambridge University Press, 2008), 49; Wilhelmus Hubertus van der Linden, *The International Peace Movement, 1815-1874* (Amsterdam: Tilleul Publications, 1987), 61ff.

3   Ralph Waldo Emerson, *The Complete Works of Ralph Waldo Emerson*, ed. E. W. Emerson, 12 vols. (Boston: Houghton Mifflin, 1903-04), 11:189.

foundations, usefulness, or value of a proposition into question. In terms of morality, it asks if structural or institutional change ever really gets at the cause of a social problem. In terms of perception it mistrusts the foundations of a practice or the motivation that is assumed to drive a proposed reform.[4] In both forms, skepticism is characterized by a strong suspicion of moral or epistemological certainty. The single-mindedness of Hawthorne's Hollingsworth, the moral assurance of his Puritans, and the confidence of the scientists, Aylmer and Rappaccini, represent a standard of certainty that is anathema, even dangerous, from the skeptic's point of view. Unless those who seek to make the world a better place, the skeptic of "Earth's Holocaust" contends, unless they "hit upon some method of purifying that foul cavern," the human heart, "forth from it will re-issue all the shapes of wrong and misery—the same old shapes, or worse ones."[5]

For purposes of literary interpretation, skepticism represents an intentional self-consciousness about the limitations of human perception and of the weaknesses that might cause one to do harm when one is trying to do good. More than a standard of humility about human powers, it is an ethic that requires individuals always to leave themselves some flexibility in interpretation and always to allow a pathway to turn a conclusion back on itself in order to establish new and more sensitive standards of observation or behavior. Thus, even as the skeptic is always saying, "not so fast, we are not done looking at this," he or she is also seeking grounds to speak in affirmative and sympathetic terms. For Hawthorne, skepticism did not imply an absence of sympathy for people's efforts to be good and to do good.[6]

---

4   Academic analysis of skepticism is often divided between an ancient tradition in which skepticism revolved around suspicion about belief systems and explicitly ideological structures, and a modern skepticism that is focused on challenging our abilities to know, perceive, and interpret accurately. See Myles Burnyeat, *The Skeptical Tradition* (Berkeley: University of California Press, 1983); Neil Gascoigne, *Scepticism* (Montreal: McGill-Queen's University Press, 2002). A. C. Grayling develops recent epistemological skepticism in *Scepticism and the Possibility of Knowledge* (New York: Continuum, 2008). David Hiley situates skepticism in the American political tradition in *Doubt and the Demands of Democratic Citizenship* (New York: Cambridge University Press, 2006).
5   Hawthorne, 10:403.
6   Sympathy is a central issue in Hawthorne criticism, see especially Brook Thomas, "Love and Politics, Sympathy and Justice in *The Scarlet Letter*," 162-85; Robert S. Levine, "Sympathy and Reform in *The Blithedale Romance*," 207-29; and Emily Miller Bidick, "Perplexity, Sympathy, and the Question of the

Indeed, his sympathy for the weakness, vanity, even hubris of behavior is a product of his skepticism because it serves as a continual challenge to see and understand how and why human endeavors fail. As Judith Shklar suggests, "There was in Hawthorne's moral world, only one supreme vice: cruelty."[7] To cause suffering intentionally is unforgivable, but to cause it unintentionally or even obliviously is simply the human condition.

Hawthorne's skepticism about people's positive powers leads him to treat weakness and failure with deep recognition and even respect. Arthur Dimmesdale in his vanity and cowardice is probably the best-known example of the sympathy Hawthorne extends to weakness, but the eponymous character of "Roger Malvin's Burial," a very early story and a kind of antecedent to Dimmesdale, is perhaps its purest example. After a battle in the wilderness, Reuben Bourne accepts the entreaty of the mortally wounded Roger Malvin, his future father-in-law, to leave him in the wilderness in order to save his own life. When Bourne returns to the settlement, his betrothed assumes he had stayed with her father until the end. He never tells her the truth. Shame and guilt wreck his life, but though Hawthorne unflinchingly acknowledges Bourne's failure, he does not excoriate or even condemn him. On the contrary, he explores the motives for his catastrophic omission and the burden he carried through life. Rather than a fable demonstrating the virtues of integrity and the dangers of its failure, "Roger Malvin's Burial" is a skeptic's articulation of the gap between ideals of character and the facts of human weakness.

Emphasizing this quality in Hawthorne's writing, his skepticism about human powers and the sympathy that it produces, is useful in a variety of classroom settings. On the most basic level in surveys of literature or American literature, his skepticism serves as a contrarian voice that challenges the narratives of courses built around processes of historical change. Second, in gateway courses for students entering the English

---

major, Hawthorne's over-determined structures combined with his epistemological restraint offer a platform on which to train students in rigorous close reading and structural analysis. Finally, in research-oriented courses, Hawthorne's resistance to progressive social reform and his skepticism even about the equality of all human beings force students to address important complexities not only in antebellum American culture but also in the relationship between literary representation and social change more generally.

Progress and Skepticism

"My Kinsman, Major Molineux" exemplifies the way Hawthorne's skepticism about the motivations that underpin historical change can add depth to introductory-level survey courses. This story conflates elements of late-Puritan society with those of the Revolutionary period, but it is also quite clearly a metaphor for democratization in Jacksonian America. "My Kinsman" articulates ambivalence about majoritarian democracy in much the same way that "Earth's Holocaust" expresses skepticism about social reform. Following its protagonist from idealism to cynicism, it juxtaposes the terms of a personal relationship against the political antagonism of the Boston community. We hardly meet Major Molineux, but we get a clear image of his connection to his nephew Robin. Pride, admiration, anticipation, even the incipient snobbery and arrogance that go with Robin's ego, reveal themselves as he wends his way through town in search of his kinsman. As his journey is being narrated, Major Molineux is being tortured. When the story finally reaches its climax, the townsmen roar with laughter. By the time the Major is displayed "in his tar-and-feathery dignity" on an open cart lighted by torches, everybody is in on the joke. Not only have they brought low the representative of Royal authority, but they have also participated in a conspiracy of silence at the expense of the Grandee's country-bumpkin nephew.

What about the Major? We only catch a glimpse of him as he is paraded in pain and humiliation. The leader of the mob, a figure who embodies the self-assured power Hawthorne also represents in the Gray Champion or in Endicott as he stands over the ruins of Merrymount, is the devilish townsman Robin had encountered colluding at the Inn. As the torchlight procession passes, he stops the procession to show Robin its trophy. Major Molineux

> was an elderly man, of large and majestic person, and strong, square features, betokening a steady soul; but steady as it was, his enemies had found the means to shake it. His face was pale as death, and far more ghastly; the broad forehead was contracted in his agony, so that his eyebrows formed one grizzled line; his eyes were red and wild, and the foam hung white upon his quivering lip. His whole frame was agitated by a quick, and continual tremor, which his pride strove to quell, even in those circumstances of overwhelming humiliation. But perhaps the bitterest pang of all was when his eyes met those of Robin; for he evidently knew him on the instant.[8]

Hawthorne presents the terror, agony, and disgrace of this victim in completely realistic terms. He is offstage for most of the action and thus has no role in the Bostonians' sly diversions that precede the parade. As brief as it is, the passage of Major Molineux through Robin's line of sight transforms the implications of this story. If democracy means laughing at that kind of suffering, if it can even include poor Robin in the joke, how good can it be? Robin's aspirations, both his and his kinsman's sense of pride, and their sense of individual selfhood stand in sharp contrast to the democratic and often demonic revelries in the street.

The challenge Hawthorne offers in "My Kinsman, Major Molineux" revolves around the exchange of tradition and personal intimacy for the majoritarian will of impersonal mass politics. For survey courses built around the representation of specific social issues that change over time, "My Kinsman" and "Earth's Holocaust" are representative of a skeptical perspective on the efficacy of that change. This same perspective characterizes Hawthorne's representations of Puritanism and science. In a course built around a value such as equality or liberty, the tension such as the relation of technology to individuality, or of gender to authority, his reservations about democracy, science, and social reform, among other topics, imply a counter narrative that allows students to think about and weigh the potential costs of social change. Hawthorne is not nostalgic—he

8   11:228-29.

tends to be sarcastic about nostalgia—and he is not usually reactionary, but he is acutely sensitive to the unanticipated implications of the social and political changes he sees taking place around him. Change is certain. Progress is not. In the arc of a survey course, paired with texts such as *The Autobiography of Benjamin Franklin* or "Song of Myself," a story such as "My Kinsman, Major Molineux" raises vital questions about the dynamics of social change and its implications for the way individuals relate to one another.

Skepticism, Allegory, and Form

Where Hawthorne's skepticism about the relationship between social change and social progress can challenge the historical narratives that drive many survey classes, his careful structural symmetries combined with the ambiguities that attend his descriptions of motivations and events are useful in helping students learn the basic analytical skills that will raise the specificity and rigor of their close reading. His "inveterate love of allegory," as he puts it early in "Rappaccini's Daughter," allows him to disconnect his own representations from empirical contexts. This porous back and forth between realistic referentiality and allegory does much to shape the structure of Hawthorne's novels. For example, in the scene at Governor Bellingham's house in *The Scarlet Letter*, the intense, high-stakes threat to Hester's custody of Pearl stands in an uncomfortable juxtaposition with the allegorical play of Pearl's taunt that she had not been made at all, but been "plucked by her mother off the bush of wild roses, that grew by the prison door."[9] On the most accessible level, this juxtaposition represents the tension between natural relationships and the conventions of Puritan society. In connection to Hawthorne's allegorical structures, however, juxtapositions like this one allow for exercises that not only facilitate students' ability to build from simple to more complex analyses, but it also compels them to determine the limits of plausible interpretations.

The Scarlet Letter is a novel about secrets, and thus, much is hidden about motives and relationships. At its very center is a public secret,

9   1:112.

Hester's, as well as a private secret, Dimmesdale's. Also, much of the pressure on the narrative comes from the secret Hester and Chillingworth keep from Dimmesdale. Hawthorne slowly unpacks the effects of these secrets as Hester, Dimmesdale, and Chillingworth move between private and public spaces. In its geography, *The Scarlet Letter* revolves around the scaffold that rises in the center of the market square. The scaffold functions to bring things into public view for display and normative judgment. It has manifold symbolic and ideological referents, but for the purpose of training students in the skills of literary analysis, it serves as a metaphor for the process of revelation that incrementally makes things accessible. Hawthorne articulates the secrets of *The Scarlet Letter* within a structure of careful symmetries built around this site of public exposure.

Asking students to map elements of the narrative through the table of contents helps students to recognize how Hawthorne's narrative eye moves from relationship to relationship. Of course, this exercise can only be done after students have read the whole novel and presumably, have studied many passages in isolation. Focusing the mapping exercise on locations or on the characters that dominate a chapter often provokes a tumult of associations; students pair chapters, articulate structural tensions, remark on chapters that manipulate romantic and realistic elements. Discussing the broad movement of the narrative from the center of town to the outskirts, from a chapter devoted to Chillingworth to one devoted to Dimmesdale, to chapters focused on Hester's relations with each of them, makes the architecture of the narrative vivid and, in effect, brings the structure of *The Scarlet Letter* onto the scaffold for analysis. And as students think and talk about this map, they return to key passages that they have addressed in earlier discussions and develop their readings more fully. Returning to these passages with a stronger command of the over-all structure of the novel helps students see ambiguities in a broader context and understand the real limitations of interpretation. Once the text is thoroughly mapped, virtually any passage that has been addressed in earlier class discussion becomes a site for more rigorous close readings that reveal Hawthorne's epistemological skepticism, especially as he intertwines allegory with realistic representation.

Asking students to return to scenes and passages that they have previously studied but are now equipped with an anatomizing structural scheme helps them situate Hawthorne's complexities, refusals, aversions, and resistances within a broader referential context. For example, it allows them to follow a path like that taken by Sacvan Bercovitch in which the relationships between the "A" and the society are paramount. In this context, the chapters that deal with Hester in solitude and Hester in Boston stand out as especially important because in Bercovitch's reading the novel is about the normalizing "office" of the scarlet letter. On the other hand, if students choose to follow a path that emphasizes the personal and ethical connections between the major characters, as Clark Davis does, then the chapters that present dialogues between Hester, Dimmesdale, and Chillingworth take on a heightened importance, and the scaffold becomes a metaphor not for the power of civil authority, as it is for Bercovitch, but rather for the intersection of conflicted personal relationships.[10] Hawthorne's epistemological skepticism leads him to maintain very tight control over his narratives. The mysteries he slowly reveals work within the structural dynamics that students can grasp and use to raise the standards of their close reading skills.

Skepticism and Hawthorne's Politics

Larry J. Reynolds concludes that Hawthorne "joined the utopian Brook Farm community at West Roxbury, Massachusetts, devoting himself for a time to the success of the project, though he was certain it would fail."[11] Judith Shklar, puzzled by a skeptic who spent so much of his life in social circles made up of radical reformers and outright utopians, reaches the similarly ambiguous conclusion that even though Hawthorne never truly believed in the Brook Farm project, he "never regretted his stay at Brook Farm and did not in the least care whether he had seemed ridiculous in trying the experiment."[12] Though there are many avenues open to students interested in pursuing research on his fiction, the combination of sympathy for the objectives of social reformers and deep skepticism that their objectives can be achieved makes for unique challenges

---

10   Sacvan Bercovitch, *The Office of the Scarlet Letter* (Baltimore: Johns Hopkins University Press, 1991); and Clark Davis, *Hawthorne's Shyness: Ethics, Politics, and the Question of Engagement* (Baltimore: Johns Hopkins University Press, 2005), 62-73.
11   *Oxford Historical Guide to Nathaniel Hawthorne*, ed. Larry J. Reynolds (New York: Oxford University Press, 2001), 6.
12   Shklar, *Redeeming American Political Thought*, 38.

to the student-scholar. For courses designed to develop research skills, Hawthorne's skepticism serves as a form of provocation. In his tendency to present compelling motives and justifications for social change but then to complicate them with reservations and objections, he frames carefully contextualized research problems for historical and theoretical analysis. Above all, his politics raise the question: how can one who is so sensitive to suffering also be so politically passive? In a recent article analyzing Miles Coverdale, Michael Borgstrom observes that "much recent scholarship focuses on the challenges Hawthorne's personal and political values pose for contemporary readers of his work. His evident endorsement of racial hierarchies, his cynicism toward social reform movements, his anti-Semitic observations, and his overriding belief that women and men should not have equal access to cultural power" would all seem to undermine his continuing claim to critical respect.[13] In perhaps his most infamous statement on slavery, for example, Hawthorne remarked that wisdom "looks upon slavery as one of these evils which divine Providence does not leave to be remedied by human contrivances, but which, in its own good time, by some means impossible to be anticipated, but of the simplest and easiest operation, when all its uses shall have been fulfilled, it causes to vanish like a dream."[14]

In advanced courses, mentoring a student doing research on a topic that contextualizes Hawthorne's representations of gender, reform movements, or patterns of historical change is a different thing than directing a student in doing research on Frederick Douglass, Harriet Beecher Stowe, Henry David Thoreau, or many of his contemporaries. The complexity of Hawthorne's participation in politics, especially his complex friendships with people as diverse as the Transcendentalist, Margaret Fuller, and John L. O'Sullivan, leader of the Young America movement, creates a cultural perspective that requires students to take his ambivalences into account. On the one hand, Hawthorne himself was a political party man and his writing explicitly engages with political life. It deals with political figures such as John Winthrop and Governor Bellingham in *The Scarlet Letter* and political aspirants such as Judge Pyncheon in *The Blithedale Romance*. Tales such as "The Maypole of Merrymount," and "The Gray Champion,"

---

13 Michal Borgstrom, "Hating Miles Coverdale," ESQ: A Journal of the American Renaissance 56, no. 4 (2011):366.
14 5:417.

among others, deal with explicit political confrontations. The civil institutions of society past and present are central to his narratives.

On the other hand, he is even more interested in representing "the truth of the human heart" as he puts it in the preface to *The House of the Seven Gables*. What thereby results is a confrontation between his skeptical understanding of human capabilities and the institutions that people create to shape their lives. In this confrontation, his skepticism, his refusal to trust positive cognitive powers, or to assume that we can understand our motivations and control their consequences, restrains him from embracing a politics that actively seeks progressive institutional change and that often condemns the good will of the philanthropist. In *Blithedale*, Coverdale demurs: "The besetting sin of a philanthropist, it appears to me, is apt to be a moral obliquity.... At some point of his career—I know not exactly when or where—he is tempted to palter with the right, and can scarcely forbear persuading himself that the importance of his public ends renders it allowable to throw aside his private conscience."[15] In a letter returning an antislavery pamphlet that his sister-in-law had written, Hawthorne expresses the same skepticism about self-awareness: "No doubt it seems the truest of the truth to you; but I do assure you that like every other Abolitionist, you look at matters with an awful squint, which distorts everything within your line of vision; and it is queer, though natural, that you think everybody squints except yourselves. Perhaps they do; but certainly *you* do."[16]

This skepticism about the opacity of perception, however, does not mean that Hawthorne preferred the status quo. Hester Prynne at one point surveys the world and finds it so unjust that she thinks about murdering Pearl. "Was existence worth accepting, even to the happiest" woman, she asks? In order to make life worth living, the world will have to be radically transformed: "As a first step, the whole system of society is to be torn down, and built up anew. Then, the very nature of the opposite sex, or its long hereditary habit, which has become like nature, is to be essentially modified, before woman can be allowed to assume what seems a fair and suitable position. Finally, all other difficulties being obviated, woman cannot take advantage of these preliminary reforms, until she herself shall have undergone a still mightier change."[17] Hawthorne describes these thoughts to

---

15   3:132
16   Hawthorne to Elizabeth Palmer Peabody, August 13, 1857, 18:89.
17   1:165.

reveal the effect of ostracism on Hester's thinking, but given her experience, these radical proposals are neither disproportionate nor unreasonable.

The tension between Hawthorne's sympathetic recognition of the price of cruelty and his refusal to embrace progressive social goals invites students studying connections between literary texts and social circumstances to address his skepticism. This means asking students to relate the specific human qualities, the "squints" and "moral obliquity," that drive Hawthorne's skepticism toward the reformers among whom he lived . Making this connection requires more than situating him within historical cultural debates. It asks students to think about social change as the acts of individuals rather than as the progress of movements. It invites students to think about events such as the schisms over women's participation that divided both the temperance and the antislavery movements. It offers a new perspective on racism within the antislavery movement and on the incompatibility of benevolent movements with bigotry, elitism, and condescension. At the beginning of *The Blithedale Romance*, Coverdale frames the issue of social change in a way that captures Hawthorne's complex attitude toward projects of social reform. Plunging "into the heart of the pitiless snowstorm" in search of utopia, he reminisces: "The better life! Possibly, it would hardly look so, now; it is enough if it looked so, then. The greatest obstacle to being heroic, is the doubt whether one may not be going to prove one's self a fool; the truest heroism is, to resist the doubt—and the profoundest wisdom, to know when it ought to be resisted, and when to be obeyed."[18] This is a particularly sensitive statement of Hawthorne's skepticism not only because of its tragic disillusionment but because it shows Coverdale trying to get back inside his own head, trying to see the world again from the point of view he had before Zenobia's death, Hollingsworth's refusal of friendship, and his own return to isolation. He orients himself in relation to a kind of wisdom that does not rule out confidence or even utopian idealism but that nonetheless expresses the resistance of Hawthorne's demanding skepticism.

The College at Brockport: State University of New York

18   3:10.

A Post-Nationalist Approach to Teaching Hawthorne

Ivonne M. García

In my twice-weekly, single-author, senior seminar on Nathaniel Hawthorne, I begin class discussion on *The Scarlet Letter* by asking the students to state the year in which the novel was published. By that moment in the semester, about the fifth week, students already know that I expect them to take note of publication dates and to locate the works within Hawthorne's historical and biographical contexts. Students are able to do this easily because, in addition to Hawthorne's major short stories, novels, and essays, as well as literary criticism about his works, I assign Brenda Wineapple's 2003 biography, *Hawthorne: A Life*. Thus, I'm not surprised when I hear a few "1850" answers around the seminar table. When I press them some more, however, inquiring about major historical events in or around 1850 that would help us further contextualize the novel, a deafening silence ensues. Students fidget and glance nervously at each other to see whether anyone can answer the question. One student ventures cautiously: "The Civil War?" "No," I say, struggling to conceal my concern that many college juniors and seniors, some of whom attended the best high schools in the United States, cannot name a single antebellum event. Finally, one student tentatively offers: "There was some sort of compromise over slavery?" "Yes!" I exclaim, relieved that at least one in about a dozen students can answer the question. This scene, which always reminds me of Santayana's warning against forgetting the past, recurs each time I teach

Hawthorne. In fact, it happens *any* time I teach early or nineteenth-century U.S. American literature.

Given the lack of basic historical knowledge most students demonstrate when stepping into the college classroom, situating Hawthorne within historical frameworks—biographical, national, and global—becomes a pedagogical imperative. This chapter describes how a post-nationalist approach, based on the premise that the nineteenth-century construct of an "American" identity was (as it continues to be) inextricably connected to national and global contexts, significantly enhances the teaching of Hawthorne's works. The development of an American national identity, a concept that both fascinated and concerned Hawthorne, developed within his lifetime in step with historical events that included the Atlantic slave trade, the expansion of slavery to newly acquired territories, the clashes with and dispossession of Native Americans, the war with Mexico, and the Civil War, to name only a few.[1] In my seminar, we seek to locate Hawthorne as an artist not only within his biographical story but also within national and transnational narratives related to the key events that marked him and the nation.

This essay argues that Hawthorne's focus on literary historicity provides an important reason why we should read and analyze his works when trying to understand nineteenth-century American culture and nation formation. In describing how a post-nationalist pedagogical approach to Hawthorne might be structured, this essay focuses on methods for reading, understanding, and teaching a selection of his works. For the sake of conciseness, I will discuss strategies for analyzing "Young Goodman Brown" (1836), "Rappaccini's Daughter" (1844), *The Scarlet Letter* (1850), and *The Marble Faun* (1860). The seminar itself, however, covers nine of the short stories published between 1835 and 1846, the five finished novels, "The Old Manse" (1846) and "Chiefly about War Matters" (1862), and concludes with the extant portions of "The Dolliver Romance" (1864). We also watch and analyze two film adaptations, the infamous 1995 *Scarlet Letter* with Demi Moore, and the 2010 film *Easy A*. In addition, we read critical essays on each work, as well as early criticism by Henry Wadsworth Longfellow, Edgar Allan Poe, Herman Melville, and Henry James. This essay's goal is to present some ways to successfully introduce students to Hawthorne by

---

1 Brinson Curiel, et al. Introduction, in *Post-Nationalist American Studies*, ed. John Carlos Rowe (Berkeley: University of California Press, 2000), 3.

connecting him not only to his own time but also to our own through his significant contribution to foundational national narratives.

In linking Hawthorne's own life and writings to the development of an "American" identity in the nineteenth century, the course contextualizes his works within local and global frameworks. Taking this approach, the class identifies the personal, familial, national, and transnational narratives that form the scaffolding of his works so that students can pinpoint the cultural building blocks that his narratives promote and/or challenge. In particular, we are interested in categories of representation that include gender, race, sexuality, national identity, and socio-economic class. In the introduction to the 2000 *Post-Nationalist American Studies*, edited by John Carlos Rowe, the collection's authors explain that "The post-nationalist is not a new critical practice; it builds upon previous work, within and outside American Studies, that is critical of U.S. hegemony and the constructedness of both national myths and national borders." Because this approach has traditionally "questioned dominant American myths rather than canonized them," it is a critical framework particularly well suited to teaching Hawthorne, who also trained his critical eye on himself, his family, and on the foundational myths of his nation.[2]

Because the focus is post-nationalist, I want students to consider how and why Hawthorne inserted portions of his own notebooks, where he kept a record of his thoughts and ideas, and recreated events in his and his family's lives in his fiction. I also want them to move beyond the biographical (this prevents the simplifying move of noting something as significant solely because it relates to the author's life). With a more focused purpose in mind, I encourage students to examine the ways in which Hawthorne contributed to and questioned the discourses of nineteenth-century U.S. imperialism. As post-nationalist scholar Amy Kaplan has noted, "imperialism has been simultaneously formative and disavowed in the foundational discourse of American studies."[3] In the introduction to the 1993 "New Americanist" edited collection, *Cultures of United States Imperialism*, Kaplan notes "the absence of culture from the history of U.S. imperialism; the absence of empire from the study of American culture; and the absence

---

2   Ibid.
3   Amy Kaplan, "'Left Alone with America': The Absence of Empire in the Study of American Culture," in *Cultures of U.S. Imperialism*, ed. Amy Kaplan and Donald E. Pease (Durham, NC: Duke University Press, 1993), 5.

of the United States from the postcolonial study of imperialism."[4] My seminar turns absence into presence by locating Hawthorne's work within the narrative history of U.S. empire formation.

Before we embark on a textual discovery of Hawthorne, students must understand what we mean by cultural analysis, the larger theoretical umbrella under which a post-nationalist approach operates. To this end, I provide the students with key terms and definitions that become the terminology we use in the class throughout the semester when analyzing Hawthorne's texts. Excerpting from Stuart Hall's 1997 textbook, *Representation*, I provide a handout that defines important terminology, including words like "culture," "representation," "meaning," "signs and signification," "discourse," "The Other," and "cultural codes" associated with representational categories. For example, Hall defines culture as

> a set of practices that produce and enable the exchange of meanings between members of a society or group. It is about feelings, attachments and emotions as well as concepts and ideas or artifacts (novels, paintings, etc.). It organizes and regulates social practices, influencing our conduct and manifesting itself in real, practical ways. Culture is produced and consumed and it helps regulate and promote social conduct.[5]

Once we have gone over these definitions in class, I ask the students to consider how social practices influence and regulate their own conduct, especially in college. Students discuss unwritten rules about using cell phones in public spaces or how to deport themselves in the college dining hall. They also discuss larger social mores within the campus that apply to race, gender, and sexuality, among others.

On the second day, using these terms as our lens, we examine two of Hawthorne's earliest and most well-known short stories, "Young Goodman Brown" and "The Minister's Black Veil." We begin doing board work, drawing on the lists I have asked them to prepare as homework, based on their own close readings of the stories. In those lists, I have asked them to identify and come to class prepared to discuss the categories of representation

---

4   Ibid., 11.
5   Stuart Hall, ed., *Representation: Cultural Representations and Signifying Practices* (London: Sage Publications Ltd., 1997), 6.

they found in common between the stories as well as those particular to each. Students comment, for instance, on the isolation of both male protagonists due to their distrust and rejection of societal conventions. In the first story and after his experience overnight in the forest with the devil, Young Goodman Brown becomes a "stern, a sad, a darkly meditative and distrustful, if not a desperate, man," who perceives unredeemable sin in everyone else.[6] Similarly, Mr. Hooper's "piece of crape" or the black veil he dons inexplicably one day "had separated him from cheerful brotherhood and woman's love, and kept him in the saddest of all prisons, his own heart" (105). In attempting to discover the significance of these similarities, we draw from Wineapple's biography, which describes how Hawthorne, who at 31 years old was still living largely secluded at home with his mother and sisters, "began to withdraw upon himself."[7] We ask ourselves what kinds of cultural meanings are promoted and challenged by these stories? Why is it significant that these male protagonists retreat from their societies for what the stories suggest are prideful reasons? (Do they feel they are better than their communities?) How do the "cultural codes" embedded in Hawthorne's prose attempt to "organize and regulate" or to interrogate social practices both at the time the story's plot develops and at the time of its publication?

When analyzing "Young Goodman Brown," in particular, students are struck by the fact that Hawthorne invests his protagonist with his own family history, specifically that of his grandfather and great-grandfather. For one, the devil tells Goodman Brown that he

> has been well acquainted with your family as with every a one among the Puritans; and that's no trifle to say. I helped your grandfather the constable, when he lashed the Quaker woman so smartly through the streets of Salem; and it was I that brought your father a pitch-pine knot, kindled at my own hearth, to set fire to an Indian village, in King Philip's war (67).

Students are intrigued by the reciprocity between history and fiction, which the Norton editor of his tales highlights by noting how Hawthorne's

---

6   Nathaniel Hawthorne, "Young Goodman Brown," in *Nathaniel Hawthorne's Tales*, ed. James McIntosh (New York: W.W. Norton & Co., 1987), 75. Subsequent citations to Hawthorne's tales are from this critical edition and are documented parenthetically.
7   Brenda Wineapple, *Hawthorne: A Life* (New York: Knopf, 2003), 82.

ancestors were implicated in the whipping of Quakers and the burning of an Indian village. Wineapple too, argues that Hawthorne, "[a]cutely aware of the power of history . . . wanted to control it."[8] Brown's story takes on a different dimension for students when they ponder the reasons why Hawthorne would have made the choice to connect his personal history with that of the nation's foundational story of the Puritans.

In exploring this question, we ask why is it significant that Hawthorne embeds so many autobiographical details, which he does not flag for his readers, into his fiction? To find some answers, students are required to read, alongside the story, an essay by Michael J. Colacurcio excerpted in the Norton edition of the tales. In this 1974 essay, Colacurcio describes the story as *"psycho-historical* fiction," noting that Brown's "insights" into the depravity and sin of his community, though they "depend on diabolical communication," are truthful, because in implicating Brown's ancestors, the devil is telling the truth; "these are, after all, the sins of Hawthorne's own fathers."[9] In doing this, Colacurcio argues, Hawthorne anticipates Freudian psychology and sets himself apart from others in his generation for dramatizing "with such compelling clarity, and with so firm a grasp . . . the psychological implications" of Puritan doctrine in the past and in his own time.[10] What students begin to discover is that history is not, as Colacurcio points out, a simple backdrop for Hawthorne's fiction but that it is actually the main preoccupation of many of his stories. History—personal, national, transnational—is the medium through which he grapples narratively with his and his nation's past and with the connections between these seemingly separate dimensions, what I have described above as his literary historicity.

In analyzing the short stories through this cultural studies lens and continuing through his major works chronologically, students find in Hawthorne not just another canonized author removed from their experience but an artist very much engaged in the controversial issues of his time, many of which are relevant today. Delving into the Norton edition of *Nathaniel Hawthorne's Tales*, edited by James McIntosh, we also read "Endicott and the Red Cross," "Mrs. Hutchinson," "Wakefield," "The

---

8   Ibid, 62.
9   Colacurcio, "Visible Sanctity and Specter Evidence: The Moral World of Hawthorne's 'Young Goodman Brown,'" quoted in *Nathaniel Hawthorne's Tales*, ed. James McIntosh (New York: Norton, 1987), 398.
10 Ibid, 404.

Ambitious Guest," "The Birth-Mark," "The Artist and the Beautiful," and "Rappaccini's Daughter." Before we get to the second set of selected stories, written after his marriage to Sophia Peabody, we read Hawthorne's first novel, *Fanshawe*, published anonymously in 1828. While reading the stories published after his marriage in 1842, we analyze Hawthorne's self-representation as a spouse and father. This allows us to continue to juxtapose, as Hawthorne himself does, the personal, the national, and the global. The latter becomes especially relevant in his later life within the context of his family's many relocations and travels.

When looking into his anxieties about family, we carefully examine "Rappaccini's Daughter," a story that has received considerable scholarly attention. Nina Baym has noted that the story functions as "an allegory of faith, an allegory of science, and an allegory of sex all at once."[11] In class, however, we focus on the problem of fatherhood and the connection between Beatrice's imaginary father, Rappaccini, and Hawthorne's actual role as father, both as creator/author and as a man. To further contextualize, students read Anna Brickhouse's essay in which she argues that the story addresses the "political and cultural confrontations between the United States and Mexico during the early 1840s."[12] Specifically, Brickhouse notes how Hawthorne directly borrowed the poisonous woman idea from Frances Calderón de la Barca's *Life in Mexico*, published in 1843, particularly the account of how the people along the Mexican coast inoculated themselves with rattlesnake poison to immunize themselves against all venoms.[13] By identifying the "Mexican genealogy" of "Rappaccini's Daughter," Brickhouse points to how Hawthorne participated in the "dense matrix of transamerican cultural exchange and literary influence emerging out of relations between the United States and the wider Americas" in the nineteenth century.[14] In this way, students begin to see the more transnational and global connections of Hawthorne's writings.

Building on Brickhouse's argument, I suggest to the students that the story can be interpreted not only within the context of and anxieties about U.S. expansionism into the Americas but also as reflecting the intersection

---

11   Nina Baym, *The Shape of Hawthorne's Career* (Ithaca, NY: Cornell University Press, 1976), 107.
12   Anna Brickhouse, "Hawthorne in the Americas: Frances Calderón de la Barca, Octavio Paz, and the Mexican Genealogy of 'Rappaccini's Daughter,'" *PMLA* 113, no. 2 (1998): 227-42.
13   Ibid, 186.
14   Ibid, 182.

of Hawthorne's own personal worries about incipient fatherhood and his related anxieties about the nation. In representing Rappaccini as a misguided father who, in making his daughter powerful, seals her tragic fate by allowing a stranger into their carefully managed garden, Hawthorne may have also represented his own fears about his first child and daughter, Una, born in 1844.[15] Along the same lines, we can read the story as alluding to anxieties over how a nation can destroy that which it seeks to protect most by opening itself to the influence of what is foreign. In our reading, we identify how "Rappaccini's Daughter" merges the personal and the national in a transnational setting to reveal deep concerns about the effects of colonial desire for the future of the nation itself and for the American family.

In contextualizing Hawthorne within his familial circle, we spend some time examining excerpts from Sophia Peabody's "Cuba Journal," as well as the joint journal that she and Hawthorne kept during their first year of marriage while living in the Old Manse. Students read sections from both manuscripts, identifying themes, such as the ways in which the couple fashioned themselves as a new Adam and Eve, a trope found in both his and her writings. For one, Peabody's letters home from Cuba between 1833 and 1835, which Hawthorne read and excerpted from before she became his wife, give students another cultural context within which to read "Rappaccini's Daughter."[16] In Hawthorne's characterization of Beatrice as having "a voice as rich as a tropical sunset," we find not only her siren-like influence on Giovanni but also hear echoes of the "Cuba Journal." Hawthorne himself

---

15 Wineapple and other Hawthorne biographers have noted that fatherhood greatly increased Hawthorne's existing anxieties, not only about the responsibility of raising a child, particularly of earning enough money to support a growing family, but also about the change that it effected on his character and on his art. As he famously told a friend, fatherhood "ought not to come too early in a man's life—not until he has fully enjoyed his youth—for methinks the spirit never can be thoroughly gay and careless again, after this great event." Wineapple identifies the story as a "biographical palimpsest," noting how Rappaccini becomes an allegory for diverse fathers within Hawthorne's circle, including Hawthorne himself. See Wineapple, *Hawthorne*, 189.

16 Claire Badaracco, who transcribed the "Cuba Journal," has suggested a connection between Sophia's descriptions of Cuban flora and Nathaniel Hawthorne's representation of the garden in "Rappaccini's Daughter." Claire Badaracco, "'The Night-Blooming Cereus': A Letter from the 'Cuba Journal, 1833–35' of Sophia Peabody Hawthorne, With a Check List of Her Autograph Materials in American Institutions," *Bulletin of Research in the Humanities* 81, no. 1 (1978): 60.

had not actually seen a tropical sunset and, as Badaracco and other scholars have pointed out, the tropical "gems" in Rappaccini's garden also seem taken directly from her descriptions and sketches of Cuban plants.[17] In considering the ways in which Peabody inspired and influenced Hawthorne and in reading Julie E. Hall's essay on how he did not wish her to become a published author, students get insight into the extent of his own anxieties about the relationship between authorship and gender roles.[18]

By repeatedly linking Hawthorne's works to his personal life and to national/global events, students can focus on how he assigns signification to categories of representation and on how his works promote and challenge specific cultural ideologies. Students examine, for example, the ways in which the ideals of Manifest Destiny are evident within *The Scarlet Letter* and learn about Hawthorne's relationship to the *Democratic Review* and its editor, John L. O'Sullivan, who coined the famous phrase. We also read Baym's essay on the emergence of *The Scarlet Letter* as an American literary classic. In that work, Baym shows how in the nineteenth century the historical novel began to be perceived as a key genre in "strengthening and guiding patriotic and nationalist sentiment."[19] More particularly, she argues that *The Scarlet Letter* fulfilled the need for just such an American novel by promulgating the nineteenth-century ideology that marked New England Puritanism as "the core of the national past, and New England aesthetics as the core of the national future." In that way, *The Scarlet Letter* contributed to a cultural project meant "to unify and construct the nation, over time and ever-expanding space, in the image of New England."[20]

With that background in mind, the class considers how by the 1850s the need for cultural unification had become more urgent, given the deep national rifts over imperial expansion and slavery, which culminated in the Compromise of 1850, several months after *The Scarlet Letter* was published. I propose to the students that, because of how it represents the ideals of the American nation and because of how it has widely disseminated such ideals through its initial and continued adoption as a textbook in high schools and colleges, *The Scarlet Letter* and its eponymous "A" represent a foundational

---

17   Brickhouse, "Hawthorne in the Americas," 199.
18   Hall, Julie E. "'Coming to Europe,' Coming to Authorship: Sophia Hawthorne and Her Notes in England and Italy. *Legacy 19.2 (2002): 137-151.*
19   Nina Baym, "Hawthorne's 'Scarlet Letter': Producing and Maintaining an American Literary Classic," *Journal of Aesthetic Education* 30, no. 2 (1996): 65.
20   Ibid, 66.

narrative of American empire and of how it has been articulated and promoted domestically and abroad.

Specifically, we focus our analysis on the novel's introduction, "The Custom House," and its concluding chapters to identify three major elements that made this novel a significant discursive literary tool for an expanding American Empire in the mid- to late-nineteenth century. First, I ask students to consider how, in investing *The Scarlet Letter* as both artifact and symbol with the character of legend and myth and by repeatedly juxtaposing its 1640s setting with its time of composition, the novel establishes a clear teleology between the nation's "dark" past and its luminous future. Second, I assist them in exploring how the ideology of Manifest Destiny is echoed in and supported by Arthur Dimmesdale's final sermon and how this is consistent with the historical context of the novel's period of composition. During Dimmesdale's last sermon, to which we are not privy except for the summary provided by the narrator, the latter tells us that its subject "had been the relation between the Deity and the communities of mankind, with special reference to the New England which they were planting in the wilderness."[21] In his sermon, it is Dimmesdale's "mission to foretell a high and glorious destiny for the newly gathered people of the Lord" (333). In articulating the ideals of a chosen people, who planted a new civilization and whose God-given destiny was to expand their glory globally, Dimmesdale appears to anticipate O'Sullivan's dictum on Manifest Destiny in "The Great Nation of Futurity" (1839):

> This is our high destiny, and in nature's eternal, inevitable decree of cause and effect we must accomplish it. All this will be our future history, to establish on earth the moral dignity and salvation of man—the immutable truth and beneficence of God. For this blessed mission to the nations of the world, which are shut out from the life-giving light of truth, has America been chosen; . . . Who, then, can doubt that our country is destined to be *the great nation* of futurity?[22]

---

21 Nathaniel Hawthorne, *Collected Novels: Fanshawe, The Scarlet Letter, The House of the Seven Gables, The Blithedale Romance, The Marble Faun*, ed. Millicent Bell (Columbus: Ohio State University Press, 1968), 332. Subsequent citations from Hawthorne's novels are taken from this edition and documented parenthetically.

22 John L. O'Sullivan, "The Great Nation of Futurity," *The United States Democratic Review* 23, no. 6 (1839): 430.

By later coining the phrase, "Manifest Destiny," in support of the annexation of Texas in 1845, O'Sullivan gave the nation a clear articulation of its imperial ideology. It is precisely this principle that Dimmesdale seems to anticipate in a sermon that serves both as his crowning achievement and the final confession of his past deceit and hypocrisy.

The connection Dimmesdale draws in his speech between a God-given or manifest mission and a national destiny is not a coincidence. In giving his protagonist the ability to foresee "an epoch of life more brilliant and full of triumph than any previous one, or than any which could hereafter be" shortly before he dies, Hawthorne links the minister's personal metamorphosis through the acknowledgement of his sin-ridden past with the nation's transformation away from its "dark Puritanic gloom" toward its bright prophesized future. By having Dimmesdale anticipate the very idea of Manifest Destiny, *The Scarlet Letter* gives credence and supports the national project of empire. This is not surprising, given that the novel's composition is contemporaneous with the articulation and implementation of this imperialist discourse, specifically through the dispassion of Native Americans, the acquisition of Texas and the resulting war against Mexico.[23]

Finally, in class we examine how the novel represents the cultural ideal of individual transformation inherent in the American experience in both its seventeenth-century, New-World iteration and in Hawthorne's own time. While neither Hester Prynne nor Arthur Dimmesdale are "Americans" by birth, the choices they make at the story's end "Americanize" them in ways that make highly persuasive cultural sense to the novel's readers, then and now. Specifically, Hawthorne uses Hester's characterization to translate her story of individual transformation into the possibility of national transformation and ultimate glorification. Scholars have noted the ways in which both Dimmesdale and Hester articulate some of Hawthorne's own personal and political anxieties, so it is not surprising that it is through these two protagonists that *The Scarlet Letter* does its most significant work for American empire. In tying Hawthorne to issues of empire and national identity and in showing how these issues are reflected in his works, the course brings him "to life" as a writer who both conformed to and struggled against the dominant national ideologies of his time.

---

23   Laura Doyle, "'A' for Atlantic in Hawthorne's *The Scarlet Letter*," in *Freedom's Empire: Race and the Rise of the Novel in Atlantic Modernity, 1640–1940* (Durham: Duke University Press, 2008), 303.

In our study of the other three published novels by Hawthorne—*The House of the Seven Gables, The Blithedale Romance,* and *The Marble Faun*—we delve critically into the symbology established by Hawthorne and attempt to decipher what these signs may signify. How do they "construct and transmit meaning" by representing cultural "concepts, ideas and feelings" in ways that enable us to "decode or interpret" meaning?[24] For instance, when analyzing Zenobia's "exotic," "rare" and "costly" "hot-house" flower, which the narrator identifies as her particular symbol, "indicative of the pride and pomp, which had a luxuriant growth in Zenobia's character,"[25] we ask ourselves why it might matter that it is not a wild flower but an expensively and artificially cultivated flower? What is the novel suggesting through this representation about Zenobia's feminism, for instance?

In addition, based on the students' annotation of the text and required class preparation, we do board work in which we identify the "Others" in racial, ethnic, national, gendered or other terms who "articulate the representation of difference" in Hawthorne's work.[26] Students must consider how these figurations simultaneously promote and challenge cultural stereotypes in his time. For instance, while Miriam and Donatello are clearly established as the racial "Others" in *The Marble Faun*, they are much more likeable and redeemable characters compared to the staid Kenyon or the compassionless and passionless Hilda. As Miriam herself proposes to Kenyon,

> The story of the Fall of Man! Is it not repeated in our Romance of Monte Beni? And may we follow the analogy yet farther? Was that very sin—into which Adam precipitated himself and all his race—was it the destined means by which, over the long pathway of toil and sorrow, we are to attain a higher, brighter, and profounder happiness, than our lost birthright gave? Will not this idea account for the permitted existence of sin, as no other theory can? (1215).

Might this be Hawthorne, theorizing about sin through Miriam, though her idea is rejected by Kenyon? Why does the novel, we ask ourselves, turn Miriam and Donatello into pariahs while simultaneously setting them up

---

24 Hall, *Representation*, 5.
25 Hawthorne, *The Blithedale Romance*, 645.
26 Hall, *Representation*, 5.

as examples of a "Fortunate Fall"? Might Hawthorne be proposing that there was value even in the worst of national sins, perhaps even in the problematic legacy of the Puritans, which so obsessed him, because it yielded the American identity with which he had such a conflicted relationship?

Such questions tend to intrigue students, and because the post-nationalist approach provides so many avenues from which to teach Hawthorne and from which to connect him to students' interests and concerns, this cultural studies-based lens becomes especially successful. Given Hawthorne's national and global influence, a post-nationalist approach is particularly well suited to creating a successful teaching environment. Students report that they enjoy reading Hawthorne's works not only in relation to his biography but also to selected critical essays, most of them from *The Cambridge Companion to Nathaniel Hawthorne*, edited by Richard H. Millington. Because Hawthorne's texts invariably engage directly with American history and identity, whether they are set in Salem or in Italy, we can follow the threads linking the individual, the national, and the global. Even when he repeatedly addresses similar themes in his writings, repeating structural pairings of opposite types of male and female characters (Hester/Pearl and Dimmesdale/Chillingworth in *The Scarlet Letter*; Hilda/Miriam, Kenyon/Donatello in *The Marble Faun*), we find that he does so in new and intriguing ways. In their evaluations, students are asked to comment on the critical structure of this seminar, and they mention it as a contributing factor to their high level of satisfaction with the course.

By the time we conclude the semester by reading Joel Pfister's essay, "Hawthorne as Cultural Theorist," most students seem persuaded by Hawthorne's relevance and the importance of reading and studying his works. As Pfister argues, while "Hawthorne was capable of being sexist, anti-Semitic, racist, and insufferably middle class—a purveyor of customs [he also] had an admirable self-critical inclination to explore beyond his own ostensible ideological preferences."[27] He adds that by shaking "up his own ideological tendencies, his social criticism often developed analytically as cultural theory."[28] More importantly, in preferring historically framed narratives,

---

27 Joel Pfister, "Hawthorne as Cultural Theorist," in *The Cambridge Companion to Nathaniel Hawthorne*, ed. Richard H. Millington (Cambridge: Cambridge University Press, 2004), 36.
28 Ibid.

> Hawthorne demonstrated a theoretically expansive grasp of the historicity of 'personal' relations, emotions, and bodies. Like some modern historians and theorists of subjective forms, he frequently concentrated on how social power was reproduced through the constitution of subjectivities . . . [and] he probed connections between these fabrications and the creation of gender, class, and individual difference in America.[29]

Hawthorne's profound interest in how social and national power structures were connected and his ability to represent such correlations makes him an ideal author to study through a post-nationalist lens. This is especially productive in a higher-level seminar where I want students to learn to identify and articulate the intersection of the global, the national, and the local as well as the literary and theoretical crossroads at which the post-nationalist approach emerges.

Ultimately, what this pedagogical approach seeks and achieves is to show students that Hawthorne was not an artist disengaged with or alienated from the "actualities" of his day that he bemoaned in his prefaces. Instead, we discover a Hawthorne who was very much involved, preoccupied, and even obsessed with some of the same concerns about American identity that we, individually and as a nation, grapple with today. The course also helps us discover how such concerns repeatedly bled into his prose. By the semester's end and in relation to the categories of representation we explore, we ask ourselves how Hawthorne produced cultural meaning through literary signs and symbols by reaffirming and challenging the cultural codes of nineteenth-century America. In our search for meaning-making, we delve into how Hawthorne produced and circulated representations that "mark out and maintain identity within and difference between groups," whether related to race, gender, or other culturally constructed categories.[30]

Kenyon College

---

29 Ibid, 54.
30 Hall, *Representation*, 3.

Hawthorne and the Brontës: A Transatlantic Senior Capstone Course

Donald Ross

During their senior year, English majors in our department are required to take a capstone seminar and write a senior paper in conjunction with the course. The first goal of these seminars is a close study of a fairly narrow literary topic and to explore that topic in depth. In addition, students use and synthesize what they have learned previously in historical surveys, genre courses, and criticism and theory. They also bring together methodologies for studying primary and secondary texts, especially how an awareness of social, historical, and political contexts helps a reader understand literary works. Each year students, based on their interests and what is available, select from the half dozen or so seminars that are offered. Some recent examples are modern detective fiction, Medieval and Renaissance drama, Keats's poetry, and "The Image and the Page" on the internet and in print.

"Hawthorne and the Brontës" is a senior seminar for English majors who will read all of Hawthorne's major novels in juxtaposition with the best five written by the Brontë sisters (*Jane Eyre, Wuthering Heights, The Tenant of Wildfell Hall, Shirley,* and *Villette*). Before the course, most students had studied or read one or two of the famous novels (*Scarlet Letter, Jane Eyre, Wuthering Heights*). Occasionally a Brontë "groupie" showed up who has been fully captivated, for example, having read all the novels and several biographies and had reverentially visited the Haworth Parsonage. But that is the exception. One of my main goals in the seminar is therefore to build an academic community with the students. In class discussion and weekly e-mails, we work together to understand the novels, accumulate information about their various contexts, and develop research sources for the required capstone paper. As the semester moves along, they accumulate connections among the writers and the students' nineteenth-century fictional worlds become more complicated. Adding to that complexity are readings in criticism, theory, history, and scholarship. Further, the topics of these novels develop from the personal and to the family to the social and economic and to the international. This sequence gives students insight into how these novelists built their careers, while revealing complex dimensions of the changing literary market and taste in the middle of the nineteenth century. The four prefaces that Hawthorne wrote for his "romances" and the "Conclusion" to *The Marble Faun* tell a story of his efforts to distance his work from actual people and places and from the competing genre of the novel. Like Hawthorne, Charlotte Brontë responded to contemporary journalists' interest in the personal lives of novelists. As "Currer Bell" she wrote prefaces to two editions of *Jane Eyre*, a "Biographical Notice of Ellis and Acton Bell" and a preface to the 1850 edition of *Wuthering Heights*. As "Acton Bell," Anne Brontë wrote a brief preface to the second edition of *Tenant* that emphasizes that the novel is not to amuse the reader but to tell the truth in a modest effort to reform society. These introductions illuminate changes in the novelists' way of seeing the world. From them and from the novels themselves, students can begin to understand the impact of differing cultural contexts on the authors' work.

Novels – sequence and pairings

The novels are assigned in this order:

1. Charlotte Brontë, *Jane Eyre* (1847)
2. Hawthorne, *Scarlet Letter* (1850)
3. Emily Brontë, *Wuthering Heights* (1847)
4. Hawthorne, *House of the Seven Gables* (1851)
5. Anne Brontë, *Tenant of Wildfell Hall* (1848)
6. Hawthorne, *Blithedale Romance* (1852)
7. Charlotte Brontë, *Shirley* (1848)
8. Charlotte Brontë, *Villette* (1851)
9. Hawthorne, *Marble Faun* (1860)

By juxtaposing novels from America and Britain, the course encourages students to be aware of transatlantic differences and similarities. The cultural practices and standards through which we view Hester Prynne and everyone's concerns about adultery's place in her seventeenth-century community, for example, are quite different from the rather casual way Rochester tells Jane about his serial adultery. The identity of Adèle's parentage is never quite explained--"not my own child,—a French dancer's bastard"—and Rochester rehearses his many European liaisons. His invitation to make Jane his mistress after bigamy destroys their marriage plan is presented as a "reasonable" arrangement. Jane, however, expresses her moral outrage: "I will *not* be yours."[1]

The transatlantic differences that students begin to distill from their reading include distinctions of class, too. In the narrower environs of *Seven Gables*, American class distinctions are straightforward and rather limited. In the seventeenth century, the Puritan Pyncheon had the great house built by the Maule carpenter, and those inherited social-class roles defined and separated the families into the nineteenth century. Then, the plucky Phoebe Pyncheon and democratic Holgrave abandon the decaying house and move to the suburbs. Social leveling through marriage is, of course, also the denouement of *Jane Eyre*, although her considerable inheritance puts her nearer to the social standing of a Fairfax second son. The range of English social classes is perhaps most evident in *Tenant of Wildfell Hall*. The chapters on the London social world feature titled nobility and the dissipated wealthy, all on the verge of economic ruin. Owners of large country estates dress and entertain well, ramble over the moors and go to the seaside; some like the narrator, Gilbert, actually work with the "servants and hirelings" to cut hay in the summer."[2]

Both Charlotte Brontë and Hawthorne develop important themes concerning the growing empires of both countries. This is most obvious and important in *Jane Eyre* with Rochester's Caribbean colonies, Jane's uncle and her inheritance, and St. John Rivers's decision to go as a missionary in India. At the end of *Villette* Lucy Snowe's fiancé goes to the Caribbean. In *Seven Gables* Hawthorne's vision of empire is limited to the United States, dramatized by the history of the Pyncheons' taking land from the Indians

---

1 Charlotte Brontë, *Jane Eyre Complete, Authoritative Text with Biographical and Historical Contexts, Critical History, and Essays from Five Contemporary Critical Perspectives*, ed. Beth Newman (Boston: Bedford/St. Martin's, 1996), 298, 300, 311.

2 Anne Brontë, *The Tenant of Wildfell Hall* (Oxford: Oxford University Press, 1991), 66.

and their absurd claims to a county in Maine. However, by mentioning the 1849 gold rush in the book's preface, he alludes indirectly to American expansion to the Pacific. Both *The Blithedale Romance* and *Shirley* deal with how the national and, in the case of *Shirley*, international political economy disrupts life in remote regions. Shirley Keeldar's ownership and management of the textile mill is central to the plot, while the Blithedale residents inveigh against capitalism, which they with their products participate in and compete with. *Shirley's* range of realistically depicted poor and working-class characters is different from the limited intellectual life of the Blithedale community. Zenobia and Priscilla are what Hawthorne critics have called "dark" and "light" heroines in interesting ways comparable to Shirley and Caroline. The romances fall apart in *Blithedale* with Zenobia's suicide and Hollingsworth's fragile marriage to Priscilla, whereas they are resolved in Brontë's novel when Shirley marries the intellectual Louis Moore after turning down a businessman and a nobleman as suitors.

Many of these texts offer female characters in various work and professional roles. Except for the two Catherines in *Wuthering Heights*, the leading women in these novels earn a living and support themselves and sometimes their children. Hester Prynne is a seamstress as is Priscilla. Phoebe had been a schoolteacher before she came to the house and became a housekeeper for her frail relatives, and Lucy Snowe was a very successful teacher of English as a second language in French-speaking Villette before setting up her own school. Jane Eyre's first job was as a governess for and teacher of Rochester's "ward." While at the Rivers' household, she briefly worked at a school for working-class girls. While servants, male and female, are in the background in the English novels, Nelly Dean in *Wuthering Heights* becomes a major character.3 Jane's paintings become an element in her courtship of Rochester, which is similar for Helen Huntington in *Tenant*; however, Helen's skill and economic necessity lead her to paint professionally and sell her work in London. Both of the women in *The Marble Faun* are artists: Hilda copies the Old Masters, while Miriam's paintings are "idealizing a truer and lovelier picture of the life that belongs to a woman, than an actual acquaintance with some of its hard and dusty facts could

---

3   An exception in Hawthorne is the dialect-speaking "black servant" in the "Alice Pynchon" chapter of *Seven Gables*; the chapter is a short story written by Holgrave.

have inspired."[4] Beyond these more traditional gender roles, Zenobia is a journalist and Shirley Keeldar is a successful factory owner and manager.

If the women in most of these novels must navigate economic shoals, they are also motivated by male physical and sexual attractiveness and power, even though the novelists' language is at times rather indirect. Thus, the modern reader of *The Scarlet Letter* can only infer a sexual motive from the fact of Pearl's existence and from Hester's wish to escape to England with her lover. Rochester's attractiveness to Jane begins with their first meeting. Catherine Earnshaw's confession to Nelly about the difference between her suitors clearly sets economic comfort with Edgar Linton against only slightly repressed desire and spiritual bonding with Heathcliff: "he's more myself than I am."[5] Isabella Linton is so swept away that she loses any sense of propriety or caution. Sexual desire motivates Helen Huntington's pursuit of Arthur, despite her aunt's well-placed warning. And sexual desire motivates Zenobia to pursue Hollingsworth, including her abandoning her feminist principles in the face of his critical attack. In *The Marble Faun*, the staid, New-England-Puritan relation between Hilda and Kenyon contrasts with Miriam's complex interactions with Donatello as well as the conflicting rumors about her past.

The dominant voice in five of the nine novels in the seminar is the first-person narrator. This begins with the curious title page: "*Jane Eyre: An Autobiography* by Currer Bell." The technique invites the reader to identify with and focus on her and is also used with Lucy Snowe in *Villette*.[6] Hawthorne's more complicated experiment is Coverdale in *The Blithedale Romance*, where what he conceals either consciously or unconsciously is more intriguing than what he reveals. The nested narrations are also interesting for their implications about how characters can be interpreted. Lockwood, the frame narrator in *Wuthering Heights*, opens up the question of what motivates a fictional "person" to talk or write for hundreds

---

4   Nathaniel Hawthorne, *The Collected Novels* (New York: Library of America, 1983), 889.

5   Emily Brontë, *Wuthering Heights: Complete, Authoritative Text with Biographical, Historical, and Cultural Contexts, Critical History, and Essays from Contemporary Critical Perspectives*. 2nd ed. Ed. Linda H. Peterson. (Boston: Bedford/St. Martin's, 2003), 86.

6   Two novels not in the syllabus are also first-person: Anne Brontë's *Agnes Grey*, and Charlotte's *The Professor*. The latter has an introductory letter that motivates the narrative. Hawthorne's *Fanshawe* is third person.

of pages. In this case, he is confronted with a mystery about Heathcliff and the two Catherines in the first chapters, which is partly solved by the loquacious Nelly Dean whose credibility is similar to Coverdale's. Technically similar but not so credibly performed is the frame narrator, Gilbert, in *Tenant of Wildfell Hall*. He also has a mystery to solve, the identity of his neighbor, Helen Huntington, whom he eventually marries. The partial solution is incredibly her diary, which he transcribes overnight for about 250 pages, more than one volume of the three-decker and twenty-eight chapters. Here, most readers will identify with the diarist's struggles, while they are not so likely to do so with Nelly, a servant with her personal prejudices, especially against Heathcliff. Yet Hawthorne's intrusive, authorial asides seem to violate the convention of third-person narration and render his voice especially ambiguous. He gives personal and apparently definitive judgments: "The truth was, that the little Puritans, being of the most intolerant brood that ever lived, had got a vague idea of something outlandish, unearthly, or at variance with ordinary fashion, in the mother and child" (*The Scarlet Letter*).[7] Again: "But what was most remarkable… in the young man [Holgrave], was the fact that, amid all these personal vicissitudes, he had never lost his identity" (*The House of the Seven Gables*).[8] In the "Conclusion" of *The Marble Faun*, the Hawthorne-narrator goes so far as "to cross-examine his friends [sic], Hilda and the sculptor, and to pry into several dark recesses of the story, with which they had heretofore imperfectly acquainted him"[9]

Another perspective that creates class discussion uses paired novels. Isolation may be the most striking feature of *The Scarlet Letter* and *Jane Eyre*. The main characters are in very small worlds, the New England town and the closed interiors in the English rural midlands. Jane is reading in the window seat and Hester emerges from physical prison. Hester's outside world is partly embodied by her husband's intrusion and partly built on her

---

7   Nathaniel Hawthorne, *The Scarlet Letter: An Authoritative Text, Essays in Criticism and Scholarship*, 3rd ed., ed. Seymour Gross, Sculley Bradley, Richmond Croom Beatty, and E. Hudson Long (New York: W.W. Norton, 1961), 65.

8   Nathaniel Hawthorne, *The House of the Seven Gables: An Authoritative Text, Backgrounds and Sources, Essays in Criticism*, ed. Seymour Gross (New York: W. W. Norton, 1967), 177.

9   Nathaniel Hawthorne, *The Marble Faun* in *The Complete Novels and Selected Tales of Nathaniel Hawthorne*, ed. Norman Holmes Pearson (New York: The Modern Library, 1937), 856.

fantasy of escaping with her lover to England. Jane's outside vision comes from stories about her distant relative, her fiancé's past in Europe and the Caribbean, and St. John Rivers's Indian fantasy. In the end her world is even more narrowed, whereas Pearl escapes. *The House of the Seven Gables* and *Wuthering Heights* are also books about houses—physical buildings and multi-generation families. The Grange and Wuthering Heights are within walking distance, but the social and economic worlds they represent create major tensions for all of the characters, from the servant Nelly down (or up) to Heathcliff. *The House of the Seven Gables* is the site of representations of the Pyncheons from Puritan times to the decaying present. The intruders, Holgrave [Maule] and Heathcliff, with their ideas and understanding of modern politics and economics, disrupt the precarious balances. In the end, the house is abandoned, while the plants from the Grange are imported by young Catherine and Hareton to civilize the Heights.

The final novels by Charlotte Brontë and Hawthorne are set in Europe, *Villette* in Belgium and *The Marble Faun* in Italy. Hawthorne uses the occasion to explore the history of Rome from its mythical past, when fauns roamed the landscape, to the contemporary carnival during the French occupation. Two fascinating chapters in *Villette* have Lucy Snowe trapped in an opiate-induced psychedelic and surrealistic vision of a political "festal night" in the Belgian city. The arts also play important roles in both books. The characters tour picture galleries, admire famous sculptures, and attend stage performances, but students need footnoted editions to identify the many references. Both novels have Protestant women trying to negotiate a Roman Catholic world. Hilda's confession in St. Peter's and Lucy's similar effort in a parish church illustrate the Protestant novelists' prejudices about what Brontë calls "honest popish superstition."[10] While their previous works are famously provincial (Yorkshire and Massachusetts), this breaking away to a cosmopolitan setting and "foreign" characters resonates with Hawthorne's frequently articulated frustration with the limit imposed on the American novelist. His complaint includes the lack of a long history in America, which he partly solved by setting *The Scarlet Letter* and several of his short stories in the seventeenth century and using that century as the starting point for *The House of the Seven Gables*. For the Brontës history was simply part of their world. Wuthering Heights has the date "1500" over the door.

---

10   Charlotte Brontë, *Villette*, ed. Geoffrey Tillotson and Donald Hawes (Boston: Houghton Mifflin, 1971), 140.

Reading these novels more or less in chronological sequence allows for some thoughtful observations about differences between Romantic and Victorian worldviews, as well as Anglo-American commonalities. If we regard the publication of Wordsworth's *Prelude* in 1850 as the last major work of high Romanticism, it is a date that fits nicely with the Hawthorne-Brontë period. It also fits with the American Romanticism that started with Transcendentalism and Emerson's *Nature*, Poe's stories, and indeed Hawthorne's early fiction, and was a generation later than its British exemplar.[11] On the other side of the Atlantic, the Brontës were writing at the same time as the clearly Victorian and urban Charles Dickens (*David Copperfield*, 1850, *Bleak House*, 1853), and William Makepeace Thackeray (*Vanity Fair*, 1848). In very broad strokes, "Romantic" is concerned with the private and personal, with intuition and imagination, rather than reason as the guide to truth (Hawthorne's "truth of the human heart"). In contrast, "Victorian," focuses on the public and social and pays attention to ethical values such as duty, responsibility, and justice. Near the Romantic endpoint are Hester Prynne and Jane Eyre whose lives are guided by their imagination, intuition, and emotion. In contrast, Hawthorne's Priscilla and Hilda and Anne's Helen Huntington and Charlotte's Lucy Snowe are respectable and repressed by their social surroundings and how others regard them—how they dress, how they talk, how they stray from narrowly defined norms and values. A short comparative exercise like this one helps students understand that literary and historical periods and movements such as Romanticism and Victorianism are retrospective generalizations that are useful but in many ways inaccurate. Yes, it's a lot of reading, but students can surprisingly be rather diligent, although their ardor tapers off toward the end of the semester. Some are graduating within a couple of weeks and they have their senior papers to write. One thing students always notice is that Hawthorne's novels are significantly shorter than the Brontës'—no "three deckers" in America.

---

11   "American Victorianism" is a valuable concept, although the phrase is rarely used.

Editions, Literary Research, and Writing

In this capstone course, students analyze literary history and scholarship, theory and criticism. Linda Peterson's edition of *Wuthering Heights* includes biographical and historical contexts for the novel. Having basic biographical facts leads to a discussion, for example, about what difference it makes that Hawthorne was raised without a father and the Brontës without a mother and how those situations might have influenced the novelists' selection and presentation of major characters (the long-lost father in *The Blithedale Romance* and mother in *Shirley* come immediately to mind). Historical information about the cultural isolation of Salem and Haworth can be seen both as affecting the novels' settings as well as the writer's careers. The theory and practice section of Peterson's edition, like others in the Bedford series, includes general introductions to different "critical approaches," including psychoanalytical, Marxist, cultural, and feminist. For each, there is a historical overview of the approach with a selected bibliography and then an article that applies the approach to the novel such as Terry Eagleton's "Myths of Power: A Marxist Study of *Wuthering Heights*." One advantage of students' having these resources at hand is that they get a sense of the range of theories that exist under one umbrella and the specificity required to perform literary analysis; it is not enough to gesture in a vague way toward "Marxism" by noting that Jaffrey Pyncheon is a capitalist who own stocks. Instead, students need to document their theoretical position as diligently as they document what they say or write about the novels. Again, pairing *The Blithedale Romance* and *Shirley* further illustrates these connections. The Bedford Cultural Edition of *Blithedale* has a useful collection of contemporary texts concerning feminism, socialist communities, and other reforms.[12] Incorporating these texts into a reading of the novel gives students experience in reading nonfiction about issues raised in the novel. At the same time, the *Blithedale* readings prepare students for Charlotte Brontë's treatment of labor-capitalist conflicts and feminist politics in *Shirley*. This pairing reveals specific ways that American and British institutions and practices differ, even though they also share some of the same influences and themes. For instance, several of the cultural texts in

---

12 See Nathaniel Hawthorne, *The Blithedale Romance*, ed. William E. Cain (Boston: Bedford/St. Martin's Press, 1996).

the Bedford edition prepares students to track down and understand the place of Luddites and frame-breaking violence in Brontë's novel.

If "Hawthorne and the Brontës" is certainly a reading intensive course, it is also a "writing intensive" one. As a capstone course, the final paper for the course itself is a kind of capstone in the form of a 25-page synthetic argument that challenges students to integrate four novels, two by Hawthorne and two by the Brontës, plus a fair number of secondary sources, all orchestrated by a single theoretical/critical perspective. Thus, for example, a paper might take a specific feminist perspective on courtship in *The House of the Seven Gables*, *The Blithedale Romance*, *Wuthering Heights*, and *Shirley*. After three short papers composed during the first half of the term, including a close literary analysis of selected texts, an annotated bibliography of at least ten critical or scholarly sources is due in the ninth week. Each time I teach the course to seventeen students, they accumulate about one hundred scholarly and critical sources, mostly articles. (I combine the citations and circulate the result as an MS Word document, which is a tangible sign of the students' collective work.) Two weeks later (in week eleven), students write a two-page prospectus and logical outline of their papers and the final essay is due at the end of the semester. By then, students will have dispensed with one major worry about whether their writing should be "original." In the setting of this course, discussions and writing that compares these multiple writers and texts are inevitably original, since fewer than half a dozen scholarly articles juxtapose Hawthorne's works with any of the Brontës'. The tendrils of connections and comparisons these texts induce are almost endless and always provocative.[13]

University of Minnesota

---

[13] I thank Professor Sarah Wadsworth for her helpful comments on several drafts of this essay.

Studying Hawthorne Abroad: The Italian Writings and their Contexts

Sandra Hughes

In the preface to *The Marble Faun* (1860), Hawthorne famously complains about an essential problem faced by American authors: "No author, without a trial, can conceive of the difficulty of writing a Romance about a country where there is no shadow, no antiquity, no mystery, no picturesque and gloomy wrong. . . . Romance and poetry . . . need Ruin to make them grow."[1] Steeped in "antiquity," "mystery," and "ruin," Italy would provide the ideal setting for Hawthorne's new romance; the country's art, history, culture, and landscape would appear in one form or another on every page of his last published novel. Indeed, Hawthorne's fidelity to the actual was so great that nineteenth-century tourists routinely used *The Marble Faun* as a guidebook, and I recently employed the same strategy with my students during a one-month summer study abroad program based in Rome and Florence. By combining traditional lectures, discussions, and research with excursions to relevant museums and historical sites, I intended to make *The Marble Faun* come alive for students by exploring the likely sources of Hawthorne's inspiration in his background

---

1 Nathaniel Hawthorne, *The Marble Faun*, in *The Centenary Edition of the Works of Nathaniel Hawthorne*, vol. 4, ed. William Charvat, et al. (Columbus: Ohio State University Press, 1968), 3. Subsequent citations from the novel are from this edition and are documented parenthetically.

reading and in his daily experience in Rome and Florence in 1858–59. Although the course in its entirety included the Italian writings of both Hawthorne and James, here I will focus on my experience of teaching *The Marble Faun*.[2]

The power of teaching the novel on-site in Italy can hardly be overestimated. I have taught my Hawthorne and James course that includes *The Marble Faun* both in the U.S. and in Italy at both graduate and undergraduate levels. Even highly motivated English graduate students from the U.S.-based course would have trouble recalling details from a photograph of a work of art they had seen three or four times. On the other hand, the undergraduates from the Italy-based course, although *eighty percent* of them were neither English majors nor minors, could easily recall details and make comparisons to other works of art or to Hawthorne's descriptions of them after one in-person viewing. Students in the Italy course were required to be actively involved in locating "context passages" from *The Marble Faun* and Hawthorne's *Italian Notebooks* in preparation for museum trips. The responsible student would read Hawthorne's observations aloud as we stood looking at the painting or sculpture. Needless to say, students are more interested in comparing Hawthorne's description of an art work with the work itself when standing in front of the piece than when looking at a photograph in Kentucky, and there is a vital three-dimensional aspect of sculpture that is lost in photographic representations. Above all, students are far more likely to be drawn into the spirit of the novel when they are literally walking in the footsteps of Hawthorne and, by extension, those of his characters.

Certainly there are many questions to be answered about *The Marble Faun*. The female characters are especially perplexing because Hilda seems too shallow and Miriam almost too deep: one is so one-dimensional as to be boring and the other so mysterious as to be frustrating to readers. I would suggest that the key to understanding both characters lies in the historical and legendary women of Rome. Scholarly attention has long been drawn to the theme of women's sexuality in Hawthorne's fiction,

---

2 I supplemented *The Marble Faun* with "Rappaccini's Daughter" and selections from *The Italian Notebooks* and incorporated the following Italian writings by Henry James: *Roderick Hudson, Daisy Miller, The Aspern Papers,* and selections from *Italian Hours*. For context, I also required students to buy the most recent edition of James Hall's *Dictionary of Subjects and Symbols in Art* (Boulder: Westview Press, 2007).

and Hawthorne's Italian travels would bring this idea to the forefront of his consciousness again, for never had he encountered more starkly defined opposites of "pure" and "impure" women as in Rome. A great deal of Roman history, reaching all the way back to the rape of the Sabine women, seems to focus on virginity and rape: the unassailable purity of the Vestal Virgins; the once soiled, yet restored honor of Lucretia; the infamous rapes of Beatrice Cenci and of artist Artemisia Gentileschi. All of these women would serve as models for either Hilda or Miriam, and the goal of *The Marble Faun* section of the study abroad course would be to tease out exactly how, when, and why their stories came to inspire Hawthorne, as well as what that would mean for our interpretation of the novel.

In the same sense that the students and I relied on *The Marble Faun* to determine our itinerary, the Hawthornes looked to the Murray Guides for background information. As these guidebooks attest, the author would have had ample opportunities to encounter artistic renderings of Vestal Virgins in Rome. For example, in the Capitoline Museums, he would have seen a large seventeenth-century fresco by Cavalier d'Arpino, which depicts *Numa Pompilius Instituting the Cult of the Vestals*. My students and I were as dazzled as Hawthorne must have been by the Numa Pompilius fresco, which frames a large glass door that admits an explosion of sunlight radiating from the same location as the fire at the center of the Temple of Vesta. Nor were the Vestal Virgins only to be encountered in museums. In the Roman Forum, we were able to visit the Temple of Vesta and the ruins of the adjoining House of the Vestals where the priestesses lived. The Courtyard of the Vestals, once part of the luxurious residence, contains numerous haunting sculptures of Vestal Virgins. The so-called Temple of Vesta described by Murray and visited by Hawthorne, now known to be a Temple of Hercules Victor, was constructed with the same round shape and colonnade as the actual Temple of Vesta in the Forum. The circular shape of the building and the central aperture in the dome directly above the sacred flame evident in the *Numa Pompilius* fresco call to mind the Pantheon, which holds so much significance for Hilda.

Encountering the legacy of the Vestal Virgins in so many forms while in Rome clearly impacted Hawthorne's conception of Hilda. He casts her in the mold of a Vestal Virgin, I would argue, because it suits both her purity and her level of religious devotion. Although she purportedly trims the lamp atop her tower in honor of the Virgin Mary, her connection to the Vestal Virgins is supported by numerous textual details that await student discovery. The Vestals were consecrated priestesses who served the goddess Vesta at the oldest temple in Rome. After a long period of training, a Vestal Virgin spent ten years watching over the sacred fire kept continually burning on the altar of Vesta.[3] Hilda, a maiden herself, likewise undertakes the duty of maintaining the perpetual flame at the shrine dedicated to the Virgin Mary, a ritual which "has for [her] a religious significance" (112). At the time of her initiation, each Vestal Virgin took a vow of chastity, which she violated only on pain of death, and the Romans boasted that during the one-thousand-year history of the Order, only eighteen women suffered punishment for violation of this pledge. In accordance with the esteem in which the Vestals were held by the Roman populace, a priestess of Vesta was offered a place of honor at all public festivals.[4] Thus, when Hilda appears at the Carnival depicted in the final pages of *The Marble Faun*, she shares a "private balcony" with an Abbate and three "English people of respectability." She "attract[s] the gaze of many," and the revelers shower her with "bouquets and bon-bons" (452–53).

The honesty and integrity of a Vestal remained above reproach. Roman law accorded her certain privileges based on her revered position, an important detail that may help students solve one of the mysteries at the heart of *The Marble Faun*. In Roman courts, a priestess swore no oath because her honesty was taken for granted.[5] Furthermore, Cato Worsfold relates that "In addition to their religious duties, the Vestals were often entrusted with wills, treaties, and other important documents," including the wills of the Emperors.[6] "This custody," according to Worsfold, "was voluntary on the part of the Vestals and regarded as a compliment to them."[7] Interestingly, Miriam asks Hilda to be the guardian of a mysterious and important packet, which she is to deliver to the Palazzo Cenci if she has not heard from her by a certain date. This plot point seems closely related to the practices surrounding the Vestal Virgins. On some occasions, Vestals intervened with the magistrates to obtain pardons for people.[8] Indeed, they could pardon a

---

3   J. E. Zimmerman, *Dictionary of Classical Mythology* (New York: Bantam, 1964), 287.
4   Ibid.
5   Ibid.
6   Thomas Cato Worsfold, *The History of the Vestal Virgins of Rome* (London: Rider, 1932), 46.
7   Ibid.
8   Ibid., 49.

criminal on the way to execution with a mere word.⁹ Hilda's long absence before the Carnival would be explained if she were acting in some way to mitigate the punishment of Miriam and Donatello. Any Vestal who retired after thirty years of service was released from her vow of chastity and allowed to marry if she wished.¹⁰ Hilda, therefore, does not violate the traditions of the Order with which Hawthorne implicitly associates her when she consents to marry Kenyon: "Another hand must henceforth trim the lamp before the Virgin's shrine; for Hilda was coming down from her old tower, to be herself enshrined and worshipped as a household Saint, in the light of her husband's fireside" (461). The notion of Hilda as a "household Saint" who will be reverenced at "her husband's fireside" not only carries connotations of domestic happiness but also establishes a final connection to the Order of Vestal Virgins since Vesta, who was worshipped through the safeguarding of a perpetual flame, was the Roman goddess of hearth and home.¹¹

Among the Vestals, purity and chastity meant everything, and that value system is equally present in the story of Lucretia, who was raped and subsequently committed suicide in an effort to preserve her honor. When students are asked to research the background for Lucretia's suicide, they learn that she was the wife of Collatinus, who was in turn a relation of King Tarquin of Rome. Tarquin's eldest son Sextus grew jealous of Collatinus when a competition of sorts determined that Lucretia was the most admirable and virtuous among the wives of Tarquin's relations. Sextus, having developed a passion for Lucretia, realized that he could have his way with her and embarrass Collatinus at the same time. He went to her house when her husband was away and tried to seduce her. When she stood firm, he used all imaginable means to persuade her. Still failing in his design, he threatened to kill her and one of her slaves, place them in bed together, and claim that he had killed the two of them when he surprised them in an act of adultery. Only under this threat to her honor did she submit. After the rape, she summoned her father and husband to her, explained what had happened to her, asked them to avenge her, and plunged a dagger into her breast, thus restoring her honor. The story of Lucretia, which represents a blending of history and legend, became one of the most popular artistic

---

9   Zimmerman, *Dictionary of Classical Mythology*, 287.
10 Ibid.
11 Ibid., 286.

subjects throughout Italy, so Hawthorne would have been surrounded by portraits of her as he visited the museums of Rome and Florence. He must have noticed a depiction of Lucretia's suicide hanging in the Capitoline Museums because it was the work of Guido Reni, whose *St. Michael Trampling the Devil* and supposed portrait of *Beatrice Cenci* figure prominently in *The Marble Faun*.

If we consider that Hawthorne might have drawn on the legend of Lucretia as a model for Hilda, it is possible to make sense of some mystifying behavior on the latter's part. I find it helpful to share with students a passage from Bayle's *Dictionary*, which Hawthorne knew well, that attributes the following analysis to one Father le Moyne:

> It was not the love of pleasure, or the fear of death, that made her transgress; It was the love of honour, and her extreme apprehension, that she should lose it. . . . Not being able with her hands to resist an armed force, she repulsed it in thought, and her soul raised itself as much as possible to avoid the stain of impurity, with which her body was defiled.[12]

Bayle himself comments on the important moral and social influence that Lucretia's actions held when he asserts that "This lady knew herself innocent, and yet would die, that no leud [sic] woman should have the face to live, under pretense, that Lucretia had the cowardice to survive her rape."[13] Overall, the story of Lucretia teaches us that even if someone is innocent, he or she is stained by the mere *proximity* to evil. Although this idea is rendered almost comic in the painting of Hilda entitled, "Innocence, Dying of a Bloodstain!" it is, in all seriousness, the principle that governs her feeling of being tainted by merely having *witnessed* the murder of the model, as well as her need for confession, a need so strong that it leads her, a daughter of the Puritans, to seek the ear of a priest in a confessional at St. Peter's.

If the legacies of the Vestal Virgins and Lucretia give us insight into Hawthorne's conception of Hilda, we should also consider which models he may have drawn on for the characterization of Miriam. Numerous critics have noted that in developing ideas for her background, Hawthorne

---

12 Pierre Bayle, *Dictionary Historical and Critical*, vol. 3 (London: J.J. and P. Knapton, 1736), 916.
13 Ibid., 912.

may have looked for inspiration to the story of Beatrice Cenci, which served as inspiration for Romantic writers ranging from Percy Shelley to Herman Melville.[14] Because it is somewhat more accessible than Shelley's play, I ask students to read Alexandre Dumas's account of "The Cenci" from *Celebrated Crimes*. As students continue to read and research, the story unfolds of a young Roman noblewoman who was infamous as a victim of incest and an alleged parricide, yet whose public execution in 1599 garnered tremendous sympathy among the Roman people. Although Beatrice almost certainly conspired to kill her father, since he had raped, abused, effectively imprisoned her, and treated other members of her family with great cruelty, the Roman populace offered her their support. This story of a woman who was greatly wronged and who did great wrong in retribution is one that resonates with the scant details we are given about Miriam's past, particularly the portion of her past involving the Model.

Hawthorne would have been reminded of the tragic circumstances of Beatrice Cenci's life and death when he saw Guido Reni's supposed portrait of her at the Palazzo Barberini. Now thought by art historians not to be a portrait of Beatrice and not even by Guido Reni, the painting is described by the Murray guidebook that Hawthorne used as "one of the most celebrated portraits in Rome." Quoting Murray, Hawthorne further relates that "According to the tradition, it was taken on the night before her execution; other accounts state that it was painted by Guido from memory after he had seen her on the scaffold."[15] Perhaps this romanticized view of the circumstances contributed to the powerful reaction that Hawthorne had to the portrait, and I ask students to consider this possibility as we stand in front of the painting while the researcher responsible for the context reads from *The Italian Notebooks*:

[I]t is the very saddest picture that ever was painted, or conceived; there is an unfathomable depth and sorrow in the eyes. . . . It is a sorrow that removes her out of the sphere of humanity; and yet she looks so innocent, that you feel as if it were only this sorrow, with its weight

---

14   For a discussion of this theme, see Diane Long Hoeveler's "Beatrice Cenci in Hawthorne, Melville, and Her Atlantic-Rim Contexts," *Romanticism on the Net*, Vols. 38–39 (May 2005), doi:10.7202/011670ar.

15   Nathaniel Hawthorne, *The French and Italian Notebooks*, in *The Centenary Edition of the Works of Nathaniel Hawthorne*, vol. 14, ed. Thomas Woodson (Columbus: Ohio State University Press, 1980), 746–47.

and darkness, that keeps her down upon the earth and brings her within our reach at all. She is like a fallen angel, fallen, without sin.[16]

Certainly, such a deeply sympathetic portrait leads us to view Miriam with a great deal more compassion than Hilda does.

A near contemporary of Beatrice Cenci, Baroque artist Artemisia Gentileschi may likewise have served as an inspiration for Miriam's character. David Mayer has done extensive research, which proves that although Hawthorne never refers to Gentileschi's work specifically, he would have had opportunities to view her canvases on exhibition in England, as well as in the Palazzo Pitti and the Uffizi Galleries in Florence.[17] Student researchers can uncover evidence that like Beatrice Cenci, the young Artemisia was raped by a father figure, Agostino Tassi, who had been employed by her father to further her art education.[18] Artemisia was subjected to a long, humiliating rape trial and a court-ordered gynecological exam, a besmirching of her reputation that would most certainly compromise her marriage possibilities. During the trial, she was accused by Tassi and witnesses for the defense of everything from general promiscuity to incest with her father.[19] Despite her "detailed description of the rape and of her active resistance, to the point of wounding her assailant with a knife," lingering doubts about her virginity at the time of the rape remained.[20] In addition to the court-ordered gynecological exam, Artemisia *voluntarily* submitted herself to a torture called *sibille,* an agonizing procedure that involved the tightening of cords around the fingers to prove that she was innocent, and her accusations were shown to be valid.[21] As the hands are the artist's means of livelihood, she was willing to risk her career as an artist in order to prove

---

16   Ibid., 93.
17   David R. Mayer, "Artemisia Gentileschi as Artist Model for Miriam in Hawthorne's *The Marble Faun," Nathaniel Hawthorne Review* 31, no. 2 (2005): 23–24.
18   Unlike the research assignments on the Vestal Virgins, Lucretia, and Beatrice Cenci, the assignment on Artemisia Gentileschi's life and art is better given before leaving the U.S. since materials on her are scarcer and less available through electronic sources that students will have access to while abroad.
19   Mary D. Garrard, *Artemisia Gentileschi: The Image of the Female Hero in Italian Baroque Art* (Princeton: Princeton UP, 1989), 404.
20   Ibid., 21.
21   Ibid., 404.

that she was telling the truth. Meanwhile, Tassi, who already had a criminal record involving incest with his sister-in-law resulting in children and who was accused of having had his wife murdered,[22] was "merely admonished by the judges to tell the truth."[23] Ultimately, Tassi escaped with a sentence of only eight months in jail.[24]

After that experience, Artemisia started painting subjects exactly like those that Donatello is shocked to find on Miriam's sketching table: Jael hammering the tent spike through Sisera's temple, Salome receiving John the Baptist's head in a charger, and *many* versions of Judith's beheading of Holofernes. As students will discover, according to the Apocryphal Book of Judith, Holofernes was an Assyrian general who had placed the city of Bethulia under extended siege. Determined to end the siege and help her people, Judith, a widow in the community, dresses herself in her finest clothes and jewels and infiltrates the enemy camp under the guise of betraying secrets to defeat Bethulia. On the fourth night, she moves as if to seduce the enemy commander Holofernes, gets him intoxicated, and when he is unconscious, decapitates him with a sword and carries it back to her people in triumph, which results in their victory over the Assyrians.

We have five autographed Judiths from Artemisia Gentileschi's hand,[25] though she may have painted as many as seven.[26] While many other Renaissance and Baroque artists painted Salome and Judith (renderings of Jael were much rarer), Artemisia distinguished herself by the passion and violence of her depictions of these scenes. In particular, the blood spraying out in wide arcs, the spattered clothes of Judith, the blood-soaked sheets in the Uffizi Judith, which, Mayer notes, Hawthorne would have had the opportunity to view eleven times,[27] stand in stark contrast, for example, to Caravaggio's treatment. The latter features a Holofernes who is being beheaded in far less realistic fashion with blood shooting out in straight lines, no blood saturating the sheets, and not a single drop of blood splattering Judith and her maid. Students who have had the chance to see for themselves both the Caravaggio *Judith* in the Palazzo Barberini

---

22   Ibid., 22.
23   Ibid., 405.
24   Ibid., 406.
25   Ibid., 278.
26   Mayer, "Artemisia Gentileschi as Artist Model," 22.
27   Ibid., 24.

Gentileschi, Artemisia (1597-c.1651). Judith and Holofernes. Ca. 1620.
Oil on canvas. 78 3/8 x 64 in. (199 x 162.6 cm).
Photo Credit: Alinari I Art Resource, NY

in Rome and the Artemisia *Judith* in the Uffizi Galleries in Florence can appreciate the differences in the two works. These can also be compared in the classroom.

Perhaps the most revealing connection to be made, though, is between Beatrice and Artemisia. Like Beatrice Cenci, Artemisia turns to violence, if only violence sublimated in art, to avenge some sort of sexual wrong perpetrated against her by a father figure. I would suggest that this similarity provides an important clue to the mysterious burden of guilt that Miriam bears in *The Marble Faun*. Two other paintings by Artemisia may also have influenced Hawthorne's conception of Miriam; both are located on the same wall in the Palazzo Pitti, which Hawthorne visited five times in 1858.[28] The first is a Judith, a far less bloody after-the-fact representation in which she and her maid are escaping with Holofernes's head in a basket. The second, hanging only a few feet above the Judith, is a Penitent Magdalen. In visiting the Pitti so many times, Hawthorne must have noticed these two paintings that hang so near to one another and by the same artist. As we stand in front of the paintings in Florence, I ask my students to imagine how the character of Miriam might grow out of the juxtaposition of these two images. Perhaps they inspired Hawthorne to conceive of a character torn between a justified desire for vengeance and the renunciation of a worldly life in order to embrace life as a penitent. These two poles define Miriam's character, and that tension, which after all ends in a choice of penitence, is what drives a great deal of the plot in the novel.

Speaking more generally, I would argue that understanding the context provided by the women of Rome's past from the Vestal Virgins and Lucretia to Beatrice Cenci and Artemisia Gentileschi changes our reading of *The Marble Faun* because it not only helps us fill in several gaps in plot and character motivation in this highly elusive and allusive novel, but it also allows, almost *requires*, us to view both Hilda and Miriam with greater sympathy. If we remember that the standard for a Vestal Virgin's purity is an absolute one, and the penalty for betrayal of her vows is, in all cases, death; and if we recall that Lucretia serves as an example to other women of purity at any cost, then Hilda's seemingly harsh judgment of Miriam, her refusal to "stain" her white robe by touching her, begins to make sense. What if Hilda wants to remain spotless not due to her prudery but because the penalty for betraying one's vows, the loss of her *eternal* life, is so severe? Significantly, a Vestal not only maintained the fire in the temple but also, by extension, the "domestic hearth of the City."[29] Therefore, according to Ariadne Staples, the Vestals' power became a "guarantor of the stability and integrity for Rome."[30] Lucretia's noble act also had important consequences for Rome because, as Bayle relates, "Brutus, who was present

---

28 Ibid.
29 Worsfold, *History of the Vestal Virgins of Rome*, 16.
30 Ariadne Staples, *From Good Goddess to Vestal Virgins: Sex and Category in Roman Religion* (New York: Routledge, 1998), 148.

at this spectacle, found the occasion he had long fought for of delivering Rome from Tarquin's tyranny and so far improved this occasion that the kingly power was abolished; thus Lucretia's death was the cause of the liberty of the Roman people."[31] Hilda's standard of behavior, then, saves not only herself but also ensures the safety of her society.[32] Further, if Miriam is modeled on Beatrice Cenci and Artemisia Gentileschi, perhaps she is *innocent* of the sin of which she is accused, not pure like Hilda, but heroic in her endurance of torturous punishment and somewhat justified in her fantasies of revenge. As we look back at the end of the course on the impact that the women of Rome had on the women of *The Marble Faun*, we might, indeed, ask whether Hawthorne had not found at least some measure of innocence abroad.

Western Kentucky University

---

31 Bayle, *Dictionary Historical and Critical*, 910.

32 In *The Marble Faun*, when the lamp goes out at the "Virgin's shrine," the Italian man who is passing by exclaims to Kenyon: "The lamp is extinguished. . . . The lamp that has been burning, these four hundred years! This surely must portend some great misfortune; and, by my advice, Signor, you will hasten hence, lest the tower tumble on our heads." Hawthorne, *The Marble Faun*, 400.

PART 4
PERFORMATIVE AND VISUAL CONTEXTS

Reading Disability in Hawthorne: Enabling Student Analyses of *The Scarlet Letter*

SARI ALTSCHULER

On the last day of a course I taught on disability and the American novel, a student approached me with the revision of a paper. In its first iteration the paper had earned a C, and the student had remained mostly silent during class discussions. I was still a graduate student teaching a full load, I had thirty students enrolled in the class, and admittedly I knew very little about this student in particular. I had suspected that she was largely disengaged. Smiling and thanking her for the revision, I reached for the paper. She withheld it. "I just wanted to say," she started to say before pausing, "I just wanted to thank you. As a woman living with HIV, I really appreciated our discussions about visible and invisible disability. They helped me think differently about my life."

Even though the course was about disability in literature, I was surprised by her confession. Many students had self-identified as impaired early in the course, using their identity in part to ground some of the perspectives they offered. Others, like my deaf student, did not need to self-identify. I had done my best to think about the material from their vantage points; however, my student's position made me reconsider the thinking I had done. In the weeks after, my thoughts about her experience in the course attached themselves particularly to Nathaniel Hawthorne's *The Scarlet Letter*.

What was it like for this student to encounter that text? What might it have been like for her to study it in high school? How might the conversation have gone differently had the course not been explicitly about disability? In what follows, I will address how we might teach *The Scarlet Letter* while remaining sensitive to disabled students in our classroom, how we might think about the way the novel insists on Chillingworth's character-defining deformity while also examining the ways in which Hawthorne troubles a collapsed reading of mind and body and how we might emphasize the openness of *The Scarlet Letter*'s symbolic logic. Finally, I will suggest how actively engaging students in these conversations can alter how they bring *The Scarlet Letter* into classrooms of their own.[1]

Disability

Disability is a political term unifying what might otherwise seem a very distinct set of conditions. Deafness, blindness, and paralysis are grouped with diabetes, dyslexia, and autism to reveal mechanisms of systemic dysfunction. These conditions are linked by a similar experience of socially constructed stigma and exclusion. Disability is distinguished from impairment in that impairment describes the condition, say paraplegia, independent of the socially constructed hindrances that make that impaired individual's life more difficult—such as stairs, tall shelves, and other problematic features of the social and built environment.

---

1   This connection between the stigma of *The Scarlet Letter* and HIV has been repeatedly drawn by American healthcare professionals involved in treating patients with HIV/AIDS. Churct et al write that children with HIV "are, despite the recommendations of the US Centers for Disease Control (CDC), being excluded from school and society, with all of the psychological implications that befell Hester Prynne, Nathaniel Hawthorne's adulteress" (423). Carr and Gramling begin their article on living with HIV/AIDS by noting that "the stigma experienced by women with HIV/AIDS is much like that of Hester Prynne in *The Scarlet Letter*" (30). See Church, Joseph A., James R. Allen, and E. Richard Stiehm. "New scarlet letter (s), pediatric AIDS." *Pediatrics* 77.3 (1986): 423-427 and Carr, Rebecca L., and Lou F. Gramling. "Stigma: a health barrier for women with HIV/AIDS." *Journal of the Association of Nurses in AIDS Care* 15.5 (2004): 30-39.

Though we are by no means finished, teachers and scholars have done an excellent job bringing race, class, gender, and sexuality into our classrooms, but when it comes to disability, many of us have a ways to go. When we teach *The Adventures of Huckleberry Finn*, we are attentive not only to Mark Twain's problematic perspective on race but also to the way that the word "nigger" works not only in the text and the classroom but also in the minds of our students. Likewise, when we teach *The Great Gatsby*, we attend to F. Scott Fitzgerald's flat representations of women and fraught representations of sexuality. Though they might once have been contentious, these are standard pedagogical activities in the contemporary English professor's toolkit. Certainly we accomplish these readings with differing degrees of skill and knowledge, and some of us are much better at it than others, but most individuals who have gone on to teach literature at the university level in the past twenty years spend time thinking about teaching in these terms. The same does not apply when we think about Ahab's whalebone leg in *Moby-Dick* or Jake Barnes's suggestive war-wound in *The Sun Also Rises*. In those cases, we tend to think less about the complicated and problematic status of disability in the works but rather about the symbolic nature of those characteristics.[2]

On an intellectual level, this move is problematic, but it is even more troubling on a practical level when we consider how many of our students care for disabled friends and relatives or are disabled themselves. Given that scholars estimate that 15%-20% of the U.S. population is disabled, many of our students have an intimate experience with disability.[3] Furthermore, as disability activists point out, able-bodied individuals are only temporarily so; we will all become disabled if we live long enough. My student, then, is

---

2   For more about the flattening representational work of disability in American literature, see Rosemarie Garland Thomson's *Extraordinary Bodies: Figuring Physical Disability in American Culture and Literature* (New York: Columbia University Press, 1997). For more about disability in American literature and culture more generally see Diane Price Herndl's *Invalid Women: Figuring Feminine Illness in American Fiction and Culture, 1840-1940* (Chapel Hill: University of North Carolina Press, 1993), David Mitchell's and Sharon Snyder's *Narrative Prosthesis: Disability and the Dependencies of Discourse* (Ann Arbor: University of Michigan Press, 2001), and Tobin Siebers' *Disability Aesthetics* (Ann Arbor: University of Michigan, 2010).

3   Lennard Davis, Introduction, *The Disability Studies Reader* (New York: Routledge, 2006), xv.

not alone and should not feel that she is. We have an ethical obligation to interrogate representations of disability in our classrooms. It is the least we can do as we strive to ameliorate the social, cultural, economic, and political conditions that structure systems of prejudice and exclusion. In what follows, I offer some thoughts about how we might do so, especially using texts like *The Scarlet Letter* that appear to resist such openness.

Before the Classroom

Whether we want to admit it or not, most of our students' readings are shaped by the internet browsing they do before they come to class. This is especially true in a survey course and even more the case with canonical texts like *The Scarlet Letter*. My best students tell me they look at online summaries before coming in to get a sense of what they are "supposed to think" about the text. This strategy is not all bad. It certainly allows us to survey conventional interpretations and engage more quickly in deeper thinking. I am also not sure I could stop them from reading these analytical summaries if I tried, but if we admit the wide-spread nature of this practice, we must also deal with its more unpleasant ramifications.

Assuming a good number of students come to class having read the SparkNotes' analysis of *The Scarlet Letter*, they would arrive armed with rigid perceptions of the relationship between body and character. With regard to positive characters, they would learn that "although the narrator pretends to disapprove" of the healthy Hester's "independent philosophizing, his tone indicates that he secretly admires her independence and her ideas."[4] About her evil husband the student learns that "Roger Chillingworth is a man deficient in human warmth. His twisted, stooped, deformed shoulders mirror his distorted soul."[5] The troubled Arthur Dimmesdale suffers "mental anguish and physical weakness" that has the virtue of "allow[ing the minister] to empathize with others" but remains a somatic symbol of the guilt he feels that "Hester takes all of the

---

4   "The Scarlet Letter: Analysis of the Major Characters," SparkNotes, last accessed 3/7/2014, http://www.sparknotes.com/lit/scarlet/canalysis. mlht.
5   Ibid.

blame for their shared sin."[6] In spite of SparkNotes's pronouncement that "By the time Hester dies, the meaning of the scarlet letter on her chest has become confused and ambiguous," its analyses are heavily dependent on conventional classroom uses of *The Scarlet Letter* to teach symbolism, and thus they do not recognize the extent of the novel's broader disruption of symbolic equivalencies.[7]

This bad reading might not be so troubling if it were not for the variety of disabled students that populate our classes or more particularly for my HIV-positive student. More than any other disease of the past few decades, HIV/AIDS has been cast as a physical condition that results from, among other causes, the sins of deviant sexual behavior and associated failings of self-control.[8] Like Dimmesdale, individuals with HIV and AIDS have been asked to understand that their bodies register their moral and sexual transgressions or those of their parents. And, like him, their conditions begin as a secret weakness that ultimately makes itself known on the body through fleshy lesions and the body's inability to care for itself that, until the advent of recent drugs, was soon followed by death. In other words, as I imagine my HIV-positive student reading SparkNotes or listening to a well-meaning high school teacher link the course of Dimmesdale's disease to his secret sin, I cannot but cringe at the invited comparisons. We have a responsibility, then, to acknowledge in the classroom that the novel does invite this interpretation while also opening up other responses for and avenues to our students.

Disability and *The Scarlet Letter* in the Classroom

As a class, we begin with a close reading of *The Scarlet Letter*'s first significant symbol: the rosebush at the prison door. "Finding it so directly on the threshold of our narrative," Hawthorne's narrator playfully describes,

---

6 Ibid.
7 "The Scarlet Letter: Chapter 23 and 24," SparkNotes, http://www.sparknotes.com/lit/scarlet/section13.rhtml.
8 See, for example, Susan Sontag's powerful discussion in "AIDS and Its Metaphors," in *Illness as a Metaphor and AIDS and Its Metaphors* (New York: Picador, 2001).

"which is now about to issue from that inauspicious portal, we could hardly do otherwise than to pluck one of these flowers, and present it to the reader. It may serve, let us hope, to symbolize some sweet moral blossom, that may be found along the track, or relieve the darkening close of a tale of human frailty and sorrow."[9] This symbol announces itself boldly. In the narrator's path, directly in the way of the "inauspicious portal" of his story, he cannot but focus on it. The rosebush, of course, sets up *The Scarlet Letter*'s central juxtapositions—nature vs. society, beauty vs. severity—but it also provides an opportunity for the narrator to circumvent those stark binaries. Hawthorne's narrator, after all, treats the rosebush as an actor might a gun accidentally left on stage by an actor in a previous scene: He must deal with it, but he is not quite sure how. His first thought is to offer it as a gift in his first flirtations with the reader, but his actions are uncertain. Phrases and words such as "may serve," "let us hope," "may be," and "or" index his uncertain handling of what the narrator insists ought to serve as a symbol.

As a class, this attention to the rosebush opens up our reading of "the scarlet letter." As the title of the book, we decide, of course, that it is the symbol on which we are supposed to focus. My students tell me that this book is used to teach symbolism in high school, and so I ask them: what does the scarlet letter mean? Well, *adultery*, of course, but also *angel* when it is associate with John Winthrop. Some students who get into what they perceive to be the game offer other "a" letter words: acceptance, ambivalent, able. We pair the opening scene introducing Hester's scarlet A with with a close reading of the novel's last scene in which Dimmesdale's own scarlet letter is implicitly compared and contrasted with Hester's in the marketplace. On its own, this connection stimulates wonderful classroom conversation, but it is especially rich for interrogating how language and bodies are connected through the work of symbolism in the novel. In "the scarlet letter," Hawthorne offers a wonderful figure for thinking about these links. The townspeople imagine that the scarlet A on her body will reduce Hester's character to her new physical marking, but when it comes to Dimmesdale's own confession, they resist making this very connection. By this point, of course, the reader has been encouraged to see Hester's "A" more capaciously, signifying "angel and apostle" (239), even as oddly

---

9   Nathaniel Hawthorne, *The Scarlet Letter* (1850. Reprint New York: Bantam, 1986), 46. Subsequent references are to this edition and are documented parenthetically.

Dimmesdale's A cannot be collapsed into a single meaning. My students have always wished—thanks to SparkNotes or not—to see it as the inward sign of the guilt he should have sooner expressed outwardly.

This reading is understandable given not only their common high school experience of being asked to read the novel in terms of straightforward symbolism but also in terms of the direct linkages between Chillingworth's body and his character. Unlike the corporeal markings of Hester and Dimmesdale, *The Scarlet Letter* seems to resist a complicated reading of Chillingworth's physicality. Scholars of disability studies agree. Rosemarie Garland-Thomson, for example, argues for the largely flattening function of disability in American literature with precisely this case:

> the rhetorical function of the highly charged trait [the character's prominent disability] fixes relations between disabled figures and their readers. If disabled characters acted, as real people with disabilities often do, to counter their stigmatized status, the rhetorical potency of the stigma would be mitigated or lost. If Hawthorne's Chillingworth made many friends, for instance, or appeared lovable to Hester, his role in The Scarlet Letter would be diminished.[10]

Thus, *The Scarlet Letter* resists the nuances of Chillingworth's character. The "deformed" man, "well stricken in years" with "the left shoulder a trifle higher than the right," haunts Hester through the narrative, and Chillingworth never deviates from the "evil principle" of revenge that is "the very principle of his life" (55, 236). Although I have argued that representations of impairment in this period are more complicated, this description offers a very useful example of the damaging work of disability representation in many works of American literature, and is more specifically productive for thinking about Chillingworth's flatly rendered character in the novel.[11]

Nevertheless, a return to "The Custom House" sketch complicates this reading of Chillingworth. In a seemingly unrelated diatribe against customhouse officers' state of dependency on the federal government, the narrator explains:

---

10 Garland-Thomson, *Extraordinary Bodies*, 12.
11 Altschuler, Sari. "'Ain't One Limb Enough?'" Historicizing Disability in the American Novel." *American Literature* 86.2 (2014): 245-274.

> An effect—which I believe to be observable, more or less, in every individual who has occupied the position—is that, while he leans on the mighty arm of the Republic, his own proper strength departs from him. He loses, in an extent proportioned to the weakness or force of his original nature, the capability of self-support. If he possesses an unusual share of native energy, or the enervating magic of place do not operate too long upon him, his forfeited powers may be redeemable. . . . But this seldom happens. He usually keeps his ground just long enough for his own ruin, and is then thrust out, with sinews all unstrung, to totter along the difficult footpath of life as he best may. (237–38)

This passage goes to great lengths to align the figure of the paid government worker with Dimmesdale, weak and leaning on the arm of Chillingworth, here standing in for "the mighty arm of the Republic." In the classroom, students quickly identify the echoes of Emerson, especially in the paragraph's final invocation of "self-reliance." Nevertheless, when pressed further, they recognize that the figure is more complicated than it appears at first. If "the Republic"/Chillingworth is slowly killing "Hawthorne"/Dimmesdale through its/his aid, the government commission is also financially supporting Hawthorne's writing as he simultaneously asserts that the Republic is killing it. This relationship to finance cannot be simply reduced to the struggle between art and the marketplace animated in *The Scarlet Letter* more generally; what appears to be a straightforward celebration of Emersonian independence is complicated by Hawthorne's earlier criticism of the "impracticable schemes" of his "dreamy brethren at Brook Farm" and his desire to leave them to "exercise other faculties of my nature" at the customhouse (24, 25). More reflective students remember that Hawthorne's condemnation of his time at the customhouse is directly motivated by his own spite at having been fired.

The analogy grows yet more complicated when we more closely examine the details. Chillingworth is an outsider and, in many ways, more of an original individual than Dimmesdale. Conversely, Dimmesdale could not be more of an insider within his society. Except for the single transgressive act that propels the plot of *The Scarlet Letter*, Dimmesdale is what Puritan society needs him to be. Filling a proscribed role, he is its pillar. In a sense then, this "Custom House" analogy reverses the roles: in *The Scarlet Letter*'s central plot, the man of society leans on the independent if dangerous outsider, whereas in "The Custom House" Hawthorne's independent outsider loses his strength from leaning too heavily on society. Certainly both figures encourage independent thought and action but, beyond an oversimplified reading of "good" and "evil," the analogy grows more complex. This relationship helps my students to see Chillingworth as a more complicated character than the novel might otherwise allow and one who is not a purely lamentable and extraneous element of the early American landscape, but inextricably bound up in its very existence. In fact, "The Custom House" sketch more generally unsettles *The Scarlet Letter*'s schema of health. Though Hawthorne's narrator fires the "gouty and rheumatic" officers who use their possibly fictitious ailments to avoid work, he cannot fully celebrate pictures of health at the Custom House (13). The customhouse "father" is an eighty-year-old man in fantastic health: "With his florid check, his compact figure . . . his brisk and vigorous step, and his hale and hearty aspect, altogether he seemed—not young, indeed—but a kind of new contrivance of Mother Nature in the shape of man, whom age and infirmity had no business to touch" (16). Though he has a "cheerful temper that grew inevitably out of his physical well-being," he has "no soul, no heart, no mind; nothing...but instincts" (17). This "legitimate son of the revenue system" is "so earthly and sensuous" that he still "smack[s] his lips over dinners, every guest at which, except himself, had long been food for worms" (17-18). This figure, more than any other in the sketch, might be said to possess the "mighty arm of the Republic" on which the narrator leans for a time, the arm aligned otherwise with Chillingworth, further complicating the symbolic logic of able-bodiedness in the text.

Moving Beyond the Classroom

While *The Scarlet Letter* will never perfectly align with the representational politics sought by disability studies scholars, it is possible to teach the text in ways that do not conspire to produce only damaging readings of physical impairment. This requires not only reading it for moments that resist and complicate such collusion, as I have tried to do in this essay, but also in foregrounding the ethical issues with our students. In my experience, they delight in tackling these problems together. Since many of my classes have included English majors who were hoping to go on to teach high school, they embraced the analytical and ethical questions raised by considering disability in *The Scarlet Letter* as issues they will need to consider in their own teaching careers. Posing the problems to them has yielded some of the most inventive papers and engaged discussions I have had teaching college. In fact, they often comment on how much they enjoy being challenged by these conversations and how they plan to incorporate them into their own lives and classrooms going forward. Since we can ameliorate but cannot fully do away with some of *The Scarlet Letter*'s distasteful representation of disability, we could do worse than to charge our students with coming up with more nuanced and ethical positions in their own teaching of the text. Whether or not we come to know about the disabilities of our students or the disabilities of those for whom they care, we must be thoughtful about our analysis and the broader ethical impact of the lessons we teach. This is the very least we owe them.

Just as I was finishing the final paragraphs of this essay, a student sent me a note to follow up on our class discussion of disability in *The Scarlet Letter*. Her words conclude this essay better than I could:

> [Dear] Professor Altschuler...
>
> I plan to go to graduate school in the future and would like to become a teacher myself. I'm not sure what level yet, but I guess it runs in my blood (cliché, I know). My mother is a high school English teacher and my father used to be a principal at a private school and also taught in colleges for years. I never thought about wanting to become a teacher until after a few years ago when I immigrated here and my daughter was born.
>
> Anyway, I was really inspired by our class discussion about *The Scarlet Letter*, I didn't really want to say anything because I knew I would burst into tears but I have an auto immune disorder (Psoriasis) that manifested itself when I was about seven years old. I came from a country that still blames the mother for something she did (or ate) during the pregnancy for a child's illness or deformity. As a child I often thought about what went wrong and "why I am getting these painful sores all over my body?" It was very embarrassing because other kids can be cruel about things they don't really understand.
>
> At one point, about two years ago, I had lesions covering about 70-80% of my body. I had no health insurance while I was working at

Walmart, but the doctor I consulted helped me get into a patient assistance program and I was able to get my medication to control my symptoms. I still have scars all over my body from having the lesions, especially on my arms and face because they got darker from sun exposure. I am off of the very strong biologics after some side effects started manifesting on me. Right now I am just trying to live healthier and take care of any lesions that appear before it gets worse.

Our discussion about the hidden illness really struck a chord. I will definitely not forget that class meeting if I ever get to teach one day. I'm never comfortable being in a box and I think giving a different reading on a widely taught piece of literature is definitely a big step…

Your student,
Janna Doyac[12]

Emory University

---

12   Janna Doyac has given me permission to publish this letter and requested that I include her name.

Puppets, Automata, and Machinery: Counter-Currents of Transnational Romanticism in Hawthorne's Short Fiction

Michael Demson

Nathaniel Hawthorne's short fiction frequently plumbs a fear of puppets, automata, and machinery. His stories are rife with figures of artificial life, simulated inspiration, and theatrical animations, manifesting a dark and anxious fascination with virtual life. Through these figures, Hawthorne develops central concerns of international Romanticism, including self-consciousness, self-individuation, and self-management, as well as liberty of action and moral agency in an American context. Indeed, Lieselotte Sauer, who surveys Romantic treatment of the automaton figure, suggests that "mechanistic metaphors" in Romantic literature became "symbols for the forces threatening man's spiritual... nature" while simultaneously satirizing the "dull and mechanical nature" of the whole of "society" as a "megamachine."[1] Hawthorne's Feathertop from the eponymous 1851 tale and Lisabetta from "Rappaccini's Daughter" (1844), for example,

---

1 Lieselotte Sauer, "Romantic Automata," *European Romanticism: Literary Cross-Currents, Modes, and Models*, ed. Gerhart Hoffmeister (Detroit: Wayne State University Press, 1990), 288–90.

terrify because they mock what is most dear: our convictions about both the transcendence of humanity and art as well as our faith in the underlying humanity of civil society. Focusing on Samuel Taylor Coleridge's "repudiation of the 'automaton poet' possessed by inspiration,'" John Savarese argues that Romantics were "deeply invested" in the proposition that writers are "full human agents" and that for them "poetry is an example—in fact, *the* example—of free human action," the reason why poets "cannot be made into automata."[2] Confidence in such Romantic assertions, however, has never been steadfast, as Savarese himself points out, and where it wavers in Romantic literature, fear creeps in. Hawthorne explores this fear in figures of puppets, automata, and machinery in tales of paranoia, doubt, and antisocial pathologies. Moreover, this fear produces an imbedded irony in Hawthorne's stories, a self-parody that both stages and undermines the positive claims of Romanticism across national traditions.

I teach Hawthorne's stories in a sophomore/junior level course that compares Romantic fiction from a variety of national traditions, including American, English, French, German, Italian, and Russian texts. To identify foundational themes, including recurrent figures of speech and philosophical questions that link this wide array, students start with a close study of several ancient texts. We read anthropogonical myths from *The Epic of Gilgamesh* (the creation of Enkidu), Hesiod's *Theogony* (the castration of man), and *Genesis* (the creation of Adam and Eve), all of which describe human creation as a four-stage process: first, a fashioning of clay into a representation or image; the second, an inspiration in the most literal sense of breathing into the clay; the third, a naming of or a speaking to the created being; and fourth, a fall from grace into a civilized state. The principal themes linking these texts include the association of the divine creation with artistry, the distinction between body and soul or body and mind, the association of life with breath and animation, the constitutive role of language in making humans human, and the necessity of rebellion as the affirmation of the autonomy of mortals. The essential figures in these myths, commonplace in subsequent literature, include clay, divine hands, wind and breath, walking, and speech, and in order to understand the primacy of these figures, we turn to a few selections from other ancient texts.

---

2   John Savarese, "Lyric Mindedness and the 'Automaton Poet,'" *Romantic Circles*, 2013, http://www.rc.umd.edu/praxis/numbers/HTML/praxis.2013.savarese.html.

Frequently, these themes and figures from the mythic origins of humanity are reworked in ancient literature in analogies to puppetry or some unseen manager, be it divine or economic in character. For example, in his description of poetic inspiration in *Ion*, Plato likens the attraction-power of poetry to that of a magnet, which "not only attracts iron rings, but also imparts them a similar power of attracting other rings," from which he concludes that a poet is not an autonomous, conscious, or knowing being but is "inspired" and "impelled" by the Muse, "a divinity moving you [the poet]" like a puppet.[3] Poetry is thus associated with the creative and animating divine speech, but it does not provide humanity with that which grants us our autonomy. In fact, it often is characterized as depriving poets of their own self-control, as Savarese discusses. Along a different line, Herodotus speaks with detectable anxiety about women parading around with phallic puppets in the Egyptian cultic worship of Dionysus:

> eighteen-inch-high images, controlled by strings, which the women carry round the villages; these images have a penis that nods and in the size not much less than all the rest of the body... Now why the penis is so much bigger and is the only thing movable in the body—about this there is a sacred story told.[4]

Through its exoticism and sexual anxiety, the passage from *The Histories* raises questions about gender roles in creation narratives, about gender subordination and discursive control of fertility, and about voyeurism and the power of the gaze. Most relevant to Hawthorne, however, is Ovid's retelling of the Pygmalion myth in *The Metamorphoses*, in which a misogynistic sculptor fashions the perfect woman from marble in order to chasten Roman women, only to succumb to a humiliating infatuation with his own lifeless creation. Through Venus's animation of the statue, Galatea, Ovid satirizes the hubris of an artist who would rival the gods in their creation, the self-absorption of lovers, and the delusions and impositions of idealism which projects fantasies while overlooking the wonders of nature.

With these themes and figures in mind, the students and I turn to the construction of the modern subject. We start with René Descartes'

---

3   Plato, "Ion," *The Internet Classics Archive*, 2009, http://classics.mit.edu/Plato/ion.html.
4   Herodotus, *The History*, trans. David Grene (Chicago: University of Chicago Press, 1987), 152.

Meditations on First Philosophy and Denis Diderot's *Rameau's Nephew* and then consider William Wordsworth's response to Enlightenment thought in his prefaces to *Lyrical Ballads*. Descartes's distinction between mind—which is immaterial and free, and body—which is entirely material and mechanistic, presents a relationship that is analogous to puppetry; *res cogitans* hold the strings to *res extensa*. Students read only a few short selections from this text but enough to introduce them to recurrent concerns in epistemology and the philosophy of mind.

Diderot's novella is short enough to be read in its entirety. His master performer, who seamlessly switches between diverse roles, remains infuriatingly aloof, highlighting that character and temperament are not natural but are, in fact, artificial and theatrical performances. In speaking of a "stupid-looking ninny," for example, he quips acerbically, "He is one of those figures who invite teasing and leg-pulling and whom God made to catch out people who judge by appearances, people whose looking-glass should have taught them that it is as easy to be a man of intelligence and look silly as to conceal a fool behind a clever-looking face."[5] As a remedy to self-bifurcation and alienation, Wordsworth promotes poetry in his prefaces and poems of *Lyrical Ballads*. Poetry, as "the spontaneous overflow of powerful feelings," aims to harmonize the poet to himself, to nature, and to the society of people around him; at the same time it draws the poet toward "A motion and a spirit, that impels/ All thinking things, all objects of all thought, / And rolls through all things," as he says in "Lines Composed a Few Miles Above Tintern Abbey."[6] Yet in celebrating the regenerative power of poetry with reverent fervor, Wordsworth returns to a figure of puppetry; the poet comes to recognize that there is a deep force that "impels... all things." Such contradictions run throughout his poetry and poetics, undermining his assertions about the solitary, independent, and transcendent poet he fancies himself to be. As Alan Richardson has argued, the Romantics were more perplexed than confident about their grasp of the human mind, about "the splitting or fragmentation of the psyche, the status of conscious volition within mental life, and the relationship between mental events and the organic body."[7]

---

5   Denis Diderot, *Rameau's Nephew and D'Alembert's Dream*, trans. Leonard Tancock (New York: Penguin Classics), 81.
6   William Wordsworth, *William Wordsworth: The Major Works*, ed. Stephen Gill (New York: Oxford University Press, 2008), 134, 598.
7   Alan Richardson, *British Romanticism and the Science of the Mind* (Cambridge: Cambridge University Press, 2001), 48.

Romantic authors from diverse national traditions took up these issues in such similar ways that it calls into question whether or not Romantics were more invested in their own traditions or in the spirit of the age. For example, the theme of self-fragmentation, which Richardson among others has identified, is addressed quite literally in Nikolai Gogol's 1836 satirical tale, "The Nose." Major Kovaliov discovers upon waking that his nose has departed from his face, that it has snubbed him and run off into town, has somehow acquired a higher social rank, and is enjoying an independent and scandalous life as a dandy:

> "Sir," said Kovaliov, with a sense of his own dignity, I don't know how to understand your words. The matter appears to me perfectly obvious ... either you wish ... Why, you are my own nose!
> The nose looked at the major and his eyebrows slightly quivered.
> "You are mistaken, sir. I am an independent individual. Moreover, there can be no sort of close relations between us. I see, sir, from the buttons of your uniform, you must be serving in a different department." Saying this, the nose turned away.[8]

Shattering Kovaliov's sense of self, the nose insists that he is an "independent individual" and then proceeds to humiliate him with a condescending dismissal. Despite his best efforts, Kovaliov is unable to be reunited with his own nose, until he wakes from his nightmare. Despite the tale's wild absurdity, Gogol is exploring a dark counter-current of Romanticism that also harkens back to the passage from Herodotus—a fear that one's own body is not under one's self-control but is somehow being manipulated by some other agent, a fear magnified by the possibility of social humiliation when the body parades before others.

In a much lighter but nonetheless similar vein, Hawthorne's "Feathertop," a tale of an animated scarecrow whose posture impresses naïve townsfolk, satirizes the nineteenth-century dandy who imagines himself to be a man of distinction. Pleased with himself, Feathertop woos the young Polly Gookin until she sees his artificial constitution reflected in a mirror. Then, suffering no delusions about his previously assumed humanity, the "fantastic contrivance" returns to Mother Rigby: "I've seen myself for the

---

8   Nikolai Gogol, "The Nose," in *The Complete Tales of Nikolai Gogol*, vol. 2, trans. and ed. Leonard J. Kent (Chicago: University of Chicago Press, 1985), 223.

wretched, ragged, empty thing I am! I'll exist no longer."[9] He then undoes himself by discarding the magic pipe that animates him. The tale involves not only many of the elements of the ancient texts in its parody of creation, but also many of the concerns of Cartesian epistemology and the paradoxes of performance enacted by Diderot's performer. Along these lines, Monika Elbert asserts, "the character Feathertop embodies all the contradictory and self-limiting poses of the gentleman in search of selfhood in the marketplace," such that Feathertop "deconstructs society" by systematically "debunking" the various "gender constructs which hide the ultimate reality—that 'We are the stuffed men... Headpiece filled with straw.'"[10] Though a testament to human ingenuity, automata can produce a contradictory anxiety about the humanity of technology and the soulless progress of industrialization. Indeed, Elbert's essay is an effective way in the classroom to shift from questions of epistemology to questions of economics, class, gender, and those dark social forces that deprive individuals of agency, the "megamachine" of which Sauer speaks. Elbert points out that Dickon, the "invisible hand" that refuels Feathertop's pipe, the source of his life, is the "'invisible hand' of capitalism, a demonic and mysterious power which controls our notion of class and gender."[11] (Although I am very selective about using secondary sources in my course, Elbert's accessible essay is an excellent way to introduce students to Marxist and feminist readings as well as to deconstruction.) Whereas Wordsworth deified the forces that impel humanity, Hawthorne offers a proto-Marxist perspective—it is the marketplace that controls our actions. I have argued elsewhere that this is the result of his familiarity with English radical culture, but in teaching "Feathertop," I focus more on its satirical dimension.[12]

Hawthorne's satirical handling of the artificial animation of life in "Feathertop" is starkly different in tone from Mary Shelley's Gothic *Frankenstein, or The Modern Prometheus* (1818), or for that matter, his own much more sober treatment of the same theme in 1846 in "The Artist of

---

9   Nathaniel Hawthorne, "Feathertop," *Mosses from an Old Manse* in *The Centenary Edition of the Works of Nathaniel Hawthorne*, vol. X, eds. William Charvat et al. (Columbus: Ohio State University Press, 1972), 249, 257.

10   Monika Elbert, "Hawthorne's 'Hollow' Men: Fabricating Masculinity in 'Feathertop,'" *American Transcendental Quarterly* 5, no. 3 (1991): 180, 169.

11   Ibid., 170.

12   Michael Demson, "The Ungovernable Puppets and the Biopolitics of Hawthorne's Gothic Satires," *Nathaniel Hawthorne Review* 38, no. 2 (2012): 72–92.

the Beautiful." This satirical dimension feels distinctively American. Klaus Benesch asserts that Hawthorne frequently expressed an "anxiety about the ongoing mechanization of American society" and that he was suspicious about "technological innovations" driving "America's metamorphosis from virgin land to capitalist market place."[13] The scarecrow, the witch at the town's edge, the town's layout, and the names are all common stock of American folk literature. Nevertheless, the core anxiety about industrialization was a common sentiment of international Romanticism, immediately identifiable, for example, in the celebration of pristine nature in François-René de Chateaubriand's wildly successful novella *Atala* (1801) or George Cruikshank's etching, *London going out of town, or, The march of bricks & mortar!* (1829) [Figure 1.]

"*London going out of town, or, The march of bricks & mortar!* designed, etched & published by George Cruikshank, 1829." Plus the credit line, "Courtesy of The Lewis Walpole Library, Yale University."

The etching is "a rendering of the ruthless devastations of the jerry-building ... The scene is Hampstead (still rural); trees and haystacks are bombarded by bricks. . . ."[14] Sympathetic haystacks and livestock retreat, trees fall—

---

13   Klaus Benesch, "Chapter 2: Machine Art Revisited: Hawthorne's Artist(s) of the Beautiful," in *Romantic Cyborgs: Authorship and Technology in the American Renaissance* (Amherst: University of Massachusetts Press, 2002), 64–71.

14   M. Dorothy George, *Hogarth to Cruikshank: Social Change in Graphic Satire* (New York: Viking Press, 1967), 180.

one crying "I'm mortally wounded"—and birds take flight as an army of sawing, digging, and brick-laying automata advance upon the countryside. Michael Rawson points out that "Cruikshank was conveying the same anxiety over the speed and scale of early British urbanization that others were expressing in prose" and that the "thin veneer of humor does not conceal the fact that his image is primarily a portrait of violence and destruction."[15] The same might be said of "Feathertop," that its humor is a thin veneer that fails to conceal how the simple rustic life is not one of independence but rather of economic subordination and control. "Feathertop" ultimately is a very disconcerting tale.

Students have little difficulty in identifying a myriad of similarities between "Feathertop" and *Frankenstein*, the text to which it is most commonly compared. In my course, I focus on Shelley's 1831 introduction to the third edition, in which she gives "some account of the origin of the story" and in which she calls her novel "my hideous progeny."[16] This preface can function as a key to counter-current Romanticism because it theorizes about the fear of puppets and automata. Here, Shelley meditates on the freedom of the imagination enjoyed in childhood but lost as one ages, on the difficulty in freeing oneself from a "common-place style," and most importantly, on artistic invention:

> Invention, it must be humbly admitted, does not consist in creating out of void, but out of chaos; the materials must, in the first place, be afforded: it can give form to dark, shapeless substances, but cannot bring into being the substance itself...Invention consists in the capacity of seizing on the capabilities of a subject, and in the power of moulding and fashioning ideas suggested to it (8).

She likens literary genesis to divine creation in an explicit analogy, and I have often used this passage to open up discussion of archetypal patterns and archetypal criticism. Her discussion of inspiration then returns to the figure of the puppet in two different configurations. First, she herself is a puppet subjugated to her inspired imagination: "My imagination,

---

15 Michael Rawson, "The March of Bricks and Mortar," *Environmental History* 17 (October 2012): 844–45.
16 Mary Shelley, *Frankenstein, or The Modern Prometheus* (New York: Penguin Books, 1992), 10. Subsequent references to this text are documented parenthetically.

unbidden, possessed and guided me, gifting the successive images that arose in my mind with a vividness far beyond the usual bounds of reverie (9). This is echoed within the novel; Frankenstein is entirely possessed by his own project of creation. In both of these cases, Shelley and Frankenstein have lost control, have abdicated moral responsibility, and plead that they have been impelled by a force other than their own reason and volition.

Shelley's novel, published and circulating around the world, is figured as a rebellious automaton, the "hideous progeny" of her imagination—not a natural child but an artificial one who has become treacherous and vengeful. This, too, is echoed in the central plot of the novel, as the monster breaks away from Frankenstein after his animation, only to wreak havoc beyond Frankenstein's control. (Discussing Mary Shelley's own scandalous elopement with Percy Shelley and her betrayal of her father, William Godwin, instances the value and the limits of biographical criticism.) Shelley explains her use of the epithet "hideous": "Frightful must it be; for supremely frightful would be the effect of any human endeavor to mock the stupendous mechanism of the Creator of the world. His success would terrify the artist; he would rush away from his odious handy-work, horror-stricken" (9). While other Romantics explore other reactions than fright (Mother Rigby is not fearful but entirely callous about her creation, for example), Shelley's formulation that there is something essentially hubristic about artistic creation is a prevalent one.

The discussion of Romantic hubris can open up many of Hawthorne's tales, particularly "The Artist of the Beautiful" (1844), which Paul Lewis identifies as Hawthorne's "retelling of Mary Shelley's *Frankenstein*."[17] Owen Warland, a watchmaker by trade but also a quiet artist seeking artistic transcendence over material reality, crafts a butterfly automaton of wondrous verisimilitude, only to have it crushed by a child. Nonetheless, in his momentary success, he achieves transcendence and is elated. Millicent Bell reads the plot of the tale as a conflict between a transcendental "Romantic worldview" and "the eighteenth-century view of the universe as a logical system of parts," an interpretation that returns to many of the central themes of the course. Perhaps what is more important, however, is to question why the butterfly, as an artificial life rather than a natural life, must be

---

17 Paul Lewis, "Victor Frankenstein and Owen Warland: The Artist as Satan and as God," *Studies in Short Fiction* 14 (1977): 279.

destroyed.[18] Why is the impulse or drive to create so commonly followed by a destructive impulse, our own or others?

These questions can occasion an introduction to psychoanalysis and in particular to Sigmund Freud's concept of the uncanny. In his essay "On the Psychology of the Uncanny" (1906), Freud's study of the uncanny takes issue with Ernst Jentsch's reading of E. T. A. Hoffmann's tale, "The Sandman" (1816), another Romantic tale of an automaton. Nathanael, a traumatized and troubled university student, falls in love with Olimpia, a dancing automaton, only to go insane upon the realization of his folly. (Hoffmann's "Automata," which features the automaton, the Talking Turk, is an optional reading choice.) In many respects, "The Sandman" is a retelling of Ovid's Pygmalion, and Jentsch insists, according to Freud's argument, that it is the ontological uncertainty surrounding Olimpia that produces the uncanny mood of the tale.[19] Freud himself, however, rejects this thesis, asserting instead that the uncanny is in fact connected to a fear of blindness (how Freud reintroduces the Oedipus Complex), and deeper still is a fear that we will not be able to distinguish between what we observe and what we desire, a conflation configured in the male gaze. Short selections from Jacques Lacan's seminars and Laura Mulvey's discussion of the male gaze in her essay, "Visual Pleasure and Narrative Cinema" (1975), are useful ways to open up further discussion of this concept, both in terms of psychoanalysis and feminism, as is a return to some of the ancient texts to reexamine how gaze and movement are essential components in the narratives of the Fall, the Herodotus passage, and Ovid's Pygmalion. Indeed, the fear of falling in love with a puppet, whose father has some diabolical plan for an inexperienced young man, is a common plot in Hoffmann's tales and is reworked as well in Hawthorne.

In "Rappaccini's Daughter," the story I assign alongside "The Sandman," a mad doctor has his daughter cultivate a collection of poisonous plants, to which she becomes immune although they are poisonous to others. While the father's science might promise to protect his daughter from lovers, it is in fact a lover, Giovanni, who attempts to cure her, killing her instead. John Hazlett argues that because "nature as seen in the tale has no readable symbolic or allegorical relation to Spirit," the tale undermines the core tenets of

---

18   Millicent Bell, *Hawthorne's View of the Artist* (New York: Dell, 1965), 13.
19   Sigmund Freud, *The Uncanny*, trans. David McLintock (New York: Penguin, 2003), 123.

American transcendentalism.[20] While this is certainly the case, the tale also offers a reconfiguration, consciously or not, of the Romantic exploration of the rights of women in terms of puppetry and machinery. For example, Mary Hays opens her novella, *Memoirs of Emma Courtney* (1795),

> The events of my life have been few, and have in them nothing very uncommon, but the effects which they have produced on my mind; yet, that mind they have helped to form, and this in the eye of philosophy, or affection, may render them not wholly uninteresting. While I trace them, they convince me of the irresistible power of circumstances, modifying and controuling [sic] our characters, and introducing, mechanically, those associations and habits, which make us what we are. . . . [21]

Indeed, the identification of women with puppets is almost so ubiquitous in Romantic literature that it is productive to see how various authors handle this figure differently. There are, of course, many other instances of puppets, automata, and machinery in Hawthorne's tales as well as in his novels, and in Romantic literature in general. One might explore Hawthorne's handling of magic lanterns in his tale, "Main-Street" (1852) from *The Snow Image* in connection with Johann Wolfgang von Goethe's *The Sorrows of Young Werther* (1774) or the procession of prisoners like parade puppets in *The Scarlet Letter* and Victor Hugo's novella, *The Last Day of a Condemned Man* (1829). My overall aim, though, is never to be comprehensive or to establish a canon of literature on these themes—quite the opposite. Rather, I want to keep the study as an open-ended, comparative exploration of world literature as well as diverse theoretical approaches.

Because the concepts and themes addressed in the course are diverse and many, I find it helpful to assign weekly two-page papers. These explications encourage the students to identify and quote a key passage from one of the texts assigned, to identify within this passage a concept or theme that has been recurrent in the course readings, to restate this concept or theme in their own words, and then to discuss briefly what is distinctive

---

20 John Hazlett, "Re-reading 'Rappaccini's Daughter': Giovanni and the Seduction of the Transcendental Reader," *ESQ: A Journal of the American Renaissance* 35 (1989): 61.

21 Mary Hays, *Memoirs of Emma Courtney* (New York: Oxford University Press, 1996), 9–10.

or compelling about its handling in that passage. These papers become the starting point for our conversations in the classroom and are often the first steps toward the longer comparative term paper in which students explore how a set of figures or themes are treated in three different national contexts. Writing is also a key component to my approach because it prompts students to reflect upon their relationship to language, the struggle of composition, the difficulties of self-expression, and the aspiration for originality and vitality which has been part of our focus. Discussion of student perceptions and issues can then circle back to a more acute awareness of the meta-fictional comments on authorship in Hawthorne's short fiction, be it Owen Warland's suffering and isolation in composing his butterfly, Rappaccini's megalomania in his transformation of his daughter, or Mother Rigby's flippancy toward her diabolical offspring, Feathertop.

Sam Houston State University

Pre-cinema in *The House of the Seven Gables*

Alberto Gabriele

The House of the Seven Gables represents a seminal text and an equally paradigmatic case-study in text/image approaches focusing on nineteenth-century fiction. Recent scholarship has identified in the character of Clifford early evidence of the emergence of the figure of the aesthete in the genealogy of nineteenth-century transatlantic aestheticism, so crucial for later rewritings by authors such as Henry James and Oscar Wilde, as indicated by Michele Mendelssohn.[1] *The House of the Seven Gables*, moreover, has attracted the attention of scholars, such as Millicent Bell, Cathy Davidson, Alan Trachtenberg, Michael Jay Bunker Noble, Michael Frank, and Susan Williams, who have focused on the representation of artists in Hawthorne's fiction and on the presence in the novel of technical innovations that transformed the tradition of the nineteenth-century portrait, such as the daguerreotype.

Not enough attention, however, has been dedicated to the wide array of pre-cinematic spectacles present in the story, next to the daguerreotype, which are frequent and appear side by side with the many other ekphrastic references to portraits of different type, size, and style that contribute to

---

1   Michele Mendelssohn, *Henry James, Oscar Wilde and Aesthetic Culture* (Edinburgh: Edinburgh University Press, 2007).

the symbolic economy of the narrative.[2] The coexistence of different modes of representing and copying reality, through portraiture and mechanical, pre-cinematic spectacles of an equally dazzling variety, constitute a significant reflection on the nature of mimesis in relation to the challenges posed by the culture of industrial modernity. Instead of extrapolating from the narrative one type of representation, as it has been the case with most of the scholars mentioned above, I wish to propose that these spectacles be examined in a more complex system of textual and visual synergies that offer important evidence of how the limits and possibilities of nineteenth-century mimesis were being redefined.[3] I shall focus here on the references

2   Michael Jay Bunker Noble in "Hawthorne's *The House of the Seven Gables*," *Explicator* 56, no. 2 (1998): 72–74 does identify a pictorial value to Hawthorne's fiction when he traces what Cathy Davidson in "Photographs of the Dead: Sherman, Daguerre and Hawthorne," *South Atlantic Quarterly* 89 (1990): 681, calls the "Manichean aspect," of the daguerreotype, which contains within its frame both a negative and a positive image, in the use of light and shaded grays in Hawthorne's stylistic palette. Susan Williams speaks of the "failed ambition" of representing both "speaking pictures" and "reality in flux" in "The Aspiring Purpose of an Ambitious Demagogue: Portraiture and *The House of the Seven Gables*," in *Nineteenth-Century Literature* 49 (1994), 244. I would rather see Hawthorne's experiments with perception inspired by the culture of industrial modernity as groundbreaking, unacknowledged attempts at redefining mimesis. Michael Jay Bunker Noble (ibid.), Michael Frank ("Photographing Ghosts: Ancestral Reproduction and Daguerreotypic Mimesis in Nathaniel Hawthorne's *The House of the Seven Gables*," *Litteraria Pragensia* 17 [2007]: 40–57), and Trachtenberg to some degree in his "Seeing and Believing: Hawthorne's Reflections on the Daguerreotype in *The House of the Seven Gables*" (*American Literature* 9 [1997]: 460–68), single out the daguerreotype without exploring the many modalities of vision and representation that the narrative includes. Trachtenberg discusses briefly the "panorama" and the "railroad-car vista" (43), in light of the "Panic of 1837," without focusing on the more complex history of pre-modernist visuality.

3   In this sense, I question Alan Trachtenberg's assumption in "Seeing and Believing" that Hawthorne's understanding of the daguerreotype can be made to identify with the echoes of the "Enlightenment rationalist ideology" (465), which he recognizes in the character of Holgrave or with typological thinking, and which he identifies in Phoebe's assumption that the old portrait is a "prophecy" (470) of the Judge. Rather than highlighting the discursive formations present in the romance, I wish to posit a new kind of intertextuality, a visual one, which is as rich in ramifications, repeated occurrences, and automatic emergences as any text-based form of intertextuality. Visual practices in nineteenth-century culture, as indicated

to panorama, proto-cinematic vision, and the daguerreotype in order to highlight the innovative form of mimesis that Hawthorne allows in the freer genre of the "romance." Interestingly, these aesthetic explorations of reality through pre-cinematic spectacles appear in the open-ended genre of the "Romance," which supposedly allows Hawthorne "a certain latitude" without the constraints of the novel, according to Hawthorne's own theorization in the preface of *The House of the Seven Gables*.[4]

The exposure to a rich variety of spectacles that characterized the rise of industrial modernity is the experiential datum for the characters in the story and, indirectly, for the reader whose inner vision is shaped by different modalities of perception. Maps, paintings, miniatures, mesmeric looking glasses, sketches, daguerreotypes, phantasmagorias, panoramas, print culture artifacts, such as books and magazine articles, all attract the attention of the observer. In order to chart the scopic regime in place in *The House of the Seven Gables*, the discussion of visual culture in the story should not focus on one form but recognize that Hawthorne alternates between fixed perspective reproductions, such as the painted portraits, and mobile ones, such as the panorama or the phantasmagoria,—to name only the patented technologies explicitly mentioned in the course of the story. In doing so, Hawthorne's experiment with the genre of the romance explores an aesthetic that challenges and problematizes the accepted modalities of vision codified by means of a long tradition of artistic theory, academic training, artistic practice, and critical appreciation. This newer "gray area" of vision and representation is a reflection of the culture of industrial modernity that exists outside of the codifications of the eighteenth-century discourse of aesthetics. In this essay, I shall exemplify some of the different modalities of vision and representation referenced in the story and point to the ways in which Hawthorne closes in on the dizzying variety of visual stimuli that the story incorporates to reintroduce a notion of structured order in

---

by Jonathan Crary in *Techniques of the Observer: On Vision and Modernity in the 19th Century*, (Cambridge, MA: MIT Press, 1990), shaped and transformed in the viewer's mind what was a naturalized notion of sight as a stable, fixed, and frontal window-view onto the world outside.

4   Nathaniel Hawthorne, *The House of the Seven Gables* (New York: Penguin Books, 1981), 1. Subsequent references are to this edition and appear parenthetically. In this sense the "Romance" cannot be said to identify only with the "atmospheric, shadowed" mimesis described by Alan Trachtenberg in "Seeing and Believing," 461.

direct opposition to the principle of multiplicity animating the culture of modernity and its new spectacles.⁵

Scholarship on text/image relations in the history of the modern novel has evolved in parallel to the discursive construction of the prestige of certain modes of artistic representation, such as the fine arts, in opposition to other lesser, more technologically based ones, such as photography. The tradition of pictorialism, the theory of the sister arts exemplified in the adage "ut pictura poesis" (like painting poetry) has built a parallel between the art of painting and the verbal translation of works of art—or of vision at large—in the codified expression of verbal signs. As new means of technological reproduction gained more acceptance in the system of aesthetic appreciation, more recent scholarship has reflected the newly acquired importance of other media, such as photography, once its artistic value gained acceptance. Pre-cinematic spectacles are forms of representation that have benefited, in the field of visual studies, from the attention of critics, historians, and scholars such as Max Milner, Werner Nekes, Jonathan Crary, and Laurent Mannoni.⁶ Their work has begun to inspire literary scholars to focus on the presence of these modalities of vision in nineteenth-century fiction.⁷ The hypothesis advanced by Max Milner in 1982, that is, that

---

5   I agree with Susan Williams who claims in "The Aspiring Purpose of an Ambitious Demagogue" that "there are moments in *Seven Gables* when the larger narrative seems to aspire to imitate the still eternity usually associated with the portrait" (229–30); I wish rather to outline the opposition not between portraits as "active agents that extend through time" and the drive to stabilize vision, but rather between the newer scopic regime of pre- and protocinematic vision and the visual intuition of metaphysical transcendence that becomes dominant as the story progresses towards its conclusion.

6   Max Milner, *La fantasmagorie* (Paris: Presses Universitaires de France, 1982); Werner Nekes, *Film Before Film* (Austria: Filförderung Nordrhein-Westfalen, documentary, 1986); Jonathan Crary, *Techniques of the Observer*; and Laurent Mannoni, *The Great Art of Light and Shadow. Archaeology of the Cinema* (Exeter: University of Exeter Press, 2000).

7   For a discussion of the phantasmagoria in relation to Gothic and nineteenth-century fiction, see Terry Castle, *The Female Thermometer* (Oxford: Oxford University Press, 1995). On the invention of the phonograph phantasy of cinema in Villiers de l'Isle-Adam, see Tom Gunning, "Doing for the Eye What the Phonograph Does for the Ear," in *The Sounds of Early Cinema*, ed. Richard Abel (Bloomington: Indiana University Press, 2001), 13–31. For the thaumatropic effect in Melville's *Pierre*, see Alberto Gabriele, "Traces and Origins, Signs and Meanings:

creativity is conditioned by the history of optics and defined by the techniques that affect perception and representation, has found several echoes in the following decade, especially for his reference to optics as a significant component in an "archaeology of knowledge."[8] Werner Nekes's *Film Before Film* (1986) and Jonathan Crary's *Techniques of the Observer* (1990) have classified and identified specific modalities of vision captivating the eyes of the urban crowds of nineteenth-century industrial modernity and reflected on the status of the observer and the epistemological purport of these innovations. They both recognize the central role of the viewer's perception in shaping and *de facto* creating the spectacle that appears by means of optical toys such as the thaumatrope, the phenakistiscope and the zoetrope, whose visual lure is based on the persistence of vision on the retina of the observer: it is only the perception of the viewer that enables the possibility of creating a life-like illusion of movement. These objects, which were called at the time "philosophical objects," demand more than an anecdotal and passing attention in relation to a material history of nineteenth-century culture, since they transformed the notion of mimesis beyond the models of pictorialism and of the frontal view of still life that photography, or, here in *The House of the Seven Gables* portraiture, made possible. By challenging the frontal, fixed, and perspectival perception of the painterly model, Hawthorne in *The House of the Seven Gables* contributes to an exploration of alternative modalities of vision based on the fast sequence of impressionistic takes that are juxtaposed in rapid sequence like in the popular forms of spectacle extending in the temporality of vision such as certain tricks of the magic lantern, the thaumatrope, the phenakistiscope, the panorama, the phantasmagoria, and later in the century, the cinematograph. [Fig. 1] By doing so, his fiction goes beyond the honored tradition of "ut pictura poesis" and the equally established notion of the sister arts suggested by the presence of portraits, which has been

---

Analogy and the Precinematic Imagination in Melville's *Pierre, or, the Ambiguities*," *Leviathan, a Journal of Melville Studies* 15 (2013): 42–62. Recent works on early cinema such as *A Companion to Early Cinema*, ed. André Gaudreault, Nicolas Dulac, and Santiago Hidalgo (Chichester, UK: Wiley-Blackwell, 2012) still ignore the importance of print culture and periodical literature in shaping both the modalities of vision and the narrative structures of the early history of cinema. See for instance the essay by Annemone Ligensa, "Sensationalism and Early Cinema," in *A Companion to Early Cinema*, 163–82.

8   Milner, *La fantasmagorie*, 5.

the topic of widespread scholarly interest.⁹ Hawthorne's experimentations with different spectacles explore the unchartered territory of a nineteenth-century aesthetics represented by the sensorium of industrial modernity that will gain currency only at the time of the modernist avant-garde. The term pre-cinema may be problematic, as it could imply a linear teleo-

logical narrative from nineteenth-century spectacle to the single patented form that became dominant in the long twentieth century, that is, the cinematograph, so much so that linguistic usage distinguishes a "before" and an "after." I use the term pre-cinematic literally, as referring to what historically preceded the advent of cinema without, however, imposing such a teleological drive to the narrative. I still use "pre-cinema" because it's a term broad enough to include phenakistiskopes, thaumatropes, zoetropes, magic lanterns, and other forms of spectacles that redefined the possibilities of vision and representation. Isolating one medium, without implicitly referring to the concomitant existence of conflicting aesthetic practices that sometimes questioned the premises of any of these spectacles, narrows down one's critical focus, running the risk of making the synecdochic

---

9   Rita Gollin and John L. Idol, Jr., in *Prophetic Pictures: Nathaniel Hawthorne's Knowledge and Uses of the Visual Arts* (New York: Greenwood Press, 1991), while privileging Hawthorne's engagement with the tradition of pictorialism, do mention other "art objects" and the importance of daguerreotype, dioramas, and magic lanterns as aides to his fiction-writing (37) and the more specific thematization of, respectively, the diorama in "Main Street," the magic lantern in "Ethan Brand" (43–44).

assumption that one technique, such as the panorama or the kaleidoscope, could become a substitute for a whole aesthetic. "Pre-cinema," being a provisional term invented by twentieth-century historians in the wake of the dominant model of vision represented by the cinematograph, can be used, I believe, against the grain. The reference to a broad pre-cinematic visual culture that the term can imply, moreover, highlights the complex and coexisting multi-mediatic reality made by intertwined and juxtaposed stimuli deriving from different forms of visuality. I use the term, therefore, to indicate a thread in the fabric of nineteenth-century visual culture that made possible the emergence of cinema, while acknowledging the many other forms of visualizations that challenged its very aesthetics. *The House of the Seven Gables* is interesting in the history of the "nineteenth-century novel" because, by absorbing and elaborating suggestions coming from the aesthetic of both traditional painting and pre-cinematic entertainment, it reflects a moment of transition between different aesthetic modes. In doing so, the new aesthetics charted in the story anticipates modernist sensitivities that at the time were not circulating as discursive formations. In this sense, *The House of the Seven Gables* helps to challenge a genealogy of the modernist avant-garde that insists, especially in the rhetoric of its early manifestoes, on its violent rupture from the past.

PORTRAITURE

The narrative convention of the family portrait in nineteenth-century fiction, which emigrates from aristocratic settings and becomes a standardized staple of the bourgeois interior, takes different turns as the modern novel developed, reflecting the specific codes of each genre of fiction. Gothic narratives, for instance, present the narrative function of the animated portrait (Horace Walpole's Castle of Otranto, or Washington Irving's "The Knight of Malta") in which the figure depicted in the painting steps down from its frame to terrorize the protagonists of the story or just to reenact a family curse on them, as in Hawthorne's "Edward Randolph's Portrait." Other narratives employ the realistic setting of nineteenth-century urban life to trace the shifting definitions of artistic value across class divides, as in Balzac's At the Sign of the Cat and Racket, where the paintings of Théodore de Sommervieux circulate among different owners belonging to the rising petty bourgeoisie and the aristocracy. In *The House of the Seven Gables*, as in "Edward Randolph's Portrait," the unshakeable weight of an ancestor's wrongdoing that haunts future generations reinforces the moral value the portrait has in shaping and constraining the lives of the descendants of the depicted figure. Portraiture, therefore, serves the social function of immortalizing rank, while leaving to the young generations the effects of the evil that may have been a necessary step in acquiring the social status so solemnly depicted in the picture. This is the case of the criminal appropriation of land by Colonel Pyncheon, the patriarchal ancestor of the family, which brings a curse on his family line: Colonel Pyncheon had the rightful owner, the workman Maule, accused of sorcery and condemned to death in order to confiscate his coveted property. No prophetic gift on the part of the painter questions the temporal linearity of the narrative by escaping the progression of everyday-life to spell out what the future of his models will be, as in "The Prophetic Pictures." The past haunts the future generations and relegates their actions to a standstill that has no outcome other than a predictable tragedy. Portraiture, therefore, is a moral reminder of the inescapable cause and effect logic of sin and retribution when perceived through Puritanical eyes.

The Panorama and the Fragmented View of Industrial Modernity

In opposition to the inescapable spatial logic of the tradition of portraiture on a two-dimensional canvas according to the conventions of line and color stand the teeming world of industrial modernity with its visual fleeting sequence of moving spectacles. The constant mobility of the observer in the industrial city of choreographed trade activities undermines any stable view, thus representing also a political challenge to the system of immobile privilege that the custom of portraying and displaying the patriarchal figures of an aristocratic family line reifies. Hepzibah is a symbol of the secluded, waning prestige of her class in the face of the culture of urban modernity. She lives in solitary pride of a long-lost family splendor, represented by the isolated and imposing location of the house; furthermore, she is quite unable, through the myopic view of her scowling gaze, to understand the dynamics that make possible the accumulation of wealth in the modern context. The new system of commodity capitalism exists far from the House of the Seven Gables, in an enveloping vision of a benumbing "panorama" (48), a 360-degrees representation of a spectacle that cannot be reduced to one single perspectival view within the safe borders of the frame of the painting. Panoramas, which allows the viewer entry into a circular space covered with a continuous depiction of subjects such as battles or landscapes, prevents vision to focus on one subject demanding the observer's full attention through its central position in a geometrically arranged setting of perspectival depth. Panoramic vision, moreover, develops in the temporality of observation, so that the observer amasses fragmentary impressions that fall within their own focus. Hawthorne interestingly uses the mode of vision of the panorama to depict commodity capitalism, the form of production, and of accumulating wealth and family fortunes that is ungraspable for Hepzibah:

> Groceries, toy-shops, dry-goods stores, with their immense panes of plate-glass, their gorgeous fixtures, their vast and complete assortments of merchandize, in which fortunes had been invested; and those marble mirrors at the farther end of each establishment, doubling all this wealth by a brightly burnished vista of unrealities! (46)

This proto-Marxist view of commodity capitalism produces, in the space of the modern store, the dizzying effect of a hall of mirrors, which multiplies the effect of unreality with the "multitude of perfumed and glossy salesmen, smirking, smiling, bowing and measuring out the goods" (49). Vision is fragmented into parceled perspectives; large synthesis organizing dominant systems of belief are reduced to long lists of replaceable items for sale. The awe-inspiring still mien emerging from a canvas is turned into a myriad of facial ticks, into fixed mechanical gestures that reproduce themselves endlessly at every street corner and in every shop. Hepzibah's store, by contrast, myopically fixates on items of quotidian use value; the economic exchanges she favors—flour, Jim Crow cookies, yeast—fall within a domestic economy of a self-sufficient maintenance of the status quo and its ideological symbols of dominance. More than once she gives away her merchandise for free, moved by sympathy and by her aristocratic ethos dictating generous acts of charity. The source of her family wealth through an illicit appropriation, which so anguishes her identity, removes her even further from contemporary life. The new scopic regime of commodity capitalism in a family of her perspective falls outside of any family narrative, to which she always recurs to make sense of family fortunes. The new reality is an alternative spectacle, defined by contemporary forms of popular entertainment, such as the panorama, that challenge the linear narrative of cause and effect and the implied moralizing temporality of sin and retribution that the cyclical evil influence portrait may produce on the onlookers from the confined space of the framed picture.

A vertical axis of influence going from a revered family ancestor hung on the wall in a prominent position is replaced by a horizontal, all-encompassing, axis of interchangeable commodities, endless transactions, new agencies that the modern city puts in chaotic motion, thus altering fixed family narratives, stable conventions of morality, logic structures of meaning. Not one of these new spectacles has a lasting influence on the retina that exceeds the fleeting glance of an enumerative, paratactic syntax that piles up one impression after the other. The view of the world outside of the premises of the cursed home presents the same percussive rhythm of repeated intermittent sensual stimuli for the ailing, passive observer Clifford who sits by the window of the house:

> The butcher's cart, with its snowy canopy, was an acceptable object; so was the fish cart, heralded by its horn; so, likewise, was the countryman's cart of vegetables, plodding from door to door, with long pauses of the patient horse, while his owner drove a trade in turnips, carrots, summer squashes, string-beans, green peas, and new potatoes, with half the housewives of the neighborhood. The baker's cart, with the harsh music of its bells, had a pleasant effect on Clifford, because, as few things else did, it jingled the very dissonance of yore. (161)

Parataxis is not only a reflection of the aesthetic experience of movement represented by the teeming activity of city merchants; syntax here implicitly resists the logic of an elaborate hypotactic explanation that may clarify the process of economic activities and the complex network of relations that the urban economy relies upon. The almost nominal sentences that describe the sequence of spectacles offered in rapid succession, in both the hallucinatory view of shop windows and in the perspective from the window, question traditional narratives and logically overdetermined developments. The view from a window, in particular, presents a view of the teeming activity of unrelated agents in the expanding urban environment that orients artistic representation in the direction of a documentary, proto-cinematographic sensitivity. The sequence of spectacles that appear within the frame of the window may proleptically coincide with the camera view of the cinematograph, in an anticipation of the early examples of film by the Lumière cinematographers or with the more elaborately edited films belonging to the genre of "a day in the life of a big city," like Charles Urban's Living London (1904) and the more canonical films produced in the 1920s like Paul Strand's Manhatta (1920–21), Walter Ruttmann's Berlin, Symphony of a Great City (1927), Mikhail Kaufman's Moscow (1926), and Dziga Vertov's The Man with the Movie Camera (1929). In both forms of vision, the view from the window and the cinematographic depiction of city life in the frame of the screen of early cinema present rapidly shifting spectacles that dictate a staccato rhythm to the narrative. Parataxis fractures the unity of complex but harmonious reality seen in landscape and genre painting; parataxis, moreover, leaves the many agents it enumerates in rapid sequence to fragmentary existences that are liberated from traditional narratives. When Hepzibah and Clifford finally venture into the outside world, without being blocked by the feared gaze of the conformist community they live in, which halted their first attempt to cross the threshold of their house directed to church, a new world of possibilities opens up to them. Clifford's enthusiastic and agitated speech moves metaphorically forward, past the existing forms of life and the dominant values of their community: he imagines a nomadic life opposed to the immured existence of their home; he also redefines morality by entertaining the possibility of a necessary evil, while their train car abolishes distances and breaks the stable urban structure of traditional life by reducing all to atomistic fragments:

> At one moment they were rattling through a solitude;—the next, a village had grown up around them;—a few breaths more, and it had vanished, as if swallowed by an earthquake. The spires of meetinghouses seemed set adrift from their foundations; the broad-based hills glided away. Everything was unfixed from its age-long rest, and moving at whirlwind speed in a direction opposite to their own. (256)

The paragraph ends with a merely enumerative sequence of human activities with no descriptive elaboration: "Sleep; sport; business; graver or lighter study;—and the common and inevitable movement onward! It was life itself!" (257). This is the final instance of a paratactic freedom of segmented agencies with no pre-existing logic to arrange them in normative narratives. While pointing to fragmentation and unrelated parcels of a larger picture that has exploded into fragments, these instances of an enumerative style of prose go in the opposite direction to the moves toward unity of traditional painting and push the dimension of movement within the spectacle of the diorama mentioned by Susan Williams to a more mechanically enhanced sensorium of disjoined fragments in rapid motion.[10] This perception is also reproduced in modernist novels that incorporate the aesthetic disorientation produced by other forms of transportation, such as the car, for instance in Proust's In Search of Lost Time when the narrator travels with Albertine in a car and sees the trees of the Raspelière fleeing the approaching car in all directions. The same sensitivity to speed that fragments the cohesive static view of the painterly classical tradition shapes also, in the context of early-nineteenth-century art, the practices of the artistic avant-garde, in performance—one can think of the futurist experiments—as well as in painting and sculpture. While the experience of the avant-garde is often presented through the narrative trope of the break of the new from the old, I want to argue that one needs to retrace this submerged aesthetics in nineteenth-century culture.

The exploration of modern spectacles in The House of the Seven Gables presents, therefore, both identifiable mechanical spectacles of mass entertainment, such as the panorama, and a kinetic sensitivity that is not contemplated by any aesthetic theory of artistic value. In this sense, the term "pre-cinema" comes to indicate not only the innovations in the long history of visual practices that were supplanted by the patented and industrial mode of vision and mass commercial entertainment of the cinematograph, but a gray area in the history of aesthetics that appears in nineteenth-century literary works without being theorized as a viable mode of artistic representation until the formulations of the twentieth-century avant-garde, which championed precisely these modes of seeing. One can also think, in this genealogy of modernity, of the verses of William Wordsworth's Prelude depicting the city of London in 1805.[11] The stroller's perspective of city crowds assembled by the early stages of industrialization is opposed to the aesthetic of rural idylls unaltered by this process. Wordsworth's representation alternates between a realistic rendition of the fragmented stimuli of the urban sensorium and an aesthetic mediation of natural landscapes

---

10   Williams, "The Aspiring Purpose of an Ambitious Demagogue," 227.
11   See Alberto Gabriele, "Visions of the City of London: Mechanical Eye and Poetic Transcendence in Wordsworth's Prelude-book 7," *The European Romantic Review* 19, no. 4 (2008): 265–85.

by means of Platonic categories. The percussive rhythm that the eye of the city flâneur registers is the rhythm of the visual "shocks" imparted by the fleeting glimpses at humanity in constant movement, by the passing look at signs, advertisements, and street scenes that rapidly parade in front of the stroller or the coach rider. Fragmentation is, therefore, an experience that goes beyond the aesthetic or subjective and acquires a new ontological value in the context of nineteenth-century industrialization that will become the esperanto of the modernist avant-garde. We can retrace the similar view of temporality in Proust's *In Search of Lost Time* when the narrator claims that "there are bits of Turner in the work of Poussin, a phrase of Flaubert in Montesquieu."[12] By turning the assumed linear and progressive evolution of temporality the other way, one discovers the traits that mark innovation in an unacknowledged predecessor. In *The House of the Seven Gables* a proto-cinematographic avant-garde aesthetics emerges as a result of nineteenth-century authors' engagement with the sensorium of urban modernity. At the other end of the spectrum that defines the "long nineteenth century" one can imagine the ironic multimedia innovations in the early collage experiments of Picasso, such as his 1912 Glass and Bottle of Suze, or the nostalgic recapturing of the montage effect of nineteenth-century print culture in the more prolonged use of the technique in Max Ernst's pictorial narratives, such as his 1929's collage novel *The Hundred-Headed Woman*. Nineteenth-century literature, therefore, does chart this new aesthetic territory without being able to read it in a larger theory that might accommodate its novelty. Both Wordsworth and Hawthorne, while experientially very engaged in the rendition of the new spectacle, shy away from its potentially unreadable fragmented perspectives by reverting to traditional aesthetics. While Wordsworth returns to the discourse of the communion with nature, briefly lost while confronting the urban sensorium, Hawthorn re-enchants the suggestions coming from the technological innovation of the daguerreotype to find an intuition of metaphysical stability.

---

12 Marcel Proust, *In Search of Lost Time: Sodom and Gomorrah*, vol. 4, ed. Christopher Prendergast, trans. John Sturrock (London: Penguin, 2002), 216.

The Daguerreotype: Mystical Unity of a Mesmeric Utopia

Holgrave's daguerreotype of Judge Pyncheon catches and reproduces more faithfully than any painting the striking similarity between the gloom emanating from the face of the dead colonel and his living descendant. The judge reveals his true nature through the new technology of the daguerreotype, which "trac[es] out human features" through the agency of "Heaven's blessed sunshine" (46). Holgrave, while at first presenting his art as a technique that "misuses" (46) divine light, later in the story more assuredly claims: "... there is a wonderful insight in heaven's broad and simple sunshine. While we give it credit only for depicting the merest surface, it actually brings out the secret character with a truth that no painter would ever venture upon, even could he detect it" (91). The daguerreotype, with its silver-plated copper surface exposed to light and fixed in a monochromatic image, offers a more precise insight into the morality of its subject, which conventional portraiture sought to construct but was subject to a time-bound deterioration that may limit its moral power; the daguerreotype, on the other hand, offers irrefutable evidence that resists the proof of time.[13] Hawthorne's use of daguerreotype, however, takes a magical meaning that inscribes the new technology within the discursive formations of neoplatonic theology. Hawthorne "gothicizes" the mechanical process of the daguerreotype by making it resonant with theological discourses on light as symbol of divine presence, which appear also in *The Marble Faun*.

> It is the special excellence of pictured glass, that the light, which falls merely on the outside of other pictures, is here interfused throughout the work; it illuminates the design, and invests it with a living radiance; and, in requital, the unfading colours transmute the common daylight into a miracle of richness and glory, in its passage through

---

13 As Mia Fineman reminds the reader: "Invented by Louis-Jacques-Mandé Daguerre in France, the daguerreotype process was the first photographic method to be revealed to the public, in 1839. Daguerreotypes, with their mirror-like surfaces and astonishing detail, enjoyed widespread popularity in Europe, especially in France, in the 1840s and in the U.S. throughout the 1850s." See Fineman, *Faking It. Manipulated Photography before Photoshop* (New York: Metropolitan Museum of Art, 2012), 271.

the heavenly substance of the blessed and angelic shapes, which throng the high-arched window.[14]

The modern technology of the daguerreotype, as seen by Hawthorne, does not question the spiritual attainment of a higher plane of vision and knowledge made possible by the mystical workings of light. This is how Hawthorne, by inverting the ominous valence that supernatural events have in his story, makes his "gothic" fascination with supernatural elements the turning point in the narrative that will bring conflicts to a resolution sealed by a happy ending. The divine power of light is opposed to the gloom that reigns in the Pyncheon household; the daguerreotype-portrait painted by sunlight reveals the evil nature of the Judge and his similarity to the image in the old colonel's picture. Judge Pyncheon will die in the end while sitting on the chair his ancestor died in, hoping to cheat his cousin Clifford of his life and rightful claim to the family possessions. The mechanically reproduced portrait of the daguerreotype does not signify the loss of the aura the individual painting had, or its recuperation, which Walter Benjamin discussed in The Work of Art in the Age of Its Mechanical Reproducibility.[15] The mystical associations between the daguerreotype and the gothic theology of light present in The House of the Seven Gables makes it a process by which, in employing the metaphysical manifestation of the divine par excellence, sunlight, modern technology acquires a metaphysical value.[16] The artist is only a conduit open to the workings of light that can explore and expose the darkness of sin; the metaphors of good

---

14 Nathaniel Hawthorne, *The Marble Faun* (London: Everyman, 1995), 243. Terry Castle in *The Female Thermometer* recognizes the long-lasting trace of spiritualism that is not excluded in the seemingly rationalist discourses of the modern disciplines. Instead of taking as a departure point the popularity of gothic fiction, I want to turn the temporal plane of the scholarly narrative to the "gothic" medieval elements that are woven in the fabric of the modern novel, and thus point to a larger discursive field.

15 Walter Benjamin, "The Work of Art in the Age of Its Mechanical Reproducibility," in *Walter Benjamin: Selected Writings, Volume 4: 1938–1940*, eds. Howard Eiland and Michael W. Jennings (Cambridge: Harvard University Press, 2003). See also Susan Williams' discussion in "The Aspiring Purpose of an Ambitious Demagogue."

16 For the tradition of gothic neo-platonism, see Erwin Panofsky, *Gothic Architecture and Scholasticism* (New York: Meridian Press, 1957).

and evil associated to the neoplatonic theology of light place human action in the region of human agency that is further removed from the ultimate source of all things, light. Nature, in being the active agent in the production of images, reclaims its primacy in Hawthorne's view of modern technology. The daguerreotype, therefore, is suffused with a magical halo that creates also a fantasy of moral transparency around it, since the true self of its subjects become visible to all; it supplants both the metaphorical portrait of a public persona and the traditional painted portrait: the first has an inflated currency that does not allow one to catch a comprehensive view of its subject and can therefore be misleading; the latter spells a predictable course of history that draws the action towards the past. The medium of the daguerreotype is a new form of realistic representation, which, precisely because its modalities of representation do not seem yet stereotypically realist, appears more insightful both in reproducing existing reality as it had never been seen and in projecting through its mesmeric, reflecting, mirror-like surface a glimpse into the future course of events.

The modality of vision of the daguerreotype, through the apparently reflecting surface of its mirror-like appearance, makes the looking-glass in the narrative of the book take part in the gothic associations that the form of portraiture through sunlight can convey.[17] The "large, dim looking-glass" in the hall of the house, "contain[ing] within its depths all the shapes that had ever been reflected there" (20), resembles the modality of vision of the oval reflecting-surface of the daguerreotype itself. An object of everyday usage, like a mirror, when looked from a specific angle, may produce the vision that daguerreotypes would let surface, here through the Gothic associations that the descendants of the old colonel evoke when appearing "some in the garb of antique babyhood, and others in the bloom of feminine beauty, or manly prime, or saddened with the wrinkles of frosty age" (20). The images mentioned here look like the standard photographic pictures that the daguerreotype would make canonical. Hawthorne "gothicizes" the process of photographic reproduction, not only because the new technology of the daguerreotype alluded to here makes the dead visible, but because the dead can even become alive and interact with the living through the mediation of a "mesmeric process" (21). In the book, therefore,

---

17 Frank, in "Photographing Ghosts," 49, elaborates on the link between mesmerism and the daguerreotype and calls this tradition in the early reception of the medium of photography "photo-fantastic," without, however, identifying the discourse of the mysticism of light that Hawthorne refers to also in *The Marble Faun*.

photographic vision and mesmeric insight work in parallel to expose the evil hidden behind bourgeois respectability: mesmeric processes "... could make its inner region all alive with the departed Pyncheons; not as they had shown themselves to the world, nor in their better and happier hours, but as doing over and over again some deed of sin, or in the crisis of life's bitterest sorrow" (21).[18] At the end of the book Hawthorne suggests that Holgrave gained access to the crucial information on where the document proving the possession of the eastward territories lies from "one of those mesmeric seers, who, now-a-days, so strangely perplex the aspect of human affairs, and put everybody's natural vision to the blush, by the marvels they see with their eyes shut" (311). Mesmerism and psychic insights do not simply offer a valid narrative function to lead the conflict of the plot to a resolution sanctioned by the power of love and domesticity. Mesmerism and the many associations to it that the daguerreotype, the looking-glass, and dream visions suggest, also challenge, I want to argue, the fragmented views of modernity that the story incorporates by representing the sensorium of urban popular forms of entertainment. Mesmerism and the spiritual powers it unleashes constitute a force of intuited unity that transcends the fragmented materiality of chaotic sensations. In this sense the daguerreotype does not seem to be emblematic of the "flitting" and "flickering" nature of the Present that Hawthorne's preface describes, as indicated by Alan Trachtenberg and Cathy Davidson, so that the medium can be seen in their eyes as a "heuristic analogy to Hawthorne's writing of romance."[19] The daguerreotype needs to be seen as one in a wide array of visual phenomena present in the novel, each of which problematizes vision and its epistemological implications. Rather than matching the fleetingness of the present, the daguerreotype appears as a powerful and mystical synthesis of visible and invisible reality, which is not mediated only through an over-determined use of typology, as indicated by Trachtenberg, but rather through

---

18 On the mesmerist use of mirrors, see Robert Darnton, *Mesmerism and the End of the Enlightenment in France* (Cambridge: Harvard University Press, 1968), 133.

19 Trachtenberg, "Seeing and Believing," 461–465. In analyzing the visual motif of the "ephemeral, vanishing" figures, Alan Trachtenberg mentions Maule's Well, but he omits the reference to the phantasmagoria made by Hawthorne and by doing so does not expand his focus to the equally shifting visual culture of pre-cinematic spectacles at large that create a stark opposition to the visual language of traditional modes of representation.

the discourse of the mysticism of light that Hawthorne describes also in
The Marble Faun. Daguerreotype-mesmeric vision has the power to dispel
the gloom that reigns within the precincts of the family home; it supplants
the fixed conventions of painted portraiture and the likewise stereotypi-
cal notion of reputation-as-portraiture.[20] Mesmeric associations, therefore,
offer a reliable, quasi-documentary access to reality; they are coated in a
rhetoric that re-enchants modern technology and at the same time escapes
the challenging principle of fragmentation and multiplicity that hinders
any access to a single truth. The theological discourse of light gives added,
moral value to technological innovation; together with the pseudo-science
of mesmerism it recreates connection and fuses what urban fragmentation
separates. Mesmerism implies also a democratizing principle that can dis-
solve class divides and alter social hierarchy, therefore dispelling the gloom
of "psychological domination" that interpreters such as Samuel Chase
Coale insist on identifying in the work of Hawthorne whenever mesmerism is thematized in his fiction.[21] Since mesmerism can give access to the
dream-state of people belonging to different classes, it equalizes them and
reverses social hierarchies as Hawthorne himself suggests:

> The Pyncheons ... haughtily as they bore themselves in the noonday
> streets of their native town, were no better than bond-servants to
> those plebeian Maules, on entering the topsyturvy commonwealth
> of sleep. Modern psychology, it may be, will endeavor to reduce these
> alleged necromancies within a system, instead of rejecting them as
> fabulous (26).

Mesmerism, from the very beginning of the story, appears as a key factor in understanding the actions of its characters through their dreams
and the conditionings that oneiric states can exert on their waking life.
Mesmerism can allow to cross class divides and make sleepers from opposing families less distant, in anticipation of the marriage between two
scions of the feuding families. In this sense, the tradition of mesmerism

---

20   As Hawthorne writes in *The House of the Seven Gables*, "Tradition—which sometimes brings down truth that history has let slip, but is oftener the wild babble of the time, as was formerly spoken at the fireside, and now congeals in the newspapers—tradition is responsible for all contrary averments" (26).
21   Samuel Chase Coale, *Mesmerism and Hawthorne. Mediums of American Romance.* (Tuscaloosa: University of Alabama Press, 1998), 18.

that Hawthorne seems to align with is not filtered through what Samuel Chase Coale calls Hawthorne's "neo-Calvinist sensitivity" reverberating his "Puritan leanings" 22 but rather associated with the radical meanings of mesmerism that animated the life of pre- and post-revolutionary French utopian thinkers, explored by Robert Darnton in his Mesmerism and the End of the Enlightenment in France. I want to suggest that this other hidden trail, the history of mesmerism, needs to be seen as the cultural background of Holgrave and his company of "reformers, temperance lecturers, philantropists" which Hepzibah dismisses as "baditti-like" (84). Although The House of the Seven Gables ends with the triumph of bourgeois domesticity that absorbs Uncle Vedder's project of communal living, and at the same time cools the Saint-Simonian fervor of Clifford's ramblings during his attempted escape from the cursed house on a train, the reconciliation of the two families and the class conflict that marred their previous histories is made possible through the power of mesmeric forces and the political message of equality that the movement often advocated. In dreamworld all achieve democratic equality.

Tel Aviv University

---

22   Ibid, 7.

Being Viewed and Viewing Oneself: Gendered Discourse in Two Contemporary Hawthorne Adaptations

Nassim Winnie Balestrini

Adaptations of Hawthorne's fiction have been proliferating ever since the 1850s, be it in genres associated with "elite" art forms such as opera or in more widely accessible appropriations in verbal narratives (or partially verbal narratives) available in periodicals or book publications.[1] Two vehicles provide the complementary roots of this essay. First, *The Scarlet Letter*, as featured in the 2010 high-school film, *Easy A*, plays a dual role: on the one hand, it is a classic American high school text referenced as such in a contemporary high school setting. On the other hand, elements of Hawthorne's romance merge with the broader social world of twenty-first-century adolescence. In other words, the film explicitly addresses one particular context of the romance's continued reception and canonization, namely through institutions of learning, and while high school readers may find this text dusty and outdated, the film innovatively recontextualizes the romance

---

1 Regarding stage adaptations, see Nassim W. Balestrini, *From Fiction to Libretto: Irving, Hawthorne, and James as Opera* (Frankfurt: Peter Lang, 2005).

by highlighting its surprisingly relevant treatment of recurrent patterns of social interaction.

My second vehicle is Hawthorne's tale "The Birth-mark" as appropriated in "Birthmark," a 2003 short story (revised in 2007) by the West Coast writer and multimedia artist, Miranda July (b. 1974). Again, perhaps especially relevant to high school readers, this appropriation invites reflections on ideologies of scientific and medical prowess as well as on the psychological and physical consequences of aesthetic norms imposed upon and potentially absorbed by women. *Easy A* and "Birthmark," both works of art in their own right, demonstrate the continuing "cultural work," to adopt Jane Tompkins's well-known term which she applied to Hawthorne's contemporary competitors, of a canonized literary work whose reception may suffer because of students' preconceptions regarding the irrelevance of mid-nineteenth-century literature and of Hawthorne's preoccupation with Puritan notions of guilt. Adaptations and appropriations of his works may thus contribute to conveying the fact that scholars and students continue to discover hitherto unrecognized layers of meaning in these texts, which bespeaks their potential significance in our efforts to reflect on current realities and ideologies.

Teaching *Easy A*: A Viral *Scarlet Letter* of the Digital Age

Director Will Gluck's and screenplay-writer Bert V. Royal's film, which is set in a California high school, cleverly plays with backbiting and rumor as effective tools for ruining a person's reputation.[2] Proliferating accusations and imagined faults cooked up in the cauldron of rumor become so varied and illusory that, like multiple (re-)interpretations of Hawthorne's text by readers and adapters alike, these eventually require a readjustment of perspective on the object of scrutiny. And this readjustment only occurs because the protagonist takes matters into her own hands and uses a variant of the technology that was used against her: texting as a viral process of disseminating "information" to distribute her version of the alleged

---

2 Bert V. Royal, *Easy A*, directed by Will Gluck (Screen Gems; Olive Bridge Entertainment, 2010), DVD.

tale by providing a home-made video of her own story, which culminates in a closing statement broadcast online at a publicly announced point in time. In the process of intermingling elements of Hawthorne's romance with high school student Olive Penderghast's performative selves, escalating into harassment and temporary social exclusion, the film parodies the popularity of watching a movie adaptation instead of reading the adapted epic text by implying that neither the "original" text nor any of the adaptations can be fully appreciated without an acute sense of the relations among various versions of the tale. Thus, one version cannot replace another version, but each potentially opens up new perspectives on any other rendering. *Easy A* stresses that terms such as "original" and "faithful," which have been discarded from the field of adaptation studies, disregard the potentially continuous stream of interrelated versions of those narratives which have become part of a larger archive of cultural heritage.

Ironically, Olive's film within the film becomes the medium through which she explains how misconstruing partial knowledge, manipulating seemingly condemnatory evidence of misconduct as well as combining and distributing "framed" images of a person's character, whether they verbal or visual, may falsify individual reality and truth. In other words, if only Hester Prynne had had access to YouTube or Vlogs, she may have defended herself through her own digital trail of self-representations rather than being subject to other people's or a narrative voice's accounts of her actions and character. As an introduction to studying the film, students may want to discuss the opening monologue in which Olive explains her motivation for digitally distributing her own version of her experience.[3]

The following five suggestions for discussion questions and classroom activities are geared toward encouraging students to engage with Hawthorne's novel as a work that includes themes and issues whose relevance transcends time and as a work that has been interpreted and reinterpreted in adaptations with specific ideological underpinnings in mind. At the same time, students would be asked to scrutinize *Easy A* as a work

---

3   See 1:05 through 2:13 of the film. Among other things, Olive comments on being a high school student in the digital age: "The rumors of my promiscuity have been greatly exaggerated. I used to be anonymous—invisible to the opposite sex. If Google Earth were a guy, he couldn't find me if I was dressed up as a ten-story building [1:05–1:14]. . . . What better way to share my private thoughts than to broadcast them on the Internet? [1:50–1:52]. . . . There are two sides to every story. And this is my side—the right one [2:10–2:13]."

that negotiates how an American classic like Hawthorne's romance may be understood by an early twenty-first-century high school student, how film adaptations participate in the reception of American classics by this age group, and how constructing one's own identity as well as constructing another person's supposed identity involves the perception and interpretation of *topoi* found within specific cultural matrices.[4]

Suggestion #1: Adaptation and/as Adultery?

Considering a-historically and tongue-in-cheek that "adaptation" is one possible meaning of the scarlet "A," which Hawthorne's narrator fails to mention, should serve as a somewhat whimsical introduction to the notion that, while adaptations have had the reputation of "adulterating" their source texts, the phenomenon of adaptation is both ancient and current. Why and how does Olive integrate clips from and references to several film adaptations of Hawthorne's romance? What is the point of her insistence on Victor Sjöström's 1926 silent film being "the original," whereas she rejects Roland Joffe's 1995 film as inauthentic? What is the significance of showing Olive trying to read a movie theater marquee, sporting the title of Wim Wenders's 1973 film, *Der scharlachrote Buchstabe*? To her, this German film version is simply not understandable, primarily because of its German title, which Olive can neither pronounce nor relate to Hawthorne, at least not in any obvious fashion. This veiled reference to yet another adaptation is thus a joke on her, which could be explored in terms of adaptation across cultural and linguistic boundaries as well as in terms of the multiple levels of reality in the film. Students could view clips from the above-mentioned films and discuss them in relation to the romance, to each other, and to *Easy A*. They could in this context contemplate their own practice when it comes to studying literary works through film adaptations. Should the instructor wish to ground the discussion in adaptation theory, Robert

---

4 Some of my suggestions derive from what I wrote about *Easy A* in Nassim W. Balestrini, "Adaptation Studies and American Studies: Interfaces," *Adaptation and American Studies: Perspectives on Research and Teaching*, ed. Nassim Winnie Balestrini (Heidelberg: Winter, 2011), 18–24.

Stam's "Introduction: The Theory and Practice of Adaptation" would be an appropriate choice, as Stam stresses the hybridization of multiple discourses in adaptations.[5]

Suggestion #2: The 1980s in 2010

Early in the film, Olive wishes that her life followed the script of a 1980s teen film, particularly when it comes to fulfilled romantic aspirations. Which functions do the teen films (such as *Ferris Bueller's Day Off* [1985], *The Breakfast Club* [1985], and *Can't Buy Me Love* [1987]), excerpts of which are included in *Easy A*, assume within Olive's attempts at self-definition? Can they be related to the references to the *Scarlet Letter* films? What happens when someone like Olive, who assumes that popular culture at least partially determines her West-Coast-teenage experience, tries to adopt a seventeenth-century persona (Hester Prynne) created by a nineteenth-century author while also yearning for romantic love as depicted in 1980s movies and, through designing revealing bodices decorated with red As, parodying "living history" as used in contemporary high school instruction? Furthermore, how does a comparison of the social constraints limiting Hester Prynne and the social constraints in Olive's environment that touts its belief in individual liberty and natural rights, such as the pursuit of happiness, possibly change students' perception of the time and society in which they live? How does the Puritans' desire to live free of persecution compare to the depiction of Ojai, California, as a small town characterized by esoteric circles as well as small churches? Does the fact that, at the end of the film, Olive happily joins her new boyfriend in reenacting a scene from a teen film (they drive off happily on a lawn mower) imply that Olive simply imitates popular culture and thus admits that her agency is limited after all? Does classic as well as popular culture, as depicted in *Easy A*, influence self-perception and potentially stifle creativity and agency, or do Olive's acts of adaptation and appropriation rather imply the opposite?

---

5   Robert Stam, "Introduction: The Theory and Practice of Adaptation," in *Literature and Film: A Guide to the Theory and Practice of Film Adaptation*, ed. Alexandra Raengo and Robert Stam (Malden: Blackwell, 2005), 1–52.

Suggestion #3: Controlling Voice and Image

How do the various levels of adaptation in *Easy A* address issues such as (female) ventriloquism and Bakhtinian authoritative (versus internally persuasive) discourse? For instance, Olive switches from the involuntary role of the ugly duckling unnoticed by boys to the semi-involuntary role of an early twenty-first-century Hester Prynne who proudly wears the, in Olive's case erroneous, emblem of socially unacceptable sexual activity outside specific constraints—in Hester's case outside of marriage, in Olive's, outside a stable love relationship. She wrongly assumes that the others will catch the parodic and partially ironic twists of her role-playing, only to realize that her performance triggers a chain reaction that turns her into an advisor and pretended sexual partner for boys who are socially marginalized because of their homosexuality, weight, ethnicity, or other features, whereas Hester assumes the role of advising young women. In contrast to Hester's voicelessness in the 1926 silent film, which is, of course, partially due to the technical limitations of film in that era but which also contributes to the filmic depiction of patient suffering, Olive turns from a "mere" actor following a script into the director-producer of a film-within-the-film, which features her performance as protagonist-narrator and which she decides to release and distribute.

This assumption of a more powerful position, then, happens on two levels. First of all, the viewer of *Easy A* perceives Olive as presenting and structuring her story, partially adopting silent-film aesthetics through the use of decidedly amateurish chapter titles that resemble the textual segments interspersed throughout a silent film. Secondly, the viewer of the movie knows that s/he is watching Olive's take on her own story, which she describes as "the right one," but within the fictional world of the movie, Olive's amateur film and webcast become weapons against libel and against voyeurism because she first lures viewers in her own community to their computer screens by promising an illicit webcast, then disappoints the viewers' voyeuristic expectations, corrects the "false" versions of her personality hitherto promoted by her detractors. and insists on her agency when it comes to making decisions about love relationships and sex.

SUGGESTION #4: PRIVATE V. PUBLIC SELVES

How does *Easy A* assess the issue of adultery or sexual promiscuity as juxtaposed to the issue of exposing either one's own or another person's sinfulness to public scrutiny as found in Hester's forced submission to public shaming in contrast to tearful admissions of personal wrongdoing by early twenty-first-century politicians (i.e., in contrast to filmed performances meant to be replicated and distributed in the media)? Olive's nemesis, a Christian fundamentalist classmate whose boyfriend has an affair with the high-school counselor who is married to Olive's English teacher, comes across as an updated reincarnation of hypocrites who point their finger at others rather than adhering to their own principles. More importantly, the fact that this girl eavesdrops on a conversation—during which, in an effort to stop her inquisitive girlfriend's curiosity, Olive makes up a story about having lost her virginity during a reckless weekend with a community college student—and then spreads rumors regarding Olive's excessive sex life by starting a wave of text messages rippling through the high school community grounds the film's emphasis on protecting an individual's private life from judgmental public exposure. Thus, the film lends itself to a discussion of Hawthorne's romance not merely as a historical novel that allows a mid-nineteenth-century perspective on the seventeenth century, but also as a text that expresses slowly evolving notions of personal responsibility, individuality, and privacy in matters of the heart.

"BIRTHMARK": MEDICINE AND ART, PHYSICAL NORMS AND SOCIAL ACCEPTANCE

Miranda July's story,[6] which I regard as an appropriation of Hawthorne's nearly eponymous tale, lends itself to illustrating the notion that Hawthorne was attuned to current issues of his artistic and political environment such

---

6   Miranda July first published "Birthmark" in *The Paris Review* 45 (Spring 2003): 45–51. A revised version, which I will use for my argumentation, appeared in her prize-winning short story collection *No One Belongs Here More Than You* (2007; New York: Scribner, 2008), 169–76.

as the twisted relation between aesthetics and ethics, contradictory attitudes regarding science and a metaphysically centered world view, nature and nurture, and gender relations. Like studying *The Scarlet Letter* through *Easy A*, the comparative analysis of Hawthorne's and July's stories encourages students to broaden their understanding of adaptation and appropriation and consider the creative potential inherent in transforming texts by canonized authors in unprecedented ways.[7] For this project, I suggest a three-step approach. First, students need to understand that scholars have recently been offering readings of Hawthorne's story that are thoroughly grounded in the cultural history of the 1830s, thus going beyond the psychoanalytical interpretations that used to dominate Hawthorne reception. Second, students should be introduced both to 1830s medical discourse and to turn-of-the-millennium discourse on aesthetic surgery. Third, by reading the two stories with the respective contemporary attitudes toward medicine, ethics, and beauty norms in mind, students can contemplate the ways in which ethical judgments of the natural sciences intersect with aesthetics-based ideas of social acceptance, specifically for women.

As indicated, recent scholarship on Hawthorne includes interpretations of "The Birth-Mark," which divert attention from psychoanalytical vantage points and from the potentially undifferentiated discussion of Hawthorne's obsession with evil and the dark side of man. For instance, Leland Person's "racialized reading" of the story reflects on Hawthorne's contemporaries' debates about "genetic hygiene" and other concepts of social inclusion and exclusion, which were applied particularly to women and to non-whites.[8] Indeed, Person is among the few scholars who have linked Aylmer's desire to change Georgiana's body to plastic surgery,[9] Regarding attitudes toward

---

7   Julie Sanders distinguishes "adaptation" from "appropriation" by crediting the latter with the creation of a work that may represent "a wholly new cultural product and domain" (*Adaptation and Appropriation* [Milton Park: Routledge, 2006], 26). For an extended discussion of July's story as an appropriation of Hawthorne's tale, see Nassim W. Balestrini, "Appropriating 'The Birth-mark' in the Twenty-First Century: From Aylmer's Experiment to Aesthetic Surgery," *Nathaniel Hawthorne Review* 38:1 (Spring 2012): 58–84.

8   Leland Person, "The Birth-Mark," *The Cambridge Introduction to Nathaniel Hawthorne* (Cambridge: Cambridge University Press, 2007), 57.

9   In this regard, also see Steven Youra, "'The Fatal Hand': A Sign of Confusion in Hawthorne's 'The Birth-Mark,'" *American Transcendental Quarterly* 60 (June 1986): 46.

the medical profession and aesthetic surgery, students need to become aware that in the antebellum period numerous Americans considered a physician's virtuous character the central feature of his healing power and rather distrusted medical and other scientific training as possibly corrupting influences.[10] While early twenty-first-century patients may demand rigorous medical studies from a qualified physician, cosmetic surgeons in particular are also concerned with establishing and preserving their reputations through establishing a relationship of trust with their patients, a relationship which is frequently understood as being grounded in a sound combination of manual skill and good character. Furthermore, Rhian Parker points out in her study of cosmetic surgeons and their patients that the notions of "normalcy" and of "natural beauty," which are promoted by physicians and believed by (particularly female) patients, are strongly linked to the patients' sense of social acceptance filtered through the superior perceptive and aesthetic faculties of the surgeon.[11]

In order to engage students in discussing the implications of perceived medical authority, of a trusting surgeon–patient relation, and of standards of beauty, one could ask students to define their own understanding of "natural beauty" in order to then contemplate, first, the cultural coding of such notions and, second, their link to equally culturally coded ideas of social inclusion. They could then go on and define "aesthetic/cosmetic surgery" and express their attitude towards its social implications. In order to base their thinking regarding the larger social significance of these issues, students could select advertisements (among other things but not solely for cosmetic surgery) or other visuals as evidence for the origins and the perpetuation of such norms and their implications. In order to direct their attention to the interrelatedness of medicine and norms of beauty, the discussion could then focus on whether a cosmetic surgeon

---

10 In order to familiarize themselves with the reputation of the medical profession in this time period, students could read John Harley Warner's "Science, Healing, and the Physician's Identity: A Problem of Professional Character in Nineteenth-Century America," *Essays in the History of Therapeutics*, ed. W. F. Bynum and V. Nutton, special issue of *Clio Medica* 22 (1991): 66–77. Parts of this essay are reprinted in *Major Problems in the History of American Medicine and Public Health: Documents and Essays*, ed. John Harley Warner and Janet A. Tighe (Boston: Houghton Mifflin, 2001), 143–49.

11 Rhian Parker, *Women, Doctors and Cosmetic Surgery: Negotiating the 'Normal' Body* (Houndmills: Palgrave Macmillan, 2010).

is primarily a physician or an artist and on the implications of stressing one or the other designation. As a philosophical follow-up question, they could consider possible links between the negotiation/promotion of norms of beauty and of a Declaration of Independence ideal such as "the pursuit of happiness."

Having discussed beauty and its possible consequences, students will be prepared to think more critically about how Hawthorne's and July's stories address the role of feminine beauty in love relationships. As a first step in the comparative analysis, the following questions should be helpful. What is the function of visual perception in the stories? Who perceives what/who, when, why, how, and to what effect? Where do visual images of the stories overlap? In particular, students may focus on references to light and whiteness, that is, regarding Aylmer's elixir for Georgiana and the surgical laser with which July's protagonist is confronted and, keeping Melville's *Moby Dick* and its chapter on "The Whiteness of the Whale" in mind, contemplate the tensions between allegorical and symbolical, unambiguous and ambiguous readings. Although instructors may wish to avoid implying that they are concerned with faithfulness to Hawthorne's text or that they see the two texts as hierarchically juxtaposed as in the outdated idea of the qualitatively preferable "original" over the "appropriation," comparing changes and reversals of details is a worthwhile endeavor. What are the implications, for instance, of July's decision to present a story of a birthmark that is first removed but then returns in a moment of surprise or shock? How do the facts that the marriages take place after the surgery, that the husband has never seen his wife with the birthmark, and that the wife suspiciously wonders whether he would have fallen in love with her before her surgery influence the way we interpret the relationship between husband and wife as well as the significance of the birthmark for them?

Whereas Aylmer is the central agent in the attempt to remove the blemish and whereas Georgiana dies in the process, July's protagonist's husband has nothing to do with the surgery, and July's protagonist awakens to a new life after accepting her birthmark. Here, students should look at images of inward or upward motion, such as Aylmer's nightmare of unsuccessful surgery that reaches towards Georgiana's heart, the narrator's rendering of Georgiana's spirit's ascent to heaven, and the description of July's nameless protagonist's imagining herself as piloting an airplane that transcends and diminishes the birthmark that used to control her. Finally, students could be encouraged to tackle the difficult question as to how the stories approach the issue of human beings as manipulators or amenders of nature. Remarks in Hawthorne's notebooks and in interviews with July invite reflection on of how the authors assess this relation.[12]

Teaching Hawthorne through twenty-first-century adaptations and appropriations does not simply dust off texts against which students may be prejudiced; rather, continued interest in his works among artists demonstrates one manner in which canonization works. It also illustrates that some narratives that travel through the centuries, on the one hand, are deeply rooted in the cultural and political histories of their time of origin and, on the other hand, appear refreshingly new and current when reimagined in different times and places. Students can thus learn to appreciate Hawthorne in a variety of ways, they can rethink the phenomenon of adaptation, and they can combine their close-reading skills of both verbal and cinematic texts with a cultural studies–informed perspective on literature.

University of Regensburg

---

12 See Balestrini, "Appropriating 'The Birth-mark,'" 78–79, 84 n.31.

Hawthorne, Scientific Anxiety, and American Mad Scientist Films

WALTER SQUIRE

At least since the publication of Mary Shelley's *Frankenstein*, fears regarding science have inhabited literature and subsequent narrative media such as motion pictures. Less attention, however, has been paid to Hawthorne's contributions to narratives of scientific anxiety. Perhaps this is due to the dominance of *The Scarlet Letter* within literature courses, especially at the high school level,[1] resulting in a perception of Hawthorne's being obsessed with America's Puritan past rather than its medical, scientific, and technological present and future.[2] Given our cur-

---

1   Although *The Scarlet Letter* has fallen somewhat in prominence over the past 25 years, it remains one of the most frequently taught texts in high school English classes. See Arthur N. Applebee, *Literature in the Secondary School: Studies of Curriculum and Instruction in the United States* (Urbana: National Council of Teachers of English, 1993), 70–71, and Sandra Stotsky, Joan Traffas, and James Woodworth, "Literary Study in Grades 9, 10, and 11: A National Survey," *Forum: A Publication of the ALSCW* 4 (2010): 9 and 14–17.

2   Taylor Stoehr's *Hawthorne's Mad Scientists: Pseudoscience and Social Science in Nineteenth-Century Life and Letters* (Hamden: Archon Books, 1978) provides a superb starting point for those who would like to explore connections between Hawthorne's texts and the popular science (such as mesmerism and phrenology) of his day. Stoehr notes references to science in each of Hawthorne's novels and in short stories ranging from "Alice Doane's Appeal" to "Young Goodman Brown," as well as in the *American, English,* and *Italian Notebooks*.

rent moment, where questions of medical and technological ethics are fervently debated, students may find entry into study of Hawthorne easier and more enjoyable if focus is placed upon his medical and technologically focused texts and contemporary media, such as popular film, and concerns relevant to their own time. In particular, I have had success with "Rappaccini's Daughter" and "The Birth-Mark," both of which feature scientists whose experiments produce fatal results.[3] Since these two stories focus upon human loss, they may encourage students to consider medical and scientific ethics in terms of effects upon people instead of within abstract notions of morality.

In suggesting this focus, I do not mean to suggest that science and ethics are the only realms worthy of student exploration in "Rappaccini's Daughter" and "The Birth-Mark." Students in my classes frequently assess the power dynamics in these texts and in particular the sexual politics at play in the stories. In both stories, male scientists experiment upon female bodies.[4] Dr. Rappaccini does so without his daughter Beatrice's consent, and although Georgiana consents in "The Birth-Mark," her husband Aylmer withholds information from her regarding his experiments upon

---

[3] By no means are these two stories the only ones within the Hawthorne corpus to feature scientists of questionable ethics. Two lesser known tales are "Dr. Heidegger's Experiment" and "The Haunted Quack." But one does not have to turn to obscure Hawthorne to find more mad doctors. Roger Chillingworth in *The Scarlet Letter* is a key example, for he uses medicine not to heal, cure, or ease but to cause suffering. Students might move from an analysis of Chillingworth to an exploration of current conflicts between governmental, military, legal or ideological interests and medical ethics as expressed, for instance, in Hippocratic and Physician's Oaths.

[4] Given current political debates regarding the justness of male legislators determining women's access to health care (reproductive, sexual, or otherwise), I would argue that this dynamic in "Rappaccini's Daughter" and "The Birth-Mark" illustrates how frequently "disinterested" science or even the supposedly compassionate science of medicine is subject to and constrained by ideology. Students and instructors interested in further exploring literary depictions of physicians imposing treatments upon patients without considering patients' feedback might look to "The Yellow Wallpaper," a story Charlotte Perkins Gilman wrote as a critique of the rest cure made popular by S. Weir Mitchell. The Bedford Critical Edition of *The Yellow Wallpaper*, ed. Dale Bauer (Boston: Bedford/St. Martin's, 1998), provides, among numerous other cultural contexts, selections from works by Mitchell that describe the rest cure.

her. In one of their final exchanges, she asks her husband, "Why did you hesitate to tell me this?" to which he responds, "Because, Georgiana . . . there is danger!"[5] Since both of these stories involve male family members claiming a prerogative to determine the fates of female relations, they expose patriarchy at work within the family unit. Beatrice's indictment of her father, for example, at the end of "Rappaccini's Daughter" is striking: "My father, . . . wherefore didst thou inflict this miserable doom upon thy child?" (1005). While Aylmer is hesitant to provide Georgiana the potion she drinks to remove her birthmark because he considers it dangerous, Giovanni assaults Beatrice in the following manner before she decides to consume the antidote he provides, which proves to be fatal: "Yes, poisonous thing! . . . Thou hast done it! Thou hast blasted me! Thou hast filled my veins with poison! Thou hast made me as hateful, as ugly, as loathsome and deadly a creature as thyself —a world's wonder of hideous monstrosity!" (1002).

Furthermore, each text contains a love plot in which the male considers the female beautiful but flawed, Georgiana by her birthmark and Beatrice by being poisonous. These males, Aylmer and Giovanni, respectively, attempt to perfect the "flawed" women, an enterprise which leads to the women's deaths.[6] Students in my courses frequently think of these stories in terms of impossible standards of beauty, produced by airbrushed and otherwise altered photographs of models, for instance, as well as in terms of infatuation, where the lover, rather than loving her/his beloved as s/he is, is in love with her/his own idea of a perfect mate. While the gender,

---

5   Nathaniel Hawthorne, *Tales and Sketches: Including Twice-told Tales, Mosses from an Old Manse, and The Snow-Image, A Wonder-Book for Girls and Boys, Tanglewood Tales for Girls and Boys; Being a Second Wonder Book*, ed. with notes by Roy Harvey Pearce (New York: The Library of America, 1982), 777. Subsequent citations from "The Birth-Mark" and "Rappaccini's Daughter" appear parenthetically. The Library of America edition more affordably combines in one volume the texts of Hawthorne's tales from *The Centenary Edition of the Works of Nathaniel Hawthorne*, eds. William Charvat, et al., vols. 7 (*A Wonder Book and Tanglewood Tales*), 9 (*Twice-told Tales*), 10 (*Mosses from an Old Manse*), and 11 (*The Snow-Image and Uncollected Tales*) (Columbus: Ohio State University Press, 1972, 1974).

6   Margaret Hallissy devotes the final chapter of *Venomous Woman: Fear of the Female in Literature* (New York: Greenwood Press, 1987), 133–41, to an analysis of "Rappaccini's Daughter," which she considers "the most sophisticated treatment of the venomous woman theme in Western literature" (133).

familial, and relationship dynamics of "Rappaccini's Daughter" and "The Birth-Mark" may seem tangential to expressions of scientific anxieties, they actually coalesce rather well. The two stories posit science as a power whose use becomes destructive when imposed upon nonconsenting subjects, when scientists determine without consulting others what is best for humanity, and when scientists attempt to "perfect" nature, all fears expressed through the mad scientist genre of horror films.[7]

Exploring Scientific Anxieties

Evaluating the consequences of a lack of informed consent on the part of test subjects, whether in Hawthorne's mad doctor stories or historical cases such as the U.S. Public Health Service Syphilis Study at Tuskegee,[8] may lead students to a cursory determination of ethics as well as a satisfaction that institutional review boards will prevent future potential abuses. However, explorations of the concept of informed consent as it is currently practiced could lead to interesting debates. In addition to considering conditions under which informed consent may be waived, students may also want to explore the ethical validity of animal testing. The most basic debate regarding animal testing, whether or not it is ethical for humans to experiment upon non-humans since consent is impossible, can be directed back to Hawthorne for, beyond Rappaccini largely experimenting upon plants, the human test subjects in "Rappaccini's Daughter" and "The Birth-Mark" have considerably less political, social, and economic power than do the

---

7 There have been a few film and television adaptations of Hawthorne's mad scientist tales, such as *Twice Told Tales* (1963), starring Vincent Price and composed of three segments: "Dr. Heidegger's Experiment," "Rappaccini's Daughter," and "House of the Seven Gables." Screen adaptations of Hawthorne's mad scientist tales tend to be rather faithful to the texts and thus do not provide the connections to twentieth and twenty-first century anxieties expressed in the films I will describe. A brief annotated bibliography of relevant films is appended to this essay.

8 An excellent resource for those unfamiliar with the study is "U.S. Public Health Service Syphilis Study at Tuskegee," *Centers for Disease Control and Prevention*, last updated 30 December 2013, http://www.cdc.gov/Features/Tuskegee/. Change URL to http://www.cdc.gov/tuskegee/index.html.

scientists. This tendency is represented within recent film as well, such as in *Hysteria* (2011), where Dr. Mortimer Granville and Lord Edmund St. John-Smythe first test their vibrator on a maid and former prostitute, although the invention is developed for middle-class clients.

To guard against easy arguments that humans have a prerogative, even if only through self-interest, to engage in animal testing or, contrarily, that all testing upon subjects that cannot provide consent must stop, the 2002 film, *28 Days Later,* may be used to examine thornier issues of research. While both the intention of the research performed at the beginning of that film to develop medical control of emotions and the means of conducting that research upon chimpanzees may be questioned, the spread of the Rage virus within human populations results from the actions of an animal liberation group, since that group frees the infected chimpanzees. *28 Days Later* certainly exhibits cultural fears that science may produce previously non-existent threats, and yet the film also presents a lack of communication or willingness to communicate between scientific and non-scientific communities as a threat to human safety.

Beyond lack of consent, a second fear expressed in Hawthorne's mad doctor stories is that scientists suffer as much from hubris as non-scientists do, but they have far more power to enforce what they believe is best for all humanity. As Aylmer boasts in "The Birth-Mark," "No king, on his guarded throne, could keep his life, if I, in my private station, should deem that the welfare of millions justified me in depriving him of it" (773). Despite his claims, scientists do not actually have this power. Rather, this is the province of government, although scientists may have the ability to persuade governments, corporations, and individuals to fund research. While at various times in the past several decades numerous American citizens have been skeptical of government-mandated fluoridation of water, vaccines, and control of substances, interestingly enough these fears have tended not to be exploited in film and are sometimes even mocked, such as through the character General Jack D. Ripper in *Dr. Strangelove, Or: How I Learned to Stop Worrying and Love the Bomb* (1964).

Part of the horrific irony of *Dr. Strangelove*, however, is that Ripper obsesses about fluoridation to the point that he initiates a nuclear holocaust, unleashing the most destructive products of science to end benefits to human health provided through science. *Dr. Strangelove*, although decidedly different from other nuclear war films produced during the 1950s and

1960s,[9] does share a key trait with other mad scientist films of the 1950s and early 1960s. According to Andrew Tudor, who analyzes 169 mad scientist films between 1931 and 1984 in *Monsters and Mad Scientists: A Cultural History of the Horror Movie*, "Science is still frightening" in films during the years 1951–64, "but increasingly it is its accidental and unanticipated consequences which threaten the world."[10] *Them!* (1954), a film in which radiation from atomic bomb tests produces enormous ants, and *Gojira* (1954), later partially re-shot and released as the English-language *Godzilla, King of the Monsters* (1956), are classic examples. *Dr. Strangelove* expands the horror further through noting that once technology leaves the controlled environment of labs and becomes controlled by bureaucracies, non-scientists not only may use the technology unethically but also nonsensically.

Although the dangers of nuclear war and radiation from nuclear power plants and radioactive waste may lead many students to believe nuclear physics to be an especially threatening field of study despite its uses in medicine, unintended consequences of applied science often occur within those scientific areas most concerned with improving the human condition, such as medicine, agriculture, and control of insect populations. Beyond researching the consequences of thalidomide and DDT use, students may want to examine current research regarding the consequences of antibiotics.[11] In terms of narratives, though, genetic engineering is perhaps the most fruitful realm for exploring fears of scientific innovation. Through his manipulation of plants, Dr. Rappaccini engages in genetic engineering

---

9   For a thorough assessment of *Dr. Strangelove*'s departures from standard filmic depictions of nuclear warfare, see Charles Maland, "*Dr. Strangelove* (1964): Nightmare Comedy and the Ideology of Liberal Consensus," *American Quarterly* 31.5 (1979): 697–717, subsequently reprinted in *Hollywood as Historian: American Film in a Cultural Context*, ed. Peter C. Rollins (Lexington: University of Kentucky Press, 1983), 190–210.

10   Andrew Tudor, *Monsters and Mad Scientists: A Cultural History of the Horror Movie* (Oxford: Basil Blackwell,1989), 141. Subsequent citations from *Monsters and Mad Scientists* appear parenthetically.

11   Two excellent introductory articles on this issue are Michael 'Specter's "Germs Are Us," *The New Yorker*, 22 October 2012, http://www.newyorker.com/reporting/2012/10/22/121022fa_fact_specter, and Carl Zimmer's "Tending the Body's Microbial Garden," *New York Times*, 18 June 2012, http://www.nytimes.com/2012/06/19/science/studies-of-human-microbiome-yield-new-insights.html?pagewanted=all&_r=0.

even before he is able to effectively intertwine human and plant genetics in his daughter Beatrice and her "sister" flower. There is a rich cinematic history of mad-scientist, genetic-engineering films dating at least as far back as *The Island of Lost Souls* (1932), the first feature-length and sound version of H. G. Wells's *The Island of Dr. Moreau* (1896), through 1950s films such as *The Fly* (1958), to eco-horror films like *The Swarm* (1978) and *Piranha II: The Spawning* (1981), and to more recent releases like *Jurassic Park* (1993) and *Splice* (2009). What is interesting about these films is that they tend to posit genetic engineering as both unethical and highly dangerous,[12] yet humans have benefited enormously from the manipulation of animal and plant species through artificial selection. While certainly a distinction could be made that manipulation of non-humans is acceptable and beneficial whereas genetic manipulation of humans is not, a study of fears expressed by genetic engineering narratives might also reveal a process by which older technology culturally is deemed non-controversial and at worst neutral whereas newer technology is deemed highly controversial and believed to be potentially dangerous. Just as newer developments in genetic engineering produce fear, whereas older developments often are accepted as "natural," older developments in computing tend not to produce anxiety whereas newer and speculative developments in artificial intelligence are often treated as producing existential risks, such as in *The Terminator* (1984) and its sequels.

Playing God

When I ask students to list the new technologies which trouble them most, far and away the most frequently mentioned are those technologies which have to do with manipulation of human bodies and particularly those which would alter human reproduction—stem cell research, cloning, and human genetic engineering. When pressed to answer why they are troubled

---

12 Andre Delambre in *The Fly* conducts experiments in electrically disintegrating and reintegrating matter, but the end result of his becoming part fly links the film to (fears regarding) genetic engineering. *Jurassic Park* is unusual for in that a group of scientists oppose the cloning of dinosaurs, expressing anxieties regarding genetic manipulation often voiced by non-scientists.

by these technologies beyond quick reactions of "That's creepy," students tend to claim that the technologies are "unnatural" or scientists are "playing God." Those who respond that scientists "play God" suggest that scientists use powers they should not. Foremost among these is the power to create life, a power supposedly reserved for a deity. The 1931 Universal Pictures production of *Frankenstein*, directed by James Whale, highlights this fear when Henry (changed from Shelley's Victor) Frankenstein declares upon animating his monster, "It's alive! In the name of God now I know what it feels like to be God."[13] Andrew Tudor notes that many mad scientist films from the 1930s and 1940s "postulate commitment to science as a central source of disorder, and their key protagonists are devoted to the pursuit of knowledge at the expense of human values. This science is dominantly medical, concerned particularly with creating life or with transforming the already-living" (137). However, Tudor continues, since these scientists are engaging in medicine with potential benefits to humanity, they "are permitted the luxury of partly defensible scientific motives" (137).

Hawthorne likewise connects scientists to forbidden knowledge. When Giovanni first sees Rappaccini at work in his garden, he muses, "Was this garden, then, the Eden of the present world?—and this man, with such a perception of harm in what his own hands caused to grow, was he the Adam?" (979). The end result of Rappaccini's pursuit of forbidden knowledge is the onset of human death within his garden, the punishment for learning what deities know. Although no deities make themselves known within "Rappaccini's Daughter," the doctor's single-minded pursuit of knowledge is foreshadowed as his downfall, for, as his colleague Baglioni comments, "But as for Rappaccini, it is said of him . . . that he cares infinitely more for science than for mankind. His patients are interesting to him only as subjects for some new experiment. He would sacrifice human life, his own among the rest, or whatever was dearest to him, for the sake of adding so much as a grain of mustard-seed to the great heap of his accumulated knowledge" (982). Similarly, Hawthorne introduces Aylmer in "The Birth-Mark" as placing scientific inquiry at least equal to interpersonal connections: "In those days, when the comparatively recent discovery of electricity, and other kindred mysteries of nature, seemed to open paths into the region of miracle, it was not unusual for the love of science to rival the love of woman, in its depth and absorbing energy" (764).

---

13   *Frankenstein*, 1931, Dir. James Whale, film.

Unnatural Bodies, Unnatural Desires

Upon reflection, however, it seems to me that a more universal opposition to scientific production is not based upon the assumption that scientists "play God" but rather their creations are "unnatural." To even attempt to improve upon nature is deemed dangerous, whether in the narrative art we see or hear or in the very food we put in our mouths if it has been genetically modified or grown/raised with the assistance of antibiotics, fertilizers, herbicides, and pesticides. Not only are the labors of food-production scientists deemed unnatural, thus hostile to nature and human health, but their products get labeled "Frankenfoods." Given this tendency to deem scientific production unnatural and inorganic, we should not be surprised that it is a doctor, Nicole Allgood, who rails against organicism in the 2010 film, *The Kids Are All Right*: "And do you know we're composting now? Oh yeah. Oh no, don't throw that in the trash. You have to put it in the composting bin. Where all the beautiful little worms will turn it into this organic mulch and then we'll all feel good about ourselves, you know. I can't do it."[14]

Beyond opposing nature and science, in many mad scientist movies, especially those from the 1930s, the creation of new life forms or the alteration of existing ones is linked to non-normative sexualities, which opponents of such sexualities often deem "unnatural."[15] The danger of science in these movies would seem to be the production or alteration of human bodies other than through heterosexual coitus, which pits science against a naturalizing discourse that would claim there are natural humans with natural bodies, there is a natural sexuality, and humans are or should at least be produced heterosexually. James Whale's 1931 film, *Frankenstein*, for example, would seem to contain an absence of desire, as Dr. Frankenstein creates/births a man asexually, but I would argue that the film still depicts an opposition between science and heterosexuality, for Frankenstein is determined to finish creating/birthing a human prior to

---

14 *The Kids are All Right*, 2010, Dir. Lisa Cholodenko, film.
15 I am indebted to Rhona J. Berenstein, who examines in depth homoeroticism of mad scientist movies in *Attack of the Leading Ladies: Gender, Sexuality, and Spectatorship in Classic Horror Cinema* (New York: Columbia University Press, 1996), 120–59. Subsequent citations from Attack of the Leading Ladies appear parenthetically.

his wedding to Elizabeth and the assumed consummation of that marriage. In other words, he is rushing to give birth before engaging in heterosexual intercourse, and his science delays and cannot exist simultaneously with heterosexuality.

If the "unnatural desire" in *Frankenstein* is asexual reproduction, 1935's *Bride of Frankenstein* appears to foreground homosexual reproduction. Early in the film, Henry Frankenstein and his fiancée Elizabeth are interrupted in Henry's bedroom on what was originally to be their wedding night by Dr. Pretorius, a man from Henry's past whom he has never mentioned to Elizabeth. The two men leave together that night, and Pretorius begins the process of persuading Henry to create another human, this time together with him. Though successful in reproduction, their parenting is brief, the time between the birth of their daughter and her intended wedding collapsed into barely a minute of screen time.

While it may be sensible that in *Frankenstein* movies non-heterosexual reproduction indicates, at least implicitly, non-heterosexual desires, seemingly any scientific manipulation of human anatomy indicates non-normative or unnatural desires. The 1932 film, *Doctor X*, presents a tawdry tale of an amputee, Dr. Wells, who creates masks and artificial limbs from synthetic flesh in order to disguise himself when collecting samples of human flesh for his experiments. The film foregrounds cannibalism and voyeurism, and since Wells's guilt is not discovered until the end of the film, all members of his medical academy, including Dr. Xavier for whom the film is titled, are suspects of the murders Wells has committed. In one scene Xavier's daughter Joan discovers her father and then another doctor with the body of one of the murder victims. She later tries to recount the scene to another character, but can only muster, "Oh, it's a terrible thought." As Rhona Berenstein phrases it in *Attack of the Leading Ladies*, "Whatever happened is too horrible for her to articulate, too evil to say out loud. The only information given is that the event took place at night, on a bed, and between men" (127–28). (As compared to the 1930s, in the post-Stonewall era mad scientists are less frequently portrayed as gay. One notable exception is the bisexual Dr. Frank-N-Furter, but in *The Rocky Horror Picture Show* (1975) Frank's sexuality entices rather than horrifies other characters. However, recent mad scientist films continue to portray scientists as possessing "unnatural" sexualities; for example, both members of the geneticist couple in *Splice* (2009) engage in bestiality with a creature they create.

On the surface, "Rappaccini's Daughter" and "The Birth-Mark" would not seem to configure scientists as having "unnatural" sexual desires, but a closer examination of the relationships between the scientists and experimental subjects yields interesting results. Rappaccini claims to have made his daughter poisonous to protect her, and yet he confines her to their home even after she has achieved adulthood. Furthermore, no mention is made of Beatrice's mother nor any other woman, aside from herself, in Rappaccini's life. Given these circumstances, once could easily argue Rappaccini might have incestuous desires.[16] Since Aylmer is married to Georgiana, "unnatural" sexual desires might seem to be absent from "The Birth-Mark," and yet his desire for a mate with perfectly uniform skin suggests agalmatophilia, a sexual attraction to statues, dolls, or mannequins.

A Matter of Perspective

While mad scientist films seem to present scientific inquiry as dangerous and "unnatural," Andrew Tudor argues, "Fear of science is not straightforward here, for it is tempered by ideas about the need for progress and the inevitable price of that need" (139). Hawthorne's mad scientist stories are not straightforward, either. Aylmer and Rappaccini are flawed and dangerous characters, but it is not their science that makes them so. Aylmer destroys his wife not out of scientific inquiry but through an obsession with purity, assuming as he does that a perfect human face is one without a birthmark. Rappaccini's failing is being an overprotective and domineering father who is certain he knows what is best for her. However, he is not even the most visible villain in "Rappaccini's Daughter:" Rappaccini at least claims to act out of concern for Beatrice, but Giovanni propels her toward taking the fatal antidote through his anger. Ultimately, though, Baglioni is the character who distributes the means of Beatrice's death as well as counsels Giovanni to provide her with that antidote. He is the only character to claim that Rappaccini "cares infinitely more for science than for mankind" (982), and he also speculates that Beatrice "is already qualified to fill a professor's chair. Perchance her father destines her for mine!" (983). He sees

---

16   For a full examination of the incest theme within "Rappaccini's Daughter," see Oliver Evans, "Allegory and Incest in 'Rappaccini's Daughter,'" *Nineteenth-Century Fiction* 19.2 (1964): 185-95.

Beatrice as a threat, and the narrator has previously noted, "The youth might have taken Baglioni's opinions with many grains of allowance, had he known that there was a professional warfare of long continuance between him and Doctor Rappaccini, in which the latter was generally thought to have gained the advantage" (983). That is to say, Baglioni has a vested interest in turning Giovanni against both Rappaccini and Beatrice, in order to accomplish his ends of eliminating a threat and to exact revenge. If students are encouraged to shift from reading the story as solely a mad scientist narrative to reading it as a revenge narrative, then, they might begin to consider the vested interests of those who oppose scientific inquiry, for humans tend not to reject science and technology overall but only specific technologies and specific areas of scientific experimentation for often quite local reasons and purposes.

Filmography

28 Days Later. Directed by Danny Boyle. 2002. Beverly Hills, CA: 20th Century Fox Home Entertainment, 2002. DVD.
  Although the majority of *28 Days Later* is devoted to a survival plot, the opening scene is useful for sparking debate regarding the ethics and wisdom of animal testing as well as the dangers of animal liberation activism.

Bride of Frankenstein. Directed by James Whale, 1935. Universal City, CA: Universal Studios Home Entertainment, 1999. DVD.
  This sequel to *Frankenstein* (1931) highlights the frequent linking of science with homosexuality in mad scientist films, since two men, Henry Frankenstein and his mentor Dr. Pretorius, produce a woman together.

Doctor X. Directed by Michael Curtiz, 1932. Burbank, CA: Warner Home Video, 2006. DVD.
  Dr. Wells is an amputee murderer who uses human flesh in experiments. The film also alludes to cannibalism and homosexuality. It is one of the finest examples of the tendency within mad scientist films to link scientists to non-normative bodies, desires, and sexualities.

Dr. Strangelove, Or: How I Learned to Stop Worrying and Love the Bomb. Directed by Stanley Kubrick, 1964. Culver City, CA: Columbia Pictures, 2001.DVD.
  Dr. Strangelove demonstrates humans' tendency to steer scientific inquiry and technological development toward increasingly more catastrophic weaponry.

Additionally, the film indicates the relative inability of governmental officials to comprehend fully the implications of nuclear weaponry. A focus on Dr. Strangelove, the weapons theorist and unreconstructed Nazi, could be useful for interrogating notions of value-free science.

The Fly. Directed by Kurt Neumann, 1958. Beverly Hills, CA: 20th Century Fox Home Entertainment, 2007. DVD.
Scientist Andre Delambre accidentally engages in the disintegration and reintegration of matter, with horrific consequences. Extended discussions beyond Andre and his wife focus upon the potential benefits and questionable ethics of his experiments.

Frankenstein. Directed by James Whale, 1931. Universal City, CA: Universal Studios Home Entertainment, 1999. DVD.
In this most famous film adaptation of Mary Shelley's novel, Henry Frankenstein simultaneously seeks the power of deities and seemingly rejects heterosexuality, for he postpones his marriage in order to create life by himself.

Gojira. Directed by Ishirô Honda, 1954. New York, NY: Classic Media, 2006. DVD.
In this cautionary tale regarding the unforeseen consequences of applied science, nuclear testing awakens a dormant prehistoric monster.

Godzilla, King of the Monsters. Directed by Terry O. Morse and Ishirô Honda, 1956. New York, NY: Classic Media, 2006. DVD.
A partially re-shot English-language version of *Gojira*.

Hysteria. Directed by Tanya Wexler, 2011. Culver City, CA: Sony Pictures Home Entertainment, 2012. DVD.
Dr. Mortimer Granville creates the first vibrator in order to treat "female hysteria." The film illustrates the degree to which medical professionals are subject to gender and sexual ideology.

The Island of Lost Souls. Directed by Erle C. Kenton, 1932. New York, NY: The Criterion Collection, 2011. DVD.
In this first feature-length and sound film adaptation of H. G. Wells's novel *The Island of Dr. Moreau* (1896), Dr. Moreau conducts experiments upon animals to accelerate evolution.

Jurassic Park. Directed by Steven Spielberg, 1993. Universal City, CA: Universal Studios Home Entertainment, 2012. DVD.
Genetic scientists clone dinosaurs for a theme park, and, predictably, the dinosaurs attack humans.

The Kids Are All Right. Directed by Lisa Cholodenko, 2010. Universal City, CA: Universal Studios Home Entertainment, 2010. DVD.
Explores the relationship between a lesbian couple, their teenaged children, and the donor whose sperm helped produce those children. There is an interesting

opposition between science and biological reproduction in the film, for the obstetrician Dr. Nicole Allgood is the only member of the family not enchanted by the sperm donor, and her wife Jules even has an affair with the donor.

Piranha II: The Spawning. Directed by James Cameron, 1981. Culver City, CA: Sony Pictures Home Entertainment, 2003. DVD.
Genetically mutated piranhas that can fly are developed as a weapon by biochemists.

The Rocky Horror Picture Show. Directed by Jim Sharman, 1975. Beverly Hills, CA: Twentieth Century Fox Home Entertainment, 2000. DVD.
In the character of Frank-N-Furter, *The Rocky Horror Picture Show* makes explicit the suggestions of mad scientists' sexual perversity within classic mad scientist films.

Splice. Directed by Vincenzo Natali, 2009. Burbank, CA: Warner Home Video, 2010. DVD.
Two genetic engineers develop animal hybrids and animal-human hybrids which turn violent and attack the engineers.

The Swarm. Directed by Irwin Allen, 1978. Burbank, CA: Warner Home Video, 2002. DVD.
This film dramatizes Africanized ("killer") bee panic yet it can also serve as a starting point for discussion of threats posed by invasive species. Contrary to many mad science films, *The Swarm* may suggest that too little scientific knowledge is a dangerous thing.

The Terminator. Directed by James Cameron, 1984. Santa Monica, CA: MGM Home Entertainment, 2001. DVD.
In this classic AI (artificial intelligence) panic film, a cyborg time-travels to try to kill the future savior of the human race before he is born.

Them! Directed by Gordon Douglas, 1954. Burbank, CA: Warner Home Video, 2002. DVD.
Atomic bomb testing results in gigantic irradiated ants.

Twice-Told Tales. Directed by Sidney Salkow, 1963. Santa Monica, CA: MGM Home Entertainment, 2001.
Vincent Price stars as Alex Medbourne, Giacomo Rappaccini, and Gerald Pyncheon in adaptations of "Dr. Heidegger's Experiment," "Rappaccini's Daughter," and *The House of the Seven Gables.*

Marshall University

Teaching Gender Dynamics in *The Scarlet Letter* through Film Adaptations

Danuta Fjellestad and Elisabeth Herion Serafidis

How to understand Hester Prynne in Nathaniel Hawthorne's *The Scarlet Letter*? Why does she decide to remain in the Boston that has judged her so harshly? Why does she endure what the narrator refers to as the "dismal severity of the Puritanic code of law"?[1] And why does she choose to return to the site of her suffering and resume wearing the scarlet letter "A" long after the community has changed its view of her, the "scorching stigma" (175) having lost its "original signification" (117). Worrying our undergraduate students, questions like these are of course entangled in a set of issues at the heart of Hawthorne's masterpiece. In what follows, we present a couple of ways in which we help our students to better understand this historic classic by focusing on some aspects of gender, aspects that are most clearly brought up in film adaptations of *The Scarlet Letter*.

To teach American literature in a European cultural context and at the undergraduate level means that most of our students are non-native

---

1 Nathaniel Hawthorne, *The Scarlet Letter, A Norton Critical Edition*, 2nd ed., ed. Sculley Bradley, et al. (New York: W. W. Norton, 1978), 43. Hereafter cited parenthetically in the text.

speakers of English, whether they are Swedes or other European nationals. While lacking a common intellectual and educational background, what students generally do share is a somewhat patchy knowledge of the sociocultural and historical context against which Hawthorne's story of Hester Prynne is played out. As their experience of reading the literature of earlier periods is limited, their language proficiency in English uneven, it is only to be expected that they not only find the complexity of the interpretive endeavor daunting but the very narrative style of a novel like *The Scarlet Letter* frustrating. They consider Hawthorne's sentence structures convoluted or meandering, and the lack of consistency and coherence of the narrative perspective confusing, even irritating. Indeed, discerning the basic structure of this novel often proves something of a challenge.

Clearly, an intricately woven verbal tapestry like Hawthorne's romance, one that explores rather than establishes, that suggests rather than claims, that traffics in ambiguity, provides very real obstacles for contemporary inexperienced readers. A sentence like the following (from "The Market Place") might serve as a case in point: "Morally, as well as materially, there was a coarser fibre in those wives and maidens of old English birth and breeding, than in their fair descendants, separated from them by a series of six or seven generations; for, throughout that chain of ancestry, every successive mother has transmitted to her child a fainter bloom, a more delicate and briefer beauty, and a slighter physical frame, if not a character of less force and solidity, than her own" (41). Here the comparison between morally coarse women of the 1640s and their more refined descendants some two hundred years later, which seems obvious at the beginning of the sentence, is complicated, in fact almost undermined, by the conditional phrase, "if not a character of less force and solidity," a phrase that introduces doubt as to the moral progress over time. This example of Hawthorne's style of long sentences strung together by multiple commas, of extensive use of subordinating conjunctions, and of comparisons that leave a lot to interpretation, creating ambiguity, indicates some of the formidable difficulties that face first-time readers of the novel.

While our students may find dealing with a verbal classic challenging, like most students around the world nowadays, they also tend to be rather sophisticated readers of visual forms of narration. Moreover, in line with a general cultural shift, they often access classic literary texts via film. "What used to be an exclusively print-based activity," Jim Collins observes, "has become an increasingly image-based activity in which literary reading has been transformed into a variety of possible literary experiences."[2] Gone are the days in which book reading was believed to be "naturally" antagonistic to watching films. In our teaching, we therefore try to tap into students' image-based reading experiences and use film adaptations as a means to re-visit the novel, the overall goal being to assist their move from a mere expression of opinions to being able to ground their claims in the text, paying close attention to and learning not only to tolerate but to appreciate its complexities and nuances.

Since we teach *The Scarlet Letter* in a second-term undergraduate course and have but two seminar sessions of ninety minutes each at our disposal, we have to be highly selective in what we focus on. We center the discussions on what constitutes three stumbling blocks for contemporary non-expert readers that film adaptations can help to overcome. First, the novel lacks a robust story line, something most students expect. A film adaptation, generally, tends to extract the novel's main characters and condense the events—that is, to focus on what Roland Barthes calls "nuclei" and Seymour Chatman "kernels."[3] What film critic Pauline Kael said many years ago still holds: "movies are good at action; they're not good at reflective thought or conceptual thinking."[4] The second hindrance is students' insufficient understanding of the historical embeddedness of texts in general. Engaging with Hawthorne's novel through its film adaptations allows us to underscore the impact of various contexts on the reader's understanding and interpretation of narratives. And finally, the shifting narrative perspective on Hester can be illuminated by comparing flattened filmic representations to this complex literary figure.

Like many classic novels, *The Scarlet Letter* has of course been translated from print to screen numerous times; the period between 1910 and 1979 alone saw ten film versions, according to Bruce Daniels, six of which were silent movies.[5] One useful source of information about some of these

---

2 Jim Collins, *Bring on the Books for Everybody: How Literary Culture Became Popular Culture* (Durham, NC: Duke University Press, 2010), 49.
3 Roland Barthes, "Introduction to the Structural Analysis of Narratives," *New Literary History* 6, no. 2 (1975): 237–72; Seymour Chatman, *Story and Discourse: Narrative Structure in Fiction and Film* (Ithaca, NY: Cornell University Press, 1978), 53.
4 Quoted in Robert Stam, "The Dialogics of Adaptation," in *Film Adaptation*, ed. James Naremore (New Brunswick, NJ: Rutgers University Press), 59.
5 Bruce Daniels, "Bad Movie / Worse History: The 1995 Unmaking of *The*

adaptations is Laurence Raw's *Adapting Nathaniel Hawthorne to the Screen* in which he discusses eight adaptations: the 1926 blockbuster silent movie by Victor Sjöström, Robert Vignola's adaptation of 1934, the 1950 TV version by Franklin J. Schaffner, the 1973 German version directed by Wim Wenders entitled *Der Scharlachrote Buchstabe*, the four-episode-long TV series by Rick Hauser (1979), and finally Roland Joffé's 1995 adaptation.[6] A more succinct presentation of the filmic revisions of Hawthorne's romance is offered by Michael Dunne, who covers the adaptations by Sjöström, Vignola, Wenders, Hauser, and Joffé.[7] These, clearly, are the most significant screen versions of *The Scarlet Letter*.[8]

We find it particularly productive to engage students in a discussion of two radically different movie versions of the novel. For our purposes, we use Robert Vignola's 1934 version and Roland Joffé's 1995 "free adaptation" of Hawthorne's novel, both of which are also called *The Scarlet Letter*.[9] Neither of these films is a markedly impressive adaptation, but as Hollywood productions, these versions of *The Scarlet Letter* are singularly useful for initiating a discussion about the representation of Hester, as each film culls from Hawthorne's novel only one aspect of this multifaceted heroine, either the penitent and submissive embodiment of a womanly woman or the independent and rebellious proto-feminist. Offering provocative representations of Hester, both these filmic portraits of Hawthorne's character are securely grounded in the concerns and ideological climate of the particular times in which the respective film was produced. We treat the encounter between the novel and its film adaptations from different historical periods

---

Scarlet Letter," *Journal of Popular Culture* 32, no. 4 (Spring 1999): 1–11. Roger Bromley, however, claims that there have been eight film adaptations and one mini TV series since 1904; he names five (not six) silent versions; "Imagining the Puritan Body: The 1995 Cinematic Version of Nathaniel Hawthorne's *The Scarlet Letter*," in *Adaptations: From Text to Screen, Screen to Text*, ed. Deborah Cartmell and Imelda Whelehan (London: Routledge, 1999), 71.

6 Laurence Raw, *Adapting Nathaniel Hawthorne to the Screen: Forging New Worlds* (Lanham, MD: Scarecrow Press, 2008).

7 Michael Dunne, "*The Scarlet Letter* on Film: Ninety Years of Revisioning," *Literature/Film Quarterly* 25, no. 1 (1997): 30–39.

8 The high-school comedy, Will Gluck's *Easy A* (2010), although inspired by Hawthorne's novel can hardly be regarded a remake of the classic.

9 *The Scarlet Letter*, directed by Robert Vignola (1934; Alpha Video 2003), DVD; *The Scarlet Letter*, directed by Roland Joffé (1995; Burbank, CA: Buena Vista Home Entertainment, 2002), DVD.

as a dialogue that highlights how the past is screened through present ideas and ideals and how it is used to comment on twentieth-century American life, be it the 1930s or 1990s.

Needless to say, Hawthorne himself can be said to have "screened" the Puritan past through the concerns of his own time. Of these we mention but two: a "typically" Romantic interest in the complex psychology of a rebellious individual and a fascination with the figure of the artist, Hester's artistic "taste for the gorgeously beautiful" realized in the "exquisite productions of her needle" (64). Hawthorne's systematic shifting between two time-frames, those of fictional events (1642–49) and narrative commentary (the late 1840s), is established from the beginning, perhaps nowhere more powerfully than in the second chapter of the novel ("The Market Place") in which the narrator repeatedly brings to the reader's attention the fact that he imagines the seventeenth-century Puritans from a distance of two hundred years. The reader is offered explicit contrasts, similarities, and continuities between the mid-seventeenth century of the fictional events and the mid-nineteenth-century scene of writing. Since in general we cannot rely on our students' knowledge of history, we provide some basic contextualizing information about such matters as the turmoil of Cromwell's revolution in England and the American Puritan venture as well as on the "Red Scare" of the revolutions that were underway in France, Austria, and Italy and the pre-Civil War tensions.

Neither of the two film versions of Hawthorne's novel can be called "faithful," nor has the ambition to be a "faithful" rendition of the text, whatever one may mean by "fidelity," and however futile such discussions may seem today, in the era of what Collins terms a "*cine*-literary culture" (122).[10] Keeping in mind that all discussions of adaptation tend to be "bedeviled by the fidelity issues,"[11] we are not concerned with the issue of whether or not the novel is superior to its film versions and disregard the

---

10 Collins, *Bring on the Books*, 122. There is a considerable body of criticism on adaptation in which the question of fidelity features prominently. A brief but very helpful introduction is offered by Imelda Whelehan, "Adaptations: The Contemporary Dilemmas," in Cartmell and Whelehan, eds., *Adaptations*, 3–19. See also Stam, "The Dialogics of Adaptation," Bruce McFarlane, *Novel to Film: An Introduction to the Theory of Adaptation* (Oxford: Clarendon Press, 1996), and Míreía Aragay, ed., *Books in Motion: Adaptation, Intertextuality, Authorship* (Amsterdam: Rodopi, 2005).

11 McFarlane, *Novel to Film*, 8.

question of whether we are dealing with a "proper" adaptation or a translation, transformation, or refraction of the original,[12] but we do focus on the two adaptations' most pronounced departures from Hawthorne's text as a means toward engaging students in a close scrutiny of this literary romance, keeping a steady focus on various aspects of gender.

Interestingly, both films enhance Hawthorne's story with extratextual characters, incidents, and themes. The most pronounced addition in the 1934 adaptation is the comic subplot that runs parallel to the main story line, a subplot centrally concerned with the love triangle between the harridan, Abigail Crackstone (played by Virginia Howell), and the two friends, Bartholomew Hockline (Alan Hale) and Samson Goodfellow (William Kent). The wooing scene in which Bartholomew acts as an intermediary between Abigail and Samson and the scene in which Bartholomew is coerced into marrying Abigail bring out important aspects of gender relations in the Puritan community that the film seeks to recreate. The lengthy 1995 version is set to begin in 1667 rather than in 1642 and opens on a prequel to the events dealt with in Hawthorne's novel, about an hour's worth of Hester's (played by Demi Moore) early adventures in the colony and the rapidly developing love story between her and the minister Arthur Dimmesdale (Gary Oldman). The additions and alterations also include a Native American plotline, a community of "outcast" women forming around Mistress Hibbins (Joan Plowright), Hester's black slave girl Mituba (Lisa Joliff-Andoh), and a grown-up Pearl as a voice-over narrator.

Due to all these additions, it is not always easy for first-time readers of Hawthorne's novel to pinpoint what features and aspects of the text each adaptation has focused on, so we initially discuss the basic dynamics of each film before addressing the question of what, actually, happened to the gender representations of the verbal text when, in different historical moments, it was mediated into the hybrid medium of film.[13] One way to

---

12   Cf. Stam, "The Dialogics of Adaptation."
13   Discussing the issue of medium specificity is beyond the scope of both our teaching parameters and this essay. Suffice it to point out the obvious: unlike the novel, the film employs moving photographic images as well as soundtracks (conversations, music, and other sounds). The nature of the relation between the verbal and the visual has been the subject of discussions for centuries, but is of little—if any—interest to us in our teaching of Hawthorne. For a succinct survey of the set of issues related to the word-image relation in film studies, see Kamilla Elliott, "Novels, Films, and the Word/Image Wars," in *A Companion to Literature and*

open up the discussion of the films is to cite Michael Dunne's observation that the Joffé adaptation "is the clearest evidence to date that filmmakers continually revision *The Scarlet Letter* in the terms provided by their own cultures."[14] Do the liberties that the films take with Hawthorne's text signal such revisions? What purpose can they be said to serve? And what do they reveal about the values, preoccupations, and prejudices of the times in which these films were produced? By considering the contemporary gender sensibilities behind each moment of filmic production of *The Scarlet Letter*, we aim to underscore how our own cultural preconceptions inevitably are brought to bear on the novel.

The main points of the ensuing discussion (which we, naturally, both monitor and steer) can be summarized as follows. The 1995 adaptation heavily foregrounds individual agency: individuals are presented as having absolute freedom to determine their own fates. This provides an occasion to talk about the very real precariousness of the historical Puritan settlements, whose physical survival depended on the very opposite of manifestations of individuality, on community members sticking together; any form of individuality was thus perceived as a threat to the community and immediately suppressed. The theocratic social structure cemented an understanding of the world in terms of binaries: chaos vs. order, emotions vs. reason, the natural (irrational) world vs. manmade (rational) culture, the female vs. male. Such binary oppositions, as feminist criticism has pointed out, are heavily imbricated in the patriarchal value system. The clarity and simplicity of these oppositions, however, which seemingly organize *The Scarlet Letter*, are consistently undermined and questioned by Hawthorne. Hence, we explain, the tensions and ambiguities.

In Joffé's adaptation, however, Hester is portrayed as a free agent, not a soul racked by sorrow and doubt, but one unfettered by communal or religious concerns and with a clear political (feminist) agenda that she shares with the community of outcast women. Students have actually little difficulty in arriving at a conclusion echoing Raw's observation that "Roland Joffé's *Scarlet Letter* transforms the novel into a quasi-feminist tract, advocating the creation of women-only communities as a way of resisting patriarchy."[15] As instanced by the conversation during Hester's first dinner

Film, ed. Robert Stam and Alessandra Raengo (Malden, MA: Blackwell Publishing, 2004), 1–22.
14   Dunne, "*The Scarlet Letter* on Film," 36.
15   Raw, *Adapting Hawthorne*, 146.

in the new community, dialogues as well as events testify to the gender-conscious nature of this film; even the change from the novel's male narrator to the female voice of Pearl in the adaptation can be read as a gesture accommodating feminist concerns and perspectives.

The film is equally conscious about a set of ethnic issues. The extensive presence of Native Americans in the film, which opens on an extended sequence of the ritual burial of the historical chief of the Wampanoag people, Massasoit, the sentiments about the need to love one's neighbor irrespective of race or religion that Dimmesdale forwards in his sermon are redolent with the sensibilities of the 1990s multiculturalism debates. The insertion of the black slave girl can be productively read in the context of Toni Morrison's *Playing in the Dark: Whiteness and the Literary Imagination* (1992), in which she explores the presence of Africanism in the work of canonical white authors. The figure of Mituba in the film might be seen as a response to the neglect of African-American presence in white American literature that Morrison is concerned with, the muteness of the slave girl an uncanny literalization of some of Morrison's arguments.[16] The ethnic concerns in Joffé's version are braided together in a story line more or less reduced to a love story,[17] the focus on the romantic affair informing even the representation of nature: the forest is not a wilderness to be feared but a space associated with enchantment and sensuousness. In a word, by adding elements absent in Hawthorne's text and rewriting others, Joffé reinvents the novel to accommodate a blend of contemporary (1990s) concerns; the preoccupation with individualism, feminism, and ethnicity all find their way into his adaptation of *The Scarlet Letter*.[18]

---

16 Mituba, it should be mentioned, is a composite character drawing on Tituba in Arthur Miller's play *The Crucible* (1953) and Maryse Condé's novel *I, Tituba, Black Witch of Salem* (1986). The representation of Mituba in Joffé's film is one of the most disturbing elements of this adaptation, fraught as it is with racial stereotypes, but its exploration is largely outside the scope of our course.

17 Students are generally bewildered by Henry James's famous assertion that "no story of love was surely ever less of a 'love-story'" than the relation between Hester Prynne and Arthur Dimmesdale ("Densely Dark, with a Spot of Vivid Colour" from *Hawthorne* [1879], rpt. in *The Scarlet Letter, A Norton Critical Edition*, 288).

18 Roger Bromley's scathing condemnation of Joffé's adaptation is worth quoting, since it offers yet another possibility to elicit an animated classroom discussion: "For all its apparent immersion in 'feminist' discourses and multiculturalism, the

In the discussion of the 1934 adaptation, we foreground such points as the representation of Hester as the archetypal mother figure, a nurturing woman who sacrifices herself for others: her child, her lover, the sick and dying members of the community. Her nurturing character is well summarized by Mistress Allerton pronouncing Hester an angel of mercy (in the novel, the narrator comments on Hester's being "self-ordained a Sister of Mercy" [117]). This highly traditional gender script of self-abnegation, piety, domesticity, and submissiveness makes her the very opposite of Joffé's heroine; unlike his Hester, Vignola's character never questions the codes of patriarchal society. It is actually incomprehensible how she ever came to transgress the code in the fashion she clearly did. Her badge of shame, the letter "A," modestly pinned to her bosom, this Hester merges with rather than stands outside the Puritan community. She is, in fact, very much of this society. Hawthorne's complex story about the repentant adulteress, a passionate and rebellious woman with strange and radical ideas about the relation between men and women, has here been dramatically toned down and transformed into the tale of a meek and penitent mother-woman. The harshness of Puritan life, indicated in the opening sequences of the film where we witness the public punishment for what a contemporary audience might consider trivial infractions like gossiping or laughing on the Sabbath, is justified in the very first shot of the movie in which a snippet of text informs the viewer that what is to follow "is more than the story of a woman—it is a portrait of the Puritan period in American life. Though to us, the customs seem grim and punishments hard, they were a necessity of the times and helped shape the destiny of a nation."[19] We suggest that this initial text seeks to link the severity of the Puritan era with the moral austerity of the time of the Depression, another period when outside threats required that people rally together and think of the common good, when national identity was under pressure, which was of course also the case in the period in which Hawthorne was writing, the 1840s, as Sacvan Bercovitch has eloquently pointed out.[20]

1995 version of the film ultimately succumbs to a set of patriarchal and racist values which, although generated out of Hollywood, would not have been out of place in seventeenth-century New England." See Bromley, "Imagining the Puritan Body," 66.
19   *The Scarlet Letter*, 1934, dir. Robert G. Vignola, Larry Darmour Productions. DVD.
20   Sacvan Bercovitch, "Hawthorne's A-Morality of Compromise," in *Nathaniel Hawthorne The Scarlet Letter: Complete, Authoritative Text with Biographical*

As the audience of the 1930s desired entertainment as much as moral edification, national necessity had to be tempered by the antics of comic characters and the humorous love triangle subplot that consistently parallels the relations between the threesome of Hester, Dimmesdale, and Chillingworth.[21] In this context, what most students would consider an unhappy ending (the film ends on a Pietà-like scene of Dimmesdale's dead body in Hester's embrace) could, in fact, be regarded as satisfying the expectations of the 1930s audience: Dimmesdale is punished by death, but since his last word is "peace" and since he has both Hester and Pearl at his side, the community members bowing in reverence, the hardships of his earthly life seem to end in salvation. While this family does not truly become a family until his final dying moment, the film does offer up one that is; in the scene preceding the final scaffold one, we have witnessed the widow Abigail and Bartholomew, her new betrothed, walking together into town hand in hand with her two children.[22]

Background and Critical History plus Essays from Five Contemporary Critical Perspectives with Introductions and Bibliographies, ed. Ross C. Murfin (Boston, MA: Bedford Books of St. Martin's Press, 1991), 344–58.

21 In the 1930s, the film industry came under serious attack for the brazen indecency of its productions. Pressure was brought to bear on Hollywood to make films that promoted traditional moral values, not least as related to gender roles and interactions between the sexes. In the early 1930s, a committee of bishops, The National Legion of Decency, was formed to combat immoral movies. It became highly influential, reviewing all films and grading them according to a three-grade scale: A: Morally unobjectionable; B: Morally objectionable in part; C: Condemned by the Legion of Decency. The industry responded with self-regulation, creating the Motion Picture Production Code that would remain in place until the late 1960s. As a consequence, the 1930s saw a considerable number of cheerful films foregrounding courtship and marriage, and family life. "Correct entertainment" was to aim at helping people to "rebuild" themselves "morally, spiritually, and intellectually." See Richard Maltby's discussion of the Hollywood censorship issues in the late 1920s and 1930s in "'To Prevent the Prevalent Type of Book': Censorship and Adaptation in Hollywood, 1924–1934," *Film Adaptation*, 79–105.

22 Students need some information about the early 1930s as a period of increasing moral conservatism in American culture. As Richard Maltby notes, "an instrumentalist" view of culture dominated the decade of Depression: films should demonstrate how people ought to behave, invariably punishing the guilty rather than, as was the case in the movies of the 1920s, glamorizing crime and

Since our students are generally savvy about relations between men and women and tend to speak with confidence about the oppressive nature of patriarchy, we focus on film scenes that problematize and perhaps even reconfigure the glib equation of patriarchy with maleness. We want to make students aware of the fact that both men and women are caught up in patriarchal structures that shape the behavior and attitudes of both genders. For example, in the 1934 adaptation, we also discuss the humorous scene in which Bartholomew by accident has seen Abigail's "nether-garments" and is coerced into marrying her as reparation of this presumed sexual trespassing. Abigail, a widow with two children, is in need of a provider, and Samson, the one who did want to marry the widow and who, the viewer may assume, blames his friend for the rejection of his marriage proposal to Abigail, both have personal reasons for trapping Bartholomew into a union he very emphatically does not desire and both characters quote the law that regulates interaction between genders. Though clearly a comic interlude with stock characters, this is a scene that simply oozes control and discipline of male and female interaction. Their minutest move and glance are checked for the violation of codes. Importantly, it is Abigail rather than a male character who is the community's most vigilant and militant agent; unlike Bartholomew, she remains unforgiving of Hester's wrongdoing to the very end. This is actually in line with Hawthorne's writing that it was the women who "appeared to take a particular interest in whatever penal infliction might be expected to ensue" (41), although it is unclear if the interest is grounded simply in a lack of compassion for Hester or fear and curiosity about what may happen if they themselves trespass in a similar way. Soon, though, the novel will detail a variety of female responses, from the pitiless to the compassionate.

Should we consider the positively wolfish Abigail an embodiment of patriarchy's oppressiveness or is she a victim of a misogynistic take on women? Does her aggressive presence perhaps serve to put Hester's humble unselfishness in sharper relief? Why this need to regulate behavior, discipline the body, and control gender relations? Perhaps the humor in this scene prevents us from noticing how patriarchal structures ensnare

sensationalizing sexuality; "More Sinned Against than Sinning: The Fabrications of 'Pre-Code Cinema,'" *Senses of Cinema* 29 (Dec. 2003), http://sensesofcinema.com/2003/feature-articles/pre_code_cinema/. What we present below assumes that Hawthorne's novel is discussed by newcomers to his text and that the pedagogy is focused on eliciting their responses rather than offering the class a lecture.

men into unwanted marriages while women or at least *some* women, such as in this case Abigail, can achieve their goals only by cunningly navigating the confines of the system? The regulatory gaze that is so caricatured in Vignola's version of the novel is given an interesting twist in the 1995 movie. We screen the romantic sequence from the beginning of the film in which Hester, roaming the forest on a Sunday morning, in secret feasts her eyes on an unknown male, who will presently be revealed as the Reverend Mister Dimmesdale, she comes upon swimming naked in a pond. The erotic charge of this voyeuristic scene is heightened by two things: first, there is a reversal of the conventional dynamics of the gaze with a woman watching a man; second, the prolonged dwelling of the camera eye on Hester's gaze creates an intriguing voyeuristic triangle as if in preparation for the film's most troubling scene where Mituba spies on Hester and Dimmesdale's love-making in the barn.[23]

If the gaze in Joffé's film is often, though not exclusively, charged with eroticism and in Vignola's film underscored by the punitive gaze, how is it presented in the novel? To answer this question, we return to chapter 2, "The Market-Place," which stages the exchanges of gaze that will run throughout the novel. Here, the town's community "thronged to see" Hester step up on the scaffold is a diversified one: kind and malicious women, young and old, common and powerful men, curious but ignorant schoolboys all stare at her, infant child in her arms, the badge of shame, the letter "A," glimmering outrageously in red and gold on her bosom. She is looked at "not without a mixture of awe," we learn, solemnly and rigidly; it is the community's relentlessly regulatory gaze, "all fastened upon her," that Hester finds "almost intolerable" to bear. This unremittingly somber collective scrutiny, however, is complicated by two other types of gaze that are brought into play by the narrator: a sympathetic gaze of a "sensitive observer" who may register Hester's pain rather than focus on her sin and the admiring gaze of a "Papist" who in Hester with her child might perceive "the image of Divine Maternity." Hawthorne complicates the gaze further by letting the reader see what Hester herself sees for her inner eye

---

23 This may be a good moment to either remind the students or introduce them to the basic argument of Laura Mulvey's important, if much contested, 1975 essay, "Visual Pleasure and Narrative Cinema" (*Screen* 16, no. 3 [1975]: 6–18). As is well known, Mulvey claims that classic Hollywood cinema puts the spectator in a masculine subject position, with the figure of the woman on screen as the object of desire and "the male gaze."

as she recollects a diversity of scenes from her earlier life: her native village, her parents' faces, her own face as a young girl, the figure of a "misshapen scholar." Hawthorne makes the reader privy to Hester's power to obliterate, if not quite to fend off, the gaze of the community in order to get relief "from the cruel weight and hardness of the reality." As she thinks about her past, the townspeople thus "vanish from her eyes," turning into "a mass of imperfectly shaped and spectral images." The target of both male and female gazing, Hester gazes back at her watchers; her glance, the narrator tells us, "would not be abashed" (43). Although Hawthorne never suggests that the public and private gaze can be reciprocal (not only do we have a scene with one individual pitched against a crowd, but the townspeople's gaze is active while Hester's is escapist), he does signal that an individual can deflect the disciplining public gaze by subterfuge. This, perhaps, is the foremost concern of the Puritan society that its gaze cannot be sure to fully exercise fully its controlling office. And indeed, Hester's child is a palpable proof of its failure.

As each of the film adaptations, then, has an agenda of its own, the teasing out of these compels us to return to Hawthorne's novel to understand better its transformations into narratives that inadvertently tell us about the cultural contexts in which the adaptations were produced. By now students generally realize that, unlike many other novels that they are familiar with, Hawthorne's narrator, to quote Suzan Last, "seems to speak in many voices, to present multiple points of view, and to share sympathies with them all just as much as he reveals them flawed."[24] This allows us to return to the question of the two radically different representations of Hester in Vignola's and Joffé's films. To set up this focus in the films, we turn to chapter 13, "Another View of Hester," to an oft-cited passage in which the narrator lets the reader access Hester's radical speculations on the necessity of a fundamental social change for equality between the sexes ever to be realized:

> As a first step, the whole system of society is to be torn down, and built anew. Then, the very nature of the opposite sex, or its long hereditary habit, which has become like nature, is to be essentially modified, before woman can be allowed to assume what seems a fair and

---

24 Suzan Last, "Hawthorne's Feminine Voices: Reading *The Scarlet Letter* as a Woman," *The Journal of Narrative Technique* 27, no. 3 (Fall 1997): 349.

suitable position. Finally, all other difficulties being obviated, woman cannot take advantage of these preliminary reforms, until she herself shall have undergone a still mightier change; in which, perhaps, the ethereal essence, wherein she has her truest life, will be found to have evaporated. (120)

Clearly, Hawthorne's text does provide material that might serve as inspiration for the kind of representation of Hester that Joffé's film offers.

What about Vignola's version? We alert students to the fact that the above passage follows upon an extended description of Hester Prynne's showing "neither irritation nor irksomeness" at the abuse she receives from the Puritan community. Instead, we are told, "She never battled with the public, but submitted uncomplainingly to its worst usage; she made no claim upon it, in requital for what she suffered; she did not weigh upon its sympathies" (116). Not only does Hester not complain, but she also unfailingly serves the community tending to the sick and the dying with a "well-spring of human tenderness," her nurturing a traditionally "womanly" virtue. Her two seemingly contradictory sides, submissive creature or rebellious woman, are brought together by the narrator in the following observation: "It is remarkable, that persons who speculate the most boldly often conform with the most perfect quietude to the external regulations of society" (119). The novel in other words lends itself to radically different interpretations of Hester due to the shifting perspective of a narrator who insists on presenting a complex, multifaceted, ambiguous portrait of his heroine. Throughout the novel, the narrator mixes championing of patriarchal values with expressing sympathy for the suffering to which women (and men) are submitted by patriarchal structures. As T. Walter Herbert, Jr. insightfully puts it, *The Scarlet Letter* is "a powerful book not because it resolves . . . gender conflicts but because it draws us into them and forces us to deploy our own ways of seeking to manage them."[25]

As any seasoned reader of *The Scarlet Letter* knows, one of the main challenges of this novel is precisely that we are forced to make up our own mind about what to make of Hester, since Hawthorne insists on destabilizing meaning, resisting the conclusive statement and the omniscient

---

25 T. Walter Herbert, Jr., "Nathaniel Hawthorne, Una Hawthorne, and *The Scarlet Letter*: Interactive Selfhoods and the Cultural Construction of Gender," *PMLA* 103, no. 3 (May 1988): 295.

narrator, offering instead interpretations and conjectures. Indeed, in the concluding chapter the narrator, provocatively enough, tells the reader to *choose* from among the various explanations of what has transpired in the scene of Dimmesdale's public confession that he has just recounted. Teaching the novel to newcomers to the text, it is to the instability of meaning in Hawthorne's masterpiece that we aim to sensitize them so that they become aware of how interpretation is dependent on cultural and historical contexts. Approaching the novel via its two film versions has proven particularly helpful in achieving this pedagogic goal. The films offer radically different paradigms of womanhood, although anchored in specific passages in the novel, which reveal themselves to be one-dimensional and thus forcefully distinct. Positively humming with the ideological concerns that defined the time of its production, the 1990s, Joffé's adaptation, a flatly feminist recasting of Hawthorne's text, stands in a stark contrast to Vignola's film, whose overall aim seems to be a desire to unify and temper rather than challenge traditional values. While these two films delineate vastly divergent gender scripts, what they have in common is that there is little more to their representations of Hester than meets the eye; no enigma she, interpretation is not required.[26] The novel, on the other hand, is about nothing else; as very little here actually is what it first appears to be, the act of exploration and investigation resides at the very core of this psychological classic.

Uppsala University

---

26 We are aware that this may appear to be a gross simplification for film studies scholars who may point to the intricate work of camera work, music score, lighting, and other filmic devices that trouble and complicate the representation of Hester in both adaptations. The constraints of the course—and of this essay—as well as the context in which we teach *The Scarlet Letter* make us bracket such discussions related to the filmic medium of representation.

Notes on Contributors

Sari Altschuler is an assistant professor of English and Health & Humanities at Emory University. Her work has appeared in the *Journal of the Early Republic, Disability Studies Quarterly, American Literature,* and *PMLA* and is forthcoming in *American Literary History* and *Nineteenth-Century Literature*. Her book *"Science on the Wing": Literature, Medicine, and the Imagination in the Early American Republic* is under contract with the University of Pennsylvania Press.

Nassim Winnie Balestrini is Professor of American Studies and Intermediality at the University of Graz, Austria. She has held positions at Johannes Gutenberg University Mainz, Germany, at the University of California, Davis, and at the universities of Paderborn and of Regensburg, Germany. She has published in Europe and the United States on various topics in American literature and culture (predominately of the nineteenth through the twenty-first centuries), on Vladimir Nabokov's Russian and English works, and on adaptation and intermedial relations (as in her monograph _From Fiction to Libretto: Irving, Hawthorne, and James as Opera_ [2005], in the edited volume _Adaptation and American Studies_ [2011], and in an essay on Hawthorne's "The Birth-mark" which appeared in the _Nathaniel Hawthorne Review_ [2012]). Her current research interests include hip-hop artists' life writing across media, intersections between socially oriented art and interactive websites, Asian American poetry, African American theater and performance, and the poet laureate traditions in the United States and in Canada.

Nancy Bunge holds an AB in Philosophy from Radcliffe College (Harvard University) and a PhD in American Literature from the University of Wisconsin at Madison. She is a Professor at Michigan State University where she teaches interdisciplinary general education courses and has won two teaching awards. She has held senior Fulbright lectureships at the University of Vienna, the University of Ghent, the Free University of Brussels and the University of Siegen and was a Visiting Scholar at Harvard Divinity School. She has published over eighty-five articles and book chapters and six books, including *Nathaniel Hawthorne: A Study of the Short Fiction*. Her most recent book is *The Midwestern Novel: Literary Populism from* Huckleberry Finn *to the present*. In 2015, the Society for the Study of Midwestern Literature gave her the MidAmerica award for distinguished contributions to the study of Midwestern Literature.

Aaron D. Cobb earned his Ph.D. in Philosophy from Saint Louis University. He is an Assistant Professor of Philosophy at Auburn University Montgomery, where he has taught since 2010. He has published several articles on the History and Philosophy of science appearing in the journals *Philosophy of Science, Studies in History and Philosophy of Science, Synthese, Perspectives on Science,* and the *International Journal for the History of the Philosophy of Science*. He regularly teaches Applied Ethics with a focus on issues in Biomedical Ethics and Technology.

Jason Courtmanche was a high school English teacher for twelve years before he received his PhD in English from the University of Connecticut. Today, as the Director of the Connecticut Writing Project and a Lecturer in English at the University of Connecticut, he is a writing specialist who works extensively with both pre-service and veteran K-12 teachers. His publications include *How Nathaniel Hawthorne's Narratives Are Shaped By Sin: His Use of Biblical Typology in His Four Major Works* (Mellen 2008) and a chapter in *What Is 'College-Level' Writing? Volume 2* (NCTE 2010). Recent awards include a Fellowship from Teachers for a New Era (2011), a Literacy Award from the New England Reading Association (2012), and a Teaching Scholar Award from the Institute for Teaching and Learning (2013). He is a newly certified program reviewer for the National Council for Accreditation of Teacher Education and the president-elect of the Nathaniel Hawthorne Society (2013-14).

Michael Demson is an Assistant Professor of English at Sam Houston State University where he teaches courses in Romanticism, World Literature, and Literary Theory. He has published articles in European Romantic Review, Romanticism, Nathaniel Hawthorne Review, among others, has a forthcoming graphic novel on Percy Shelley with Verso Publishing, and is at work on a monograph on transatlantic Romanticism and radical agrarian politics.

Monika Elbert is Professor of English and University Distinguished Scholar at Montclair State University (NJ) and editor of the *Nathaniel Hawthorne Review*. She has published widely on nineteenth-century American authors, especially on women writers and on Hawthorne, as well as on the Gothic and on children's literature. She has recently co-edited a collection, *Transnational Gothic: Literary and Social Exchanges in the Long Nineteenth Century* (2013), and a special issue on Hawthorne's Gothic.

Scott Ellis is currently Associate Professor of English at Southern Connecticut State University, where he teaches pre-20th-century American literature. He has published on Hawthorne, Charles Brockden Brown, early American authorship, and digital pedagogy, and he is currently working on a project that examines print culture and literacy in New Haven, Connecticut, from 1800-1850.

Rosemary Fisk is professor of English and associate dean of Arts and Sciences at Samford University in Birmingham, Alabama. She served as president of the Nathaniel Hawthorne Society (2012-14) and organized the international conference *Transatlanticism in American Literature: Emerson, Hawthorne, and Poe* at Oxford University, UK, in 2006, and the *Hawthorne in the Berkshires* conference in North Adams, MA, in 2014. In 2011 she was named Fulbright Scholar to work on general education reform in the Hong Kong public universities. She is co-editor of the two-volume anthology *Cultural Perspectives: A Sourcebook* and has published articles in *Studies in the American Renaissance, Resources for American Literary Study*, and *Legacy: A Journal of American Women Writers*.

Danuta Fjellestad is Professor of American Literature at Uppsala University, Sweden. Her main research interests are twentieth- and twenty-first century fiction; visual culture; intellectual auto/biography; and new media. Her latest publications include "Nesting, Braiding, and Weaving: Photographic Interventions in Three Contemporary American Novels" in *Handbook of Intermediality: Literature – Image – Sound – Music* (De Gruyter 2015) and "The Paradoxes of 'Unnatural' Mimesis in Gordon Sheppard's *HA!*" (*Studia Neophilologica* 2015). She is completing a book-length study, *A Culture of Bookish Surplus, or Multimodal American Fiction Today*.

Alberto Gabriele is Assistant Professor at the English and American Studies Department at Tel Aviv University. He is the author of *Reading Popular Culture in Victorian Print: Belgraviaand Sensationalism* (2009), which has been included in the select list of 'works of reference' of the Societé pour l'Histoire des Medias. His next book *Pre-cinema and the Literary Imagination* is forthcoming. He is currently working on his next project 'Crossing Borders: Mary Elizabeth Braddon and the Global Circulation of Books and Periodicals in the 1860s-70s.' His article 'Traces and Origins, Signs and Meanings: Melville's Pierre and the Precinematic Imagination' is forthcoming in *Leviathan, a Journal of Melville Studies*.

Ivonne M. García is Assistant Professor of English at Kenyon College in Ohio, where she specializes in nineteenth-century U.S., Trans-American, and postcolonial literatures. She is a founding member of the new Latin@ Studies Concentration at Kenyon, and recently received the Board of Trustees Junior Faculty Teaching Excellence Award and the Whiting one-year research fellowship. Dr. García has published work on Sophia Peabody Hawthorne, and teaches a senior seminar on Nathaniel Hawthorne. Her book manuscript, titled "Haunted by Cuba: U.S. Imperialism, Slavery, and the American Colonial Gothic, 1830-1898," is currently under consideration.

T. Gregory Garvey is Professor of English at the College at Brockport, State University of New York. He is Author of *Creating the Culture of Reform in Antebellum America* and editor of *The Emerson Dilemma: Essays on Emerson and Social Reform*. He has served as Fulbright Senior Scholar and as Director of the SUNY Center on Russia and the United States in Moscow. Working with Russian Colleagues he edited *American Society: Essays in History and Culture* for use in Russian Language Universities.

Sandra S. Hughes is an Associate Professor of English at Western Kentucky University, where she specializes in American Romanticism. She recently taught a graduate course on Hawthorne's and James's Italian Writings at WKU, as well as an undergraduate study abroad version of the course in Rome and Florence. She has published articles on Hawthorne, James, Poe, and L. M. Alcott, and she has presented conference papers on Hawthorne in five countries. She serves as president-elect of the Nathaniel Hawthorne Society (2014-16).

Richard Kopley, Distinguished Professor of English, Emeritus at Penn State DuBois and former president of the Poe Studies Association and the Nathaniel Hawthorne Society, is the author of *The Threads of "The Scarlet Letter"*, *Edgar Allan Poe and the Dupin Mysteries*, and a variety of articles on Hawthorne and on Poe. He has lately written an introduction and compiled appendices for an edition of Ebenezer Wheelwright's 1842 novel *The Salem Belle*. He also writes etc. He is also the editor of *Poe's Pym: Critical Explorations*, *Prospects for the Study of American Literature*, and Poe's *The Narrative of Arthur Gordon Pym*. He co-edited the second volume of *Prospects*, has co-edited *Poe Writing / Writing Poe*, and co-edits *Resources for American Literary Study*. He also writes short stories and children's books.

Chikako D. Kumamoto is professor emerita of English at College of DuPage where she taught literature and college writing. She received her Ph.D. from Loyola University Chicago and her Master of Liberal Arts degree from the University of Chicago. Her research interests include sixteenthth- and seventeenth-century British literature and rhetoric with concentration on Shakespeare, as well as on Japanese North American literature and contemporary mystery fiction. The genesis of her Hawthorne article for AMS Press is one of the conference presentations at the Midwest Modern Language Association (M/MLA).

Zachary Lamm is a Lecturer in the Departments of English, African American Studies, and Gender and Women's Studies at the University of Illinois at Chicago. His manuscript, "Visionary Affect: The Queerness of the Romance in Antebellum America," is currently under review, and he has published articles and reviews in journals such as *Nineteenth-Century Literature*, *Mosaic*, *GLQ*, and *Genders*, and in the collection *Reading Rocky Horror*.

Jonathan Murphy is an Assistant Professor at Texas A&M International University in Laredo, Texas, where he teaches courses in Early and Nineteenth-Century American Literature and Literary Theory. He has published articles in the Nathaniel Hawthorne Review, the Edgar Allan Poe Review, the Comparatist, and the Arizona Quarterly. He has had book review articles published in Romanticism, the Emerson Society Papers, the Canadian Review of American Studies, and Studies in Romanticism. He is currently working on a book-length manuscript called "At the Tomb of the American Renaissance."

Donald Ross is professor of Writing Studies and English at the University of Minnesota. His focus is on nineteenth-century American literature, with special emphasis on the decade of the 1850s. With Stephen Adams he published a book on the composition of Thoreau's major works. He also co-edited two volumes in the DLB series on American travel writers.

Elisabeth Herion Sarafidis was Associate Professor at Uppsala University, Sweden. Her main research areas are ethnic American literatures; contemporary Southern and Caribbean fiction; memory studies; Americanization/influence studies; literature and medicine studies.

Jennifer Schell received her Ph.D. from the University of Pittsburgh in the English Department's Critical and Cultural Studies Program in April of 2006. She also has an M.A. in English from the University of Georgia and a B.A. in Anthropology from Emory University. Her specialties include eighteenth- and nineteenth-century American literature, print culture, maritime/frontier writing, masculinity studies, and labor history. She also has expertise in ecocriticism and literatures of the Far North. She has published articles on J. Hector St. John de Crèvecoeur's *Letters from an American Farmer*, Herman Melville's *Moby-Dick*, William Wells Brown's *Clotel*, James Dickey's *Deliverance, and the History Channel's Ice Road Truckers*. Her book, *"A Bold and Hardy Race of Men": The Lives and Literature of American Whalemen"* is forthcoming from the University of Massachusetts Press.

Gabriela Serrano is an Assistant Professor of English at Angelo State University in San Angelo, Texas. Her area of scholarship is early American literature, and she specializes in Hawthorne studies. Her research and teaching interests extend to issues of religion in early American literature, gothic American literature, and gender studies. During the summer of 2013, she will be working on a research grant at the American Antiquarian Society and the Phillips Library at Peabody Essex Museum examining nineteenth-century lady's journals to determine how the contents within these journals, such works of fiction, color plates, and editorials, reflect shifts in gender identities for women during the nineteenth century. She is currently working on a book manuscript for Scarecrow Press titled *The Prophet, Historian, Idler, Sentimentalist, and Romantic's Tale: Hawthorne's Use of Frame Stories to Develop Narrative Identity*.

Walter Squire is an Assistant Professor of English at Marshall University, where he teaches courses in film and American literature. His publications include essays on Disney adaptations, labor literature, and L. Frank Baum's *The Wonderful Wizard of Oz*.

Eric Sterling earned his Ph.D. in English from Indiana University. He is Distinguished Teaching Professor of English at Auburn University Montgomery, where he has taught for 19 years. He has published an essay collection on Arthur Miller (*Arthur Miller's Death of a Salesman: Dialogues*) in 2008, as well as essays on Miller, August Wilson, Edward Albee, Bernard Malamud, and other American writers. His essay "Overcoming Racism: Perspectives on Race in Jacob Abbott's Stories of Rainbow and Lucky and in Antebellum America" appeared in Monika Elbert's *Enterprising Youth: Social Values and Acculturation in Nineteenth-Century American Children's Literature* (Routledge, 2008). He teaches Hawthorne's fiction regularly, primarily in Survey of American Literature I.

Robert T. Tally Jr. is an associate professor of English at Texas State University, where he teaches American and world literature. He is the author of *Spatiality (The New Critical Idiom)*; *Utopia in the Age of Globalization: Space, Representation, and the World System*; *Kurt Vonnegut and the American Novel: A Postmodern Iconography*; and *Melville, Mapping and Globalization: Literary Cartography in the American Baroque Writer*. The translator of Bertrand Westphal's *Geocriticism: Real and Fictional Spaces*, Tally is the editor of *Geocritical Explorations: Space, Place, and Mapping in Literary and Cultural Studies* and *Kurt Vonnegut: Critical Insights*.

Patricia Dunlavy Valenti is Professor Emerita at the University of North Carolina at Pembroke where she was head of the Graduate Program in English Education and directed a year-long NEH Humanities Focus Grant on *The Scarlet Letter*. She is the author of *Understanding The Old Man and the Sea* in the Greenwood Press Literature in Context Series (2002), *To Myself a Stranger: A Biography of Rose Hawthorne Lathrop* (Louisiana State University Press, 1991), and *Sophia Peabody Hawthorne, A Life*, 2 vols (University of Missouri Press, 2004, 2015). Valenti's extensive publications on the Hawthornes include articles on Nathaniel Hawthorne's fiction and Sophia's influence upon it. She can be contacted at (910) 257-2663 or patricia.valenti@uncp.edu.

Sarah Wadsworth is an Associate Professor of English at Marquette University. She is the author of *In the Company of Books: Literature and Its "Classes" in Nineteenth-Century America* (University of Massachusetts Press, 2006) and co-author (with Wayne A. Wiegand) of *Right Here I See My Own Books: The Woman's Building Library at the World's Columbian Exposition* (University of Massachusetts Press, 2012). A specialist in American literature before 1900, she has published articles in *Library Trends, The Henry James Review, Signs, Libraries & Culture, The Lion and the Unicorn, Nathaniel Hawthorne Review, Victorian Periodicals Review, Harvard Library Bulletin, Biography,* and *SHAW* in addition to an array of edited collections and reference works. Her honors include a P.E.O. Scholar Award from P.E.O. International (1998), a Houghton Mifflin Fellowship in Publishing History from the Houghton Library, Harvard (2000), an American Fellowship from the American Association of University Women (2002), a Carnegie-Whitney Award from the American Library Association (with Wayne A. Wiegand, 2002), and a Reese Fellowship for American Bibliography and the History of the Book in the Americas from the Bibliographical Society of America (2010). In 2000 she received the A. Garr Cranney Outstanding Dissertation Award from the International Reading Association (History of Reading SIG), and in 2001 she was awarded the Leon Edel Prize by *The Henry James Review*. A past president of the History of Reading Special Interest Group of the International Reading Association, she currently serves on the board of directors of the Nineteenth-Century Studies Association.

Index to Hawthorne Texts

A
"Alice Doane's Appeal," 63, 69
"The Ambitious Guest," 108, 203
"The Artist of the Beautiful," 203, 255

B
"The Birthmark," xxii, xxiii, xxiv, 63, 124–125, 129, 133–134, 145–146, 150–158, 203, 280, 285–286, 288, 292–294, 298, 300
The Blithedale Romance, xiv, xix, 37–49, 52, 55, 57, 60, 63, 68–70, 138, 194–196, 208–209, 212, 214–215, 218–220

C
"The Celestial Railroad," 135, 140
"Chiefly About War Matters," 198
"The Custom-House," 165–170, 206, 241–243

D
"The Dolliver Romance," 198
"Dr. Heidegger's Experiment," 135, 165, 167, 304

"Drowne's Wooden Image," 138

E
"Earth's Holocaust," 185–186, 189–190
"Edward Randolph's Portrait," 265–266
"Endicott and the Red Cross," 202
"Ethan Brand," xxii, 124–125

F
"Feathertop," xxviii, 138, 247, 251–254, 258
The French and Italian Notebooks, 222, 227

G
"The Gentle Boy," x
"The Gray Champion," 187, 194
"The Great Carbuncle," 108

H
The House of the Seven Gables, xiv, xix, xxix, 25–30, 32–36, 63, 65, 68–69, 133–134, 137–138, 140, 195, 208, 212–213, 216–217, 220, 259, 261, 263, 265–277

M

"Main-Street," 257
The Marble Faun, xiv, xx, xxvi, xxvii, 63, 65, 71–73, 198, 208, 209, 212, 214–218, 221–229, 231–232, 272–273, 276
"The May-Pole of Merry Mount," xiii, xxii, 127, 194
"The Minister's Black Veil," xiii, xxi, xxii, 77–78, 80–91, 93, 165, 167, 169–170, 200–201
"Monsieur du Miroir," 138
Mosses from an Old Manse, 97
"Mrs. Hutchinson," 202
"My Kinsman, Major Molineux," xiii, xxii, 125–126, 189–191

O

"The Old Apple Dealer," 135
"The Old Manse," 198

P

"The Prophetic Pictures," 266

R

"Rappaccini's Daughter," xxi, xxii, xxiv, xxvii–xxviii, 63, 72, 87–89, 91–93, 124–125, 134, 140, 145–150, 152, 158, 168–169, 191, 198, 203–205, 247, 256, 258, 292–296, 298, 300–302

"Roger Malvin's Burial," xxii, 108, 112, 115–119, 188

S

The Scarlet Letter, ix, xi, xiii–xiv, xviii–xxi, xxiv–xxviii, xxx, 4–6, 8–12, 15–16, 18–23, 26–27, 32, 36, 51, 55, 58–60, 63, 65–68, 70, 72, 77, 89, 161, 164–166, 169, 173, 175–176, 178–182, 188, 191–198, 205–207, 211–213, 215–218, 235–236, 238–244, 257, 279–280, 282–286, 291, 305–319
Septimius Felton, 133
"Sights from a Steeple," 89–90
The Snow Image, 257

T

Tanglewood Tales, 45
Twice-Told Tales, 89

W

"Wakefield," 202
A Wonder-Book for Girls and Boys, 44–45

Y

"Young Goodman Brown," xiii–xix, xxii, 95–97, 99–101, 103–107, 112–117, 126, 164, 168–169, 198, 200–201

www.ingramcontent.com/pod-product-compliance
Lightning Source LLC
Chambersburg PA
CBHW071150300426
44113CB00009B/1155